We Cannot Escape History

WE CANNOT ESCAPE HISTORY: STATES AND REVOLUTIONS

Neil Davidson

Haymarket Books
Chicago, Illinois

© 2015 Neil Davidson

Published by
Haymarket Books
P.O. Box 180165
Chicago, IL 60618
773-583-7884
info@haymarketbooks.org
www.haymarketbooks.org

ISBN: 978-1-60846-467-8

Trade distribution:
In the US through Consortium Book Sales and Distribution, www.cbsd.com
In the UK, Turnaround Publisher Services, www.turnaround-uk.com
In Canada, Publishers Group Canada, www.pgcbooks.ca
All other countries, Publishers Group Worldwide, www.pgw.com

This book was published with the generous support of the Wallace Action Fund and
Lannan Foundation.

Cover design by Eric Kerl. Cover image of a large group of workers gathered outside
a factory during World War II. Copyright Bettmann/Corbis/AP Images.

Printed in Canada by union labor.

Library of Congress CIP Data is available.

10 9 8 7 6 5 4 3 2 1

RECYCLED
Paper made from
recycled material
FSC
www.fsc.org FSC® C103567

For Michelle Campbell:
some of your questions answered (at last)

CONTENTS

PREFACE

The preface to *Holding Fast to an Image of the Past* (2014) announced that a second volume of essays, called *We Cannot Escape History*, would appear in 2015.[1] The book of this title that you are now reading is, however, slightly different from the one advertised. Originally subtitled "Nations, States, and Revolutions," it now focuses solely on the latter two terms, and to an extent on the overarching modal transitions within which social revolutions occur. There are both practical and political reasons for this. The practical one is that, since I recently subjected the world to one 370,000-word epic (*How Revolutionary Were the Bourgeois Revolutions?*), my editors at Haymarket quite reasonably felt that another book of similar size might test the endurance of all but the most dedicated readers. The political reason was that, in a way quite unexpected by me or indeed anyone else, the Scottish referendum of 2014 saw the emergence of a powerful social movement for independence, particularly in the six months leading up to the ballot of September 18. The vote was ultimately for remaining in the United Kingdom. That result is unlikely to be permanent, but in any event the extraordinary nature of the Yes campaign, the panic it produced among the British ruling class, and the transformed political landscape it left behind meant that any reflections on nation-states and nationalism must take account of these developments. A collection dedicated solely to these issues, with material on recent events in Scotland and the UK, will therefore appear later this year under the title *Nation-States: Consciousness and Competition*.

As in the preceding volume, the pieces included here have been reproduced with only minor alterations, such as the correction of factual errors, the rewording of ambiguous passages, the addition of material previously omitted for reasons of length, and the elimination of repetition. As with most essay collections, the contents of this one were written for a number of different outlets and occasions, but since I believe that political writing should be as rigorous as the best academic work, and that academic work should be as comprehensible as the best political writing, the chapters do not greatly vary in terms of style, although they do vary in length. The chapters are reproduced in broadly chronological order, with the exception of the section comprising chapters 4, 5, 6, and 7, which discuss individual revolutions and follow the order of their occurrence rather than when I happened to write about them. The opening and closing chapters were, however, respectively, the earliest of my writings to be delivered as a lecture and latest to be written as an article, and are directly related to each other. Chapter 1 is based on my 2004 Deutscher Memorial Prize Lecture and formed the basis of what, eight years later, would become *How Revolutionary Were the Bourgeois Revolutions?* Chapter 12 is my response to criticisms of that book from comrades within the British Socialist Workers Party (SWP). The book therefore opens with one major theoretical disagreement and closes with another. The former is a debate *between* two traditions, those of Political Marxism and International Socialism (IS); the second is a debate *within* the latter tradition. The remainder of this preface explains the different contexts in which the chapters were written and concludes with my reasons for republishing them. Inevitably, then, it has some of the characteristics of a memoir.

The first section consists of a single (admittedly very long) chapter, which, as noted above, was originally a lecture given in 2004. At the time I was not employed as an academic but as a full-time civil servant for what was then the Scottish Executive (now the Scottish Government) in Edinburgh, while maintaining a marginal presence in the world of higher education as a part-time tutor/counselor for the UK's main adult distance-learning institution, the Open University. In addition to my day and evening jobs I was also a member of the SWP and an activist in my trade union, the Public and Commercial Services Union. As can be imagined, these commitments did not leave me with a great deal of spare time. Nevertheless, I managed to write and have published two books: *The Origins of Scottish Nationhood* (2000), which advanced the deeply unpopular thesis (at least among Scottish nationalists) that Scottish national identity only emerged *after* the union with England in 1707; and *Discovering the Scottish Revolution* (2003), which tried to establish that Scotland had undergone a bourgeois revolution between the Glorious Revolution of 1688 and the suppression of the last Jacobite Rising in 1746. Both were products of a larger research project on the transition to capitalism in Scotland, which I had been conducting on free evenings and weekends for around eight years, but which—because of my then-publisher Pluto's concerns about word count (readers may detect a theme here)—was unpublishable as a single work.

I had however amassed a large amount of additional material, most of it dealing with the transformation of Scottish agriculture after 1746, that I naturally wanted to publish in some form. Early in 2003, I duly submitted it to what seemed the most suitable academic publication, the *Journal of Agrarian Change*. In the cover letter I mentioned that *Discovering the Scottish Revolution* was about to appear in print, and the editor, Terry Byres, emailed back asking if I could send him a copy of the manuscript. It turned out that, in addition to being a fellow-Aberdonian, Byres was on the jury that awarded the Isaac and Tamara Deutscher Memorial Prize, and after reading the manuscript, he nominated it for that year's award. Shortly before the 2003 lecture, at which the prize winner was to be announced, he rang me to say that it had been won jointly by me and Benno Teschke for his book *The Myth of 1648*—the first and so far only time the jury has been unable to agree on a single winner.

Until 1996 the published version of the Memorial Prize Lecture had appeared only in *New Left Review*. After a six-year hiatus it was delivered at the Historical Materialism (HM) annual conference and subsequently published in that journal. Teschke and I had written books that were quite different in terms of both disciplinary approach and attitude to Marxism. Teschke's book was a critique, from within the discipline of international relations, of its founding assumption, namely that the modern states system emerged with the Treaty of Westphalia. To this end he drew on both the definition of capitalism and the explanation for its emergence associated with Robert Brenner. My book was a work of history, analyzing a particular example, perhaps the earliest example, of bourgeois revolution "from above." My own influences lay in the classical Marxist writings on this subject: Engels on Germany, Gramsci on Italy, and Lukács more generally, together with more recent considerations of the nature of agency in the bourgeois revolutions by Deutscher, Christopher Hill (in his later work, at least), Geoff Eley, and Alex Callinicos. I did admire the writing of some Political Marxists—above all Brenner's work on the contemporary US labor movement and Ellen Meiksins Wood's own Deutscher Prize–winning *The Retreat from Class*—but not their central historical thesis.[2] It was not entirely clear to me exactly *how* much I disagreed with it until I arrived at the School of Oriental and African Studies in London for the Memorial Prize Lecture on October 9, 2004, which was also the occasion of my forty-seventh birthday.

Rather than simply giving separate lectures on the respective subjects of our books, Teschke and I had decided to hold what was, in effect, a debate about the one issue common to both of them: the validity or otherwise of the concept of bourgeois revolution. This at least offered the possibility of those attending being able to participate in the discussion, since I suspected that, with the exception of Terry Byres, they were unlikely to be familiar with eighteenth-century Scottish history. The debate was, however, somewhat unbalanced from the outset when the HM editorial board invited another Political Marxist, George Comninel, to act as moderator. In addition to the lopsidedness of the speaking arrangements, by the time the debate took place I had been on the receiving end of undisguised hostility from some of the other Political Marxists attending the conference, who seemed to resent the fact that Teschke had to share the Deutscher Prize with me. In my innocence, I found this puzzling, since none of them appeared to have read my book, which in any case contained precisely two references to Brenner, one quoting (with approval) his description of the English merchant Maurice Thompson and the other a rather ambivalent endnote on the Brenner Debate itself.[3] Nevertheless they all presumed to know my position—because apparently anyone who disagreed with Brenner "must" be either a supporter of Adam Smith's "commercialization thesis" or a technological determinist. Since I am neither of these I found their assumptions to be patronizing and infuriating in equal measure. What I had encountered was not the political sectarianism of the left, with which I was quite familiar, but rather an *academic* sectarianism with which I had no experience at all, where a particular theory—on the origin of capitalism!—was made the point of difference.[4] Outnumbered on the platform, and confronted with an extraordinary level of audience partisanship for what was primarily a historical debate, I felt I had no recourse but to—in the words of my partner, Cathy Watkins—"come out swinging." The organizers later informed me that the event was one of the livelier Deutscher Memorial Prize Lectures of recent years, but I felt it was also one that was unnecessarily polarized, since I actually agreed with Teschke's position on the Treaty of Westphalia, and in other circumstances I would have attempted to find more common ground with him over the international spread of capitalism from the mid-1700s onward in response to pressure from British expansion.[5]

I had taken holiday leave from my job to stay down in London for the European Social Forum (ESR), which started the following weekend. So in the four days between the close of the HM conference and the opening of the ESR, I camped out at the Scottish Executive outpost in Whitehall, Dover House, and wrote up a much-expanded version of my remarks as an article that a remarkably tolerant *Historical Materialism* published the following year in two parts. The argument is a defense of the concept of bourgeois revolution, or at least the "consequentialist" version of it, on the grounds that it corresponds to a real historical process, albeit one that has taken a number of different forms. But preparing the lecture and then writing the article also made me consider in detail the historical development of modern theories of revolution, from the writings of James Harrington onward. And because of this wider focus, the article makes a useful starting point for this collection. It establishes two important distinctions—between political and social revolutions on the one hand, and among different kinds of social revolution ("feudal," bourgeois, and socialist) on the other—that recur throughout many of the subsequent chapters. One conclusion with which I hope readers will agree is that it is impossible to make statements about "revolutions in general," in the way that is so often done in academic surveys of the subject.[6]

◆ ◆ ◆

The next two chapters are concerned with states rather than revolutions, although both explore the wider issue of modal transition before the emergence of capitalism. The first, written around the same time as the Deutscher Memorial Prize Lecture, is also related to debates over Political Marxism, but in a quite different way. I was responding to what I regarded as the exaggerated concerns over its influence expressed by Chris Harman, a long-standing leader of the SWP who had recently reassumed the editorship of the party's journal, *International Socialism* (*ISJ*). Harman had contributed in a typically robust style on my behalf during the Deutscher Memorial Prize Lecture debate. Earlier in 2004 he had invited me onto the editorial board of the *ISJ*, and he began to regularly commission articles and reviews from me, including chapters 5 and 7 below. Although Harman was an interventionist editor, he usually printed the articles I sent him unaltered in meaning even when he disagreed with them, although (no surprises here) they were regularly shortened. Only one piece, on the contemporary significance of the Enlightenment, was substantially changed—indeed, partially rewritten—by him prior to publication.[7] Harman was important in my development as a Marxist, as of course he was for many other comrades, and his work deserves a full-scale critical appraisal. While that is impossible here, I do want to briefly comment on the strengths and weaknesses of this outstanding figure on the British revolutionary left.

With the decline of the independent intellectual, there are essentially three ways in which Marxists—or thinkers on the radical left more generally—can produce scholarly work outside the academy.[8] One, which I attempted between 1995 and 2008, is to work in a nonliterary, nonpolitical occupation and essentially write in your spare time—something that is difficult to sustain for a prolonged period without damage to both health and personal relationships. Most people who find themselves in this situation consequently end up, as I did, becoming academics themselves if possible, although with the massive increase in temporary contracts in both the UK and the US this is becoming more difficult for the present generation to do with any degree of security. A second, represented by Isaac Deutscher, is to make a living as a writer, usually in journalism or other media, so that you are at least practicing your craft, and it is at least possible for your scholarly work to overlap with your professional role. People in these two situations may or may not have organizational affiliations. But a third group, of which Harman was an exemplar, *always* functions within a party context, conducting intellectual work not only for the benefit of the movement in general but of the revolutionary organization to which they belong in particular, their work primarily appearing in party publications. Political partisanship is one reason many of Harman's important intellectual achievements, notably in relation to the analysis of Eastern European Stalinism—which, for me at any rate, is his most enduring contribution—remained unrecognized outwith the IS tradition until relatively late in his life. As we shall see, there are dangers associated with the too-close identification of a theoretical position with a political tendency, but they are not those of academic contemplation or passive commentary. Harman had nothing but contempt for the disciplinary confines of the bourgeois academy: he wrote historical and economic analysis, but he was not a historian or an economist. Indeed, one of the qualities for which I most admired him was the way in which, if he thought an issue needed to be explored, he was prepared to research and write about it himself, even though he had no previous grounding in the subject.[9]

Harman could, however, also be deeply unwilling to abandon positions once he had committed himself to them—an attitude well encapsulated by the excellent

Scottish word "thrawn." Of course, there is much to be said for maintaining positions until they have been decisively proved wrong, rather than light-mindedly abandoning them at the first opportunity. In some respects conservatism can be an underappreciated revolutionary virtue: it can, for example, prevent the launching of inadequately thought-out initiatives or the adoption of fashionable stupidities, particularly those that exaggerate the extent to which conditions have changed. But in periods when conditions *have* actually changed in significant ways, refusing to recognize it can be enormously disabling. It is one thing to argue, for example, that neoliberal ideology does not accurately express the nature of the contemporary capitalist system; it is quite another to deny that any significant changes have taken place in that system. Harman's adherence to the latter position struck me as an example of this counterproductive kind of refusal.[10]

It was another example of this attitude that provoked me into writing chapter 2. Harman was unwilling to accept that there were any obstacles to capitalist development that could have prevented it from becoming a global system. This stance determined his attitude toward the existence or otherwise of the so-called Asiatic mode of production. He claimed that Marx and Engels were wrong to argue for the existence of the Asiatic mode, because in doing so they had to make claims about socioeconomic stagnation in large parts of the world (notably China and the territories covered by the Mughal and Ottoman Empires) that contradicted their core position about the tendency of the productive forces, and consequently of capitalism, to develop. He regarded the most common alternative to it, the tributary mode of production, as simply a relabeling, which furthermore conceded ground to Political Marxism by suggesting that there could be precapitalist but nonfeudal societies in which the state acted as a collective exploiter. Harman made these claims in a number of places but summarized them all in a long footnote to an otherwise admirable article for the *ISJ*, on the origins of capitalism, to which I then responded.

Harman's position was an example of what Tom Nairn in another context once called "all-the-same-ism."[11] In the case of the Asiatic mode, it amounted to holding that there were no fundamental differences, only purely contingent ones, between geographical regions of the precapitalist world, and that the prospects for capitalist development in all of them had therefore been equally good. While I could see a plausible case for the widespread *emergence* of capitalism as a subordinate mode, I found far less convincing the claim that capitalism would inevitably have become *dominant* in a sufficient number of states to establish a new global system. I agreed with Harman that the Asiatic mode was an actively misleading concept, at least as it was usually understood, but also thought that he had misunderstood the point of the tributary mode, which had nothing to do with the stagnation or nondevelopment of the productive forces, but was rather about how certain particularly powerful types of states were able to prevent capitalism from developing beyond a certain point, in a way that the weaker feudal states in Western Europe could not. There *was* therefore a link between the tributary states of the East and the absolutist states of the West, in the sense that the latter were attempting to achieve the same degree of control over economic development as the former. The degree to which capitalism had already developed before the absolutist states were consolidated was one of the main determinants both in the timing of the bourgeois revolutions and in whether or not they would be successful. In any event, after extensive email exchanges whose subject matter ranged from subterranean assumptions about human nature in the work of Wood through to possibilities for capitalist development in medieval Poland, Harman accepted my response for publication on the *ISJ* website.

Chapter 3 requires less explanation. It was part of a symposium on Chris Wickham's magisterial work *Framing the Early Middle Ages* (2005), to which Harman also contributed. Although it was originally delivered as a contribution to a panel discussion of the book at the HM conference in December 2006 and submitted as an article the following year, it and the other papers only appeared in print in 2011, by which time Harman's untimely death had occurred and Wickham had produced an equally monumental and impressive sequel. Of all the themes Wickham discusses, my focus—as the chapter title suggests—was on the question of the transition from slavery to feudalism and the extent to which class struggle played any role in it.

There is one aspect of my argument in both chapters 2 and 3 that I now no longer accept. In both pieces I had followed the work of John Haldon in characterizing the tributary mode of production as a variant of the feudal mode, largely because both involve the forcible extraction of a surplus from peasants. In retrospect, as I note in chapter 12, this fails to recognize that modes of production, in addition to involving relations between exploiters and exploited, also involve relations among the exploiters themselves—in Brenner's terms, they involve both "vertical" and "horizontal" relations.[12] Since ruling-class relations under the tributary mode are quite distinct from those under the feudal mode, the former cannot be considered as a variant of the latter.

The next section consists of four chapters reflecting on individual social revolutions: three successful bourgeois revolutions and one failed socialist revolution. Chapter 4 was originally written for a *Capital and Class* symposium on passive revolution, edited by Adam David Morton and published in 2010. I noted earlier that this concept of Gramsci's had influenced my theoretical approach to the Scottish Revolution, although I use it in a more restrictive way than Gramsci himself did, confining it to instances of "bourgeois revolution from above" rather than extending it to cases of subsequent capitalist reorganization. Morton's invitation to contribute to this collection allowed me to present a condensed version of all my research on revolution and transition in Scotland (excepting the material on national identity), explicitly framed in Gramscian terms.

My attempts to persuade the world, or even the Scottish historical profession, of the existence of a Scottish Revolution between 1692 and 1746 have not, as yet, been crowned with total success, although I remain optimistic. With regard to the French Revolution, however, the problem has never been one of dating, since the period is universally recognized as falling between 1789 and 1815, but rather of the significance of what occurred within those dates. Chapter 5 was a review for the *ISJ* of Henry Heller's *The Bourgeois Revolution in France* (2006), the title itself indicating the author's defiant opposition to revisionist attempts—including those by Political Marxists—to argue that the revolution was neither consequence nor cause of capitalist development. Admiring though I am of Heller's book and subsequent work on this theme, his approach differs from my own in being a highly sophisticated version of the "orthodox" view of bourgeois revolutions, in which they have to be carried out by the bourgeoisie themselves. For reasons that I explain both here and in several other chapters in this book, particularly 1, 11, and 12, this seems unnecessarily restrictive as a general position, although it is valid in the case of France where the bourgeoisie actually played a leading role.

The bourgeoisie also played a leading role in the subject of chapter 6, the US Civil War. Uniquely, in this case it was the industrial bourgeoisie who did so. Unlike the French Revolution, which was treated as the preeminent example of bourgeois revolution virtually from the formation of historical materialism, the Civil War was never discussed explicitly in these terms until after the Second World War. One major recent attempt to do so is John Ashworth's two-volume *Slavery, Capitalism and Politics in the Antebellum Republic* (1995 and 2007). Chapter 6 was originally written for an HM symposium on Marxism, the US Civil War, and slavery that marked the publication of Ashworth's second volume, but like several of the other contributions it was not so much a review of the book as a meditation suggested by its themes. As in the case of Heller's work, I approached Ashworth's in a spirit of admiration while questioning his definition of bourgeois revolution, which for me—in the second volume at least—relies too heavily on the motivations and ideology of the leading social actors in the North. For Ashworth, as for Heller, these characteristics are valid in the particular example he is discussing—the Northern industrialists were indeed thoroughly capitalist in their worldview—but this was not true of the forces that led most of the other great bourgeois revolutions of the 1860s, in Italy, Germany, and Japan.

Finally, later in this section, we leave the bourgeois revolutions behind for one of what Harman called the great "lost" socialist revolutions of the twentieth century: the German Revolution of 1918–23. Chapter 7 was originally a 2007 review for the *ISJ* of Pierre Broué's *The German Revolution* (2005), which had finally been translated into English thirty-four years after its initial French publication. In the context of an otherwise extremely favorable review I criticize Broué's epic work for surveying the events of these years almost entirely through the prism of debates within the Communist Party of Germany (KPD). There is one respect, however, in which Broué's remarkably detailed exposition of the KPD's internal affairs is of more than historical interest. Intentionally or not, his study of this most important of all the Western Communist parties makes it quite clear that there is not, and cannot be, a single model of revolutionary organization with eternally valid forms of election, decision making, and leadership.[13] This point has still to be fully absorbed by today's revolutionary left.

◆ ◆ ◆

The final group of essays all deal, in different ways, with themes of permanent revolution and uneven and combined development. As will soon become abundantly clear, this is a field where controversies abound, so for purposes of clarity I should make clear what I understand by these terms. "Permanent revolution" indicates both a possible *outcome*—the attainment of socialism in a context where the bourgeois revolution has yet to be achieved—and a *strategy* for achieving that outcome. "Uneven and combined development" also does double duty, signifying both a historical *process* involving the unstable fusion of archaic and modern forms that made permanent revolution possible, and the *theorization* of that process. My position on their contemporary relevance, which I only arrived at around the time the last two chapters in this section were written, is that while permanent revolution can no longer be meaningfully invoked, uneven and combined development is likely to continue for as long as capitalism itself.

Chapter 8 was originally written for a 2006 commemorative collection edited by Bill Dunn and Hugh Radice, *100 Years of Permanent Revolution*. Despite the title, the majority of its essays were concerned with uneven and combined development more than permanent revolution. This shift in emphasis is recent and, for me at least, very welcome. Trotskyists, of whatever degree of orthodoxy, had previously shown very little interest in this aspect of Trotsky's theoretical legacy. The revival—or perhaps I should say the commencement—of discussion on the subject came from a quite unexpected source, the academic discipline of international relations, beginning with Justin Rosenberg's 1995 Deutscher Memorial Prize Lecture.[14] Many previous accounts of uneven and combined development had failed to distinguish it from the earlier, far more widely accepted concept of uneven development—a frequent error being the assumption that the former is primarily about "the advantages of backwardness," whereas this focus has in fact been associated with uneven development as such. This has been true since Gottfried Leibniz's first tentative formulation of the concept, interestingly in relation to Russia, in the early 1700s. My chapter simply attempts to distinguish between uneven development and combined development, while tracing the actual relationship between the two down to Trotsky's distillation of the latter in chapter 1 of *The History of the Russian Revolution*.

Chapter 9 was also originally published in *100 Years of Permanent Revolution*, but it is not concerned with the theory of uneven and combined development so much as with the process itself, in the country where it currently has the greatest significance: China. In particular, it examines the political consequences of the two great waves of uneven and combined development in Chinese history, first from 1911 to 1931 and then from 1978 until now. Of all the nation-states in the global South, China is the one where the possibility of achieving parity with those in the heartlands of capitalism has the best prospects. Yet for all the breathless hype about how China is set to dominate the twenty-first century, even it is unlikely to do so in any overall sense, although individual cities like Shanghai may now resemble Los Angeles or Tokyo more than Mexico City or Nairobi.[15] This is one reason why uneven and combined development promises to be an ongoing phenomenon.

Chapter 10 was another essay written in 2006, this one originally published in the SWP's monthly magazine, *Socialist Review*. It was less about the Third World revolutions of the title than an attempt to argue that the Third World still exists, and that—despite growing internal differentiation—it remains collectively distinct from the First World in several ways. One conclusion it draws is that, contrary to the adherents of the Zapatistas, strategies developed in Chiapas are unlikely to be transferable to Glasgow or Chicago, even if we accept that they were successful in their place of origin—a highly contestable claim. But does the continuing distinctiveness of the Third World also mean that revolution there needs to be conceived of as a separate process of *permanent* revolution? This question brings us to the last two essays, which require some contextualization.

Those familiar with the travails of the British revolutionary left will be aware that the SWP experienced two waves of crisis in the last decade: the first in 2008–09, when its malfunctioning democratic structures finally provoked large-scale opposition, and the second in 2012–13, when the revulsion that a large minority of comrades felt at a badly mishandled disciplinary inquiry into allegations of sexual harassment reawakened all the unresolved issues from the first wave. When it became apparent that these issues would never be resolved in a way that responded to the concerns of the opposition, to which I belonged, the majority of us left and regrouped as Revolutionary Socialism for the 21st Century (rs21). Chapter 11 was written early in 2010, during a lull between these two crises. Chapter 12 was written early in 2014, after the resolution of the second, by which point I had resigned from the SWP after having been a member since 1978. Although neither chapter directly refers to these events, the anguish and exhaustion attendant on the factional struggle and its outcome inevitably surface in the second, although I did try when writing it to remain focused on the theoretical issues at hand.

Chapter 11 first appeared in the *ISJ* in 2010. It took as its starting point an article by Leo Zeilig, a comrade whose work I usually find interesting and informative. On this occasion, however, he had taken Tony Cliff's modification of permanent revolution, the notion of *deflected* permanent revolution, which was first developed in the late 1950s and early 1960s, and applied it to explain contemporary events in Africa. I found the result not only overly reverential to Cliff, but also irrelevant to the situation of Africa, or indeed any part of the global South today. To me, this was indicative of a more widespread conservatism within the SWP that treated all major theoretical problems as having been solved. It was as if there could be no new situations that required the development of existing theories or the formulation of new ones. Harman's attitude to neoliberalism, to which I referred above, was a case in point.

The IS tradition rested on Three Whales: the theories of state capitalism, the permanent arms economy, and deflected permanent revolution.[16] These theories did not, however, all have the same status. State capitalism was the most complete of the three and the least open to criticism. If there was a problem, then it lay not in the theory itself but in the way Cliff originally formulated it—for entirely understandable reasons—to explain the nature of the Stalinist regimes, rather than to describe a tendency within the world system as a whole that merely reached its highest stage of development under Stalinism. But even this overemphasis was later corrected, notably in Harman's later work.[17] The permanent arms economy was different. Although inseparable from the theory of state capitalism (since military preparation for war was the main form taken by competition between Washington and Moscow and their respective camps), it sought to explain a different aspect of the system since 1945, namely the extent of the postwar boom. It was, however, only a partial account. Michael Kidron, who had provided the most sophisticated explanation of the permanent arms economy during the 1960s, later described it as an "insight" rather than a "theory."[18] Ironically, Harman identified the nature of the problem more precisely than Kidron himself in an article criticizing the latter: "There is a valid criticism of this argument, which Mike may be trying to make. He could argue that, while the permanent arms economy explains the lack of crises and the slow rise in the organic composition of capital after the war, other factors need to be invoked to account for the *extent* of the boom in the 1950s and 1960s. He might be right—but this would not invalidate the theory of the permanent arms economy."[19] I think this assessment strikes the right balance: while the permanent arms economy did explain the absence of slump, it did not explain the existence of the boom and therefore needed to be supplemented with other explanations.[20] Whatever the greater or lesser degree of explanatory power respectively possessed by the two theories, however, it was obvious by the onset of crisis in the mid-1970s, and certainly by the time Stalinism collapsed in Eastern Europe and Russia, that they were no longer central to explaining how the system worked—whether or not you thought that capitalism had in other respects entered a new period.

Deflected permanent revolution was different again, since it could be argued that, unlike its companion theories, it had not only historical but contemporary relevance. The plausibility of this claim very much depended on how you regarded the parent concept, since this is what any scrutiny of the concept of deflection forced one to reconsider. Cliff's article "Permanent Revolution" was one of the first theoretical pieces I read as a young socialist in the mid-1970s, and it made an enormous impression on me. However, I had always understood the process of deflection as occurring where permanent revolution was a possibility but for whatever reason so-cialism was not achieved, and the process only ever resulted in a bourgeois revolution, understood in this context as the destruction of the precapitalist state and the con-struction of a new one geared to the accumulation of capital. In other words, there was a double deflection: class agency moved from the working class to a section of the bourgeoisie, and the outcome changed from that of a socialist to that of a bour-geois revolution. In this perspective, both permanent revolution and its deflected variant were now irrelevant, since the bourgeois revolutions had been accomplished everywhere by the mid-1970s at the latest. Working-class revolutionary movements can still be *defeated*, alas, but when they arise within an existing capitalist state there is no possible alternative class outcome other than socialism. In cases where the state remains bourgeois, the ascendancy of one wing or fraction of the bourgeoisie in place of another is therefore not "deflection" but simply an example of political revolution.

Yet there was an ambiguity in Cliff's argument, which can be traced back to Trotsky himself, whose conception of permanent revolution underwent two signifi-cant changes in the late 1920s and early 1930s.[21] On the one hand, he finally theo-rized the underlying social process, which he then named as uneven and combined development, and this in turn provided what I call the enabling conditions for revo-lution in China, as it had for Russia: this was a major scientific advance. On the other hand, he extended the applicability of permanent revolution far beyond Russia and China, and beyond any of those parts of the colonial and semicolonial world subject to uneven and combined development, detecting it even within long-established capitalist states—not merely in relatively weak capitalisms such as that of Spain, but in those at the very heart of the system, in the United States itself. This was not a major scientific advance but the cause of massive confusion. Trotsky's discovery of the near-universal applicability of permanent revolution seems to have two sources.

One was his highly conventional conception of bourgeois revolution, which involved the accomplishment of a series of "tasks," usually understood as democracy, agrarian reform, and national unification: where these had not been established, or had been less than perfectly achieved, then it was still permissible to talk of perma-nent revolution being on the agenda. Thus he at least retained a link with the notion of an unaccomplished or incomplete bourgeois revolution, but at the cost of calling into question whether it had actually been achieved anywhere. Most if not all states, even in Western Europe and North America, retained some characteristics which could be classified as unresolved issues from the bourgeois revolution, including monarchies and unelected second chambers, unresolved national questions, ma-jority peasant populations, restrictions on democratic participation, and forms of discrimination against minorities on racial, ethnic, or national grounds. So in effect Trotsky had to invoke a normative conception of capitalism, an "ideal type" in We-berian terms, which existed precisely nowhere and which, conversely, opened up the possibility of permanent revolution being applicable everywhere.[22]

The other source was his struggle against Stalinism. A strategy of class alliances with the "progressive" wings of the bourgeoisie, and what seemed to be a return to the stageist theory of the Second International, had been discernible in Comintern policy between 1924 and 1928–29. It emerged in fully developed form with the advent of the Popular Front in 1934–35. Trotsky instead counterposed the necessity for socialist revolution: any attempt to confine the revolution to prior stages would effectively disarm the working class, with fatal consequences. This correctly predicted the disasters that followed when the socialist revolution was not consummated, but nevertheless misunderstood the Stalinist position. It was not that the Stalinists had adopted an incorrect position about socialism being on the immediate agenda (owing to lack of confidence in the working class, for example, or a desire to retain alliances with "democratic" bourgeois states); *they were opposed to the very idea of socialist revolution, understood as a process of working-class self-emancipation.* To declare that permanent revolution was the alternative to the Stalinist strategy was therefore to declare that it was applicable in every situation, for when did they *ever* consider that conditions were right for socialism?

Permanent revolution originally meant a strategy applicable in one very specific case, that of Russia, where, as John Rees puts it, "the bourgeoisie really did have to clear away elements of a pre-capitalist state machine."[23] It was later extended to societies, above all China, with comparable conditions—or at least where the conditions produced comparable effects to those in Russia. Finally, it was made virtually coterminous with the strategy of "revolution" as such. Trotsky was not of course the only major Marxist figure to overstretch his own concepts and then to have them posthumously extended still further by his admirers: I have already suggested that Gramsci did the same in relation to his notion of "passive revolution."[24] In the case of permanent revolution, Cliff incorporated the overextension into his notion of deflection, first by severing any connection between permanent revolution and uneven and combined development, then by dissolving the distinction between political and social revolutions. The absence of democracy was the key, a stance made explicit by Joseph Choonara in a response to my article.[25] I responded to some of Choonara's criticisms in *How Revolutionary Were the Bourgeois Revolutions?* but also incorporated positions with which I agreed, for example on the difficulty of identifying the precise moment at which a capitalist state comes into being in countries lacking a single historical moment of revolutionary transformation.[26]

The only aspect of this chapter that I now regret is not following through the logic of my own position and simply arguing that permanent revolution is as historical a concept as state capitalism and the permanent arms economy, an issue the chapter fudges towards the end. I do think countries that are subject to the process of uneven and combined development are more likely to experience revolutionary situations than those that are not, but to describe these as being examples of permanent revolution is to imagine the future as an endless repetition of the past.

Chapter 12 was originally written for the *ISJ* as a response to criticisms of *How*

Revolutionary Were the Bourgeois Revolutions? by Alex Callinicos and Donny Gluck-stein. I had known Gluckstein since 1984, when I arrived in Edinburgh, where he was already a leading member in the SWP district and emerging as a national figure. I had joined and drifted out of the party in Aberdeen, then done the same again in London, but had now decided to mark my latest geographical relocation by making a more definite commitment. Gluckstein encouraged me to speak at meetings and to write, which he may now regret, but for which I remain grateful—indeed my first published article was a piece from 1990, jointly written with him, about the history of the class struggle in Scotland.[27] A modest and highly disciplined figure of great personal integrity, Gluckstein has focused as a historian on significant individuals (Bukharin), institutions (the Labour Party, the Soviets), and events (the Paris Commune, the British General Strike, the Second World War) in socialist history, not on ideas. If, as he suggested, I had indeed attempted to write about the latter without situating them in their historical context, then his criticisms on this score would have been perfectly legitimate. As it is, I disagree with the claim that this was what I had done—although ultimately this is for readers of the book to judge.[28]

Callinicos took over as editor of the *ISJ* after Harman's death. I think it is fair to say that his theoretical work influenced me more than that of any other SWP thinker, not least in relation to the bourgeois revolution and to the theory of revolutions more generally.[29] I had always been particularly impressed by his willingness, from the early 1980s, to test the boundaries of the IS tradition by incorporating new subjects and intellectual developments from elsewhere on the left, for which he was subjected to a degree of uncomprehending criticism by the more orthodox. His subsequent resistance to rethinking our central concepts beyond a certain point seems to be inspired by a concern that this would lead to an unraveling of the IS tradition, and perhaps aspects of classical Marxism more generally. Understandable though these concerns may be, I think they are misplaced. I accepted some of Callinicos's criticisms, but others illustrate our theoretical disagreements more than any doctrinal "mistakes" on my part, and such disagreements—here the lapse into cliché is unavoidable—can only be resolved in practice. I agree with Callinicos that the question of democracy will be central to revolutions, and indeed the class struggle in general, in the future.[30] I do not agree, however, that the struggle to achieve it necessarily makes the prospect of moving towards socialism any more likely. The historical record since the overthrow of the Mediterranean dictatorships in the 1970s, through to the establishment of majority rule in South Africa and beyond, suggests that bourgeois democracy has a retarding effect on revolutionary movements, in the short term at least, as newly enfranchised populations wait to see what democracy can do for them. This is evidently a subject on which detailed work is urgently required.

◆ ◆ ◆

The afterword was specially written for this volume. It attempts to examine the question of tradition, in a more reflective way than in the more polemical pieces gathered here. The central challenge is always to recognize the moment when maintaining this tradition in spirit involves departing from the ways it has previously been understood. The parallels the essay draws between Lincoln and Lenin do not of course extend to their specific policies. Lincoln, ignorant of the term *bourgeois revolution*, was nevertheless engaged in making one. Lenin, who perhaps wrote more on the subject of bourgeois revolution than any other Marxist, initially expected the Russian Revolution to fall into this category. But there is otherwise no overlap between their personalities or politics. Parallels between them can be seriously made in only one respect: their willingness, in a moment of crisis, to assess a changing situation and abandon previously held—often very long-held—positions in order to resolve it. The necessity for revolutionary leadership, in this sense at least, is perhaps the one element of continuity across the eras of the bourgeois and the socialist revolution, which, as I have tried to explain elsewhere in the book, are otherwise so different.

Neil Davidson
West Calder
West Lothian
Scotland
UK
March 31, 2015

1

How Revolutionary Were the Bourgeois Revolutions?

Introduction

I owe at least two debts to Isaac Deutscher. The first is general: his personal example as a historian. Deutscher was not employed as an academic and for at least part of his exile in Britain had to earn his living providing instant Kremlinology for, among other publications, *The Observer* and *The Economist*. It is unlikely that the Memorial Prize would be the honor it is, or that it would even exist, if these were his only writings. Nevertheless, his journalism enabled him to produce the great biographies of Stalin and Trotsky, and the several substantial essays that are his real legacy. For someone like me, working outside of the university system, Deutscher has been a model of how to write history that combines respect for scholarly standards with political engagement. I did not always agree with the political conclusions Deutscher reached, but the clarity of his style meant that, at the very least, it was always possible to say what these conclusions were—something that is not always true of the theoretical idols of the left.[1]

My second debt to Deutscher is more specific and directly relates to my theme: his comments on the nature of the bourgeois revolutions. Deutscher was not alone in thinking creatively about bourgeois revolutions during the latter half of the twentieth century, of course, but as I hope to demonstrate, he was the first person to properly articulate the scattered insights on this subject by thinkers in what he called the classical Marxist tradition.[2] I am conscious of the difficulties I face, not only in seeking to defend the scientific validity of bourgeois revolution as a theory but also in attempting to add a hitherto unknown case (and potentially others) to the existing roster. Since Scotland never featured on the lists of great bourgeois revolutions, even in the days when the theory was part of the common sense of the left, arguments for adding the Scottish Revolution to a list whose very existence has been called into question might seem quixotic, to say the least. Therefore, although I will occasionally refer to the specifics of the Scottish experience, my task is the more general one of persuading comrades—particularly those who think me engaged in an outmoded form of knight errantry—of the necessity for a theory of bourgeois revolution.

Bourgeois revolutions are supposed to have two main characteristics. Beforehand, an urban class of capitalists is in conflict with a rural class of feudal lords, whose interests are represented by the absolutist state. Afterward, the former have taken control of the state from the latter and, in some versions at least, reconstructed it on the basis of representative democracy. Socialists have found this model of bourgeois revolution ideologically useful in two ways. On the one hand, the examples of decisive historical change associated with it allow us to argue that, having happened before, revolutions can happen again, albeit on a different class basis. (This aspect is particularly important in countries like Britain and, to a still greater extent, the US, where the dominant national myths have been constructed to exclude or minimize the impact of class struggle on national history.) On the other hand, it allows us to expose the hypocrisy of a bourgeoisie that itself came to power by revolutionary means but now seeks to deny the same means to the working class.

Whether this model actually corresponds to the historical record is, however, another matter. For it is doubtful whether any countries have undergone an experience of the sort that the model describes, even England and France, the cases from which it was generalized in the first place. This point has been made, with increasing self-confidence, by a group of self-consciously "revisionist" writers from the 1950s and, particularly, from the early 1970s onward, in virtually every country where a bourgeois revolution had previously been identified. Their arguments are broadly similar, irrespective of national origin: prior to the revolution, the bourgeoisie was not "rising" and may even have been indistinguishable from the feudal lords; during the revolution, the bourgeoisie was not in the vanguard of the movement and may even have been found on the opposing side; after the revolution, the bourgeoisie was not in power and may even have been further removed from control of the state than previously. In short, these conflicts were just what they appeared to be on the surface: expressions of inter-elite competition, religious difference, or regional autonomy.

Even though the high tide of revisionism has now receded, many on the left have effectively accepted the case for the irrelevance of the bourgeois revolutions—perhaps I should call them the Events Formerly Known as Bourgeois Revolutions—to the transition from feudalism to capitalism. There are, of course, different and conflicting schools of thought concerning why they are irrelevant, four of which have been particularly influential.

From society to politics

The first retains the term "bourgeois revolution" but dilutes its social content until it becomes almost entirely political in nature. The theoretical starting point here is the claim by Arno Mayer that the landed ruling classes of Europe effectively remained in power until nearly halfway through the twentieth century, long after the events usually described as the bourgeois revolutions took place.[3] One conclusion drawn from Mayer's work by Perry Anderson was that the completion of the bourgeois revolution, in Western Europe and Japan at least, was the result of invasion and occupation by the American-led Allies during the Second World War.[4] The wider implication is that the bourgeois revolution should not be restricted to the initial process of establishing a state conducive to capitalist development, but should be expanded to include subsequent restructuring in which the bourgeoisie assume political rule directly, rather than indirectly through the landowning classes.

But if the concept can be extended in this way, why confine it to the aftermath of the Second World War, when direct bourgeois rule had still to be achieved across most of the world? In *The Enchanted Glass* (1988), Anderson's old colleague Tom Nairn also drew on Mayer's work to date the triumph of capitalism still later in the twentieth century, "to allow for France's last fling with the quasi-Monarchy of General de Gaulle, and the end of military dictatorship in Spain, Portugal and Greece."[5] If the definitive "triumph" of capitalism requires the internationalization of a particular set of political institutions, then it had still not been achieved at the time these words were written. By the time the second edition was published in 1994, however, the Eastern European Stalinist states had either collapsed or been overthrown by their own populations, events that had clear parallels with the end of the Mediterranean dictatorships during the 1970s.

These revisions mean that the theory no longer applies only to those decisive sociopolitical turning points that removed obstacles to capitalist development. Instead, it now extends to any subsequent changes to existing capitalist states that bring them into more perfect alignment with the requirements of capital accumulation. But there can be no end to these realignments this side of the socialist revolution, which suggests that bourgeois revolutions are a permanent feature of capitalism, rather than a feature associated with its consolidation and extension. On this basis we would have to categorize events like the Indonesian Revolution or the revolutions now opening up in the former Soviet Republics as bourgeois revolutions, when in fact they seem to me far better understood as examples of the broader category of *political* revolution—political because they start and finish within the confines of the capitalist mode of production. In other words, I am suggesting that the bourgeois revolutions are, like socialist revolutions, examples of that very rare occurrence, a *social* or *societal* revolution. These are epochal events involving change from one type of society into another—not merely changes of government, however violently achieved.[6] But there are political as well as theoretical problems involved. If we accept that the US could bring about the—or "a"—bourgeois revolution in Germany or Japan during the Second World War, there is no logical reason why they cannot bring one about "from above" in Iraq (or Iran, or Syria, or Saudi Arabia) today. Christopher Hitchens used precisely this argument to justify his support for the invasion and occupation of Iraq.[7] Here, "bourgeois revolution" simply means conforming to the political arrangements acceptable to the dominant imperialist powers.

FROM EVENT TO PROCESS

A second way in which the meaning of bourgeois revolution has been reduced in significance is through extending its duration in time until it becomes indistinguishable from the general process of historical development. The first interpretations of bourgeois revolution as a process were serious attempts to deal with perceived weaknesses in the theory.[8] And there is nothing inherently implausible about bourgeois revolutions taking this form rather than that of a single decisive event. (In fact I argue precisely this in relation to the Scottish Revolution.[9]) The problem is rather that adherents of "process" have tended to expand the chronological boundaries of the bourgeois revolutions to such an extent that it is difficult to see how the term "revolution" can be applied in any meaningful way, other than, perhaps, as a metaphor. As a general proposition this dovetails with the influential views of the French Annales School of historiography, which has always been distrustful of event-based history. Whatever there is to be said for these views, they are incompatible with any conception of bourgeois revolution involving decisive moments of transition, particularly where, as in several recent variants, there is no concluding episode.

On this basis bourgeois revolutions are no longer even political transformations that bring the state into line with the needs of capital, but can be detected in every restructuring of the system, including the prior process of economic change itself. Some writers on the left have even begun to speak of capitalist globalization as "a second bourgeois revolution."[10] But by now enumeration is clearly meaningless, since "bourgeois revolution" has simply become a metaphor for an ongoing process of capitalist restructuring that will continue as long as the system exists. Aside from trivializing the analytic value of the concept, such a redefinition is—once again—open to appropriation by ex-revolutionaries seeking a "progressive" justification for supporting the system. Nigel Harris, one ex-Marxist convert to neoliberalism, writes that the "original" bourgeois revolutions were "far from establishing business control of the state": "Thus, it is only now that we can see the real 'bourgeois revolution,' the establishment of the power of world markets and of businessmen over the states of the world."[11]

"THE CAPITALIST WORLD SYSTEM"

The third position that I want to consider is a component of the capitalist world-system theory associated with Immanuel Wallerstein and his cothinkers. Here, the focus completely shifts from revolution—however conceived—to the transition to capitalism itself. Unlike those who hold the first two positions, Wallerstein thinks that bourgeois revolutions are no longer necessary, but his position is also more extreme in that he thinks they have *never* been necessary. Wallerstein regards the feudal states of the sixteenth century, like the nominally socialist states of the twentieth, as inherently capitalist through their participation in the world economy. Bourgeois revolutions are therefore not irrelevant because they failed to completely overthrow the feudal landed classes but because, long before these revolutions took place, the lords had already transformed themselves into capitalist landowners. Capitalism emerged as a conscious response by the lords to the fourteenth-century crisis of feudalism, the social collapse that followed, and the adoption, by the oppressed and exploited, of ideologies hostile to lordly rule. The lords therefore changed the basis on which they extracted surplus value over an extended period lasting two centuries.

Two aspects of this account are notable. One is that the key social actors are the very class of feudal lords regarded as the enemy to be overthrown in the conventional model of bourgeois revolution. Although Wallerstein and his school do not deny the existence of a bourgeoisie proper, it is the self-transformation of the lords that is decisive, not the actions of the preexisting bourgeoisie. The other is that the nature of the capitalist world system, which the lords are responsible for bringing into being, is defined by the dominance of commercial relationships. Indeed, Wallerstein defines "the essential feature of the capitalist world economy" as "production for sale in a market in which the object is to realize the maximum profit."[12] Although wage labor certainly exists at the core, it is insertion into the world market that defines the system as a whole as capitalist, since productive relations in the periphery continue to include modified forms of slavery and serfdom, in addition to wage labor. Anyone who produces for the market can therefore be described as a capitalist.

The strengths of this position should not be underestimated. It treats the question—so important for Mayer and those influenced by him—of whether the ruling classes possessed land and title or not as less significant than whether income from these sources was derived from feudal or capitalist methods of exploitation. It also gives due weight to the fact that the advanced nature of the "core" of the system is at least partly dependent on the enforced backwardness of the "periphery."

But there are problems too. World-systems theory certainly does not see episodes of bourgeois revolution in every political upheaval that changes the relationship of the state to capital, but it equally wants to dissociate them from the ascendancy of capitalism. Wallerstein himself continues to use the term, but it has lost all relation to the creation of a capitalist world economy. Theoretical pluralists, for whom there are no necessary connections between aspects of human existence, might find this acceptable, but Marxists surely cannot. However, there are also difficulties with the theory that must be equally evident to non-Marxists. One is the voluntarism that underlies it. Capitalism apparently arose because the existing class of lords made a conscious decision to transform the basis on which they exploited their tenants and laborers. But, if they were already in such a commanding position, why did they feel the need to change? The most fundamental issue, however, is whether the system described by Wallerstein is actually capitalist at all. It is not only in relation to the periphery but also to the metropolitan centers themselves that a definition of capitalism based on the realization of profit through trade is problematic. The key issue, which Robert Brenner more than anyone else has placed on the agenda, is whether the formation of a world market is equivalent to the establishment of capitalism. As Brenner has pointed out, the argument that expansion of trade is the prime mover in generating capitalist development is often assumed to be that of Marx himself, but it is in fact derived from Adam Smith. Hence, despite their differences, Brenner can legitimately describe Paul Sweezy, Gunder Frank, and Wallerstein as "neo-Smithian" Marxists. Brenner's own definition of capitalism, to which we will turn next, is also deeply unsatisfactory, but his negative critique is well founded in this respect.

"Capitalist social property relations"

The fourth and final position that I want to consider is the "capitalist social property relations" approach of Brenner himself. Unlike Wallerstein, Brenner does not see the mechanism by which capitalist development occurs as being the expansion of trade and commerce, but rather the introduction of a distinctive set of "social property relations." (He uses the latter term in place of the more conventional Marxist concept of "relations of production," although the two are by no means synonymous.) So distinctive are these relations that, rather than encompassing the entire world by the sixteenth century, as capitalism does for Wallerstein, they were still restricted to a handful of territories even a hundred years later. Where Wallerstein is broad, Brenner is narrow. But there are also similarities. Like Wallerstein, Brenner treats bourgeois revolution as irrelevant and does so for essentially the same reasons, namely that capitalist development—albeit confined to a very limited number of countries—occurred prior to and independently of the events that are usually described in this way.

I regard the Brenner thesis as the most serious of the four theoretical tendencies under review here. No serious attempt to construct a defensible version of the theory of bourgeois revolutions can avoid meeting the challenge it poses. I should perhaps begin by saying that the comments that follow are not offered, as it were, in self-defense of my own views. In fact, my position on Scottish capitalist development is—and I choose my words carefully here—not incompatible with the Brenner thesis. Nevertheless, I think the thesis is wrong, although wrong in a stimulating and productive way that has forced those of us who disagree with it to think rather more seriously than we might otherwise have done about, for example, the very nature of capitalism. Discussion of the thesis is complicated by the fact that there is far from complete unanimity among Political Marxists, by which I mean those hard-core supporters—Ellen Meiksins Wood, George Comninel, and my fellow Deutscher Memorial Prize winner Benno Teschke—who in many respects have taken up more extreme positions than Brenner himself. We cannot hold Brenner directly responsible for every interpretation they have made of his original thesis, or even assume that he is necessarily in agreement with all of them. In what follows, I will therefore try to distinguish between Brenner's own positions, those that are common to the entire school, and those that are held by individual members.

Elements of the Brenner thesis are less original than some of his supporters appear to realize.[13] Nevertheless, it is also true that these elements have never before been brought together into such a coherent synthesis. Originality may in any case be an overrated virtue in these days of instant revisionism. What is more important is that Political Marxism has rightly challenged several positions that Marxists have carelessly adopted in common with their intellectual opponents—above all, the assumption that capitalism is somehow innate, always existing in some subordinate form and only waiting to be released from feudal or other constraints. Many Marxists make this assumption by default through their inability to explain how capitalism comes into existence, thus inadvertently aligning themselves with the position of Adam Smith and his contemporaries, for whom the emergence of capitalism is, in Brenner's own words, "human nature reassert[ing] itself."[14] If it were true that capitalism had existed virtually since the emergence of civilization, then the possibility of socialism, at least in the form of anything but a totalitarian dictatorship, would be nonexistent, for capitalism would indeed have been shown to be congruent with human nature—a point that bourgeois ideologues have been making with increasing stridency since the fall of Stalinism in 1989–91. The insistence of the Political Marxists on the radical break that capitalism involves in human history therefore retains all its relevance. On a less obviously ideological level, Brenner's work has made it more difficult—if not, alas, impossible—for historians of the late medieval or early modern periods to write about "economic development" or "economic growth" as if these automatically involved capitalist economic development and growth, without specifying the social relations within which economic activity took place. These qualities have ensured Brenner's work an acceptance that is wide, but often not, I think, very deep. Beyond the fairly narrow ranks of the Political Marxists proper, his thesis is often cited approvingly but without the full implications necessarily being understood. In fact, in its initial form at least, the thesis is not one that can be accepted in part or synthesized with other interpretations. On the contrary, its rigor and internal consistency is such that the positive alternative it offers can really only be accepted or rejected in full. Although Brenner has correctly identified major problems with the way historians, including Marxist historians, have dealt with the development of capitalism, his alternative involves a different set of problems.

Brenner argues that "modern economic growth"—the systematic growth associated with capitalism and with no other exploitative mode of production—only takes place when two conditions are satisfied. One is that the direct producers are separated from both their means of production and their means of subsistence, and therefore have no alternative but to satisfy their needs by recourse to the market. The other is where the exploiters can no longer sustain themselves by simply intensifying extra-economic pressure on the direct producers, but instead have to increase their efficiency. Unlike in precapitalist economic formations, both sides are compelled to be competitive, most importantly by cutting costs. Without these conditions there is no incentive for either class to innovate. Any direct producers who attempted to introduce new techniques would meet resistance from their fellow agriculturalists who would regard it as a breach of collectivist solidarity. Any exploiters who attempted to introduce new techniques would require a labor force motivated to adopt them and, in its absence, they would be more likely to invest instead in more effective methods of coercion. Even if new methods were successfully adopted by individuals of either class, there is no reason to expect that they would be adopted by anybody else, not least because technical advances introduced once and for all do not themselves bring economic development or the compulsion to innovate with a view to reducing costs. Brenner is of course aware that, for example, peasants adopted more efficient ploughs from the eleventh century onward, but denies that this had any significant impact on social relations because community control resisted systematic improvement, specialization, and market dependence. "The only significant method by which the feudal economy could achieve real growth was by opening up new land for cultivation."[15] Nor was the situation different in the towns, since they were also unable to act as spontaneous generators of capitalism: "Their potential for growth was strictly limited because urban industry was almost entirely dependent upon lordly demand (as subsistence-oriented peasants had only limited ability to make market purchases) and lordly demand was itself limited by the size of agricultural surplus, which was itself constrained by limited growth potential of · the agrarian productive forces."[16]

How could this closed circuit, in which the same feudal relations of production are endlessly reproduced according to a given set of "rules," ever be broken? In the case of peasant communities where the means of production were collectively owned, Brenner thinks that it never would have been. Where peasants possessed the means of production individually, he proposes three possible alternatives, all unintended consequences of actions designed to produce quite other results. First, peasants could lose land through selling it or through demographic growth. Second, the lords could increase the level of surplus extraction to such an extent that peasants could no longer pay their rent or, if they could pay it, could no longer retain enough produce for their own subsistence. Third, the lords might be forced to expropriate those peasants who had asserted their independence to such an extent that they were virtually defining themselves as owners, not merely existing in a state of effective possession. From the enormous difficulties involved in subverting feudal "rules for reproduction," Brenner draws two conclusions: "The first is that pre-capitalist economies have an internal logic and solidity which should not be underestimated. The second is that capitalist economic development is perhaps an historically more limited, surprising and peculiar phenomenon than is often appreciated."[17] If Brenner is right, peasant small production could have carried on almost indefinitely beneath the surface of precapitalist social structures had it not been for the unhappy accident that gave rise to capitalism. What was the nature of this apparently unfortunate series of events?

Recall the two sets of economic actors that Brenner claims must be present and compelled to accumulate capital: an exploited class of direct producers who are forced to sustain themselves through the market and an exploiting class of property owners who cannot sustain themselves through forcible extraction of a surplus. In England, both classes become simultaneously subject to these conditions. Following the non-Marxist historian Lawrence Stone, Brenner argues that, by the accession of the Tudor dynasty in 1485, non-economic coercion was of declining significance to the English lords, since the peasantry was no longer subject to the serfdom that required it and, in the aftermath of the Wars of the Roses, an exhausted nobility faced a strengthened state that would no longer tolerate magnate insubordination. But they could increase their incomes through the exploitation of their lands or, more precisely, through the exploitation of the commercial tenants who increasingly came to occupy their lands.[18] We are offered an explanation here as to why the lords were increasingly compelled to turn to systematic commercialization of their estates—but what allowed the peasants to abolish serfdom while preventing them from successfully resisting when the lords attempted to turn them into commercial tenants? Brenner has a two-fold answer to this question, both parts of which involve comparisons with nations that did not take the road to capitalist development at the same time as England.

The first part concerns different outcomes of the class struggle in Eastern and Western Europe. After the period of demographic collapse during the second half of the fourteenth century, the lords attempted to discipline a numerically reduced peasantry, which was consequently in a much stronger bargaining position. Success-ful peasant resistance to these impositions permanently ended serfdom in Western Europe, but failed to do so in Eastern Europe, where it was either reimposed in areas where it had been weakened or imposed for the first time in areas that had previ-ously escaped subjugation. These differences could be seen most clearly on either side of the Elbe. Brenner rejects the relative weight of the urban sector as the main explanation for this divergence.[19] Instead he identifies another factor as decisive: "The development of peasant solidarity and strength in western Europe—especially as this was manifested in the peasant's organization at the level of the village—ap-pears to have been far greater in western than in eastern Europe; and this superior institutionalization of the peasant's class power in the west may have been central to its superior ability to resist seigniorial reaction."[20] But outcomes were by no means uniform even within Western Europe.

The second part of his answer identifies the source of this further divergence as the extent to which the various peasantries of Western Europe were able to retain possession of the land that was won during the late feudal revolts from actual or potential exploiters: "This is not to say that such outcomes were arbitrary, but rather that they tended to be bound up with certain historically specific patterns of the devel-opment of the contending agrarian classes and their relative strength in the different European societies: their relative levels of internal solidarity, their self-consciousness and organization, and their general political resources—especially their relationships to the non-agricultural classes (in particular, potential urban class allies) and to the state (in particular, whether or not the state developed as a class-like competitor of the lords for the peasants surplus)."[21] It is the last point that is crucial for Brenner in explaining the difference between England and France. The English feudal state was centralized, but not in the sense that it drew in power from the periphery. It was established with the consent of the feudal ruling class and largely ruled in alliance with it. As a result its power was less than that of the French state, which centralized later on an absolutist basis and in opposition to the individual interests of the lords. In England, the absolutist project was aborted, leaving the peasants free from the burden of state taxation but also without protection from the lords: "It was the English lord's inability either to re-enserf the peasants or to move in the direction of absolutism (as had their French counterparts) which forced them in the long run to seek novel ways out of their revenue crisis."[22] In France, "the centralized state appears to have developed (at least in large part) as a class-like phenomenon—that is as an independent extractor of the surplus, in particular on the basis of its arbitrary power to tax the land."[23] The very success of the French peasantry in resisting the power of the lords left them exposed as potential sources of taxation to a much more powerful opponent, the absolutist state, which was in competition with the lords for surplus that the peasants produced. Paradoxically, however, the French state also protected the peasants from lordly impositions, in rather the same way as a farmer protects his chickens from the fox. The English lords, constrained by neither peasant ownership nor absolutist restriction, were able to consolidate their lands in the interest of economies of scale by forcing some peasants to accept competitive leases. Those peasants who were unsuccessful in gaining leases were either compelled to become wage laborers for now-capitalist farmers or to leave the land altogether in search of work elsewhere. In both cases their labor power had become a commodity to be bought and sold on the market.

In the Brenner thesis the emergence of capitalism is therefore an unintended outcome of the actions of the two main feudal social classes, peasants and lords. One former Deutscher Memorial Prize winner, James Holstun, has written that this position provides socialists with an approach that "resists the binary blackmail threatened by revisionists or postmodernists, for the results are neither inevitable nor purely contingent."[24] But contingency is precisely what is involved. In a position that has curious parallels with Althusserianism, Brenner conceives of feudalism as a self-enclosed, self-perpetuating system that cannot be undermined by its own internal contradictions. It is claimed that Brenner has an explanation for the—in his terms, highly unlikely—appearance of capitalism: the class struggle. Even outside the Political Marxists proper the claim is repeated by writers with quite different attitudes to the thesis. Consequently, many socialist readers must have gone to Brenner's key articles, eagerly anticipating detailed accounts of peasant resistance to the lords, only to be disappointed by the scant attention that he actually devotes to the subject. In fact, it is the outcome of such class conflicts that Brenner is interested in, not the conflicts themselves. The rural class struggle is merely a mechanism for explaining why capitalist social relations of production emerged in England and not in Prussia, France, or China. But why does Brenner need such a mechanism?

Marxists have previously argued that capitalism emerged in the countryside through a series of transitional forms, initially combining different modes of production but progressively becoming more purely capitalist in nature. Lenin's discussion of Russian agriculture after the abolition of serfdom in 1861, in *The Development of Capitalism in Russia*, is one of the most outstanding examples of this type of analysis. Brenner might well agree with this assessment in relation to nineteenth-century tsarist Russia. From his perspective such gradual transformations were possible because the system that began in England established an international context in which other countries were both pressurized into adopting capitalist social property relations and provided with a model to which they could aspire. Russian landowners therefore had a motivation for introducing capitalism, albeit under tightly controlled conditions. But since English landowners and peasants were the first to be subject to these relations they could have had no such motivation. The outcome of class struggle provides Brenner with the situation in which the necessary determinations come into effect.

Marx saw no need for a special mechanism with which to explain the appearance of capitalism in England (or the United Netherlands and Catalonia, the other areas where Brenner, if not his followers, concedes that capitalism had emerged). The most obvious explanation for this omission on his part is that he did not think the development of capitalism was unique to England but rather saw it as a general phenomenon, at least in Europe. Consequently, the entire elaborate hypothesis about the different outcomes of the class struggle is totally unnecessary. In effect, Political Marxists do not seem to recognize that there is an abstract model in *Capital*. Brenner himself apart, they think that England was the only site of endogenous capitalist development and therefore assume that Marx takes English development as a model for the origin of capitalism because, in effect, it was the only example he had. Now, I do not dispute that England was the country where capitalism developed to the greatest extent. It was for this reason that Marx made it the basis of his analysis, in the same way that he always took the most developed form of any phenomenon as the basis of his analysis. But in his mature work Marx repeatedly states that capitalist development took place beyond England in space and before England in time.[25] He certainly believed that by 1648 the capitalist mode of production had become *dominant* in England to a greater extent than anywhere else, but that was perfectly compatible with believing that capitalist production had developed elsewhere, within otherwise fundamentally feudal economies.[26]

If, as I have suggested, the argument from contingency is a speculative answer to a non-question, then it may explain why Brenner has some difficulty explaining why the class struggle resulted in such different outcomes across Europe. His attempts to deal with this problem are among the least convincing aspects of the entire thesis. Brenner points to the different capacities deployed by the classes involved: these lords had better organization, those peasants displayed less solidarity. But without an explanation for the prior processes by which these classes acquired their organizational or solidaristic qualities, these are mere descriptions, which, to borrow a favorite expression of Wood's, "assume precisely what has to be explained." His inability to explain the differing levels of peasant resistance to the lords (as opposed to the consequences of that resistance) means that he has to fall back on what Stephen Rigby calls "a host of particular historical factors which cannot be reduced to expressions of class structure or of class struggle."[27] It was for this quite specific reason that Guy Bois described Brenner's Marxism as involving "a voluntarist vision of history in which the class struggle is divorced from all other objective contingencies."[28] But he is only a voluntarist in relation to the part of the period that took place before the different-settlements-of-the-land question occurred. Afterward, precisely the opposite applies, and his interpretation becomes overly determinist. In the case of England, far from being free to opt for a particular course of action, he sees no alternative for either the lords or the peasants but to become market-dependent. As soon as the mechanism has produced the required result, the element of choice disappears from his account, to be replaced by that of constraint.

However, let us accept, for the sake of argument, that capitalist social property relations arose only in the English countryside and that they did indeed do so as a result of the indeterminate outcome of the class struggle. There are still other problems. Brenner is surely right to reject the counterposition of a supposedly feudal countryside to supposedly capitalist towns, but are we not being asked to accept an equally implausible reversal of these terms? Indeed, it is difficult to envisage how there could have been an inescapable "market compulsion" in the countryside in the first place while the urban economy remained untouched by capitalist social property relations, given that the former was not and could not have been isolated from the latter. Furthermore, it is by no means clear how capitalist social property relations were then extended to the towns, which presumably remained feudal, or postfeudal, or at any rate noncapitalist, until something—but what?—brought about the introduction of these relations. Political Marxists are either silent on this issue or apparently fail to realize that it represents a problem. To whom did the dispossessed peasants sell their labor power, given that no capitalist class existed outside of the landlords and tenant farmers in the English countryside? In order to buy the commodities they required, the new work force needed jobs. Who employed them? Could it be that enterprising merchants or artisans saw—whisper who dares—an *opportunity*? For urban employers could not, at this stage, have been subject to market compulsion. At the very least there is a missing link in the chain of argument. I am not suggesting, of course, that agrarian capitalism had no effect on other sectors of the economy. It both transformed the existing service sector and generated a requirement for new services, but this does not explain the emergence of capitalist production in the towns and the non-agricultural areas of the countryside. I understand how Political Marxists account for the establishment of capitalism in the English countryside. I also understand how Political Marxists account for the spread of capitalism beyond Britain. I do not understand how capitalist social property relations spread from the English countryside to the rest of England. Nor, for that matter, how the same process took place in Holland or Catalonia, the other areas where Brenner himself thinks that capitalism existed.

This is not a problem in Marx's own discussions of the rise of capitalism. In a section of the *Grundrisse* ("The Chapter on Capital") much admired by Political Marxists, Marx argues that "the dissolution of the old relations of production" has to take place in both the towns and the countryside, and that the process in the former is partly responsible for it in the latter: "Urban labor itself had created means of production for which the guilds became just as confining as were the old relations of landownership to an improved agriculture, which was in part itself a consequence of the larger market for agricultural products in the cities etc."[29] Marx had earlier presented this argument specifically in relation to England in an 1850 review of François Guizot's *Why Was the English Revolution So Successful?* (This review should, incidentally, be required reading for anyone who believes that Marx simply adopted the views of the French Restoration historians as to the nature of bourgeois revolutions.) Two aspects of this argument are particularly interesting. First, Marx is already fully aware of the capitalist nature of the majority of the English landowners, but he does not consider them the only capitalists in England. Second, despite the preexistence of capitalist social relations, Marx did not regard the transition to capitalism as having been completed, even by 1688: "In reality . . . the momentous development and transformation of bourgeois society in England only began with the consolidation of the constitutional monarchy."[30] In other words, Marx conceptualizes an uneven but broadly simultaneous development across the rural and urban sectors with mutually reinforcing results. Such an explanation is impossible for Political Marxists, however, as it would involve conceding that, in some circumstances at least, people could willingly choose to become capitalists rather than only do so when the role was imposed on them. As a result they have no explanation at all for urban capitalist development, other than osmosis.

For the members of the Political Marxists, capitalism is defined by the existence of what they call market compulsion—the removal of the means of production and subsistence from the direct producers so that they are forced to rely on the market to survive. There is of course a venerable tradition of thought that defines capitalism solely in market terms, but it is not Marxism; it is the Austrian economic school whose leading representatives were Ludwig von Mises and Friedrich von Hayek. In the Hayekian version of this argument the reductionism involved has a clear ideological purpose. It is to declare any forms of state intervention or suppression of market mechanisms, from the most modest public provision of welfare services through to full nationalization of the economy, as socialist, incompatible with capitalism and consequently liable to lead down "the road to serfdom." Political Marxists are obviously on the other side of the intellectual barricades from Hayek and his followers, but this is why I find it so curious that they similarly define any kind of economic activity that does not involve "market compulsion" as noncapitalist, particularly since Hayek's position is extreme even by the standards of contemporary bourgeois ideology. It might be worth recalling, in this connection, what John Maynard Keynes said of Hayek, since the remark evidently has wider application: "It is an extraordinary example of how, starting with a mistake, a remorseless logician can end up in Bedlam."[31] For Marx, capitalism was defined not as a system of market compulsion but as one of *competitive accumulation based on wage labor*. Both aspects are equally important.

Marx starts with wage labor. He writes in the first volume of *Capital* that the emergence of capital as a social relation is the result of two types of commodity owners: on the one hand, "the owners of money, means of production, means of subsistence" and "on the other hand, free workers, the sellers of their own labor power, and therefore the sellers of labor." He concludes: "With the polarization of the commodity market into these two classes, the fundamental conditions of capitalist production are present."[32] Wage labor was by no means universal in England by 1789, let alone by 1688. But since the Brenner thesis is insistent that capitalist social relations were already completely dominant in England before the Civil War, what were these great social struggles for "moral economy" against "political economy" and for "just price" against "market price," which occurred as late as the end of the eighteenth century, actually about? The logic of this position is that the origins of capitalism need not involve wage labor. Wood in particular has followed this logic through to its conclusion and claimed that, rather than being constitutive of capitalism as Marx had thought, wage labor is in fact a consequence of it:

> In the specific property relations of early modern England, landlords and their tenants became dependent on the market for their self-reproduction and hence subject to the imperatives of competition and increasing productivity, whether or not they employed wage-labor. . . . The fact that market-dependence and competition preceded proletarianization tells us something about the relations of competition and their autonomy from the relations between capital and labor. It means that producers and possessors of the means of production, who are not themselves wage-laborers, can be market-dependent without employing wage-labor.[33]

For Wood, the removal of the means of *subsistence* from the direct producers is the fundamental moment in their subjection to market compulsion. It is true, of course, that in a context where the economy is already dominated by the capitalist mode of production, tenant farmers can play the role of capitalists whether or not they employ wage labor, but this has nothing to do with whether or not they possess the means of subsistence. Independent farmers in the southwest of Scotland, and even in parts of the Highlands, were already dependent on the market long before the transition to capitalism was imposed during the second half of the eighteenth century, for the simple reason that they were restricted by environmental constraints to pastoral farming and could not meet their needs in any other way. If capitalism is based on a particular form of exploitation, which is the extraction of surplus value from the direct producers through wage labor, then I fail to see how capitalism can exist in the absence of wage laborers. Where does surplus value come from in a model that contains only capitalist landlords and capitalist farmers? Surplus value may be realized through market transactions, but it can scarcely be produced by them. The only means by which Wood proposes that surplus value can be extracted is the competition for leases among tenant farmers (in that the latter compete to hand over the greatest proportion of their output to the landlord in order to acquire or retain a tenancy). But there is nothing distinctly capitalist about this mechanism. In seventeenth-century Scotland it was common for feudal landlords to conduct a "roup" or auction of leases that included the full panoply of labor services as part of the rent. Indeed, pioneering improvers like Fletcher of Saltoun and Seton of Pitmedden regarded this as one of the main means through which the peasantry was exploited.[34]

Is Wood therefore right to claim that all critiques of Brenner, including this one, assume "that there can be no such thing as a Marxist theory of competition"?[35] By no means; but it important to be clear what such a theory must involve. I referred earlier to competitive accumulation, rather than market competition. The watchword of Moses and the prophets, it will be recalled, was "Accumulate! Accumulate!" Accumulation takes place in the context of competition, but not all competition between capitals is market-based. Nikolai Bukharin pointed this out in *The Economics of the Transition Period* (1920), one of a series of classic works that, it seems, have still to be fully absorbed into the Marxist tradition:

> Every economic phenomenon in the capitalist world is, in some way or another, bound up with price and, hence, the market. This does not mean, however, that every economic phenomenon is a market phenomenon. It is the same with competition. Up to now, the chief consideration has been of market competition, which was characteristic of the pattern of horizontal competition in general, but competition, i.e., the struggle between capitalist enterprises, can also be waged outside the market in the strict sense of the word. Such, for example, is the struggle for spheres of capital investment, i.e. for the very opportunity to expand the production process. In this case too, it is clear that other methods of struggle will be used than those of the classical case of horizontal market competition.[36]

What were these "other methods of struggle"? The most important, at least among state capitals, is war and preparation for war. Contrary to a widely held misconception, the classical Marxist theory of imperialism, to which Bukharin made a significant contribution, was not mainly concerned with the domination of the colonial or semicolonial world by the advanced capitalist states. Its main concern was with interimperialist conflicts *between* the advanced capitalist states, and these conflicts were seen as the inevitable expression of their capitalist nature.

An overemphasis on markets as the defining characteristic of capitalism is not the only curious affinity between the Political Marxists and the Austrians. There also appears to be a common conception of human nature. Hayek focused on the emergence of a market order—"the spontaneous extended human order created by competitive capitalism"—and held that it was a formation that evolved over several thousands of years with the gradual development of institutions, rules, and laws that are quite contrary to the instincts of human beings.[37] These instincts remain essentially egalitarian and collectivist, biological remnants of the attitudes that were appropriate to tribal groups of foragers, but would be destructive of the market order if they were given free rein, as he believed would happen under socialism. According to Hayek, the very amorality of the market order, the fact that it often rewards the worst and penalizes the best, means that it runs counter to the instincts of the mass of people. But the market is the only rational means of economic organization, and so these instincts must be suppressed in the interests of what Hayek calls, following the terminology of Adam Smith, "the Great Society." For Hayek, capitalism is only possible through the transformation of human nature, or rather the suppression of the behavior that has been characteristic of human nature across almost the entire period since we completed our evolution from the primates.[38]

Political Marxism obviously rejects the positive value that Hayek ascribes to the overthrow of these supposedly ancient human characteristics, but it nevertheless makes very similar assumptions. As Ricardo Duchesne writes: "[Wood] thinks that capitalism is too unnatural and too destructive of human relations for anyone to have wanted it, least of all a collectivist peasantry."[39] But there are as many problems with a conception of human nature that sees it as being uninterested in economic development as there are with a definition of capitalism based on the existence of market compulsion. The rejection of one form of bourgeois ideology should not blind us to the dangers of accepting another, albeit with the inversion of its value system; there is no advantage to us in rejecting Smithian Marxism only to embrace Hayekian Marxism instead.

No mode of production is intrinsically alien to human nature. This is not to imagine that human nature is infinitely plastic or malleable, and has no stable qualities at all. The point was made in a wonderful passage—perhaps my favorite from the entire Scottish Enlightenment—by Adam Ferguson in *An Essay on the History of Civil Society*: "If we are asked therefore, where the state of nature is to be found? We may answer, it is here; and it matters not whether we are understood to speak in the island of Great Britain, at the Cape of Good Hope, or the Straits of Magellan. While this active being is in the train of employing his talents, and of operating on the subjects around him, all situations are equally natural."[40]

In other words, human beings may not have a "natural propensity to truck and barter," as Adam Smith thought, but they can develop such a propensity under certain conditions. What I am suggesting, therefore, is that the entire elaborate edifice of the Brenner thesis is based upon a conception of human nature in which it is seen as innately opposed to capitalism—indeed, in which it is seen as innately opposed to economic development as such—and will only be induced to accept capitalist relations under duress. While this may allow us the comforting thought that capitalism need not have happened, it also has certain implications for socialism. For if capitalism is essentially a contingent or accidental historical outcome, then so too is the possibility of socialism. One does not have to accept, in classic Second International or Stalinist style, that human social development has gone through a succession of inevitable stages in order to reject the ascription of absolute randomness to key historical turning points as a viable alternative. Marx's own position lends support to neither of these positions. For Marx, the core human quality, the one that distinguishes us from the rest of the animal world, is the need and ability to produce and reproduce our means of existence. This is why production, not property, is the *sine qua non* of Marx's own Marxism, and why his theory of social development privileges the development of the productive forces over productive relations.

For several decades now the left has tended to downplay or deny altogether the significance of the development of the productive forces and the Political Marxists have played a leading role in providing intellectual support for this tendency. Whatever their differences with the capitalist world-system theorists, members of the Political Marxists are equally dismissive of the development of the productive forces in explaining the transition from feudalism to capitalism. One consequence is a tendency to portray peasant life before capitalism as essentially based on a natural economy of self-governing communities, which have no incentive to develop the productive forces, and into which the lords or the Church only intrude superficially and occasionally in order to acquire their surplus. I do not recognize this picture. In a great passage from one of the early classics of Scottish vernacular literature, *The Complaynt of Scotland*, published anonymously in 1549 (I have here translated it into modern English), the character of "the laborer" rages against the misery of his life: "I labor night and day with my hands to feed lazy and useless men, and they repay me with hunger and the sword. I sustain their life with the toil and sweat of my body, and they persecute my body with hardship, until I am become a beggar. They live through me and I die through them."[41]

Four centuries later the power of that final sentence is undiminished. Developing the productive forces seems to me to be at least as rational a response to the feudal exploitation it so vividly describes as "fight or flight," the alternatives that are usually posed. Let us assume, as Brenner does, that fear of risk is the main factor preventing peasants from opting for profit maximization. What could overcome these concerns? Only such insecurity that the risk was worth taking because it could scarcely be worse than current conditions. In situations where the direct producers have to hand over part of what they have produced to someone else, a part that tends to fluctuate upwards, they clearly have a motive—one might almost say an imperative—to increase their output, a motive that need not have anything to do with markets. Increasing production, if it leads to greater disposable income, might give peasants the wherewithal to buy their way out of performing labor services, to hire wage labor to carry out work that would otherwise destroy the health and shorten the life of family members, or perhaps even to acquire heritable property that would remove them from feudal jurisdictions altogether. "Rather than retreating from the market," writes Jane Whittle, "peasants used the market to escape from serfdom."[42] And in conditions of crisis, such as those that shook European feudalism in the fourteenth and seventeenth centuries, the pressure on the ruling class to raise the level of exploitation, and consequently on the peasantry to look for ways of escape, was of course heightened still further.

There is a very limited number of ways in which human beings can economically exploit each other. "Slavery, serfdom and wage labor are historically and socially different solutions to a universal problem," writes Fernand Braudel, "which remains fundamentally the same."[43] Given this highly restricted range of options, the chances of something like capitalism arising were actually rather high, given certain conditions. The slave, tributary, and feudal modes of production emerged directly from preclass societies and so did the elements—wage labor, commodity production, market competition—that eventually combined to create the capitalist mode. Political Marxists are quite right to insist that the existence of these elements does not indicate the existence of capitalism as such. One can further agree that the socioeconomic activities that ultimately ended in producing capitalism were not, initially at any rate, necessarily undertaken with capitalism as a conscious goal. One can, however, explain the original making of the capitalist system without reference to either the commercialization model or to the prior necessity for changed "social property relations" by drawing on Marx's own model of the development of the productive forces. The desire of peasants to escape from feudal constraints was only one cause for the development of those forces. Another cause, much more important for industry than agriculture, was the increased need for armaments and other instruments of war by absolutist states engaged in the great dynastic and territorial struggles of the early modern period. Cannon, let alone battleships, could not be manufactured by a handful of artisans in a workshop. And from this certain necessities followed, including the expansion of wage labor and dismantling of feudal guild restrictions on who could be involved in production.

If, as I have suggested, Brenner is wrong about the geographically limited and socially contingent nature of capitalist development, then this has certain implications for his critique of the theory of bourgeois revolution. Brenner claims that the theory is "based on a mechanically determined theory of transition" that "renders revolution unnecessary in a double sense": "First, there really is no transition to accomplish: since the model starts with bourgeois society in the towns, foresees its evolution as taking place via bourgeois mechanisms, and has feudalism transform itself in consequence of its exposure to trade, the problem of how one type of society is transformed into another is simply assumed away and never posed. Second, since bourgeois society self-develops and dissolves feudalism, the bourgeois revolution can hardly play a necessary role."[44] The first point is valid as a criticism of many accounts of the transition from feudalism to capitalism, but the second misses its target. The theory of bourgeois revolution is not about the origins and development of capitalism as a socioeconomic system, but about the removal of backward-looking threats to its continued existence and the overthrow of restrictions to its further expansion. The source of these threats and restrictions has, historically, been the precapitalist state, whether estates-monarchy, absolutist, or tributary in nature. It is perfectly possible for capitalism to erode the feudal social order in the way Brenner describes while leaving the feudal state intact and still requiring to be overthrown if the capitalist triumph is to be complete and secure. Fortunately, there is no need for me to pursue this argument because Brenner himself has already done so.

In his critique of the work of Maurice Dobb, Brenner suggested in a footnote that an interpretation of the English Civil War as bourgeois revolution was not "ruled out."[45] The postscript to his massive monograph, *Merchants and Revolution*, is essentially an attempt to substantiate that footnote. In order to maintain consistency with his earlier work, Brenner has to maintain that feudal relations had been virtually overcome in England by 1640. The effect, however, is that he also has to treat the English state as virtually an autonomous body. It apparently has interests opposed to that of the dominant capitalist class, but these neither embody those of a feudal class nor balance between the capitalist and feudal classes, since the latter no longer exists. There were, of course, states based on what Brenner calls "politically constituted property" at this stage in history, but these were the great tributary empires of China, Byzantium, and Russia. In these cases the state acted as a collective feudal overlord, exploiting the peasantry through taxation and, where capitalist production had begun to emerge (as it had in China), successfully preventing it from developing to the point where a capitalist class might challenge the political rule of the dynastic regime.

Any serious comparison of the resources available to the Ming emperors and the Stuart kings would show the sheer *absence* of autonomous state power available to the latter. According to Brenner, Charles I relied for support on three forces—his courtiers, the High Anglican clergy, and the traditional merchants—but it is difficult to believe that the war would have lasted longer than a handful of months if this was all that he could muster. Brenner places great emphasis on the fear of popular intervention in forcing capitalist aristocrats into supporting the Crown. This certainly took place, and Charles consciously played on these fears in his search for support among the nobility and gentry. Yet this will not do as a complete explanation. First, Charles had already assembled formidable forces to his side before the interventions of the London crowd in December 1641. Second, Parliament was just as anxious as the Crown to gain the support of the (decidedly feudal) Scottish Covenanting armies after hostilities broke out, precisely as an alternative to relying on the people. Third, even after the Independents had taken over from the moderate Presbyterians, Cromwell was ultimately prepared to crush the Levelers, who were the largest but by no means the most radical of the social movements. In short, distrust and opposition to the mass movement was quite compatible with support for Parliament, even after its radicalization and militarization. The most obvious answer to the question of where royal support came from, which Brenner is unable to accept, is that at least part of it came from sections of English society whose socioeconomic position derived from local "patrimonial" (that is, feudal) interests comparable to those of Charles himself. Charles did not, after all, invoke only the general threat of disorder in his search for support but also the fact that any weakening of the monarchy, even such as that proposed by Parliament prior to the outbreak of the Civil War, would lead to commensurate weakening of the aristocracy. But weakening in what sense? Not their position as capitalists, surely.

Even with these difficulties, Brenner's complex argument shows why a revolution—let us leave aside for the moment whether the designation of "bourgeois" is appropriate or not—was necessary in England, even though the economy was already largely capitalist. However, Brenner's position *only* allows for revolutions under such conditions. Effectively, this reduces the field to England and the similarly capitalist United Netherlands, where the threat to capitalism came not from the native dynasty but from the foreign rule of the Spanish Habsburgs. What happened in the rest of the world? Brenner has not explicitly dealt with this question, but his fellow-thinkers have offered answers based on his theoretical framework.

For most of these like minds, as with Brenner himself, the autonomous role of the state is decisive, although in the opposite direction from that of the English state under the Stuarts. Benno Teschke claims that European capitalist development was entirely due to the competitive pressure of the British state on other states and did not, even to a limited extent, emerge from processes internal to the latter. Teschke talks about "revolutions from above," but not bourgeois revolutions, presumably on the grounds that the bourgeoisie was not involved in these events, although they did lead to the development of capitalism. His timing, however, closely resembles that of the Mayer thesis with which I began this survey: "This long period of transformation lasted from 1688 to the First World War for Europe, and beyond for the rest of the world."[46] In short, Brenner's insistence that the transition to capitalism was virtually complete by the time of the English (and possibly Dutch) revolutions is matched by his follower's insistence that it had barely begun by the time of subsequent "revolutions from above."

I have no difficulties with the concept of bourgeois revolution from above and have used the concept in my own work. Yet, as I have already noted in relation to the theory of "process" discussed earlier, it is difficult to say whether the notion of "revolution" (even if "from above") is appropriate here, when dealing with such an extended period of time. There are difficulties too with the periodization. Identifying the crucial period as lying between 1688 and 1918, as Teschke does, rather elides the inconvenient fact that, outside of Scotland, the major transitions to capitalism occurred not after 1688 but after 1789. And here we come to the elephant in the sitting room or, if you prefer an allusion to the Scottish Play, the ghost at the feast. I say inconvenient because every Political Marxist, without exception, is committed to the proposition that the Great French Revolution had nothing to do with the development of capitalism either at home or abroad. (This is another respect in which they are at one with Wallerstein and the capitalist world-system theorists.) Why?

Because the people who made the revolution were not capitalists. One response might be that at least some of the revolutionaries were people who *wanted* to exploit peasants and artisans in new capitalist ways, but were prevented from doing so by the Old Regime. George Comninel will have none of this: "The French Revolution was essentially an *intra-class* conflict over basic political relations that at the same time directly touched on relations of surplus extraction."[47] By "intra-class conflict" Comninel means that the revolution involved a struggle over the possession of state offices between different wings of a ruling class that combined both nobles and bourgeoisie. So the most cataclysmic event of the eighteenth century, perhaps of human history down to that point, whose effects were felt across the world from Ireland to Egypt, and which, until 1917 at least, defined the very nature of revolution itself, was ... a squabble over who gets to be the local tax farmer in Picardy.

I find these arguments deeply unsatisfactory. Apart from anything else, the parallels between the English Revolution, which took place in a society where capitalism was supposedly almost fully developed, and the French Revolution, which took place in a society where capitalism had supposedly not developed at all, are remarkable, even down to quite specific incidents, yet these must presumably be coincidental, if the societies were as different as the Political Marxists would have us believe. But the difficulties here are not simply reducible to empirical questions about England in the seventeenth century or France in the eighteenth; they stem from a fundamental misunderstanding about what is meant by bourgeois revolution in the Marxist tradition. It is to this issue that I will now turn.

Theories of Bourgeois Revolution 1: The Enlightenment

Bourgeois thinkers had been attempting to understand the process that was bringing their class to power for at least two hundred years before the emergence of Marxism in the 1840s. The first successful bourgeois revolution, the Dutch, took the form of a war of liberation against the external power of Habsburg Spain. Consequently, the political theories that emerged, notably those of Hugo Grotius, were less concerned with identifying the relationships between different social classes and forms of private property than with outlining the rights of the state over its own citizens and in relation to other states. Discussion of revolution as an internal process only came in three subsequent moments of theorization, as the focus of bourgeois revolution shifted consecutively from Holland to England, from England to Scotland, and finally from Scotland to France.

In England, the development of capitalism preceded the revolutions of the seventeenth century, if not so completely as Brenner claims. In this respect there are interesting similarities between the writings of the moderate republican James Harrington before the Restoration and those of the moderate Royalist Edward Hyde, First Earl of Clarendon, afterward. Harrington wrote in grand theoretical terms, while Clarendon left a rather more empirical reconstruction of landowner behavior in Somersetshire; but both men made essentially the same point: changes to political attitudes had followed changes in the nature of property ownership, and the conflict between representatives of different forms of property was the underlying cause of the Civil War.[48] But it was only one of two conflicts that emerged in the years between 1640 and 1660. The other arose mainly within the revolutionary camp and concerned the franchise. "Property, generally, is now with the people," said Adam Baynes in Parliament during 1659; "government must be there." But, as Hugh Stubbe in effect replied, "it is necessary to know who the PEOPLE are."[49] Baynes identified the key issue as being the triumph of a particular form of property; Stubbe, how much of that form of property people had to possess before they could be said to belong to the People. The first issue was decisively resolved by the Revolution of 1688; the second only by the Reform Act of 1832.

The Scottish moment fell between these two dates. Capitalism had scarcely developed in Scotland before the kingdom was incorporated into the British state in 1707. The Scottish Revolution involved neither decisive popular insurgencies, such as had accompanied the defense of London, nor wide-ranging debates on the limits of democracy, such as had taken place within the New Model Army at Putney. Instead, it took the form of the military repression and juridical abolition of feudal power by the British state following the civil war of 1745-46. "Power follows property," wrote John Dalrymple in 1757, in a phrase redolent of Harrington: England had developed commercial property while Scotland had not, and this accounted for the difference between them, a difference that the thinkers of the Scottish Enlightenment believed could now be overcome.[50] The transition to capitalism in Scotland was therefore a conscious and highly controlled exercise in revolution from above with the specific objective of introducing commercial property, first in agriculture, then more generally. I say "from above" because it did not involve the popular masses in any sense, but it was not state led either. On the contrary, this was one of the purest bourgeois experiences in history, precisely because it did not involve the lower orders with their inconvenient demands for representation. Instead, it involved an overlapping alliance of feudal lords and clan chiefs who had been forced to transform themselves into capitalist landowners, Enlightenment intellectuals concerned with national development, and a *cadre* of improving tenant farmers who leased land from the former and drew theoretical inspiration from the latter. The main difference between the English and the Scots in theoretical terms was that the former were simply justifying the outcome of a process that had taken hundreds of years to complete, while the latter were concerned with producing a blueprint for how the process could be reproduced in a period of decades.[51] Interestingly, Adam Smith shared with Brenner a disbelief in the necessity for bourgeois revolution. Smith certainly saw the suppression of noble power as essential for the rise of what he called "commercial society." As he explicitly stated in his lectures at Glasgow University during the 1750s, the nobles must be "brought to ruin," "greatly crushed," before liberty and security could be secured.[52] In his view, however, this had already been largely carried out, at least in England, by the absolutist state whose ascendancy was followed by the gradual growth of commerce in the towns, once these were freed from the parasitism and wastefulness of the feudal nobility. The specifics of how the lords had been defeated in Scotland—which of course depended on their prior transformation in England—was never really discussed in the theoretical works of the Scottish Enlightenment, although it is an essential component of the novels of Sir Walter Scott, the last great representative of the Scottish Historical School.

French theory was different again. The one hundred fifty years between the outbreak of the English and French revolutions is at least partly due to the fact that, initially at least, the French ruling class was capable of learning from history and made conscious attempts to prevent the growth of forces similar to those that had overthrown the Stuarts. (In this respect there are parallels between the Chinese tributary state and French absolutism that do not exist between the former and English absolutism.) French capitalism in 1789 was therefore much less extensive than English capitalism in 1640, especially in the countryside, but as forthcoming work by Henry Heller will demonstrate, it did exist and often involved far more advanced forms of industrial wage labor than English capitalism had during the previous century.[53] In a speech to the National Assembly of September 1789, the Abbe Sieyès portrayed a world in which "political systems, today, are founded exclusively on labor: the productive faculties of man are all," and described "the largest number of men" as "nothing but laboring machines."[54] Such a world would have been incomprehensible to John Lilburne and, in reality, it was still far from being achieved even in 1789. But it was the world that the French bourgeoisie wanted to achieve, a world that they saw emerging in England after 1688 and in Scotland after 1746. Indeed, one semianonymous member of the National Assembly wrote an account in 1790 that enviously noted how far Scotland had advanced in fifty years, how superior Scottish intellectual life now was to that of England, and how much wealthier Scottish peasants were than those of France.[55]

The problem for the French, unlike the Scots, was that no benevolent state would intervene to remove feudal obstacles to capitalism, since the state itself constituted the main obstacle. The French bourgeoisie had less economic power and a far stronger absolutist opponent than the English. For this reason they had to rely to a greater extent on the intervention of a popular majority to overthrow the Old Regime, but they were also acutely aware that the masses upon whose strength they relied had other views about society, however unrealizable these might have been in the short term. Nevertheless, in spite of their different circumstances, the formulations used by the French theorists are still very similar to those used by their English predecessors, insofar as they see changed property relations as the social basis of the revolution. In 1791, Antoine Barnave noted that the French Revolution had only been possible because of the social forces that had grown up within the feudal system: "Just as the possession of land gave rise to the aristocracy, industrial property increases the power of the people: they acquire their liberty, they multiply, they begin to influence affairs." The revolution that "the people" would make would be democratic: "The democratic principle, almost stifled in all European governments as long as the feudal regime remained vigorous, has since that time increasingly gathered strength and moved towards its fulfilment."[56] But who would be exercising the "democratic principle"? All the bourgeois revolutions down to the French, with the exception of the Scottish (and no one outside that country considered it a process separate from the English anyway), had involved popular interventions to achieve their goals. What was unclear was whether these mobilizations were integral to the process, contingent, or merely typical of a particular stage in the development of capitalism. The bourgeois theorists themselves had not answered this question, nor could they.

By the time Marx and Engels entered political life, then, there had been for nearly two hundred years a consensus, common across quite different local circumstances, which held that the basis of political change lay in prior changes to the nature of property and in the individuals who owned that property. It is perhaps worth pausing for a moment to consider the significance of the theoretical consistency involved. I accept the point made by Lukács in *History and Class Consciousness* that the bourgeoisie can never achieve a completely scientific understanding of the world, even in its revolutionary phase. But this did not mean that bourgeois intellectuals had no insights into the historical process. It was the suppression of these insights, after all, that led Marx to identify a transition from "disinterested research" to "apologetics" by the 1830s.[57] We have seen that a common position was held fairly consistently by the greatest intellectuals of their epoch, from Harrington and Clarendon in the 1640s, to Dalrymple and Smith in the 1750s, through to Barnave and Sieyès in the 1790s and beyond. Perhaps it is therefore safe to assume that it reflected, in however incomplete a form, real changes in society that were general, in varying degrees, throughout Europe.

None of the French Liberals who survived the Revolution of 1789 doubted that it was a similar event to the English Revolution of 1640. Marx had good political reasons for disliking François Guizot (who had, among other things, arranged for him to be deported from Brussels), but for all that, this supreme representative of the postrevolutionary bourgeoisie was not a complete intellectual nullity. Writing in the early 1850s, Guizot dismissed as "superficial and frivolous" attempts to distinguish the English and French revolutions: "Originating in the same causes, by the decay of the feudal aristocracy, the Church, and the royal power, they labored to affect the same work—to secure the domination of the people in public affairs." His final judgment was that "although deceived in many premature expectations, it liberated English society, to an immense extent, from the monstrous inequality of the feudal regime;—in a word, such is the analogy between the two Revolutions, *that the first would never have been properly understood unless the second had occurred.*"[58] In this respect at least he was in agreement with his class enemies, Marx and Engels. The latter were also quite clear that, apart from the common presence of the absolutist state, there were differences between the class forces involved in the English and French cases. Nevertheless, the patterns of development were similar enough for these to be classifiable as the same kind of event. Does this level of agreement mean that Marx and Engels simply endorsed the views of their bourgeois forerunners and contemporaries, that they were responsible for perpetuating a "bourgeois paradigm," and the rest? No.

THEORIES OF BOURGEOIS REVOLUTION 2: MARX, ENGELS, AND THE CLASSICAL TRADITION

Political Marxists claim that although Marx and Engels used different terminology, they initially conflated two bourgeois explanatory models to produce the theory of bourgeois revolution. On the one hand, they used the same commercial model of socioeconomic development as the political economists of the Scottish Enlightenment to explain how capitalism emerged from within feudal society. On the other, they used the same revolutionary model of political development as the liberal historians of Restoration France to explain how the bourgeoisie were able to overcome the absolutist obstacles to their ascendancy. Marx (Engels tends to vanish from these accounts) supposedly produced his own model of capitalist development, based on the establishment of changed social property relations rather than commercial expansion, only during the 1850s, while drafting the notebooks subsequently published as the *Grundrisse*—which then formed the basis of the discussion in *Capital*. The theory of bourgeois revolution, however, retained the impress of its liberal origins and therefore remains at odds with his mature critique of political economy. Opinion within the Brenner camp seems to be divided over whether Marx actually abandoned the theory or not, but the issue is in any case irrelevant for them, since they claim it was rendered redundant by Marx's discovery that the key to the origin of capitalism lay in social property relations.[59]

Before discussing these claims, it is perhaps worth pointing out, for those who imagine that influences only come from books, that Marx was born and lived until young manhood in the Prussian Rhineland, one part of the German states where the influence of the French Revolution was most directly experienced, not least because of the French occupation. For Marx, therefore, the French Revolution was not just something to be absorbed from the works of French Liberals but a historical experience only recently past, whose effects and unfulfilled promises still defined the politics of the time. In particular, they defined the debate over the forthcoming German Revolution. And this was not an abstract debate. There was going to be some sort of revolution—everybody but the dullest Prussian bureaucrat knew that. But what kind of revolution? What would its objectives be? What should "extreme democrats"—socialists like Marx and Engels—argue for its objectives to be? In other words, Marx and Engels had to develop a theory of bourgeois revolution at least partly because they expected to be taking part in one and needed to establish what the attitude of the working class movement should be in these circumstances. This is the context. However, even if we attempt to isolate their theoretical influences from their social environment, neither of the claims made by the Political Marxists can be sustained.

First, Marx and Engels arrived at their mature theory of socioeconomic transition long before the composition of the *Grundrisse*, and it remained unchanged afterward. Marx and Engels did, of course, inherit a series of important distinctions from their Enlightenment forebears. The distinction between one stage of subsistence and another (pastoral, agrarian, agricultural, and commercial) they inherited from the French and the Scots; the distinction between no property and property they inherited from the Dutch and the English. But they abandoned the term "mode of subsistence" and subsumed the process it describes within what they called the productive forces. And while they continued to refer to property relations, it was now as part of the broader category that they called productive relations. When did the break from—or rather, the radicalization of—their Enlightenment inheritance take place? Political Marxists are correct to say that *The German Ideology*, jointly written between 1845 and 1846, is in some ways still heavily dominated by the Scottish Historical School. Here, the concept of the productive forces is not yet twinned with the productive relations, but with "forms of intercourse," which include, in addition to property relations, such aspects of "social intercourse" as methods of transportation, which Marx would subsequently assign to the forces of production. Nevertheless, although the terminology is sometimes inconsistent and consequently confusing, it is not the case that Marx and Engels simply identify economic development with the expansion of commerce and the resulting increased complexity of the division of labor. On the contrary, the latter has another source altogether: "How far the productive forces of a nation are developed is shown most manifestly by the degree to which the division of labor has been carried."[60] In other words, the extension of the division of labor is a function of the development of the productive forces, not the expansion of trade. But whatever problems there are with *The German Ideology*, it is clear that their mature position on socioeconomic development was fully worked out by 1847 at the latest, in *The Poverty of Philosophy* and the original lecture upon which *Wage Labor and Capital* is based. That position did not subsequently change, as can be seen by comparing these texts with subsequent works from the *Grundrisse* through the "Preface" to the *Contribution to the Critique of Political Economy*—a text that has always proved rather inconvenient for the Political Marxists—to *Capital* itself.[61] As can be seen by checking the dates of publication, most of the references to bourgeois revolution by Marx and Engels postdate the turning point of 1847. Indeed, as late as *Capital* Volume 1 (1867), Marx refers to total dominance of the money-form only being implemented "on a national scale" toward the end of the eighteenth century "during the French bourgeois revolution."[62]

Second, Marx and Engels did not simply take over the theory of bourgeois revolution from the French Liberals and give it a name for the first time. Marx famously wrote in a letter of 1852 to Joseph Weydemeyer: "Long before me bourgeois historians had described the historical development of this class struggle and bourgeois economists the economic anatomy of classes."[63] But these comments refer to the class struggle, not to the bourgeois revolution. The bourgeoisie's own conception of their revolution had in any case begun to change by the early 1830s, a process that coincides too closely with the end of political economy as a science and the turn to naked ideological support for the system to be accidental. We can see the change, in a British context, in the writings of Thomas Babington Macaulay. On March 2, 1831, Macaulay made an incendiary speech in the House of Commons in support of the Reform Bill, in which he argued that political forms had to adapt to changed property relations. He gave examples from history, including the French Revolution, of how this had happened. Yet if we turn to his great work, *The History of England from the Accession of James II* (1848–1857), which actually describes how those property forms were consolidated in the Revolution of 1688, the subject has changed to that of constitutional liberty, and it is the continuity of English history—from which both James and his uncle had temporarily broken—that is both celebrated and contrasted with that of France, where continuity was lost. Is it too much too suggest that this change in attitude was produced, even unconsciously, by the new fear of working-class revolution? The English were of course fortunate in having what Macaulay called the "preserving revolution" of 1688 to point to as their decisive turning point. The French did not have such a subsequent "preserving revolution" to play the same role and consequently could not simply ignore or downplay the events of 1789 as the English did those of 1640. Nevertheless, we are dealing here with a general ideological shift. The consolidation of capitalist society increasingly led to the separation of economics and politics. In parallel, the bourgeoisie increasingly rewrote the history of their own revolutionary rise to power so that each individual moment appeared to be a political rather than social revolution.

In other words, by the time Marx and Engels came to consider the issue, bourgeois thought had begun to reinterpret the great revolutions in terms that gave greater emphasis to "liberty," or the achievement of constitutional government, than to "property," or the unshackling of a new economic order. Faced with this retreat, to have retained the original insights of the revolutionary bourgeois thinkers would in itself have been an intellectual achievement, but in fact Marx and Engels moved beyond their predecessors. Just as they did not restrict themselves to defending classical political economy from the "hired prize-fighters of capital" but rather undertook a critique of the entire intellectual tradition, neither did they confine themselves to restating the political doctrines of French (or more properly, Franco-British) liberalism, but separated out the issues of liberty, property, and agency in a way that bourgeois thinkers themselves were ideologically incapable of doing. As a result they transformed conceptions of revolutionary change to at least the same extent as they did to, say, the law of value.

Confusion over this issue may be due to the fact that Marx and Engels theorized both bourgeois and proletarian revolutions at the same time, and in both cases drew heavily from the example of the French Revolution. This is not in itself a problem, since, as Lukács later noted: "From the Great French Revolution on, all revolutions exhibit the same pattern with increasing intensity."[64] Marx and Engels drew, however, on different aspects of the French experience in relation to these two types of social revolution. If the *form* of the French Revolution (mass popular democratic upheavals) foreshadowed the process of proletarian revolution, the *consequences* (overthrow of absolutist restrictions on capitalist development) defined the nature of bourgeois revolutions. It was this consequentialism that they saw as linking the French with the Dutch and English revolutions, despite their other differences. And it is in this respect that Marx and Engels differ most significantly from their contemporaries like Guizot. As far as I am aware, their position was anticipated only once, by Pierre-Louis Roederer (1754–1835), a participant in the French Revolution who, unlike Barnave, survived to re-enter political life during the Restoration.

We should first note Roederer's exasperated dismissal of the argument that the French Revolution was simply a political squabble—a view that was already circulating in the 1830s: "And what a goal for a nation of twenty-five million men, what a deplorable goal for such a deployment of forces and wills—the overthrow of a king and his replacement by some upstart!" Like Barnave, Roederer too noted the ideological change that had already taken place prior to 1789: "The revolution was made in men's minds and habits before it was made into law." And Roederer thought he knew in whose minds these changes had occurred: "It was the opinion of the middle class that gave the signal to the lower classes." But Roederer did not believe that the revolution had been made for economic reasons: "The principal motive of the revolution was not to free lands and persons from all servitude, and industry from all restraint. It was not in the interest of property nor that of liberty. It was impatience with the inequalities of right that existed at that time; it was the passion for equality."

But just because the revolution was not directly made for economic reasons did not mean that it had no effect on economic development: "What the nation did for liberty and property was only the consequence and side effect of what it did to achieve equality of rights." Here Roederer was breaking new ground by suggesting that the release of new forms of property and production by the overthrow of absolutism might not have been the intention of the majority of actors, who may have had quite other objectives.[65] I have no idea whether Marx and Engels read Roederer or not, but this is relatively unimportant. Roederer's insight, to which he refers only in passing, is central to Marx and Engels's conception of bourgeois revolution.

Take, for example, the "Manifesto of the Communist Party" itself. One interesting fact revealed by actually reading this immortal work is that it mentions the French Revolution precisely twice, once in passing as an example of changes in property relations, and once on the final page in the context of a discussion on the nature of the forthcoming German revolution. The latter page also contains the only reference to the bourgeois revolution in the entire pamphlet.[66] Moreover, if we turn to the pages in which Marx and Engels discuss the achievements of the bourgeoisie, the revolutions to which it does refer are "in the modes of production and exchange." The hymns of praise to the bourgeoisie with which the "Manifesto" itself opens refer to its economic and social achievements, not to its political capacity for seizing power. In this context, it is by no means clear that Marx and Engels expected the bourgeoisie itself to burst asunder the fetters invoked in the famous metaphor that follows.[67] Marx and Engels did invoke the revolutionary role of the bourgeoisie, for quite specific reasons closely related to the politics of the time. During the brief revolutionary period between 1847 and 1849, Marx and Engels took every opportunity both to identify and to explain the inadequacies of the German bourgeoisie, which "had developed so sluggishly, so pusillanimously and so slowly, that it saw itself threateningly confronted by the proletariat, and all those sections of the urban population related to the proletariat in interests and ideas, at the very moment of its own threatening confrontation with feudalism and absolutism."[68] One way of drawing attention to the shortcomings of the contemporary bourgeoisie in Germany was by highlighting the virtues of the historical bourgeoisie in England and—especially—France. "Reading these texts," comments Michael Löwy, "one often gets the impression that Marx only extolled the virtues of the revolutionary bourgeoisie of 1789 the more effectively to stigmatize the 'misbegotten' German version of 1848."[69] Comprehensible in the context of arguments over political alliances at the time, these claims nevertheless involved a degree of exaggeration. In 1848, for example, Marx wrote of the English and French revolutions that "the bourgeoisie was the class which was genuinely to be found at the head of the movement"—a statement that is true only in a very qualified sense. And Marx does indeed go on to qualify it. Marx points out that what he called "plebeian" methods were required to achieve and defend both the English and French revolutions, methods from which the bourgeoisie themselves shrank, but that these could not have been successful if the economic conditions had not themselves developed to the extent that the new social order of the bourgeoisie could inherit; otherwise absolutist rule would simply have re-established itself.[70]

None of this suggests a fixation on the revolutionary bourgeoisie. Indeed, Engels much later generalized "a law of evolution of bourgeois society" from these observations in a discussion of the English case.[71] Whether Engels is actually describing a general law is open to doubt; it seems rather to be one specific to the early period of capitalist development, since plebeian activity is no longer decisive after the Revolutions of 1848. Marx made the same point more generally in *Capital*: "The knights of industry, however, only succeeded in supplanting the knights of the sword by making use of events in which they had played no part whatsoever."[72]

However, it was not only plebeians or protoproletarians that could clear the way for capitalist development on behalf of the bourgeoisie. "Since it is an army of officers," wrote Engels of the bourgeoisie, "it must ensure the support of the workers or it must buy political power piecemeal from those forces confronting it from above, in particular, from the monarchy."[73] As Engels subsequently noted, however, there were situations where money was insufficient, and sections of the existing feudal ruling class were prepared to take political action to advance the development of capitalism, action that the bourgeoisie itself was unwilling or unable to take. The notion of "revolution from above" was first used by Engels in relation to Germany and took two forms. First, that brought "from above and outside" by the French Revolution.[74] Second, those brought "from above and within" by a section of the old Prussian ruling class.[75] This involved an ironic reversal of roles: "The grave-diggers of the Revolution of 1848 had become the executors of its will."[76] Nor was his analysis restricted to Germany: "The Revolution of 1848, not less than many of its predecessors, has had strange bedfellows and successors. The very people who put it down have become, as Karl Marx used to say, its testamentary executors. Louis Napoleon had to create an independent and united Italy, Bismarck had to revolutionize Germany and to restore Hungarian independence, and the English manufacturers had to enact the People's Charter."[77] Such an analysis is as incompatible with "bourgeois paradigms" as Marx and Engels's earlier discussions of 1649, 1792, and 1848.

Marx and Engels's own analysis was continued by those Marxists who remained faithful to their method. Lenin's starting position, for example, was the same one with which Engels finished: "If you want to consider the question 'historically,' the example of any European country will show you that it was a series of governments, not by any means 'provisional,' that carried out the historical aims of the bourgeois revolution, that even the governments which defeated the revolution were nonetheless forced to carry out the historical aims of that defeated revolution."[78] This position had specific implications for Russia. In his reflections on the fiftieth anniversary of the "peasant reform" of 1861, Lenin described it as "a bourgeois reform carried out by feudal landowners," at the instigation of the greatest feudal landowner of all, Tsar Alexander II, who had "to admit that it would be better to emancipate *from above* than to wait until he was overthrown *from below*." Lenin identified three main reasons for these initiatives: the growth of capitalist relations of production through the increase in trade, military failure in the Crimea, and the rise in peasant insurgency in the countryside. But even the reforms were only achieved through "a struggle waged *within* the ruling class, a struggle waged for the most part *within the ranks of the landowner class*." As a result, "the year 1861 begat the year 1905," the period in Russian history that Lenin describes as "the era of her bourgeois revolutions."[79]

Lenin here introduces the idea that a bourgeois revolution can be spread over a prolonged period—an "era"—although it is a period that has a definite end point. Characteristically, however, he envisages the resolution of the Russian bourgeois revolution as one that could take more than one form. Lenin saw "revolution from above" as one of two alternative paths to bourgeois revolution in Russia, based on the "two types of bourgeois agrarian evolution" that had occurred in Europe and its overseas extensions. In the first, the "Prussian" (or reformist) path, the landowners of the great estates would gradually replace feudal methods of exploitation with those of capitalism, retaining feudal instruments of social control over their tenants (at

least in the medium term) but ultimately transforming themselves into large capitalist landowners or farmers. In the second, the "American" (or revolutionary) path, the
landowners are overthrown, feudal or other precapitalist controls are removed, and
the estates are redistributed among the previous tenants, who now emerge as a new
class of medium-scale capitalist farmers.[80] The "Prussian" path had been underway
in Russia since 1861. Was the alternative American path a possibility? If so, who
would lead it?

> Does not the very concept "bourgeois revolution" imply that it can be accomplished
> only by the bourgeoisie? . . . A liberation movement that is bourgeois in social and
> economic content is not such because of its motive forces. The motive force may
> be, not the bourgeoisie, but the proletariat and the peasantry. Why is this possible?
> Because the proletariat and the peasantry suffer even more than the bourgeoisie
> from the survivals of serfdom, because they are in greater need of freedom and the
> abolition of landlord oppression. For the bourgeoisie, on the contrary, complete vic-
> tory constitutes a danger, since the proletariat will make use of full freedom against
> the bourgeoisie, and the fuller that freedom and the more completely the power of
> the landlords has been destroyed, the easier will it be for the proletariat to do so.
> Hence the bourgeoisie strives to put an end to the bourgeois revolution half-way
> from its destination, when freedom has been only half-won, by a deal with the old
> authorities and the landlords.[81]

During the same period Trotsky took the argument still further, asking in 1906:
"Is it inevitable that the proletarian dictatorship should be shattered against the barriers of the bourgeois revolution, or is it possible that in the given *world-historical* conditions, it may discover before it the prospect of victory on breaking through those
barriers?" His answer was that such a self-denying ordinance should be rejected by
socialists for the strategy of permanent revolution made possible by the growth and
interconnectedness of the world economy.[82] Like Engels, Trotsky rejected the idea
that the bourgeoisie itself had ever been at the forefront of revolutionary struggle,
writing in 1923: "When the movement of the lower layers overflowed and when
the old social order or political regime was overthrown, then power dropped almost
automatically into the hands of the liberal bourgeoisie." Unlike the petty bourgeoisie
who actually carried out the early bourgeois revolutions, they had no need to consciously organize for the seizure of power: "The liberal bourgeoisie (the French in
1789, the Russian in 1917) can content itself with waiting for the elemental mass
movement and then at the last moment throw into the scales its wealth, its education, its connection with the state apparatus, and in this way seize the helm."[83]

Other Marxists associated with the early years of the Third International advanced the analysis further. What if a mass movement of the petty bourgeoisie was
not forthcoming? In this connection Georg Lukács made a number of important
observations in *History and Class Consciousness* (1923), at one point going beyond
even the notion of "revolution from above":

The true revolutionary element is the economic transformation of the feudal system of production into a capitalist one so that it would be possible in theory for this process to take place *without a bourgeois revolution*, without political upheaval on the part of the revolutionary bourgeoisie. And in that case those parts of the feudal and absolutist superstructure that were not eliminated by "revolutions from above" would collapse of their own accord when capitalism was already fully developed. (The German situation fits this pattern in certain respects.)[84]

In fact, the "feudal and absolutist superstructures" rarely "collapsed of their own accord," but they certainly collapsed. When the Habsburg Empire disintegrated under the weight of military defeat and nationalist and working-class pressure, Austria-Hungary fragmented into several different states that were already dominated by the capitalist mode of production to a greater (Austria, Czechoslovakia) or lesser (Hungary) extent. No revolution was required, and indeed, the only ones that threatened were socialist revolutions that were in each case defeated. But the essential point is correct: not every country is required to undergo a bourgeois revolution. Once a sufficient number of countries had undergone the process to establish a capitalist world economy, the need to compete within it ensured that most ruling classes would implement a series of incremental adaptations to the new order. But the creation of such a capitalist world economy was not in the gift of Britain alone to deliver; it only emerged in the last quarter of the nineteenth century—indeed, the opening of the imperialist stage of capitalist development is itself indicative of the fact that such an economy had formed. The dominance of capitalist economy does mean, however, that the bourgeoisie has to be in direct control of the state: "The necessary link between the economic premises of the bourgeoisie and its demands for political democracy or the rule of law, which—even if only partially—was established by in the great French Revolution on the ruins of feudal absolutism, has grown looser."[85] However, as Lukács explains elsewhere, the bourgeoisie, more than any previous ruling class, has never needed to take direct control of the state apparatus; all it required was that the apparatus functioned on its behalf.[86]

A similar point was made independently by Antonio Gramsci in his Fascist prison during the late 1920s and early 1930s. In these writings Gramsci developed the analysis of Germany that had first been made by Engels. Gramsci draws a comparison between the English and German revolutions that may appear counterintuitive, but only to those who mistakenly consider sociopolitical developments in the former country to be unique. In fact, as Gramsci suggests, the link is in the continued role of the nobility, in the case of England where a majority had already made the transition to capitalist forms of exploitation by the revolutionary era, and in the case of Germany, where a majority saw the necessity to make such a transition. Gramsci extended the analysis to his native Italy, where the kingdom of Piedmont played the role taken by Prussia in relation to Germany: "This fact is of the greatest importance for the concept of 'passive revolution'—the fact, that is, that what was involved was not a social group which 'led' other groups, but a State which, even though it had limitations as a power, 'led' the group which should have been 'leading' and was able to put at the latter's disposal an army and politico-diplomatic strength."[87] The concept of "passive revolution" is perhaps the most evocative one to describe the process of "revolution from above" developed within the classical tradition: the dignity of action is reserved, in the main, for the state and the forces that it can bring into play, rather than the masses themselves.

These views were not, however, restricted to the writings of a handful of important theorists. They were widespread in the scholarship of the Lenin era. One work of the early 1920s by O. V. Pletner, *The History of the Meiji Era*, noted that "the class of feudal lords remained in power" in Japan after 1868, but that they "rejected all outmoded feudal norms and started the rapid development of capitalism on the new economic basis." Pletner took the view that it was the consequences that were important rather than the role of the bourgeoisie: "Hence the term 'revolution' may be used in relation to the Meiji Ishin only conventionally. It may be called 'bourgeois' only from the viewpoint of its results, which does not mean at all that the bourgeoisie played the most important role at that time."[88] Perhaps the most interesting comments of all, however, were made relatively late (1932) by Georges Lefebvre, one of the historians often criticized for presenting too heroic a picture of the "rising bourgeoisie." Here he is criticizing the interpretation of the French Revolution associated with Jean Jaurès:

> Today this view strikes us as excessively summary. In the first place, it does not explain why the advent of the bourgeoisie occurred at that moment and not at some other time, and, more particularly, why in France it took the form of a sudden mutation, whereas it could well have taken the form of a gradual, if not an entirely peaceful, evolution, as occurred elsewhere. . . . It is thus clear that the economic interpretation of history does not commit us to simple views. The rise of a revolutionary class is not necessarily the only cause of its triumph, and it is not *inevitable* that it should be victorious or, in any case, victorious in a violent manner. In the present case the Revolution was launched by those whom it was going to sweep away, not by those who were to be its beneficiaries.[89]

I could go on, but it should be clear by now that the classical Marxist tradition was never committed to the conventional version of the bourgeois revolution, in which a fully conscious bourgeois class announces the abolition of feudalism, executes the king, and then proclaims the republic to the thunderous applause of Parliament, the Assembly, or their local equivalents. Insofar as the French Revolution could be described in these terms, it was seen as an exception.

If there was a weakness in the classical tradition, it stemmed from adopting a polemical strategy of unfavorably comparing the historical and contemporary bourgeoisie, similar to the one that had earlier been adopted by Marx and Engels themselves. In 1905, for example, Trotsky used the French example to attack the Russian bourgeoisie, which was then displaying even greater political cowardice than the German bourgeoisie had sixty years earlier. These modern liberals were repelled by their Jacobin ancestors, Trotsky noted, but the working class was not: "The proletariat, however radically it may have, in practice, broken with the revolutionary traditions of the bourgeoisie, nevertheless preserves them, as a sacred tradition of great passions, heroism and initiative, and its heart beats in sympathy with the speeches and acts of the Jacobin Convention."[90] In addition to invoking the heroic bourgeois past, Trotsky also introduces a notion to which we will have cause to return, that of the "revolutionary traditions." These could be turned against not only the modern bourgeoisie but reformist tendencies within the working class. In "Where Is Britain Going?" (1925), Trotsky was careful to state that Cromwell and the Independents are in no sense forerunners of socialism, but nevertheless he uses their revolutionary example to expose claims by Ramsay MacDonald and others that British development is characterized by "gradualness." What emerges is the idea—which Trotsky elsewhere rejected—that Communists within the working-class movement play the same role as the Independents and Jacobins played within the bourgeoisie: "It can be with some justice said that Lenin is the proletarian twentieth-century Cromwell."[91]

Overall, however, the theoretical resources of classical Marxism in relation to this subject are therefore far richer, far subtler, than is usually supposed by critics. It comes as no surprise to discover, therefore, that whatever their specific conclusions, all attempts to revise or abandon the theory of bourgeois revolution have one aspect in common: the theory that they criticize is significantly different from the one held by Marx and Engels and their followers in the classical Marxist tradition. What the revisionists are criticizing is therefore itself a revision, a departure from the complexity of the original position. How and why did it take place?

Theories of bourgeois revolution 3: From the Second International to Stalinism

The origin of what I will call the conventional theory of bourgeois revolution also lies within classical Marxism, but not in the discussions that I have just surveyed. Rather, it is derived from the general formula contained in the first section of the "Manifesto of the Communist Party": "The [written] history of hitherto existing society is the history of class struggles."[92] More precisely, it derives from how this formula was codified within the Second International. In the opening paragraphs of the pamphlet, Marx and Engels give a list of pairs of antagonistic classes. The list is so familiar, and the rhetoric in which it is presented so overwhelming, that the difficulties it represents are often overlooked. Partly these stem from inconsistencies within the pairings: as Geoffrey de Ste Croix has pointed out, insofar as the opposing classes are divided between exploiters and exploited, the first couple identified by Marx and Engels should be slave owners and slaves, rather than freemen and slaves.[93] Nevertheless, with this exception, the pairs listed are indeed "exploiter and exploited." Marx and Engels, however, refer to them as "oppressor and oppressed." Furthermore, they claim that these are binary oppositions in which the victory of one side is associated with "either a revolutionary reconstitution of society at large, or . . . the common ruin of the contending classes."[94] Let us leave aside—for now—questions of whether slaves or serfs were capable of "reconstituting society," and of the absence of the bourgeoisie from the list, a point to which I will return below.[95] The problem is that we are invited to view history not only as involving a series of class struggles but as involving a series of class struggles in which one hitherto subordinate class overthrows and takes over from its predecessor, until the working class, the "universal class," overthrows the bourgeoisie and puts an end to the process by initiating the dissolution of all classes. These paragraphs tended to be read together with a set of key texts that appeared to suggest that history was a succession of ever more developed modes of production. In the 1859 "Preface" to *A Contribution to the Critique of Political Economy*, Marx famously wrote that "the Asiatic, ancient, feudal and modern bourgeois modes of production may be designated as epochs marking progress in the economic development of society."[96] Marx is not proposing a universal succession of modes of production. Those listed here are only chronological in two senses. One is that, as Eric Hobsbawm puts it, "each of these systems is in crucial respects further removed from the primitive state of man."[97] The other is that this is the order in which these modes of production arose historically. Neither sense suggests that every social formation is fated to pass under the dominance of each mode of production in succession. Nevertheless, this passage was interpreted to mean that history should be understood as a universal succession of increasingly more developed modes of production—an understanding compatible with broader, non-Marxist notions of evolutionary progress. In other words, the conventional theory of bourgeois revolution arose as a specific application of the general theory of historical development, in this case that the defeat of the lords by the bourgeoisie leads to (or even is equivalent to) the supersession of feudalism by capitalism.

What made this application more plausible than it might otherwise have been was the fact that Marx, Engels, and some later Marxists like Trotsky did invoke the revolutionary role of the bourgeoisie, for quite specific reasons closely related to the politics of the time. The danger was that, shorn of context or qualification, statements like those I quoted earlier by Marx and Trotsky could be used to license not only an overly heroic view of the bourgeoisie's political role but the notion that the bourgeois revolution was essentially the same kind of experience as the socialist revolution, complete with political leadership and organization, the only real difference being their class basis. The point here is not to deny the significance of the Independents or the Jacobins, or to dispute their relevance to the bourgeois revolutions, but to question how typical they were of the bourgeoisie and how typical their revolutions were of the ways in which capitalism was consolidated.

The second source of the conventional theory of bourgeois revolution emerged from the historic memory of the broader labor movement. The early Atlantic working class was by experience and instinct international in orientation, as Peter Line-baugh and Marcus Rediker have shown in *The Many-Headed Hydra*. But as the same authors also demonstrate, after the initial period of formation it fragmented on an increasingly national basis.[98] As these movements stabilized in the second half of the nineteenth century and moved to establish permanent parties and trade unions, re-formism emerged as a coherent form of ideology and organization. One consequence was the search for predecessors from which to construct a native radical tradition—a tradition that was, by definition, non–working class. Where Marxism distinguished between historical classes on the basis of different positions within the relations of production and consequently the different capacities that each possessed, these tradi-tions made "the people" their central category. What then was their unifying theme, if not the succession of classes? It was democracy. It became important to identify struggles that could be retrospectively endorsed and assimilated into a narrative of democratic advance, the closing episode of which had opened with the formation of the labor movement. In most cases the radical traditions were directly inherited from left liberalism, particularly in those countries—above all Britain, but also France—where Marxism was initially weakest and where liberal connections with labor were political and organizational as well as ideological. In effect, these traditions tended to become a populist alternative to what one early radical liberal historian, John Rich-ard Green, called "drum and trumpet" histories.[99] In Britain, for example, the offi-cial ruling-class conception of "Our Island Story" highlighted the Magna Carta and the Bill of Rights as the foundations of English liberty; but in "The People's Story" it was the Peasants' Revolt and the Cromwellian Commonwealth that featured as the crucial episodes. (Discussion of divisions *within* the Parliamentary side, notably those between the Levelers and Independents, only really began after the First World War.) The view of history as the unfolding of representative democracy was deeply influential within the emerging workers' movements over the second half of the nine-teenth century—understandably, since gaining the male franchise was one of its main objectives. And of course there was a Marxist justification for this emphasis, since the "Manifesto" had argued that winning the "battle for democracy" was the road to working-class power.[100] "Between the 1860s and the First World War," writes Geoff Eley, "socialist parties became the torchbearers of democracy in Europe."[101]

Two strands of thought about historical development had therefore emerged within the socialist and labor movement by the second half of the nineteenth century. One, embedded in the codified Marxism of the Second International but accepted in diluted form far more generally across the movement, saw history as a progression of successively more advanced modes of production, emerging and overtaking their predecessors through the mechanism of the class struggle, which would culminate in socialism. The other, which predated the widespread adoption of Marxism by the movement but maintained its influence afterward, saw history as the ongoing strug-gle for democratic representation for the majority of the population that would also culminate in socialism. By the period between the founding of the Second International in 1889 and the outbreak of the First World War in 1914, most national labor movements, even those nominally committed to Marxism, had incorporated both strands, which converged on periods of bourgeois revolution. In the resulting synthesis, the bourgeoisie were presumed to have been the leading actors in the struggle to supplant the feudal lords and to have done so (in alliance with other classes) through the demand for democracy. The failure of the bourgeoisie to establish full democracy meant that it now had to be accomplished by the working class and that so doing would open up the road to socialism. The problems with this conception, both in respect of the role of the bourgeoisie in the bourgeois revolutions and the relationship of the bourgeois revolutions to democracy, should not require restatement by now. A more realistic view was maintained by the left wing of Social Democracy, particularly in Russia; yet it was from Russia that the third and final component of the conventional view of the bourgeois revolution was eventually to emerge.

The Russian Marxist tradition, as it emerged from the 1880s onward, was virtually the only one within the Second International to devote serious discussion to the question of the bourgeois revolution—unsurprisingly, since Russia was the major area in Europe that still had to undergo this experience. However, with the main exception of Trotsky, virtually every tendency within Russian Marxism referred to the forthcoming revolution as bourgeois-*democratic* in nature—a compound term that had not appeared in the work of Marx or Engels. The use of this term did not mean that they necessarily regarded the earlier bourgeois revolutions as having been democratic in either their goals or their accomplishments. It meant rather that the Russian revolution would not only be bourgeois in content (i.e., it would establish the unimpeded development of capitalism) but would introduce democratic politics that the working class could use to further its own demands. In the early 1920s the Communist International—still a revolutionary organization at this point, of course—extended this analysis to the colonial or semicolonial world in which (with some important exceptions like China and India) the working class was even weaker than it had been in Russia forty years earlier. In these countries socialism was not immediately on the agenda, but democratic rights were a necessary prerequisite for the organization of movements for socialism and national liberation. (In his early theses on the subject Lenin insisted that the phrase "bourgeois-democratic" be replaced by "national-revolutionary," as the former tended to disguise the reformist, if not totally accommodating, role that the local bourgeoisie played in relation to the colonial powers.[102]) This was a serious strategy at the time, as not even Trotsky believed that permanent revolution was feasible outside of Russia. Furthermore, the conception did not distort the understanding of historical bourgeois revolutions within the Communist International—indeed, as we have seen, this achieved a new level of sophistication, particularly in the work of Lukács.

However, as the Communist International degenerated along with the Russian Revolution that gave it birth, the concept of the "bourgeois-democratic revolution" began to shift from one that advocated allying with bourgeois (or even prebourgeois) forces only where they were genuinely involved in fighting imperialism, to a stages theory in which support had to be given to the supposedly "revolutionary" bourgeoisie as a matter of course, in line with Stalin's foreign policy. This was disastrous enough politically, most of all in the Chinese Revolution of the late 1920s, but it also affected how history was written. From the onset of the period of the Popular Front in 1935, there was effectively a fusion of Stalinist conceptions with the two preexisting theories of historical stages on the one hand and the struggle for democracy on the other. This involved two retreats from the classical Marxist conception of bourgeois revolution.

One was that the notion of a "bourgeois-democratic" revolution was now read back into history and applied to England, France, and the other countries where bourgeois revolutions had been identified. The main problem is that, although a minority of the bourgeois revolutions involved episodes of democracy, none resulted in the establishment of permanent representative institutions; most did not involve popular insurgencies of any sort. Nor was this the only distortion. In the Stalinist model, democracy became one of a checklist of "tasks" borrowed from the French Revolution—the others were the agrarian question and national unification—that had to be ticked off before the bourgeois revolution could be declared complete. If these "tasks" were really taken seriously, then the Japanese Revolution, which began with the Meiji Restoration in 1868, was incomplete until the agrarian reforms imposed by the US occupiers after 1945. Unfortunately this introduces further problems, since the American Revolution itself was presumably unfinished until the black civil rights legislation of the mid-1960s. And in relation to my own country, the Scottish Revolution has presumably still to be consummated in the absence of an independent Scottish state. The absurdity of such notions should be obvious. There are still important unresolved democratic issues in most countries in the world, but they have nothing to do with the accomplishment or consolidation of capitalism. It is important to understand how widely these misconceptions about "the tasks of the bourgeois revolution" were accepted, even by Trotsky, Stalin's greatest opponent. As we have seen, Trotsky was clear that, in terms of agency, the French Revolution was led by the petty bourgeoisie rather than the bourgeoisie as such; but he still accepted that the "tasks" it allegedly accomplished were necessary components of any bourgeois revolution. It was for this reason that he tended to treat events like the Meiji Restoration—which of course failed to accomplish all of these "tasks"—as substitutes for or means of avoiding bourgeois revolutions, rather than bourgeois revolutions themselves.[103] But as Alex Callinicos writes: "Surely it is more sensible, rather than invoke the metaphysical concept of a 'complete and genuine solution' [to the tasks of the bourgeois revolution], to judge a bourgeois revolution by the degree to which it succeeds in establishing an autonomous center of capital accumulation, even if it fails to democratize the political order, or to eliminate feudal social relations."[104]

The other shift was, if anything, even more damaging to historical understanding. Rather than being the beneficiaries of the revolutions that bear their name—revolutions in which they played a greater or lesser role depending on specific circumstance—the bourgeoisie was presented as the social class directly responsible for bringing them about. But to discuss the bourgeoisie as if it had been a revolutionary class then in the same way that the proletariat is a revolutionary class now is to go beyond making an analogy between bourgeois and proletarian revolutions: it is to claim that they share a common structure.

ISAAC DEUTSCHER AND THE RECOVERY
OF THE CLASSICAL TRADITION

I want now to return to my starting point in the work of Isaac Deutscher. As a survivor of the "midnight in the century" who had been personally involved in the Communist movement at the end of the classical epoch, he stood in direct line of continuity with the traditions of pre-Stalinist Marxism on bourgeois revolutions. Deutscher's work is not above criticism; indeed, he also claimed that bourgeois and proletarian revolutions shared a common structure, but in his case it was because he thought that the proletarian revolution could be assimilated to the bourgeois revolution, rather than the other way around. In other words, the difficulty is with his top-down conception of socialism, not his view of the bourgeois revolutions, which was uncompromisingly realistic and quite unencumbered with fallacious assumptions about the relationship between them and popular democracy.[105] Deutscher specifically wrote about the subject in two lengthy passages. The first is from his 1949 biography, *Stalin*:

> Europe, in the nineteenth century, saw how the feudal order, outside France, crumbled and was replaced by the bourgeois one. But east of the Rhine, feudalism was not overthrown by a series of upheavals on the pattern of the French Revolution, by explosions of popular despair and anger, by revolutions from below, for the spread of which some of the Jacobins had hoped in 1794. Instead, European feudalism was either destroyed or undermined by a series of revolutions from above. Napoleon, the tamer of Jacobitism at home, carried the revolution into foreign lands, to Italy, to the Rhineland, and to Poland, where he abolished serfdom, completely or in part, and where his code destroyed many of the feudal privileges. *Malgré lui-meme*, he executed parts of the political testament of Jacobitism. More paradoxically, the Conservative Junker, Bismarck, performed a similar function when he freed Germany from many survivals of feudalism which encumbered her bourgeois development. The second generation after the French Revolution witnessed an even stranger spectacle, when the Russian Tsar himself abolished serfdom in Russia and Poland, a deed of which not so long before only "Jacobins" had dreamt. The feudal order had been too moribund to survive; but outside France the popular forces arrayed against it were too weak to overthrow it "from below"; and so it was swept away "from above."[106]

Here Deutscher identifies two different types of revolutions from above. One is where states established by revolutions from below, like those of Cromwell or Napoleon, spread the revolution externally by military intervention. The other is where the ancien régime itself—or elements within it—imposes capitalist social relations internally through their control of the existing state apparatus.

The second passage comes from the 1967 Trevelyan lectures, which formed the basis of his last book, *The Unfinished Revolution*:

> The traditional view [of the bourgeois revolution], widely accepted by Marxists and non-Marxists alike, is that in such revolutions, in Western Europe, the bourgeois played the leading part, stood at the head of the insurgent people, and seized power. This view underlies many controversies among historians; the recent exchanges, for example, between Professor Hugh Trevor-Roper and Mr Christopher Hill on whether the Cromwellian revolution was or was not bourgeois in character. It seems to me that this conception, to whatever authorities it may be attributed, is schematic and unreal. From it one may well arrive at the conclusion that bourgeois revolution is almost a myth, and that it has hardly ever occurred, even in the West. Capitalist entrepreneurs, merchants, and bankers were not conspicuous among the leaders of the Puritans or the commanders of the Ironsides, in the Jacobin Club or at the head of the crowds that stormed the Bastille or invaded the Tuileries. Nor did they seize the reins of government during the revolution nor for a long time afterward, either in England or in France. The lower middle classes, the urban poor, the plebeians and *sans culottes* made up the big insurgent battalions. The leaders were mostly "gentlemen farmers" in England and lawyers, doctors, journalists and other intellectuals in France. Here and there the upheavals ended in military dictatorship. Yet the bourgeois character of these revolutions will not appear at all mythical, if we approach them with a broader criterion and view their general impact on society. Their most substantial and enduring achievement was to sweep away the social and political institutions that had hindered the growth of bourgeois property and of the social relationships that went with it. When the Puritans denied the Crown the right of arbitrary taxation, when Cromwell secured for English shipowners a monopolistic position in England's trading with foreign countries, and when the Jacobins abolished feudal prerogatives and privileges, they created, often unknowingly, the conditions in which manufacturers, merchants, and bankers were bound to gain economic predominance, and, in the long run, social and even political supremacy. Bourgeois revolution creates the conditions in which bourgeois property can flourish. In this, rather than in the particular alignments of the struggle, lies its *differentia specifica*.[107]

The second type of revolution from above is important in relation to his more general argument concerning the definition of bourgeois revolutions. These cannot be defined by reference to the class position of the social forces that carried them out, since in neither case were these composed of capitalists or even members of the bourgeoisie. Nor can they be defined by their intentions, since neither the English Independents nor the French Jacobins were primarily motivated by establishing capitalist relations of production; the Prussian Junkers and Japanese Samurai were concerned with this outcome, but more as a means of strengthening the international political and military positions of their respective states than of increasing the profitability of their individual estates.

Deutscher was one of the first figures after the classical Marxists to identify two important but neglected characteristics of bourgeois revolution: one, that it could take the form of "revolution from above"; the other, that it was their *consequences* or outcomes which constituted the decisive factor in assessing whether or not a bourgeois revolution had actually occurred. But he was not alone. Several other writers from the Trotskyist tradition—including those who were the most critical of his views on Stalinism, like Max Shachtman and Tony Cliff—took essentially the same positions. In relation to the first, Cliff wrote in 1949: "The 'Bismarckian' path was not the exception for the bourgeoisie, but the rule, the exception was the French revolution."[108] This scarcely suggests an obsessive focus on the French Revolution as a model. In relation to the second, Shachtman wrote during the same year: "Once the work of destruction was accomplished, the work of constructing bourgeois society could proceed automatically by the spontaneous expansion of capital as regulated automatically by the market. To the bourgeoisie, therefore, it could not make a fundamental difference whether the work of destruction was begun or carried out by the plebeian Jacobin terror against the aristocracy, as in France, or by the aristocracy itself in promotion of its own interests, as in Germany."[109] These remarks were made in the course of a very critical review of Deutscher's *Stalin*, but on this point both the criticized and the critic were as one. What this indicates, I think, is that in this, as in so many other respects, Trotskyism was responsible for preserving important elements of the classical Marxist tradition that would otherwise have been even more deeply buried than they were. In 1965, Edward Thompson wrote that "mill-owners, accountants, company-promoters, provincial bankers, are not historically notorious for their desperate propensity to rush, bandoliers on their shoulders, to the barricades. More generally they arrive on the scene when the climatic battles of the bourgeois revolution have already been fought."[110] At the time, these comments may have seemed simply another example of the iconoclasm with which Thompson tended to approach what he regarded as Marxist dogma. In this occasion, however, it was actually Thompson, rather than the targets of his critique (Perry Anderson and Tom Nairn), who was nearer to the classical tradition.

It was rare for Thompson to theoretically converge with Trotskyism. It is ironic, therefore, that one of the first historians outside the ranks of that movement to recognize the importance of Deutscher's comments on the bourgeois revolution was one of Thompson's comrades from the Historians Group of the Communist Party of Great Britain: Christopher Hill. Hill is a historian usually identified as one of the stalwarts of the conventional model of bourgeois revolution, and it is true that his early writings, particularly his famous essay of 1940, "The English Revolution," are in this mode. The problem here is not in his claim that the revolution allowed free capitalist development, but that it placed the bourgeoisie in power. Yet it is also true that Hill abandoned this aspect of his interpretation, and much more quickly than is usually thought. In writings of the 1950s, such as *Economic Problems of the Church* (1956) and "Recent Interpretations of the Civil War" (1958), he had already separated capitalism and democracy. It was in an essay of 1971 commemorating Deutscher's work as a historian of revolution, however, that Hill noted the significance of his conception of "revolution from above" ("although he never seems to have worked it out fully") and his consequentialism, commenting that "Deutscher was quite right to say that historians of seventeenth-century England have spent too much time in analyzing the participants rather than the consequences of the Revolution."[111] By 1974 Hill had come to regard Deutscher's comments on his own earlier work in *The Unfinished Revolution* as legitimate criticism and subsequently quoted them in defense of his revised definition.[112] Finally, by 1980, Hill had abandoned the conscious role of the bourgeoisie entirely: "'Bourgeois revolution' is an unfortunate phrase if it suggests a revolution willed by the bourgeoisie." In the same essay Hill noted that he drew on Deutscher, not as an innovator but as a representative of the classical Marxist tradition.[113] And as we have seen, in this respect he was entirely accurate.

Ellen Meiksins Wood claims that the term "bourgeois revolutions" has "undergone many redefinitions," to the point that it now means "any revolutionary upheaval that, in one way or another, sooner or later, advances the rise of capitalism, by changing property forms or the nature of the state, irrespective of the class forces involved."[114] If these claims were true then attempts to defend the theory of bourgeois revolution would be examples of what Imre Lakatos called a "degenerating research program," involving the construction of endless auxiliary hypotheses to protect an inner core of theory that has in fact little or no explanatory value.[115] But we can see that they are completely false. In fact, writers who regard the theory as retaining its scientific value have returned to the *original* research program, after decades in which it was gradually abandoned. Far from "redefining" the term bourgeois revolution we have in effect rediscovered the pristine meaning of the term.[116] Nor is the term simply an all-embracing redescription of the events that preceded the establishment of capitalism in individual countries: the class forces involved are limited to two main configurations, each with its own distinct form of the revolutionary process, but both of which were directly connected with transformation of the state into one capable of fostering capitalist development. It is possible to add a third variant, which only emerged during the twentieth century in the postcolonial world. But even so, this scarcely involves the infinite permutations suggested by Wood.

THE PLACE OF THE BOURGEOIS REVOLUTION IN HISTORY

Is there a general process through which societies move from the dominance of one mode of production to another? If so, what aspects are specific to the bourgeois revolution? Marx initially considered the issue solely in relation to the transition from capitalism to socialism: "While this general prosperity lasts, enabling the productive forces of bourgeois society to develop to the full extent possible within the bourgeois system, there can be no question of a real revolution. Such a revolution is only possible at a time when *two factors* come into *conflict: the modern productive forces* and the *bourgeois forms of production*."[117] Subsequently, he generalized the argument to transitions more generally, most famously in the 1859 "Preface": "At a certain stage of development, the material forces of society come into conflict with existing relations of production or—this merely expresses the same thing in legal terms—with the property relations within the framework of which they have operated hitherto. From forms of development of the productive forces these relations turn into their fetters. Then begins an era of social revolution."[118]

Marx is describing here what Daniel Bensaïd calls a "law of tendency" (Bensaïd is thinking of "the law of the tendency of the rate of profit to fall" introduced by Marx in the third volume of *Capital*): "In an open system, like political economy, the empirical regularities and constant conjunctions of events are in fact manifested as tendencies."[119] There are reasons specific to the German politics of the period why Marx emphasized structure rather than agency in these passages, but even so, it does not represent a fundamental break from or retreat behind the positions he and Engels had worked out in the late 1840s.[120] For the sake of variety I will take an example from outwith the Political Marxists, in this case by Cornelius Castoriadis, once a leading figure in the French post-Trotskyist group "Socialism or Barbarism." Castoriadis argues that the contradictions between the forces and relations of production do not apply to any period of history except that of the bourgeois revolution:

> It more or less faithfully describes what took place at the time of the transition from feudal society: from the hybrid societies of western Europe from 1650 to 1850 (where a well-developed and economically dominant bourgeoisie ran up against absolute monarchy and the remains of feudalism in agrarian property and in legal and political structures) to capitalist society. But it corresponds neither to the breakdown of ancient society and the subsequent appearance of the feudal world, nor to the birth of the bourgeoisie, which emerged precisely outside of and on the fringes of feudal relations. It corresponds neither to the constitution of the bureaucracy as the dominant order today in countries that are in the process of industrialization, nor finally to the evolution of non-European peoples. In none of these cases can we speak of a development of the productive forces embodied in the emergence of a social class within the given social system, a development which "at a certain stage" would have become incompatible with the maintenance of the system and would have led to a revolution giving the power to the "rising class."[121]

This is more generous than most critiques, since it at least grants that the bourgeois revolution can be explained in these terms; most critics would deny even that. Yet the problem is essentially the same: critics assume that Marx is illegitimately generalizing from the experience of the transition to capitalism and from the bourgeois revolutions that both resulted from and further stimulated this process. In fact what Marx is saying is far less prescriptive than is usually thought. He did not think, for example that the "eras of social revolution" had taken the same form in the past or would do so in the future. Eras of social revolution—understood as the decisive moment in the transition between one mode of production and another—are in any case extremely rare, as rare as modes of production themselves, and class struggle has not always played the decisive role in bringing them to a conclusion. As Perry Anderson notes: "The maturing of such a contradiction [between the forces and relations of production] need involve no conscious class agency on either side, by exploiters and exploited—no set battle for the future of economy and society; although its subsequent unfolding, on the other hand, is likely to unleash relentless social struggles between opposing forces."[122] The outcome of such a crisis can vary. What is decisive? "In the first place historical materialism specifies the structural capacities possessed by agents by virtue of their position in the productive relations, i.e. their class position. Secondly, it claims that these capacities, and also the class interests which agents share, have primacy in explaining their actual behavior."[123] The decisive issue is therefore the role played by social classes and, in particular, by their very different capacity to transform society in their own interests. In other words, to what extent were these different social revolutions brought about by the triumph of one class over another?

There is one final consequence of shifting the definition of bourgeois revolutions onto their outcomes, which relates to the bourgeoisie itself. In this interpretation, while it is always the beneficiary of the bourgeois revolutions, it is not always the agency that brings them about.[124] I am not, of course, claiming that the bourgeoisie has *never* played a revolutionary role, simply that there is no *necessity* for it to do so in order for a revolution to qualify as bourgeois. Does this not contradict the notion of class struggle that is central to Marxism? It is indeed important to understand that the history of all hitherto existing society is the history of class struggles, but it is equally important to understand that these struggles have taken two different forms, identified by Claudio Katz as exemplifying, respectively: "The antagonism within a class system and that between class systems."[125] One is where the classes involved are exploiter and exploited. The issues here are relatively straightforward. Slave owners extract surplus value from slaves; feudal lords and tributary bureaucrats do the same to peasants; and capitalists do the same to workers. In each case the exploited class resists to the extent that material conditions allow, but it is not always possible for them to go beyond resistance to create a new society based on a different mode of production. Exploited classes, in other words, do not always have the structural capacity to make a social revolution: slaves did not; the majority of peasants did not; the working class does, and in this respect—among several others—it is unique among the exploited classes in history. The other is where the classes involved are oppressor and oppressed. The issues here are considerably more complex. For one thing, while all exploited classes (slaves, peasants, workers) are oppressed, not all oppressed classes are exploited, and they may even be exploiters themselves. The class struggle can therefore be between two exploitative classes, but nevertheless still be the means of bringing about social revolution, provided that the modes of production represented by these classes are different and one is more "progressive," in the Marxist sense of involving the greater development of the productive forces. However, the number of oppressed classes that have the capacity to remake society is as limited as the number of exploited classes with that capacity. Among oppressed classes it is the bourgeoisie that is unique. The class struggle in history has therefore taken multifaceted forms. It is a permanent feature of the relationship between exploiting and exploited classes, but can also occur between dominant and subordinate exploiting classes, or between existing and potential exploiting classes. And these different class struggles have taken place simultaneously, have intertwined and overlapped. The precise combinations have been or (in the case of socialism) will be different in relation to the case of each of the great social revolutions.

The fall of the Roman Empire and the transition to feudalism

The first transition involved the passage from primitive communism through "Asiaticism" to a variety of social formations dominated by different modes of production: a relatively short-lived slave mode; the tributary mode or its feudal variant; or combinations of some or all of these. Can we therefore speak of a feudal revolution? In parts of the north and far west of Europe, such as Scandinavia and Scotland, clearly not: feudalism evolved spontaneously out of primitive communism and through the Asiatic mode. But even if we accept (as I do) that feudal relations of production also existed within the territories of the Roman Empire in the West before barbarian invasions, it is clear that feudalism only became the dominant mode there after 500 AD. The rise of feudalism in the former territories of the empire therefore represents the first direct passage in history from one exploitative mode of production (slavery) to another. How was it accomplished? For our purposes there are five important aspects to this initial transition from one exploitative mode of production to another.

First, the impetus for the transition came from the increasing failure of the previously dominant slave mode of production to sustain, let alone increase, levels of ruling-class income. The decisive element in the crisis is therefore the inability of the existing ruling class to further develop the forces of production. The decline of slavery began toward the end of the second century AD. What caused it? Once the territorial limits of the empire were reached, the only way in which landowners could expand was by acquiring land from other, usually smaller landowners who would then be reduced in status. From the reign of Augustus, the freedom of the peasant-citizen began to be eroded, as the state no longer permitted him to vote or required him to fight, with the restriction of the franchise to what were now openly called the *honestiores* ("upper classes") and the recruitment of armies by enlistment rather than as a duty of citizenship. Increasingly taxed to pay for the wars and the burgeoning bureaucracy, including that of the Christian Church, peasants began to seek the protection of great landowners, protection that came at the price of their independence and what remained of their citizenship. In other words, an unfree labor force now began to emerge that rendered slavery redundant. The end result, through a series of mediations too complex to trace here, was the collapse of political super-structure of the Roman Empire in the West, and the failure of subsequent attempts, notably by Charlemagne, to recreate it on anything like the original basis. The slave owners transformed their former slaves into serfs or peasants with tenure in order to maintain or increase productivity; the latter were prepared to try new methods of production as their own subsistence—or at least continued tenure—now depended on their doing so in a way that it did not for slaves. Their success in achieving greater productivity encouraged the slave-owners-cum-lords to orient still further toward nonslave agriculture: "Slavery became extinct against a background of almost continuous and increasingly more marked development of the forces of production."[126]

Second, as these remarks suggest, the exploited class on which the dominant slave mode of production was based was not responsible for overthrowing the slave owners. Indeed we know of only three major slave revolts in Roman history, two on Sicily during the second century BC and the most famous, that of Spartacus, on the Italian mainland during the first century BC. Some other, smaller revolts have more recently come to light, but the fundamental picture remains unchanged. The class struggle in the Roman world was conducted between the free citizens, over an over-whelmingly passive slave population. But the inheritors were no more the peasants and plebeians of ancient Rome than they were the slaves (although the slaves who obtained their freedom clearly benefited). The new ruling class was rather an alliance of the two forces that had actually been responsible for the Fall: from within, the landowners who withdrew their support for the state in opposition to its increasing demands for taxation; from without, the tribal chiefs and their retinues who led the barbarian invasions. The struggles of the exploited and oppressed classes obviously continued throughout the process, but contributed little to the outcome.

Third, the transition was therefore not an accidental or unintended consequence, but one consciously achieved through a series of pragmatic adaptations in the ways production and exploitation took place. The former slave owners consciously changed the relations of production by lifting up the slaves they owned to the status of serfs while forcing down the free peasants tenanted on their land to the same level, as a response to the growing shortage of captured slaves and the expense of raising them. The tribal chiefs were unconsciously evolving into settled communities with stable and inherited social divisions between the warrior caste and the peasantry, a process hastened by the establishment of permanent settlements on the former territories of the empire. Both were moving from different directions toward what would become, over several hundred years, a new feudal ruling class. There was also a two-way movement of the exploited, particularly between the ninth and eleventh centuries. On the one hand, the supply of slaves dried up and those who did remain were settled as serfs. On the other, the previously free peasants were increasingly brought into a servile condition.

Fourth, the process took place first at the socioeconomic level and only toward the very end gave rise to the political and ideological forms (the estates monarchy, the "three orders") that we now regard as characteristic of feudalism. Indeed, we might say that the transition to feudalism *is* the feudal "revolution"; there is no seizure of power—from whom could it be seized given that ruling-class personnel were simply changing their roles?—but a gradual transformation of political forms to meet new socioeconomic realities. What Georges Duby, Guy Bois, and others refer to as the "feudal revolution" around 1000 AD is in fact the final episode in a process that had taken over five hundred years to complete.

Fifth, the societies that were transformed on feudal lines occupied a relatively small region of Western and Central Europe (although a similar society also developed independently in Japan). Feudalism did not contain an inherent tendency toward expansion. It did not require a world or even continental system, either for exploitation (the territorial acquisitions of the Crusaders in the Middle East and later of the Hispanic states in the Americas were "opportunities" rather than "necessities") or for self-defense (since the great tributary states of the East were almost completely uninterested in these undeveloped formations, so obviously inferior to them in every respect except that of warfare).

The socialist revolution

The socialist revolution will differ from the feudal "revolution" in each of these five aspects. Clearly we are at a disadvantage here, since unlike in the case of the transition to feudalism we are discussing a process that has still to occur. The only socialist revolution to have sustained itself for years rather than months, the Russian Revolution of October 1917, was thrown into reverse by the triumph of the Stalinist counterrevolution by 1928, and the transition it initiated has still to be successfully resumed. Nevertheless, from that experience and those of the brief but illuminating moments both before (the Paris Commune) and after (Germany 1918–23, Spain 1936, Hungary 1956, Portugal 1974–75, etc.), it is possible to make some general comments.

First, the impetus for the transition arises not only from the meaningless, alienating repetitions experienced at the point of production but from a tendency to regularly go into crisis and consequently subject the working class to insecurity, poverty, social breakdown, disease, repression—and ultimately starvation and war. Capitalism has no purely economic limits; unlike slavery or feudalism it cannot reach the limits of the productive forces, although once unleashed they can destroy the world through war or environmental collapse. These are excellent reasons to dispense with it, but—and here the question of consciousness is paramount—the duty of revolutionaries and their organizations is to persuade other members of the working class that capitalism is responsible for existing disasters and those that threaten us in the future.

Second, the exploited class under capitalism, the working class, will achieve the socialist revolution, or it will not be achieved at all. The working class is the first exploited (as opposed to oppressed) class in history that is able to make a revolution on its own behalf. Unlike the peasantry, the working class is structured collectively and is therefore the basis of a new form of social organization in a way that the peasantry can never be. Unlike the bourgeoisie, the working class itself has the numeric size and structural capacity to rebuild the world on its own behalf, without using another class as a battering ram to break down the existing system on its behalf. The working class is not an alternative exploiting class to the bourgeoisie and it will not be transformed into one by victory. (Even those writers who believe that socialism is impossible and that revolution will only lead to a new form of managerial or bureaucratic society do not claim that the proletariat itself will constitute the ruling class, but rather that it will consist of a technocratic elite or "new class.") Consequently, the "everyday" class struggles between exploiters and exploited, and the "transformative" struggles for social revolution, are linked by the fact that the same classes are involved. This is what Lenin meant by saying that the germ of revolution was present in every strike. Clearly the working class will not be the only class involved in the socialist revolution, although its potential allies have changed in the course of the last hundred years—if the Russian Revolution had successfully spread after 1917, then the peasantry would have played a far greater role than they will now, just as the "new" middle or technical-managerial class will play a far greater role now than they would have done in 1917.

Third, and because the transition starts with the seizure of power, it must be a conscious process. No socialist economy will blindly emerge from the struggle to develop the productive forces or to find new ways of exploiting the direct producers who set those forces to work. The struggle for power by the working class requires organization to awaken, consolidate, and maintain class consciousness. But it also requires organization to counterpose to that of the state. If there is any comparison between working class organization and that of the bourgeoisie, it does not involve their respective revolutionary organizations. As Trotsky wrote in 1923: "Consciousness, premeditation, and planning played a far smaller part in bourgeois revolutions than they are destined to play, and already do play, in proletarian revolutions. . . . The part played in bourgeois revolutions by the economic power of the bourgeoisie, by its education, by its municipalities and universities, is a part which can be filled in a proletarian revolution only by the party of the proletariat."[127] In short, what the proletariat has to match is not the organizational structures within which the bourgeoisie conducted their struggle for power (in the minority of examples where, as with the Independents and the Jacobins, it did in fact play this role) but the centralizing role of the state and ideological forms established by the bourgeoisie after its ascendancy.

Fourth, the process *begins* with the smashing of the old state and the construction of the new. If the feudal "revolution" was a process of socioeconomic transition out of whose completion new political forms eventually emerged, then the socialist revolution will be a sociopolitical struggle for power whose completion will allow a new economic order to be constructed. Because the working class is nonexploitative, there is no prior development of an alternative socialist or communist mode of production. As Lukács noted:

> It would be a utopian fantasy to imagine that anything tending towards socialism could arise within capitalism apart from, on the one hand, the *objective economic premises that make it a possibility* which, however, can only be *transformed* in to the true elements of a socialist system of production after and in consequence of the collapse of capitalism; and, on the other hand, the development of the proletariat as a class. . . . But even the most highly developed capitalist concentration will still be qualitatively different, even economically, from a socialist system and can neither change into one "by itself" nor will be amenable to such change "through legal devices" within the framework of capitalist society. [128]

Eight months after the October Revolution, Lenin noted that the Russian economy still contained five intermingled "socioeconomic structures": patriarchal or "natural" peasant farming, small commodity production, private capitalism, state capitalism, and socialism. His point—sadly lost on subsequent generations of would-be Leninists—was that state ownership of the economy did not define the nature of the workers' state, but rather whether the working class was in political control of the state. [129] Democracy is not merely a desirable feature but a necessity for socialism. Indeed, it will be defined by the way in which democracy becomes the basis for those aspects of human existence from which either the market or the bureaucratic state currently exclude it.

Fifth, the socialist revolution is a global event. As long as it remains isolated it remains susceptible to counterrevolution, either from without or from within. The latter point perhaps bears some elaboration. The threat to the Russian Revolution, which was eventually realized, was not simply the backwardness of the economy, but the fact that in the capitalist world system, the pressures of competitive accumulation would ultimately make themselves felt, to the point of determining what happened in Russian factories. Crudely, if the West has tanks and missiles, then so must we. Greater levels of economic development might enable a state to hold out from internal degeneration longer than Russia was able to, but cannot ultimately protect against this process. That is why the international nature of the socialist revolution is a necessity, not a desirable but optional extra. Space has implications for time: the territorial extent of the socialist revolution exercises severe restraints over its temporality.

The transition from feudalism to capitalism and the bourgeois revolution

Between these two polar extremes of social revolution represented by the transition to feudalism and the socialist revolution lies the bourgeois revolution itself. Behind many attempts to deny the historical existence of the bourgeois revolution lies a conception that identifies all social revolutions with the socialist revolution—a fully conscious class subject setting out to overthrow the state as a prelude to transforming all social relations. Because the bourgeois revolutions do not conform to this model, do not share these structures, it is easy to reject their revolutionary provenance and dissolve them back into the broader process of the transitions to capitalism. These arguments are valid in relation to the transition from slavery to feudalism, where, as I have argued, "revolution" does indeed have a metaphoric character. But to treat the events that I continue to call the bourgeois revolutions in this way is to reduce all of the great religious, military, social, and political struggles of five centuries to super-structural or epiphenomenal status. The bourgeois revolutions may not resemble the revolutions that we are trying to make, but they were revolutionary for all that. They do not share the same structure with either their feudal predecessors or their social-ist successors, in some respects looking back to former, in others looking forward to the latter, and in still others distinct from them both.

First, the impetus for the bourgeois revolutions also has two sources. The first examples, extending in this case down to the French, were in response to the crisis of the absolutist state, a crisis that was manifested in the attempts to impose both eco-nomic and ideological controls over society. But this crisis had still deeper roots in the periodic stagnation and decline of the feudal economy. If the "revolutions from below" were less-than-fully-conscious mechanisms for breaking out of the cycle of feudal decline, the "revolutions from above" that followed 1848 were attempts to avoid mil-itary and economic eclipse by those states that had already made the transition.

Second, a single class did not make the bourgeois revolutions. Michael Mann has suggested that a variation of the schema supposedly advocated by Lenin in *What Is to Be Done* (1902), whereby ideological leadership can only be brought to the working class "from outside," might in fact be relevant in relation to the bourgeoisie: "Left to itself the bourgeoisie was only capable of economism—in the eighteenth century of segmental manipulative deference."[130] It is nevertheless possible to argue that only out-siders, only people without direct material interests in the process of production, could supply the leadership for bourgeoisies who were by definition divided in segmented interests. The bourgeoisie includes both urban and rural capitalists, in the literal sense of those who owned or controlled capital, but also encompassed a larger social group over which this class was hegemonic. Hal Draper describes the bourgeoisie in this sense as "a social penumbra around the hard core of capitalists proper, shading out into the diverse social elements that function as servitors or hangers-on of capital without themselves owning capital."[131] The bourgeoisie needs this penumbra. For Anderson: "This mass is typically composed . . . of the gamut of professional, administrative and technical groups that enjoy life-conditions to capitalists proper—everything custom-arily included in the broader term 'bourgeoisie' as opposed to 'capital.'" But the distinc-tion between capitalist and bourgeoisie is not only one operative here. As Anderson continues, "this same bourgeoisie will normally lack a clear-cut frontier with layers of the petty bourgeoisie below it, for the difference between the two in the ranks of the small employer is often quantitative rather than qualitative."[132] But this relationship could not persist. As Gareth Stedman Jones writes: "In general, the more industrial capitalism developed, the stronger was the economic power of the *grande bourgeoisie* in relation to the masses of small producers and dealers from which it had sprung, and the greater the distance between their respective aims. Conversely, the less developed the bourgeoisie, the smaller the gulf between 'bourgeois' and 'petit bourgeois,' and the greater the preponderance and cohesion of the popular movement."[133] The earliest successful examples of bourgeois revolution, in the Netherlands and England, did involve leadership by mercantile, agrarian, and even industrial capitalists (although the latter tended to be based in the colonies rather than the metropolitan centers), but—precisely because they belonged to a minority, exploiting class—they were forced to involve other forces, who were exploited by both feudal lords and themselves, in order to overthrow the absolutist state. But this reliance brought with it the danger that these other forces would seek to pursue their own interests. The English capitalist class had learned the lesson as early as 1688, when it called on a Dutch invasion to complete their work for them, precisely to avoid the upheavals that had characterized the years 1640–60. For the European bourgeoisie who developed later, it was the French Revolution that provided the lesson. The actual involvement of capitalists was actually less in France than in the earlier events in the Netherlands or England, partly because capitalist development had been consciously restrained by the absolutist state, but partly because those capitalists who did exist were more inclined to reform, not least because of the risk that revolution posed to property, which in their case was more industrial than agrarian or mercantile. The petty bourgeoisie therefore played a far greater role, and where this was shared with classes higher in the social structure, it was with the broader bourgeoisie, the journalists, lawyers, and schoolteachers who were remote from the actual productive process, rather than with capitalists in the purely economic sense. Further shifts followed. The political semiparalysis of the European bourgeoisie after 1849 meant that the only social forces capable of forcing through revolutionary change without having to rely on the "dangerous" classes were sections of the existing ruling class, like Prussian Junkers or Japanese Samurai. In the absence of even this instrument, Lenin thought that the working class would have to accomplish the bourgeois revolution. As we know, this was not required, but there is at least a case for arguing that the counterrevolution of the Stalinist bureaucracy after 1928 was the functional equivalent of the Russian bourgeois revolution, adding another, and final, class force to the list of those responsible.

Third, the bourgeois revolutions display a range of different levels of consciousness, depending on the classes involved and the period during which each one took place. As Callinicos suggests, it is in this respect that the intermediary role of the bourgeois revolutions is most pronounced:

> The balance between the role played by structural contradictions and conscious human agency in resolving organic crisis has shifted from the former to the latter

in the course of the past 1,500 years. The transition from feudalism to capitalism occupies an intermediate position in this respect between the fall of the Roman Empire and the Russian Revolution.[134]

Although the earliest revolutions did involve actual capitalists to an extent that was later rare, their motivations were far more concerned with religious or constitutional liberties than with allowing them to exploit their workforce more effectively, although—through several mediations—that was indeed the outcome. The reason for this lies in the very fusion of the economic and political (and the ideological) that was characteristic of feudalism and reached its apogee in the absolutist state. Whatever the reason social actors had for destroying absolutism, once its integrated structures collapsed, the only viable economic alternatives left standing were those of capitalism. Full consciousness was not required in the early "revolutions from below" because behind the revolutionaries lay the solid basis of the capitalist economic development. Insofar as the capitalist leaderships were conscious of their underlying economic aims, they could scarcely declare these openly to their allies in other classes, who were the very ones likely to find themselves simply with a change of master. In the later "revolutions from above," the protagonists were interested in capitalist development as a means of competing militarily with their more advanced rivals. The only examples where a fully conscious capitalist bourgeoisie set out to establish capitalism were in the transformation of Scottish agriculture after 1746 and in the American Civil War where, exceptionally, it was also an industrial bourgeoisie. But in both cases their ability to do so was dependent on prior control of an overarching territorial state apparatus.

Fourth, the bourgeois revolution is both a product and a cause of the transition to feudalism. Ellen Meiksins Wood asks: "Was a revolution necessary to bring about capitalism, or simply to facilitate the development of an already existing capitalism? Was it a cause or an effect of capitalism?"[135] The answer, of course, is that depending upon the stage of the transition at which a specific bourgeois revolution takes place, it can be either. In some cases it was primarily a means of facilitating the development of capitalism (the Dutch Revolt, the English Civil War, the French Revolution, the American Civil War), and in others it was primarily a precondition for the emergence of capitalism (the Scottish Revolution, the Italian Risorgimento, German unification, the Japanese Meiji Restoration), but in no case was capitalism either completely dominant or completely nonexistent, even in Scotland. Early capitalist developments had been thrown back in the Italian city-states and Bohemia, and once the initial breakthroughs took place in the Netherlands and England, the forces of European absolutism mobilized both in their own domains and on a continental scale to prevent any further revolutions taking place along these lines. Consequently, in no other country after England did a capitalist economy grow up relatively unhindered until the point where the classes associated with it could lead an assault on feudal absolutism. Even in the case of England, the French state tried for decades to undo the effects of 1688, mainly by supporting Jacobite reaction in Scotland, an intervention that only stopped with their decisive defeat at Culloden in 1746. As a consequence of the relative success of the absolutist regimes in retarding the development of capitalism, when Prussian, Piedmontese, and Japanese ruling-class fractions did move to establish unified states with which to compete with Britain and France, they were staring from much further back than their competitors had done at a comparable stage in their development as capitalist economies.

Fifth, the bourgeois revolution as a whole has to be wider than a mere regional phenomenon like feudalism, but does not have to resolve at a global level like socialism. Feudalism was essentially a more backward variant of the tributary mode and consequently posed the states in which it was dominant no real threat—indeed, absolutism can be seen as the mutation of European feudalism into state forms comparable to the Chinese and Byzantine.[136] Capitalism was fundamentally different from both the Eastern tributary states and—more immediately—the Western absolutist states. That is why the Spanish tried so hard to suppress the Dutch Revolt and why the French tried even harder to overthrow the English Revolution; their rulers realized, without fully understanding why, that these new forms were their deadly enemies, were ultimately incompatible with their system. The Soviet historian Alexander Chistozvonov has argued that we need the concept of "irreversibility," since "the process of the genesis of capitalism may assume, and does assume, a reversible character whenever there are only some of the combined factors of the genetical transformational series in the country, when they happen to be subjugated to factors of the formational reproduction series and embrace only some centers (regions, branches), while the ruling feudal class and the political superstructure of the feudal society are able for the time being to regulate the development of the process with the aim of preserving the feudal basis, and to overcome or suppress socio-economic conflicts."[137] But this did not mean that the entire world had to be transformed along capitalist lines for the bourgeois revolution to be safe, let alone complete. On the contrary, for at least part of the history of the system, the capitalist states depended on the existence of areas that were forcefully prevented from repeating the experience of bourgeois revolution. The imposition of global capitalism is only really happening now, but the moment when the bourgeois revolution ended can be dated with some precision to October 1917—in other words, when it became evident that socialism was now possible, rather than simply being an aspiration for some future point. There were of course individual and often extremely important national transitions after that date, usually along state-capitalist lines, but the existence of an alternative signaled that epoch in which the bourgeois revolution as a relatively progressive phenomenon was now over.

Conclusion

I want to conclude with some considerations on why Marxists should be so anxious to dismiss the bourgeois revolutions, these events that did so much to shape the contemporary world. There is probably no single answer to this question. One is that opposition is a healthy reaction against Social-Democratic and—especially—Stalinist stages theory. Another reason, however, appears to deal precisely with the question of "relative progressiveness," to which I have just referred. I detect an increasing unwillingness to credit historical capitalism and, by extension, the bourgeoisie, with any positive contribution to human development. Understandable though this position is, given the horrors for which the system continues to be responsible, Marxists must nevertheless reject it. Without capitalism, we would have no possibility of developing the forces of production to the extent that will enable the whole of the world's population to enjoy what is currently denied most of them—a fully human life. In fact, without capitalism there would be no "us"—in the sense of a working class—to seriously consider accomplishing such a goal in the first place. To me, at any rate, it seems to be completely implausible to think that if only capitalism had not come into existence we could all be living in a happy hobbit-land of free peasants and independent small producers. You may think that I exaggerate, but at least two of the very finest Marxist historical works of recent years—James Holstun's *Ehud's Dagger* and Peter Linebaugh and Marcus Rediker's *The Many-Headed Hydra*—are undermined, in my opinion, by literally incredible claims about the possibilities of bypassing capitalism for nonexploitative societies of small commodity producers, possibly in alliance with the indigenous peoples of the Americas, whose "communism" is supposed to have affinities with European "commonism."[138] It is true that capitalism was not inevitable, of course, but the alternative was probably a world divided between endlessly warring absolutist and tributary states without even the possibility of escape that capitalism provides.

This is only a more extreme example of a reaction to the Stalinist celebration of the bourgeoisie as a revolutionary class that seeks to find more revolutionary forces with which contemporary radicals can identify. Hence, in an English context, the attempts to diminish the role of Oliver Cromwell in favor of the Levelers and of the Levelers in favor of the Diggers, and so on. (The latter two groups, which are often spoken of together, were of course different in ideology, class composition, size of membership, and virtually every other respect.) This seems to me to be both completely mistaken and completely unnecessary. In *Discovering the Scottish Revolution* I argue that we have to distinguish between two different sets of historical actors in the bourgeois revolutions. One set consists of our socialist *predecessors*–that is, those who looked toward collectivist solutions that were unachievable in their own time, like the Diggers in England or the Conspiracy of Equals in France. The other set consists of our bourgeois *equivalents*—that is, those who actually carried out the only revolutions possible at the time, which were, whatever their formal goals, to establish the dominance of capital.[139] Clearly, our attitude to these groups is very different. But since one aspect of bourgeois revolutions is to establish the most successful system of exploitation ever seen, it is scarcely surprising that the people who carried them through should, like Cromwell, leave a complex and contradictory legacy.

I want, however, to end on a note that recognizes the fact that the bourgeoisie, in the hour of their greatness, did more for the possibility of human liberation than simply provide the material basis for future socialist development. I think here of the universalism of Enlightenment thought at its best. In the context of my own country, the thinkers of the Scottish bourgeoisie were engaged in changing their world, not merely interpreting it—*The Wealth of Nations* is a program for transforming Scottish society as much as it is a history of the world economy. But what Smith and his colleagues wanted—"commercial society," in their terminology—was not the same as the capitalist society they eventually helped bring into being. Lukács once wrote of the Enlightenment hope that "democratic bourgeois freedom and the supremacy of economics would one day lead to the salvation of all mankind."[140] As we know only too well, it did not. I think that the more perceptive of the Scottish Enlightenment thinkers—above all, Smith himself, Adam Ferguson, and John Millar—were aware of this and that awareness is responsible for their studied ambiguity toward "actually existing capitalism" as it emerged toward the end of the eighteenth century. To paraphrase William Morris, the thing that they fought for turned out to be not what they meant, and other people have since had to fight for what they meant under another name.[141] We in the movements against globalization and imperialist war are those "other people." What we fight for, however, is not to accomplish outstanding "tasks of the bourgeois revolution" in the sense I have already rejected, but those universal principles of freedom and justice that the bourgeois revolutions brought onto the historical agenda, principles that, for all their epochal significance, they were unable to achieve.

Asiatic, Tributary, or Absolutist?
A Comment on Chris Harman's
"The Rise of Capitalism"

Introduction

Since the late 1970s the dominant account of the transition from feudalism to capitalism, among the academic left at least, has been that of Robert Brenner and his followers (Ellen Meiksins Wood, George Comninel, and Benno Teschke). Contributors to *International Socialism* have generally been less admiring, although responses to Brenner's work have ranged from critical support for some of his conclusions to outright rejection of them all. Chris Harman belongs to the latter camp. Much of the criticism he has directed at Brenner over the years has been justified, although the central problem is not, as Chris sometimes suggests, that Brenner is obsessed with rural class struggle to the exclusion of all else.[1] Indeed, many readers must have gone to Brenner's key articles eagerly anticipating detailed accounts of peasant resistance to the lords, only to be disappointed by the scant attention he actually devotes to this subject. In fact, Brenner is only interested in the class struggle in the countryside as a mechanism for explaining why capitalist social relations of production supposedly emerged only in England, and not in Prussia, France, or China. The central problem is rather that he treats feudalism as an enclosed, self-perpetuating system that cannot be undermined by its own internal contradictions.[2] Consequently, the emergence of capitalism, the most dynamic of all exploitative modes of production, becomes a merely contingent and highly unlikely outcome of conjunctural events.[3]

In his article "The Rise of Capitalism," Chris insists that the potential for capitalist development existed not only elsewhere in Europe but globally. By doing so he has helped remove the emergence of capitalism from the realm of accident, where Brenner left it, and return it to that of history. Chris does not engage directly with Brenner in this article, except in the footnotes, but his presence lies behind the one aspect of Chris's article that I find both unconvincing and unnecessary to his central argument, namely his discussion of the Asiatic mode of production.[4] Chris supports a particular conception of the Asiatic mode of production and denies the very existence of another mode that, over the last thirty years or so, has increasingly been invoked as a more rigorous alternative to it: the tributary mode.

Asiatic or tributary? Readers may be forgiven for thinking that they have so far managed to demonstrate against the occupation of Iraq, campaign for Respect or the Scottish Socialist Party, and attend their trade union branch on a semiregular basis without feeling the need to take a side on this question or even notice its existence. Nevertheless, despite the esoteric nature of the terminology, the debate involved is of political importance. The British medievalist Chris Wickham, one of the key contributors to these debates, once wrote: "Why do we try to categorise world history in Marxist terms at all? Leaving aside the devotional elements in such categorisations—an element that is, as is well known, still strong—the only answer can be Marx's own: that we understand the world better by doing so, so that we can change it."[5] That is the reason why, in the course of registering these disagreements, it might be worth elaborating on some of the arguments to which Chris could refer only in passing.

The use and abuse of the Asiatic mode of production

So why do we need the concept of the Asiatic mode of production? Can we not simply declare that the entire precapitalist world, with the exception of the Greek and Roman slave societies, was feudal? In fact, with the exception of the few remaining Stalinists, virtually everyone who is interested in this question recognizes that the differences between the societies involved are so vast that this position is impossible to maintain. The alternative that Chris adopts is that some of them were "Asiatic" (i.e., dominated by the Asiatic mode of production). Now, Marx himself used the term on a handful of occasions, most notably in the 1859 "Preface" to *A Contribution to the Critique of Political Economy*: "In broad outline, the Asiatic, ancient, feudal and modern bourgeois modes of production may be designated as epochs marking progress in the economic development of society."[6] The trouble is that it is by no means clear what Marx means by the Asiatic mode. Anyone who has tried to trace the evolution of his thought on the subject of modes of production—even over the relatively simple matter of how many there are—quickly discovers that Marx changed his mind at least four times, and the picture becomes even more complex when Engels is included. As far as the Asiatic mode is concerned, the confusion is deepened by the fact that both Marx and Engels spoke not only of an Asiatic mode of production but of Asiatic or Oriental Despotism, a notion out of Enlightenment thought that refers to the nature of the political regime rather than the economic basis of society. Rather than trawl through the *Collected Works* for every reference made by Marx and Engels to these issues, it might be preferable to assess which interpretations are compatible with their general theory of history and (equally important to those who reject the "devotional" attitude that Wickham refers to) which ones in any case have the greatest explanatory power, are able to account for the widest range of evidence, and so on.

So let us leave Marx and Engels aside for the moment: what does Chris mean by the Asiatic mode of production? In *A People's History of the World* Chris describes as

Asiatic those societies in which "the rulers were able, through their collective control of the state machine, to exploit entire peasant communities which farmed the land jointly without private property," including "the Mesopotamian, Egyptian, Chinese, Indian, Meso-American and South American."[7] Chris has now revised his position. He excludes India from his earlier list, claiming that Marx was wrong ever to classify it in these terms, and argues that at least some territories in India should instead be classified as feudal. The only society that Chris now explicitly wants to describe as "Asiatic" is China, but rather than "collective ownership of the state machine" in general being decisive, it is specifically because the centralized state bureaucracy collectively owned and controlled the dam and canal systems by which agricultural land was irrigated and goods were transported inland from the coastal trading regions. If the Asiatic mode is only found in "hydraulic society," then as Chris writes, not only India but also "Islamic North Africa and the Ottoman Empire" must be excluded from the category, although presumably it can still be applied to Pharaonic Egypt and pre-Columbian Mexico and Peru, in addition to China.[8]

As Chris notes, the "hydraulic society" thesis was first proposed by the erstwhile German Marxist Karl Wittfogel, during the 1930s. It has been widely criticized, not to say ridiculed, in the intervening years. In some cases, these criticisms were part of a politically inspired Stalinist campaign. A conference in Leningrad during 1931 put an end to a debate that had been running in the USSR since 1925, by declaring that the "Asiatic" mode was nonexistent. There seem to have been two reasons for this edict being issued. The first was that the possibility of an exploiting state that did not rest on private property was, to say the least, an embarrassment to the ideologues of Stalinism, whose state exploited the Russian working class and peasantry . . . without the existence of private property. The second was in relation to the contemporary situation in China, the "Asiatic" state par excellence. The Left Opposition had argued that the bourgeoisie were too weak to carry out the "bourgeois-democratic" revolution in China and that—as the theory of permanent revolution suggested—the working class would have to lead the revolutionary process all the way to socialism. Since Stalin had been allied with what he imagined was the revolutionary bourgeoisie in the shape of the Kuomintang, and he took it as axiomatic that the bourgeoisie could only emerge out of feudalism, any attempt to declare that China was not feudal but "Asiatic" undermined these assumptions and was obviously a Trotskyist attempt to criticize the alliance. The rejection of the Asiatic mode remained an article of faith in the USSR virtually down to the end of the Stalinist regime.[9] The Stalinists were able to point to the fact that Marx never again used the term "Asiatic" after 1859 and that Engels explicitly refers to only three exploitative modes of production in *The Origins of the Family, Private Property and the State* (1884).[10] During the 1950s, Wittfogel, now turned anti-Communist, seized on these discoveries to claim that Marx and Engels had in fact deliberately suppressed their knowledge of the Asiatic mode because "Marx could scarcely help recognising some disturbing similarities between Oriental despotism and the state of his program," a program realized when "the Bolshevik revolution paved the way for the rise of the total managerial apparatus state of the USSR."[11] There are, however, perfectly good reasons for rejecting the "hydraulic" model, unconnected with either Stalinist ideology or the Cold War purposes to which Wittfogel later put his ideas.

The problem is not the existence of state production and ownership over the hydraulic systems: this has been long established, and not only for China; Iran is another example. The problem is the significance that Chris ascribes to it. Dams, canals, or any other water-based aspects of the economic infrastructure belong to the forces of production. But modes of production cannot be defined solely by the forces of production involved, since the same forces can coexist with several different modes. More importantly in this context, neither can modes of production be defined by ownership of the forces of production. It is the process of exploitation, the means by which surplus value is extracted from the primary producers, that is decisive in defining a mode of production, and that is also why the societies based on them have what Chris calls "different dynamics" in the first place.[12] State ownership of canals in pre-Republican China no more determined the dominant mode of production there than private ownership of canals did in the prerevolutionary Netherlands. Chris argues that state ownership of these important resources contributed to blocking the emergence of a mercantile class, which is plausible, but completely irrelevant. Collective ownership of the economy in Stalinist Russia by a state bureaucracy certainly prevented the formation of a "private" bourgeoisie (of any significant size) until 1991, but writers in *International Socialism*—not least Chris Harman—have always argued that there is no fundamental difference *in relation to the exploitation of the working class* between the Stalinist bureaucracy and either of the private bourgeoisies that preceded and succeeded it. In other words, the Asiatic mode of production may or may not be a useful concept with which to analyze the dynamics of class society in China, or indeed anywhere else—let us leave that to one side for the moment—but either way, its existence is not dependent on state ownership of canals and other waterways.

We are therefore apparently left with two unpalatable alternatives: either reject the Asiatic mode of production and treat every nonslave society between primitive communism and capitalism as feudal, or accept the Asiatic mode on a basis that undermines the Marxist conception of the mode of production. Fortunately the choice is more apparent than real. Ironically, the solution lies in what is usually thought to be one of the greatest weaknesses of the Asiatic mode. Chris alludes to it in his summary of Marx's position: "He outlined a theoretical account of societies where the ruling class collectively exploited an oppressed class, which was engaged in collective production. He suggested that this was a transitional form between primitive communism and a fully developed class society."[13] The difficulty here, as Chris recognizes, is that whatever one thinks about the precise nature of, say, China under the Ming dynasty, it can scarcely be described as "transitional": it was "a fully developed class society." Perry Anderson has given the clearest exposition of this contradiction within the Asiatic mode:

The notion has, in effect, typically been extended in two different directions. On the one hand, it has been cast backwards to include Ancient societies of the Middle East and Mediterranean prior to the classical epoch: Sumerian Mesopotamia, Pharaonic Egypt, Hittite Anatolia, Mycenaean Greece or Etruscan Italy. This use of the notion retains its original emphasis on a powerful centralised state, an often hydraulic agriculture, and focuses on "generalised slavery" in the presence of arbitrary and unskilled labour drafts levied from primitive rural populations by a superior bureaucratic power above them. At the same time, a second extension has occurred in another direction. For the "Asiatic mode of production" has also been enlarged to embrace the first state organisations of tribal or semi-tribal social formations, with a level of civilisation below those of pre-classical Antiquity: Polynesian islands, African chieftainries, Amerindian settlements. This usage usually discards any emphasis on large-scale irrigation works or a particularly despotic state: it focuses essentially on the survival of kin relationships, communal rural property and cohesively self-sufficient villages. It deems this whole mode of production "transitional" between a classless and a class society, preserving many pre-class features. The result of these two tendencies has been an enormous inflation of the scope of the Asiatic mode of production—chronologically backwards to the earliest dawn of civilisation, and geographically outwards to the farther edge of tribal organisation.

Anderson is rightly scathing about the possibility of describing both types of social formation as being dominated by the same mode of production: "What serious historical unity exists between Ming China and Megalithic Ireland, Pharaonic Egypt and Hawaii? It is perfectly clear that such social formations are unimaginably distant from each other."[14] Anderson is wrong, however, to suggest that the twofold extension of the concept only occurred after Marx and Engels; both sides were already present in their own work. When Marx and Engels refer to the Asiatic mode they are in fact referring to *two* different modes of production under the same name: the Asiatic *and* what has come to be called the tributary.

The Asiatic mode "proper," as Anderson indicates, is simply the transitional stage between primitive communism and all of the exploitative modes of production that emerged directly out of it. Historically, class societies did not simply "arise" or "emerge" like cruise missiles from a silo; they took millennia to form. Indeed, the process almost certainly took longer to complete than the length of time for which the resulting class societies have subsequently existed. There is therefore some use in having a term for societies during this initial and (to date) most fundamental transition. The most detailed discussion by Marx is in the *Grundrisse*, the notebooks he kept between 1857 and 1858. Here he describes four different routes out of primitive communism—"Asiatic, Slavonic, ancient Classical, Germanic"—that are in effect all transitional forms in which private property first emerges, the difference being the nature of the relationship between the countryside and the city in each form.[15] The Asiatic and the Slavonic modes are essentially the same and evolve into the tributary mode, as in China and Russia; the ancient Classical mode evolves into slavery, as in Greece and Rome; and the Germanic mode evolves into feudalism, as in Scotland or Scandinavia. As the French Marxist Maurice Godelier puts it:

> Marx, without having been completely aware of it, described a form of social organ-isation specific to the *transition* from classless to class society. . . . Because of this re-lation between the situation and structure it is possible to explain the geographical and historical universality of the form of social organisation which emerges when the conditions for the transition to class society develop: maybe at the end of the fourth millennium BC in the case of Egypt with the transition of the tribal Nilotic societies first to monarchies and then to a unified Empire, or in the nineteenth century with the birth of the Bamoum kingdom in the Cameroons.[16]

In effect, Godelier is arguing that Marx came to use the term "Asiatic" to embrace all of these transitional forms, and that we should do the same. There is certainly no geographical limitation to the Asiatic mode in this "transitional" sense, despite the quite unnecessary indignation the term has produced in certain writers: "No concept of a mode of production can make its geographical location necessary," sniff Barry Hindess and Paul Hirst; "where (or *if*) a mode of production exists is a contingent and not a necessary matter": "It can only be, in the last instance, in the form of 'Spirit' that geography can be made necessity, and in the form of the Hegelian dialectic which works by exclusion and contradiction. Thus if there were an AMP there would be no reason why it should not occur in Africa, Europe, Australia or the North Pole; its ex-istence *in Asia* would be contingent."[17] At the risk of taking a sledgehammer to crack a nut, or possibly a pair of nuts, it might be worthwhile to recall the eminently sane reflections of Hal Draper: "Just as the discovery of Peking man did not mean that only the Chinese had prehuman ancestors, so too the survival of living-fossil social forms in Asia did not mean that the 'Asiatic' mode of production was an Oriental monopoly."[18] Hobsbawm similarly notes that when Marx referred to Germanic and Slavonic modes of production in the *Grundrisse*, he was not suggesting that they existed only among the Germans or the Slavs.[19]

Yet there is a problem here. Ernest Mandel writes:

> What must we think of the attempts . . . to reduce the Asiatic mode of production to a socio-economic formation marking the transition from classless society to class society? In order to do this they have to suppress, first and foremost, the key role that Marx and Engels attributed to hydraulic and other large-scale works in the es-tablishment of this mode of production. . . . What they are doing, in fact, is gradually reducing the characteristics of the Asiatic mode of production to those that mark every first manifestation of the state and of ruling classes in a society still based on the village community.[20]

The attempts to which Mandel refers must, presumably, include those of Marx himself, although typically Mandel cannot bring himself to include his name in the charge sheet. Nevertheless, the contradiction remains. In Marx's journalism of the 1850s, where the concept, if not the term, "Asiatic mode of production" was first introduced, it referred to the dominant mode in contemporary China and India, not societies thousands of years earlier in history. This is where the tributary mode is useful. It is important to recognize that the latter is not merely a more rigorous alternative to the Asiatic mode—since this would not deal with the incompatibility of social formations stressed by Anderson and Mandel—but a separate mode that, as I have suggested, directly followed the Asiatic in many parts of the world.[21]

THE TRIBUTARY MODE AS ALTERNATIVE

The concept, if not the term, originates with Marx himself: "In the case of the slave relationship, the serf relationship, and the relationship of tribute (where the primitive community is under consideration), it is the slaveowner, the feudal lord or the state receiving tribute that is the owner of the product and therefore its seller."[22] The first person to use the term was probably the Japanese Marxist Jiro Hoyakawa in 1934.[23] More recently, however, the Egyptian radical economist Samir Amin has been most responsible for popularizing its use. He characterizes the tributary mode as "the separation of society into two main classes: the peasantry, organised in communities, and the ruling class, which monopolises the functions of the given society's political organisation and exacts a tribute (not in commodity form) from the rural community."[24]

Wickham has elaborated on this basic definition, writing that the tributary mode involves a "'state class' based on a public institution, with political rights to extract surplus from a peasantry that it does not tenurially control." Wickham argues that the crucial distinction between the tributary and feudal modes lies in the means by which the surplus is collected from the peasantry. In the former, it is through payment of taxation to the state; in the latter, through payment of rent to private landowners.[25] For Wickham, there are two further differences between the tributary mode and the feudal. The first is that a tributary state taxes landowners in addition to peasants. The second is that the tributary mode allows far greater autonomy for the peasantry in the process of production than the feudal mode. As a result: "They represent two different economic systems, even if they can come together in some exceptional circumstances. Their differences, their antagonisms, lie in their divergent interventions in the peasant economy, just as their convergences lie in the fact that both are rooted in it. The same productive forces, however, can, be seen as giving rise to two separate modes of production."[26] Eric Wolf gives an example of this from India, where the operation of the tributary mode involved domination of the direct producers by the local agents of the state—either military bureaucrats with lifetime grants of land (*jagirdars*) or hereditary chiefs (*zamindars*)—responsible for collecting the tribute, part of which went toward their own revenue, part to the central state. "The critical difference from the later English practice was that these rights were not, properly speaking, rights of property in land, but rather claims on people's labour and the products of that labour." In some cases the central state bypassed the zamindars completely to extract the surplus directly; in others the zamindars had a feudal relationship with the peasants.[27]

The concept of the tributary mode has proved useful in the International Socialist tradition. Alex Callinicos, for example, follows Amin in general and Wickham in particular in several works, including *Making History* and *Theories and Narratives*. In the latter, he advances as a general thesis the case that Chris makes for China alone, namely the power of the tributary state in preventing the growth of an independent class of lords and their transformation into capitalist landlords or manufacturers. He also notes that it has, at the other end of the class spectrum, an interest in preserving the peasantry as a source of tax income. It is therefore precisely the weakness of feudal as compared to tributary societies that provides capitalism with the most fertile ground to develop, notably through the greater direct involvement of the lords in the productive process and the existence of fragmented power structures that encourage the flow of commodities.[28] (Some care needs to be exercised with this argument, however, since it is also true that the feudal societies in which the central state was weakest—Scotland in the West and Poland in the East—had even less capitalist development than China.)

The question is whether the tributary and feudal modes are different from each other on the basis that I gave earlier: the process of exploitation. Marx himself suggested that they were not. He noted that where peasants form what he called a "natural community," then "the surplus labour for the nominal landowner can only be extorted from them by extra-economic compulsion, *whatever the form this might assume*": "If there are no private landlords but it is the state, as in Asia, which confronts them directly as simultaneously landowner and sovereign, rent and tax coincide, or rather there does not exist any tax distinct from this form of ground-rent."[29] I agree with this and therefore with Chris when he argues that neither the distinction between the central state and the local lord, nor the distinction between taxation and rent, is decisive in Marxist terms:

> Otherwise you would have to conclude that there were two different modes of production in feudal Europe—one where the individual feudal lord was the exploiter, the other where the role was played by the collective institution of the medieval church. It can only be correct to identify tax-based exploitation of the peasantry as constituting a different mode of production if it results in a fundamentally different dynamic to society. You would also have to conclude that, as does Benno Teschke ... that absolutist France was not feudal, since the exploitation of the peasantry and enrichment of the nobility was mainly through the tax system of the monarchy.[30]

The reference to Teschke indicates Chris's real concern here; for behind Teschke stands the figure of Brenner, his theoretical inspiration. Why does Brenner think that absolutist France was not feudal? He argues that the state in prerevolutionary France "developed ... as a class-like phenomenon ... an independent extractor of the surplus.[31] Teschke follows him in declaring that "[Absolutism] was a *sui generis* social formation, displaying a specific mode of government and determinate pre-modern and pre-capitalist domestic and international 'laws of motion.'"[32] Characteristically, Ellen Meiksins Wood has taken the position to its logical conclusion, arguing that absolutism was not simply a state form typical of the transition from feudalism to capitalism but a distinct mode of production in its own right: "In some Western European cases, feudalism gave way not to capitalism but to absolutism, with its own non-capitalist modes of appropriation and politically constituted property."[33] Or again: "The absolutist state was a centralized instrument of extra-economic surplus extraction, and office in the state was a form of property which gave its possessors access to peasant-produced surpluses."[34] It is clear, therefore, why Chris had to change his conception of the Asiatic mode, since it would have otherwise borne too great a resemblance to both the tributary mode and absolutism as conceived by Brenner and his followers. In other words, Chris is concerned that by accepting that a centralized tax-collecting state can be characteristic of a distinct mode of production, we allow Brennerism in by the back door, because this definition effectively also applies to the European absolutist states: "Those like Alex [Callinicos] who disagree with [Brenner] over France should not embrace an essentially similar analysis to his when it comes to India."[35]

THE TRIBUTARY MODE AND THE ABSOLUTIST STATE

The solution to the problem here has been provided, in my opinion, by a historian of Byzantium called John Haldon. He argues that there is no fundamental difference between tax and rent that would justify regarding them as constituent of different modes of production: "the fundamental difference between these two forms of the same mode of surplus extraction lies in fact in a political relation of surplus appropriation and distribution." The relationship to peasants of landlords, on the one hand, and of states, on the other, do not differ fundamentally:

> The forms of intervention vary quantitatively, to a degree; but states and their agents could also be just as involved in the process of production and extraction of surplus as landlords (indeed, in Mughul India, for example, tax-farmers also involved themselves in these relationships). Where both exist it does not imply that there are two different ruling classes (for the state represents the landlords), merely that the state bureaucracy and the landlords represent different factions of the same ruling class and their conflicts are not based on a different relationship to the direct producers, but over the distribution of the surplus extracted from them.[36]

In other words, the tributary and feudal modes are variations on the same mode of production, but it is the tributary variant that was dominant, both in the sense that it embraced the majority of the world's population after the fall of the Roman Empire and that these areas remained the most economically developed until the eighteenth century. The feudal mode of production was a peripheral, mainly Western European variant of the tributary mode, although, as we have seen, it was precisely through "the advantages of backwardness" that capitalism was able to develop more freely than in the hitherto more advanced East.

It is therefore possible to see a connection between the tributary and absolutist states without, as Chris fears, claiming that the latter is some hitherto undiscovered but nonfeudal mode of production. Haldon does not discuss absolutism, but if we accept his analysis, then the emergence of absolutism can be seen as the resumption—at a higher level of development—of the form in which feudalism (that is, the "tributary" mode) had generally been experienced outside of Europe. Amin suggests that absolutism would have been the Western variant of the tributary mode, but that it arrived too late to arrest the development of capitalism in the same way that the Chinese state did after 1300.[37] Far from absolutism being a sign of the advanced nature of the West, as Anderson maintains, it was in fact an attempt to impose a similar "fetter on production" to the one that the Chinese and other non-European states had already experienced in the form of an overmighty state superstructure.[38] From this basis the main difference between Russia and China on the one hand, and England and France on the other, is that in the former two societies the state was successful in preventing new class forces from developing for such a long period that, in both cases, it was from the working class rather than the bourgeoisie that the challenge eventually came. But there was no necessity for these outcomes, as is demonstrated by the examples of Prussia from the "absolutist" West and Japan from the "tributary" East, both of which made the transition to capitalism.

To summarize an argument that is unavoidably confusing, I think that the most useful applications of the terminology we have inherited are the following: First, the Asiatic mode is the transitional stage between primitive communism and all the initial forms of class society. Second, the tributary mode emerges most directly from the Asiatic mode. It is the main form of precapitalist class society and is characterized by the exploitation of the peasantry by a centralized bureaucratic state. (The feudal mode is a variation on this mode in which power is devolved to local lords and corporate bodies.) Third, absolutism is the form taken by the feudal state during the transition from feudalism to capitalism in Europe. Because of the fundamental unity of the feudal and tributary modes, the centralizing character of absolutism allows it to play a role analogous to that of the tributary state in the Americas, North Africa, and Asia. These usages have the advantage of avoiding untenable notions of "hydraulic society" without conceding ground to the position that there were ever societies inherently resistant to capitalist development.

3

Centuries of Transition:
Chris Wickham
on the Feudal Revolution

Introduction

Why should readers of *Historical Materialism* consider reading a book by a specialist in early Italian history, containing 831 pages of text and dealing with Europe and the Mediterranean world between the fifth and ninth centuries AD? *Framing the Early Middle Ages* was awarded the Deutscher Memorial Prize for 2006, which suggests that it may interest a wider audience than the fellow medievalists Chris Wickham addresses in his introduction. There, "you the reader" is assumed to belong to a group of "experts" who "often . . . know far more than I about a given set of materials."[1] In the case of this reviewer, Wickham need have no such concerns, since my area of expertise lies in a historical period that opens nearly nine hundred years after his closes, and with a country (Scotland) that he specifically excludes from discussion.[2] My purpose here will therefore not be to dispute with Wickham over, for example, his explanation for why there are greater similarities between Syro-Palestinian and Italian ceramics than between either of these and ceramics of Egyptian origin.[3] Instead, I approach the book in the same way as most other non-specialist readers of this journal: as a Marxist interested in what a fellow Marxist has to say about a crucial but deeply obscure turning point in human history, and in what implications his work has for Marxist theory. As we shall see, his work is full of interest in both respects.

Wickham and the debate on the first transition

There have been recurrent debates over the transition from feudalism to capitalism. There have even been extended discussions over the transition from capitalism to socialism—an event that, as we are all too painfully aware, has not yet successfully taken place. As a result we have some idea of the relationship between economic transition and social revolution in both cases. By contrast, the emergence of feudalism has been relatively neglected by all the major intellectual traditions that seek to explain long-term socioeconomic development, including Marxism.[4] In the first volume of Michael Mann's *The Sources of Social Power*, for example, his conclusions concerning the decline and fall of the Roman Empire are followed by an extended discussion of Christianity and rival religions, before beginning a survey of twelfth-century Europe, considered solely insofar as it provides the setting for capitalist development.[5] Mann can at least argue that, as a non-Marxist, he does not find the concept of feudalism useful, but even a work as firmly situated within the classical Marxist tradition as Chris Harman's *A People's History of the World* deals with the subject in a summary fashion that is noticeably different from the later treatment of the transition to capitalism.[6]

In one sense this is unsurprising, since the Marxist classics are relatively silent on the subject. The most famous discussion, by Engels in *The Origins of the Family, Private Property and the State* (1884), summarizes over four hundred years of history in around twelve pages. For Engels, the pressures caused by imperial taxation had already set in motion the economic crisis of the empire, as a result of which the declining profitability of slavery, in both the great estates and artisanal workshops, led to landlords settling former slaves as hereditary tenants.[7] There is nothing uniquely Marxist about this explanation, except perhaps the stress Engels places on the Germanic invasions in embedding the "barbarian" gentile constitution that supposedly gave peasant society a community structure and an institutional means of emancipation from servitude. Important essays by Max Weber (1896) and Marc Bloch (written between the world wars, but published posthumously in 1947) also privileged the changing position of the slaves, although with different emphases. For Weber, the decisive point was when the territorial limits of the empire were reached, leading to difficulties in acquiring new slaves with which to replace the existing workforce, since actual reproduction—breeding slaves rather than capturing or buying them—would have required massive levels of investment that landlords were unwilling to make.[8] Bloch is in some ways closer to Engels, but adds an additional component in claiming that the new class of serfs arose not only from a loosening of the conditions of absolute servitude hitherto imposed on the slaves, but from a tightening of the relative liberty previously enjoyed by free peasants.[9] None of these contributions referred to revolution as such. Those that did tended to be non-Marxist and focused on a much later period. Richard Southern famously wrote of the period between 970 and 1215: "The slow emergence of a knightly aristocracy which set the social tone of Europe for hundreds of years contains no dramatic events or clearly decisive moments such as those which have marked the course of the other great social revolutions." It was the almost imperceptible quality of the transformation that led him to describe it as the "silent revolution of these centuries."[10]

Serious Marxist discussion of the subject took place over a relatively short period toward the end of the last century, culminating in a series of exchanges in *Past and Present* across 1996–97. Since Wickham made several important contributions to that discussion, it may be worth recapitulating the key positions, including his own, to contextualize his latest book. Two works, Perry Anderson's *Passages from Antiquity to Feudalism* (1974) and Guy Bois's *The Transformation of the Year One Thousand* (1989), conveniently set out the main opposing explanations and timescales for the emergence of feudalism.

For Anderson, there is a period of socioeconomic transition that begins with the barbarian settlement within the Roman Empire in the West, but is concluded only several centuries after its collapse: "The catastrophic collision of two mutually dissolving anterior modes of production—primitive and ancient—eventually produced the feudal order which spread throughout medieval Europe."[11] Given that the preexisting modes were embedded in social formations occupying geographically separate areas of Europe, feudalism was initially marked by spatial unevenness:

> In effect, the core region of European feudalism was that in which a "balanced synthesis" of Roman and Germanic elements occurred: essentially, Northern France and zones contiguous to it, the homeland of the Carolingian Empire. To the South of this area, in Provence, Italy or Spain, the dissolution and recombination of barbarian and ancient modes of production occurred under the dominant legacy of Antiquity. To the North and East of it, in Germany, Scandinavia and England, where Roman rule had never reached or had taken only shallow root, there was conversely a slow transition towards feudalism, under the indigenous dominance of the barbarian heritage.[12]

The prolonged period during which fusion took place meant that the preexisting modes were not transformed immediately, but for Anderson there is no suggestion that they continued to exist anywhere as dominant after the sixth century, although examples could of course be found of free peasant communities on the one hand, and of slaves on the other.

Anderson could draw on some passing suggestions by Marx himself in the *Grundrisse*, where the notion of "synthesis" was first deployed, as his authority.[13] The main support for this position had, however, come from Russian and Eastern European academics such as Elena Mikhailovna Shtaerman, although it was by no means universally accepted by all their colleagues.[14] Anderson refuses to contemplate the existence of feudalism prior to the fall of the Roman Empire, and he is, of course, scarcely alone in taking this position. As Moses Finley once wrote: "On any account chattel slavery ceased to be dominant even in Italy by the fourth or fifth century whereas it is improper to speak of feudalism before the time of Charlemagne, leaving a 'transition' lasting three or four hundred years."[15] Why Finley finds it improper is not clear, but the same position was also taken by his great opponent, Geoffrey de Ste Croix. The latter was prepared to acknowledge the existence of serfdom as one of the three forms of unfree labor in the ancient world (along with chattel slavery and debt bondage), but he opposed the idea that this demonstrated the existence of feudal relations of production, describing this as a "groundless connection." Again, the grounds of his objection are not entirely clear, other than this would involve the discovery of feudal-ism across the Greek world prior to the Hellenistic period, although he recognizes that there are "closely related (though not identical) forms in Graeco-Roman antiq-uity and in the middle ages."[16] Ste Croix's unwillingness to recognize the existence of feudalism may signal his adherence to a Social-Democratic or Stalinist notion of successive stages of social development. In the case of Anderson the reason is different. He is committed to the view that capitalism emerged as an indigenous system only in Western Europe. Although he sees feudalism as having a slightly wider territorial extent (it also includes Japan), the conditions for the emergence of capitalism are only present in Western Europe because the genesis of feudalism there took a peculiarly "synthetic" form, allowing what Anderson sees as the distinctive element—the cultural and juridical heritage of classical antiquity—to be transmitted into the new system.[17] As this suggests, Anderson's definition of feudalism is based on its superstructural characteristics—a necessity, in his view, since all precapitalist class societies other than slavery are based on the exploitation of a peasantry by land-lords.[18] Feudalism therefore cannot have existed during the lifetime of the Roman Empire, as these characteristics were absent. It is of course quite possible to explain the priority of capitalism in Western European history without recourse to idealist speculations about the heritage of classical antiquity. The key point in the context of this discussion, however, is Anderson's chronology: the end of the empire in the West during the fifth century sets in train a process that led to the emergence of feudalism.

Bois would agree that feudalism did not predate the end of the Roman Empire, but in every other respect his account is the opposite of Anderson's. Far from slavery beginning a long transformation virtually from the moment the social organization of the barbarian tribes began to interpenetrate with that of the Romans, Bois claims that it remained the dominant mode until the tenth century, notably in the areas where Charlemagne had attempted to preserve the political form of the Western Empire. Accordingly, Bois emphasizes not the process of transition but a moment of revolution around 1000, which he describes as a "European phenomenon."[19] Draw-ing on events in the village of Lournard in Cluny to support his thesis, he describes a situation of "dual power" between the monks of the monastery of Cluny, bearers of the new feudal order, and the existing masters, the Carolingian defenders of slavery:

> The driving force behind this movement was a faction within the aristocracy, or, to be more precise, within the high aristocracy in its monastic dimension. This was done almost despite itself. The sole concern of the first Cluniacs was to assure their independence with regard to the lay powers and to reform monasticism. However, this concern led them to develop close ties with the peasantry. There was thus an identity of interest (the peasantry feeling themselves threatened by the local gran-dees) and even an ideological rapprochement, to the extent that monastic spiritual-ity coincided with the moral needs of the peasantry. From this moment on the old order was threatened. As often happens in such cases, the signal for hostilities was given by the champions of the past, by that local aristocracy, warrior and slave-own-

ing, which formed the social base of the Carolingian system, but which saw its position being eroded. By unleashing violence, it plunged society into anarchy, thus compelling the monks to assume responsibilities in the social sphere and define a new order: the first draft of feudal society.[20]

Bois was the last in series of French historians, beginning with Georges Duby, who had introduced the notion of a feudal revolution by way of an analogy with the bourgeois revolution.[21] (Although by the time Bois's book appeared in France, Duby had rejected both the term and the notion.[22]) There are two main objections to Bois's account of the process. The first is empirical. His material is too narrowly based on one small area of France and cannot be generalized across the whole of Europe: slaves existed in estates east of the Rhine where Roman influence was minimal, and labor services were innovations in Italy during the eighth and ninth centuries, not a legacy from antiquity.[23] The second is theoretical. His definition of a slave is too fixated on the legal category and not enough on the actual relationship of the direct producers so categorized to the means of production. In other words, many of these slaves were in fact nearer to the free peasants—notably in their interest in raising output—than the slaves who labored in the fields, mines, or households of antiquity.[24] Nevertheless, a diluted version of the "feudal revolution" thesis has now been mainstreamed, shorn of the Marxism framework to which Bois at least had subscribed, to the extent that the term "revolution" can be used to describe changes around the first millennium without specifying the transition to any particular mode of production, as in Robert Moore's *The First European Revolution, c. 970–1215* (2000).[25]

Where did Wickham stand in this debate? In two important articles, "The Other Transition" (1984) and "The Uniqueness of the East" (1985), he established his own distinct position. Against Anderson, he claimed that feudalism already existed in 300 AD, so that it could not have been the result of a synthesis of German barbarism and Roman slavery. Indeed, as Wickham points out, "in so far as the German invaders had such things as a landed aristocracy, these largely resulted from Roman influence."[26] Against the French tradition of "feudal revolution," which was shortly to culminate in Bois's work, he claimed that this preexisting feudal mode of production had become the dominant mode by 700 AD, by which time "the balance shifted" from the hitherto dominant ancient mode.[27] The transition from slave to serf, through the mechanism of labor service, was, he claimed, "marginal" to the transition—indeed he sees the peasantry as major beneficiaries of the entire process. He does note that increased surplus extraction from peasants occurred during the ninth and especially tenth centuries, but this is characteristic of the end of the first phase of feudal development, not the transition to feudalism itself. Whatever happened around 1000 AD could scarcely have been a revolution, then, since the fundamental change had already been completed 300 years earlier.

Wickham began by identifying a contradiction within the Roman ruling class, which was heightened from the beginning of the fifth century. The acquisition of land made individual members liable for tax, which they tried with increasing success to evade, this reducing the resources available to them collectively as state managers. The main recipient of state funding was the army, engaged in increasingly futile attempts to repel the Germanic invasions—attempts whose lack of success provided an even greater incentive to tax evasion. Meanwhile the German invaders began to appear an attractive alternative to supporting a declining but acquisitive state apparatus. As Wickham stresses, however, "tax-evading aristocrats," although important, were not the only social actors involved in achieving the transition.[28] Peasants played a far greater role, but (despite several important risings from early in the fifth century) not principally as participants in open class struggle. Instead, they hastened the internal disintegration of the empire by placing themselves under the protection of landowners, effectively renouncing their independence on the assumption that not only would their new status as tenants not carry tax liabilities, but their new lords would be capable of avoiding such responsibilities themselves, and consequently would not pass them on. In effect, both the landowners and the peasants had reasons to choose what would later become known as feudal social relations.

These pressures also applied in the East, but the outcomes were different, mainly because in the West the crisis of taxation coincided with an additional factor: the Germanic invasions. The triumph of the barbarians did not immediately lead to total transformation: "The new Germanic states were not yet feudal."[29] Taxation continued, but without the need for a centralized army—since the new states raised armies from their own landowners and retainers—the main purpose for raising taxation no longer existed. Taxation became increasingly fragmented: inessential for supporting monarchs, whose wealth derived from their own estates, it became principally used for securing support through gifts or bribes. Previously, members of the ruling class had sought to acquire land in order to gain access to control of the state apparatus, but now it became an end in itself: "Private landowning was henceforth no longer the means to the obtaining of power; it was itself power."[30] The scene was by no means uniform: some areas, such as the British Isles, reverted to preclass agrarian societies; in others, such as the German states, preclass societies coexisted with feudal relations in a subordinate position; but in terms of the state, "all were feudal, for they were based on the politics and economics of landowning, expressed in different ways."[31]

Why then the difference with the East? Wickham originally argued that, in addition to the slave mode, the Roman Empire had at different times also involved the feudal and the tributary modes, based respectively on rent and tax. He originally argued that these two modes emerged as dominant from the fifth century, effectively maintaining different aspects of the later Roman Empire: feudalism in the West and the tributary mode in Byzantium. And while Wickham was clear that the tributary mode was not simply a relabeling of the "Asiatic" mode, which he rightly dismissed, he also emphasized that it did exist in other regions, above all in the Chinese Empire.[32] The distinction between feudal and tributary modes drew far more response than his account of the transition. In particular, Halil Berktay and John Haldon pointed out that, in terms of the central exploitative relationship with the peasantry, there was no difference between these; the difference lay in the extent and nature of state power, but Marxists do not distinguish between modes on superstructural grounds—that would be to fall into precisely the error for which all contributors to the debate criticized Anderson.[33] Wickham accepted this criticism, as he pointed out upon the re-publication of his early essays in *Land and Power*:

> The basic economic division inside class societies thus becomes simply that between societies based on taking surpluses from peasants (or, for that matter, household-based artisans) and those based on withholding surplus from wage laborers. . . . It does not mean that the Chinese or Roman empires, the Frankish kingdoms, and the feudal world of the eleventh century were exactly the same, for an essential *structural* difference remains between the first two, tax-raising state systems (with aristocracies subject to them), and the second two, polities dominated by aristocratic rent-taking and Marc Bloch's politics of land.[34]

Like the positions to which he was opposed, Wickham could find support for his alternatives in respect of both chronology and modes of production in Marx's own writings, specifically in the *Grundrisse*, that most ambiguous of his major works. As Hobsbawm wrote in an important early commentary: "Feudalism appears to be an *alternative* evolution out of primitive communalism, under conditions in which no cities develop, because the density of population over a large region is low."[35] Similarly, although Wickham derived his use of the tributary mode from Amin, the concept, if not the actual term, can also be found in the pages of Marx's notebooks: "In the case of the slave relationship, the serf relationship, and the relationship of tribute (where the primitive community is under consideration), it is the slave-owner, the feudal lord or the state receiving tribute that is the owner of the product and therefore its seller."[36] Wickham therefore had at least as much reason to claim a relationship to the Marxist classics as his opponents.

THEMES, THEORIES, ABSENCES

After a professional career as a historian principally of the Tuscan region of Italy, Wickham has now returned to the subject of the post-Roman world as a whole. During the debate on the feudal revolution, Wickham commented on Bisson's dating of that process to between 850 and 1100, noting that "250 years is a long time for a revolution," and he argued that it was preferable to see the period as one of consolidation or formalization of a feudal system that had already been established: "Like the Industrial Revolution, or the varying moments of middle-class political assertion in Europe that began with the French Revolution, this major shift could be fast or slow, (relatively) peaceful or sharply violent, and the variations themselves shed light on the structural differences between one region and another."[37] In effect, *Framing the Early Middle Ages* is a massive depiction of the prior process of feudal emergence, empirically substantiating the picture he sketched out over twenty years ago, taking into account his changed position on the modes of production debate. This is no mere coda to the earlier debate on the transition to feudalism, but a re-engagement with the issues that has greater significance than any of the original contributions.

Starting from the dissolution of the political unity and relative economic homogeneity of the Roman Empire, he traces how the constituent regions diverged from each other as successor societies adopted particular aspects of the imperial experience. As we should expect from his previous work, Wickham is particularly interested in the nature of the fiscal regime, which he sees as simplifying and in some places disappearing altogether, with obvious implications for whether society was dominated by feudal politics of land or tributary extraction by the state. Central to the book is the fate of the two great classes: the peasantry and the aristocracy, sometimes antagonistic, sometimes cooperative. The former achieved greater autonomy and, in some areas, freedom from exploitation altogether; indeed, in some respects Wickham describes a golden age for peasants, compared to both the oppression from which they had been released and the oppression to which they would eventually be subjected. A condition of peasant freedom was the weakening power of the aristocracy, the character of which also changed, becoming more narrowly focused on its military role and abandoning the literary culture that had been just as important to the Romans. This too was only a temporary condition, before the reassertion of their dominance by the end of the period. Throughout it, however, Wickham is clear that the aristocrats are in most respects the key social actors. Large-scale production at the regional level, let alone interregional long-distance exchange, was structured by "elite consumption," in the absence of mass peasant demand: the wealthier the aristocracy, the greater the demand. But that wealth was in turn determined by two of the elements Wickham sees as constitutive of the transitional economy: the extent, reach, and effectiveness of the tax system, and the level of exploitation of the peasantry by the lords. To these must be added two more elements, one contingent and the other deeply structural: the retarding effect of war and the extent to which a region continued to be integrated into the post-imperial Mediterranean world system.

The scope of this survey, and the command with which Wickham presents it to the reader, means that *Framing* will inevitably and rightly be compared to the other great Deutscher Prize–winning work of premodern history, Ste Croix's *The Class Struggle in the Ancient Greek World*. That work famously begins with a lengthy consideration of the theoretical concepts that Ste Croix then uses to structure his argument.[38] Wickham does not adopt this strategy. Although there is of course a theoretical apparatus at work behind the scenes, Wickham draws back the curtain to reveal it only in tantalizingly short passages, usually where some sort of definition is required. Typically, this was also the approach taken by the earlier generation of British Marxist historians like Rodney Hilton—to pick one specifically identified as an influence by Wickham—at least in their substantive works.[39] This approach has much to recommend it, especially when compared to the endless theoretical preliminaries that were typical of the work of, for example, Barry Hindess and Paul Hirst, at the time when Wickham began to publish. But here the very richness of empirical detail means that underlying theoretical positions have sometimes to be inferred. This lack of explicit discussion creates a barrier for the reader, not to checking Wickham's conformity to some Marxist orthodoxy or other, but to assessing how his assumptions have shaped his use of the material. On one methodological issue, however, Wickham is explicit: his rejection of teleological explanations of capitalist development, particularly, "the metanarrative of medieval economic history which seeks to explain the secular economic triumph of north-west Europe." Instead, he emphasizes "the variegated patterns of social development" and argues that "social change is overwhelmingly the result of internal factors, not external influences."[40] By external influences Wickham seems to mean the view (which he identifies with Henri Pirenne, although it can be traced back to Adam Smith) that feudalism arose as a result of outside pressures.[41] Wickham argues that the roots of feudalism have rather to be discerned in the internal development of the regions he discusses.

These regions extend from the Irish edge of Western Europe to the present-day Middle East. The geographical compass of the book is set by the subject, the after-world of the united Roman Empire, and Wickham does full justice to the range of different societies this involves, focusing as much on Egypt and Syria as on Denmark and England. The book is not completely exhaustive: Scotland and (for the most part) Saxony are excluded without greatly affecting his argument, since similar societies to these are included, although the exclusion of the Balkans perhaps passes up an opportunity to compare tributary formations in Europe with those in North Africa and Asia. But these are minor issues. Far more important than absolute comprehensiveness is the fact that the parallels and similarities he draws to our attention help undermine another form of teleology. In this case, it is not the Western origins of capitalism so much as the broader narrative that distinguishes Europe, or sometimes simply "the West," from the rest of the world on the basis of the "Judeo-Christian" heritage, or similar inventions, which supposedly date back to this period.

For example, the societies that showed the most signs of agricultural intensification during the period lay not only at opposite extremes of the tax/rent continuum but also at opposite extremes of the territorial limits of the empire: Francia on the one hand, and Egypt and the Levant on the other. These two regions, respectively involving "a rich aristocracy in the Carolingian world, a powerful state in that of the Umayyads and the Abbasids" were "the regions with the most potential for exchange, and thus the most stimulus for agricultural intensification."[42] But the same types of parallel are also apparent in less complex forms of society, where the Roman state collapsed: Mauritania, in the Berber lands of North Africa, had a pattern of "social development" that Wickham claims "resembles Britain," although "its closest British analogues would be with more traditional highland Wales" rather than lowland England. Mauritania retained its own political traditions under the empire, while Britain wholeheartedly embraced those of Rome; yet the results were similar, not least in terms of social simplification and economic retrogression.[43] This would suggest that, whatever the origins of the differences between West and East, they are clearly not intrinsic to the societies involved and have to be traced instead in subsequent historical developments.

Wickham's account would also suggest that religious differences between Christianity and Islam are less important in determining the regional character than the material conditions upon which he focuses, but this has to be inferred since ideological issues are nowhere discussed, except briefly in relation to aristocratic hegemony. To be fair, Wickham makes clear from the outset that, because of the already great length of the book, his focus will be on the social and the economic. Take as a comparison Fernand Braudel's *The Mediterranean and the Mediterranean World in the Age of Phillip II*, in many ways a model of this kind of large-scale history. It begins with a part on the physical geography of the region, where change is "almost imperceptible," and ends with one of the political events of the fifty-year period beginning in 1550, where change occurs in "brief, rapid, nervous fluctuations." Between is a part dealing with "social history," where change is "slow" but nevertheless has "perceptible rhythms."[44] Wickham's book deals with themes similar to those in this middle-range part of Braudel's book ("Collective Destinies and General Trends").[45] Political developments are only discussed to provide essential background to the regions under discussion, and culture is excluded completely—although not cultural artifacts; potsherds appear with great regularity, but only as traces of economic activity.[46] But "politics" here has to be understood primarily as what we would now call "geopolitics"—or more simply, war—since the state, the political institution par excellence, is certainly of paramount importance to Wickham, not least because its form was "the arena that saw most change."[47] Indeed, following a brief survey of geopolitical developments, he privileges the state as the first area of discussion before analyzing the position of the two main classes, aristocrats and peasants. This is not because he sees the state as the "prime mover" in social change, "with the form of the state somehow determining every other aspect of society and the economy, in a statist version of a very traditional Marxist analysis."[48] Wickham is not proposing to substitute a superstructural determinism for one that privileges the base, but the structural focus of the book does mean that the actual moments of change—above all the moments of peasant expropriation—tend to be subsumed within discussions the main focus of which is on other aspects of the period.

STRUCTURE: SOCIAL CLASSES, MODES OF PRODUCTION, AND STATES

Wickham argues that neither slavery nor (less controversially) wage labor was of any great significance to the economy of the early Middle Ages:

> Throughout our period the slave mode was only a minor survival, everywhere marginal to the basic economic structure, of the landlord peasant relationship (where

there were landlords at all). . . . The marginality of the slave mode in our period is matched by the relative unimportance of wage labor, at least outside Egypt; essentially, throughout our period, agriculture on estates was above all performed by peasant, tenant cultivators.[49]

Slavery and unfreedom more generally had a different significance depending on the extent of peasant autonomy within the locality. Where a lord had superiority over an entire area, as in the Ile de France, it could be a status distinction, with the possibility of movement between the free and unfree. Ironically, it was where peasants were most free of lords, as in England before 700 AD, that the distinction had its greatest significance, indicating a potentially exploitative relationship within the household economy.[50] Only "potentially," Wickham argues, because the position of the unfree within the peasant household would only involve "class exploitation" in circumstances where "the members of the free family all stopped working, and simply lived of the labor of the unfree."[51] I am not sure whether this argument is sustainable. Exploitation still takes place in situations where small commodity producers supplement the labor of themselves and their families with wage labor, since wage laborers produce a surplus over and above what they receive. Why would the situation be different in the case of a peasant family supplementing their labor with that of slaves or otherwise unfree workers? If anything the surplus would be greater in the second case. This does not affect Wickham's argument about the irrelevance of slavery, but it does raise a question about his treatment of the one mode of production that he sees as seriously posing an alternative to feudalism: the peasant mode.

Wickham argues that feudalism had become a universal system across Europe, North Africa, and the Middle East by the ninth century, but what does he mean by feudalism? As I noted earlier, Wickham rejected his earlier distinction between rent and taxation as the basis for distinguishing between the feudal and tributary modes of production, and he retains that position here. He has not, however, abandoned the tributary mode itself.[52] Indeed, following Haldon, he writes: "it now seems to me that both [feudalism and the tributary mode] are sub-types of the same mode of production, in that both are based on agrarian surplus extracted, by force if necessary, from the peasant majority."[53] The process of exploitation is the same in each case, but the mechanism for rent or tax collection is different and, as Wickham stresses, this leads to corresponding differences in the state, above all in two respects. With the important exception of Merovingian and Carolingian Francia, "tax-based states were . . . richer and more powerful than rent-based, land-based, states." More important even than wealth, however, was stability, which Wickham illustrates with the Byzantine example:

> Even at the weakest point of the eastern empire, roughly 650–750, Byzantine political structures were more coherent than those of even the best-organized land-based states, such as Lombard Italy in the same period; tax-based structures had more staying-power, and the risk of decentralization, a feature of all land-based states, was less great. If taxation disappeared as the basis of any given state, then, no matter how

much cultural, ideological, or legislative continuity there was . . . it would not prevent fundamental changes in political resources, infrastructure and practice.[54]

Nevertheless, both variants stand at a far greater distance from the peasant mode of production, involving "an economic and political system dominated by peasants, in a ranked society" than they do from each other.[55]

Societies based on the peasant mode involve "clear status differences . . . but they are not necessarily stable or heavily marked, except for the distinction, always present, between free and unfree."[56] According to Wickham there were many varieties of the peasant mode, but the essential features for him are that the productive unit is the household and that each household works land that it directly controls. Relations between households are governed by reciprocal exchange, partly to consolidate community relations, partly to acquire goods to which individual households would not otherwise have access. Since communities based on the peasant mode do not have to produce a surplus for an exploiting class, the main impulse behind production is to allow maximum leisure compatible with the satisfaction of physical needs and cultural norms; indeed, there are strong social pressures on individual households not to increase production beyond certain limits, since the output will either be given away to other, less productive neighbors or, if retained, lead to the household being ostracized by the rest of the community. Society under the peasant mode should not of course be regarded as a "primitive communism," since, in addition to the use of unfree labor, it is inegalitarian with respect both to gender relations and to the act of giving itself, which confers high status or rank upon those who can give the most. The latter relationship is not, however, fixed, in that positions within the status group can change. During this period the peasant mode would have existed in two forms: either in a dominant "tribal" form, as in large parts of Northern Europe but also Spain and North Africa, where a relatively small external tribute might have to be paid to a local lord; or scattered like islands (Wickham writes about "leopard spots") among territories otherwise dominated by the feudal mode of production, as in Francia and Italy.[57]

Wickham assembles an impressive array of evidence to demonstrate the existence of the peasant mode, and his historiographical achievement also supports an important socialist argument. The existence of an original classless society, "primitive communism," is regularly denied by supporters of capitalism, for whom it is an enormously dangerous idea, suggesting as it does that inequality and exploitation are not, as it were, natural conditions. Wickham rejects both the term and, as we have seen, the implication that it involved complete equality in relation to this period; but if he is right, then it means that in some regions at least, the collapse of class societies in their slave and tributary forms did not lead to the "war of all against all," but rather to a situation in which cooperation was the dominant characteristic. Although the situation is scarcely likely to be repeated should capitalism collapse, it is nevertheless an important historical contribution to the debates over human nature. But is the peasant mode effectively the same as the "Asiatic" mode, where the latter is taken to be a general term for mode dominant in transitions between classless and class societies?[58] In other words, although the peasant mode seems to be the "fallback" position for peasants where precapitalist class society collapses, is it also a dynamic mode that would in time produce a new or revived form of class society? I will return to these issues below.

The absence of classes, or at any rate the absence of classes relating to each other as exploiter and exploited, also suggests the absence of a state, and Wickham accordingly argues that this was the case where the peasant mode was dominant. He defines the state as an institution combining a series of key elements: a centralized public authority apparently distinct from the public itself; "the centralization of legitimately enforceable authority (justice and the army); the specialization of governmental roles, with an official hierarchy which outlasted the people who held official position at any one time; the concept of a public power, that is, of a ruling system ideologically separable from the ruled population and from the individual rulers themselves; independent and stable resources for the rulers; and a class-based system for surplus-extraction and stratification." On this basis he identifies three types of state: "strong," as in the Roman, Byzantine, and Arabic empires; "weak," as in Romano-Germanic kingdoms of southern Europe like Gaul, Italy, and Spain; and nonexistent ("pre-state"), as in the non-Roman kingdoms of northwestern Europe like Ireland, England, and Denmark—in other words, where the peasant mode was strongest. As Wickham rightly remarks, the point of a definition is its usefulness: how useful is this one?[59]

It is useful insofar as it helps us to remember that state formation is a lengthy *process*, which if captured by the historian before the end will reveal an institution that is not yet a state, but is (to use Hal Draper's terminology) a "proto-government" exercising "proto-political" power. States take as long as classes to form, but this indicates my first difficulty with Wickham's definition, namely that he places too much emphasis on region-wide formal attributes. If classes do exist, and Wickham accepts that lords tended to coexist with peasants even under the peasant mode, then the imposition of coercion and control is no longer exercised entirely by the community as a whole, but by a part with separate juridical powers.[60] In this context, aristocrats and landowners more generally can act as a "state," can embody state functions, at quite local levels.

A further theoretical problem is suggested by the relationship between the fourth and fifth characteristics of a state in Wickham's definition (independent and stable resources for the rulers; and a class-based system for surplus extraction and stratification): "It is worth distinguishing between the resources of rulers and those of the ruling class, because one can often, even though not always, draw a distinction between the two (e.g., tax versus rent)." Wickham acknowledges that, where taxation was the overwhelmingly dominant method of surplus extraction, it could be subsumed into the provision of resources for rulers, "and the ruling class were simply public employees": "In practice, however, dominant classes have almost always been distinguishable from state institutions; they are independently wealthy, although they characteristically seek wealth as well as power from official positions in public hierarchies." And in landed societies where rent is the dominant method of surplus extraction, the subsumption operates in reverse, with "the resources of kings . . . nearly identical with that of the ruling class as a whole."[61] The distinction between "rulers" and "ruling classes" here seems to be unnecessary to Wickham's argument. In the analysis of contemporary capitalism, there are usually some differences of interest between those who manage the state and those who own or control capital, although these always overlap, are currently decreasing, and in any case tend to be overridden by the joint class membership of the bourgeoisie. To the extent that these differences do exist, they are a reflection of the (much exaggerated) "separation of the economic and the political under capitalism."[62] But under feudalism, or any other precapitalist mode of production, the separation does not exist. Consequently, until the emergence of the absolutist state from the late fifteenth century, the possibility of a clash of interests between what one might call the political and economic wings of the ruling class does not arise. The resistance of Roman aristocrats to being taxed by the Imperial state, to which Wickham gave a central explanatory role in his initial account of the transition, might be cited as an example that supports the rulers/ruling class distinction—indeed, it lent plausibility to the claim that the feudal and tributary modes were distinct. But precisely because it occurred at an exceptional moment of systemic breakdown, it scarcely reflects the "normal" operation of class society. It is not clear what behaviors are explained by this distinction that would not otherwise be so. Indeed, to maintain it would seem to suggest that both groups operated with potentially different "logics," which undermines Wickham's—in my view, correct—argument about the fundamental unity of the feudal and tributary modes.

AGENCY: SOCIAL REVOLUTION, SOCIOECONOMIC TRANSITION, AND THE CLASS STRUGGLE

Who were the agents behind the transition to feudalism, where it did not emerge directly from the end of the slave mode? Although Wickham broadly endorses what he calls the historiographical "cliché" of serfdom emerging as a combination of tightened constraints on formerly free tenants and loosened constraints on the formerly unfree, his own emphasis on the relative unimportance of slavery suggests that the former was of considerably greater importance.[63] The fate of the free peasantry is a central issue; the question is the extent to which it was undermined from within, by the emergence of class divisions, or overthrown from without, by submission to an existing class of aristocrats and landowners.

Wickham points to an inconsistency in Marx's own approach as to the "prime mover" behind changes from one mode to another, contrasting the more abstract formulations (such as those of the 1859 "Preface," which privilege the development of the forces of production) with actual historical analysis (such as in *Capital* Volume 1, where he shows that changes to the relations of production take priority). For this reason Wickham supports the position taken by Robert Brenner, which follows the latter aspect of Marx's own work.[64] The problem for Wickham, as for Brenner, is what drives changes to the relations of production. Wickham repeats the oft-expressed claim that, for Brenner, it is the class struggle.[65] However, as I argued in the 2004 Deutscher Memorial Prize Lecture, Brenner is actually far less interested in the class struggle than is generally supposed. Since he believes that there is no impulse for the forces of production to develop, class struggle acts instead for him as a mechanism for producing (or failing to produce) a set of "unintended consequences" that in turn lay the initial conditions for the formation of capitalist social relations of production.[66] As presented by Wickham, the peasant mode *before* the consolidation of feudalism bears a close resemblance to the description of the peasantry *under* feudalism as it is presented by Brenner, prior to the emergence of capitalism—particularly in relation to its internal stability and the lack of motivation to develop technology or increase productivity beyond a certain point.[67]

Leaving aside the question of whether both can be right, Wickham is more open to the possibility of feudalism emerging from internal developments within the peasant mode than Brenner is of capitalism emerging from internal developments within the feudal mode. Wickham allows, for example, that a "feudal economic logic" may be set in train when peasants with high status begin to require others to provide them with goods in return for more specialized but less material services, of which he specifies military protection (although presumably religious functions would also be relevant here).[68] He also notes that peasants can acquire sufficient land to be able to lease it out to tenants, thus elevating themselves into the landowning class, with the potential to ultimately join the aristocracy.[69] But these are mainly presented as hypothetical cases, rather than a process that can actually be traced. Of the two examples he offers, one is from the actual Danish village of Vorbasse and the other is from his invented archetypal village of "Malling." It is clear that evidence is lacking, and Wickham explains that he must rely on models of change because "we can so seldom see them happening in our sources."[70] Consequently, when Wickham discusses the shift to feudal relations of production, he generally does so in contexts where they are introduced by an agency from outside the peasant community, namely existing landowners and aristocrats. But it is not clear whether this was the main path to the establishment of a "feudal economic logic" or simply the most visible from this distance in time. The extent to which feudalism was a "bottom-up" in addition to a "top-down" affair remains an area that still requires further research.

There are three types of class struggle "from below" recorded by Wickham, none of which would necessarily contribute to the rise of feudalism. The first are slave revolts. Wickham gives only one example, a tantalizing reference to what he calls the "famous" Zanj slave revolt in southern Iraq during the 870s.[71] This event may enjoy fame among scholars of the medieval Middle East, but it might have received greater consideration for the benefit of nonspecialists, particularly given the emphasis Wickham places on the relative unimportance of slavery during his period.

The second are tax revolts. The examples to which Wickham devotes most attention took place in Umayyad, then Abbasid Egypt between 726 and 832 AD. These were not the actions of a particular class, like slaves, but overlapping risings, first by a preexisting religious community (the Christian Coptic sect), then by Arab settlers, and finally by an alliance of the two. Wickham argues that these were provoked not by higher levels of taxation than under the Roman Empire but rather because taxation tended to be more arbitrary and, above all, "more stringently enforced, and more aggressively policed." The reason lies in the fact that the Arab rulers did not transform the societies they occupied but established themselves as a "state class" maintained solely by taxation, "with no structural social links to taxpayers," meaning that patronage of client groups as a channel for allowing the latter to mitigate or avoid tax was not an option.[72] Peasants also rebelled against taxation, in some cases supported after the fact by local religious figures: Wickham records one episode in Eukraoi in West Galatia (modern-day Turkey), where the local bishop and "holy man," Theodore of Sykeon, dismissed the local aristocratic administrator and tax-collector after a rising by the villagers.[73] This was not, however, the main focus of peasant action.

The third are peasant revolts, but these are different from predecessors under the Roman Empire and from successors under the consolidated feudal regime. Earlier peasant revolts, above all of the Bagaudae against the Roman Empire in Gaul, were essentially directed against taxation and injustice at a time when the state was weakened, and therefore the possibility of change beneficial to the peasantry became possible. Later peasant revolts too were conducted against the state in relation to "military service, laws on status and, above all, taxation."[74] In this period, revolts have a different impetus. Wickham notes that "a detailed knowledge of peasant states of mind is largely closed to us before the fourteenth century." He nevertheless speculates that aristocratic hegemony did function in certain areas where the peasants had to rely on aristocrats for external support, as in eighth-century Lucchesia (in modern Italy), although this did not, of course exclude "small-scale signs of disobedience"—but these are compatible with overall acceptance of ruling values. At the other end of the spectrum, as in eighth-century Paris, the aristocrats dominated through "overwhelming physical force" and did not require peasant acceptance of their rule, which they any case did not receive. Between these lies a third type of area, such as sixth-century Galatia, where neither situation prevailed: that is, where aristocrats could rely on neither ideology nor violence to secure compliance. As Wickham notes, the latter situation is where revolts are most likely to take place, but "the absence of hegemony is only one reason why peasants revolt, of course; they have to have something concrete to oppose as well."[75] In this case peasant revolts are signs of resistance to attempts by the emergent ruling class to impose serfdom. England is exceptional in its lack of peasant revolt, which seems to have two causes. First, because initially both the "rulers" and the "ruling class" (to use Wickham's distinction) had less control over the peasantry than in any other part of Europe, while at the same time they exercised superiority over exceptionally large territories. Second, in that when the lords did move to subject or expropriate peasant communities they did so slowly and in piecemeal fashion, attacking the weakest while leaving the strongest and wealthiest untouched until the basis of possible collective resistance was eroded.[76] Elsewhere, the gradual encroachments of the emergent feudal state led to what Wickham calls "frequent small-scale resistance," which erupted into one of the great risings of the period: the Stellinga revolt in Saxony of 841–42 AD, a revolt that took the opportunity of a civil war among the local Saxon ruling class to launch a program for the return to the pre-aristocratic social order.[77]

Could war be treated as the functional equivalent of revolution, in the sense that revolutions from outside and above were conducted by the Cromwellian and Napoleonic armies a thousand years later? One of Wickham's critics has certainly accused him of ignoring the impact of war—indeed, of being in thrall to an "Austro-German model of explaining great transitions in human history," a model with "little or no theorization of war or violence."[78] The "Austro-German model" evidently includes Marxism, and Wickham himself has made a similar point about it in the past; but it is untrue.[79] More to the point, in this case it is also irrelevant: war can be important as an agent of social change, but it is scarcely autonomous. It is difficult to see how war could be the source of a new form of society, since all the societies involved were based on variations of the same mode of production, and the most ideologically innovative—the Arab invaders of the later seventh century—tended to allow the continuation of existing social structures in the territories they conquered. The most significant social impact of war was in fact an inadvertent consequence of the Vandal invasions of North Africa, of which Wickham writes that "Geiseric's conquest of Carthage in 439 is arguably the turning point in the 'fall' of the western empire"—the significance of the conquest being that it "broke the tax spine" connecting the Roman world economy.[80] But elsewhere the impact was muted: as Wickham notes, "only Italy in the sixth century and Anatolia in the seventh saw wars that really devastated economies and societies on the regional level for more than short periods."[81]

In short, class struggle clearly occurred in different forms throughout the period, but revolutionary movements for the transformation of society, or plausible surrogates, are absent—except of course in the form of the piecemeal revolution from above, imposed by the lords to either abolish the economic logic of the peasant mode or erode the autonomy of peasants where the feudal mode already existed.

Conclusion

Wickham has argued that the interaction between the forces and relations of production, and between them and the superstructure, may vary from one mode of production to another. Be that as it may, what he makes unmistakably clear in this work, among many other things of value to historical materialists, is that the nature of the transitions from one mode to another are certainly distinct, and that we proceed by analogy with later ones at our peril. Whatever questions *Framing the Early Middle Ages* still leaves unanswered—and many of those we are only able to *ask* because of Wickham's achievement—we should be grateful that we now have an account of the transition to feudalism that rivals those on the transition to capitalism, which have for so long been the staples of Marxist historiography.

4

Scotland:
Birthplace of Passive Revolution?

Introduction

One of the ways Antonio Gramsci used the term "passive revolution" was as a synonym for "bourgeois revolution from above."[1] The latter concept has a far longer history in the classical Marxist tradition, starting with Engels's discussion of the unification of Germany, a process contemporary with the Italian Risorgimento that inspired Gramsci's discussion, and it was later developed, for example, by Lenin in relation to Russia after the Peasant Reform of 1861.[2] As these historical parallels suggest, Gramsci was right not to regard events in Italy as an "isolated phenomenon": "It was an organic process that in the formation of the ruling class replaced what in France had occurred during the Revolution and with Napoleon, and in England with Cromwell."[3] In other words, for him the supposed differences between France, England, and Italy were less important than the similarities between them: all bourgeois revolutions involve a "passive" element in the sense that they involve larger or smaller minorities taking power in the state—the masses may have played a role, but ultimately the transition is completed from above by the exercise of state power. After 1849, however, the top-down aspect of the bourgeois revolutions became more pronounced. Typically, a fraction of the existing ruling class, under pressure from nation-states that had already undergone bourgeois revolutions, simultaneously restructured the existing state from within and expanded its territorial boundaries through conventional military conquest. Gramsci wrote of "a period of small waves of reform rather than . . . revolutionary explosions like the original French one," a period that combined "social struggles, interventions from above of the enlightened monarchy type, and national wars—with the two latter phenomena predominating": "The period of 'Restoration' is the richest in developments of this kind: restoration becomes the first policy whereby social struggles find sufficiently elastic frameworks to allow the bourgeoisie to gain power without dramatic upheavals, without the French machinery of terror."[4] The dominance of "passive revolution" after 1849 was the result of two related factors, both products of the growth and dynamism of the capitalist system.

The first was the creation of the working class. During the French Revolution even the most class-conscious members of the bourgeoisie drew back from the actions necessary to achieve victory over the Old Regime, paralyzed as they were by a fear of the urban plebeians who might—and in the event, did—push beyond the limits that the former considered acceptable. It was therefore inevitable that once the potentially even more dangerous working class appeared as a social force, as it did during the revolutions of 1848–49, the bourgeoisie would seek accommodation with the existing regimes rather than risk igniting a conflagration that might engulf them too. Gramsci noted in relation to the behavior of the Action Party during the Risorgimento, for example, that "the atmosphere of intimidation (panic fear of a terror like that of 1793, reinforced by the events in France of 1848–49) . . . made it hesitate to include in its program certain popular demands (for instance, agrarian reform)."[5]

The second factor was the availability of agencies that could provide capitalist leadership in the place of this increasingly cautious bourgeoisie. The states that had undergone revolutions during the earlier cycle—pre-eminently Britain and France—were now not merely the competitors of those that had not, but potential models for them to follow. This is a specific example of what Gramsci called "the fact that international relations intertwine with . . . internal relations of nation-states, creating new, unique and historically concrete combinations."[6] Once the system of which these nation-states were the preeminent members had achieved a certain momentum, its very success became the most decisive argument in persuading sections of the noncapitalist ruling classes that they must effect internal self-transformation or be overtaken by their more developed rivals.

Although the experiences of Germany, Italy, the US, Japan, Canada, and Russia during the period between 1859 and 1871 provided the historical material for subsequent theorizations of "passive revolution," a very similar process had been undergone by Scotland over a hundred years earlier, in a very different period. There is no evidence that Gramsci or any of his contemporaries drew on the Scottish experience. In fact, like most figures in the classical Marxist tradition after Marx and Engels themselves, he had some difficulty in distinguishing between Scotland, England, and Britain; only Trotsky showed any real awareness of the distinctions.[7] Nor does the process in Scotland seem to have directly influenced those in Europe, North America, or the Far East, other than to the extent that the British state and economy, both of which the Scottish Revolution played a major part in shaping, were the dominant models that all later developers aspired to emulate. Nevertheless, Scotland seems to have been the first nation to have experienced a "passive revolution," suggesting that the concept is applicable to a longer historical timescale than the middle decades of the nineteenth century about which it was first applied. Gramsci identifies three main characteristics of passive revolution in Italian history, all of which were prefigured, with local variations, in Scotland.

The first was a favorable geopolitical context: the very conflicts and rivalries that the emergent capitalist system engendered provided a space and opportunity for new participants to emerge. In a letter to the Fourth World Congress of the Third Communist International, dated November 20, 1922, Gramsci states:

> The Italian bourgeoisie succeeded in organizing its state not so much through its intrinsic strength, as through being favored in its victory over the feudal and semi-feudal classes by a whole series of circumstances of an international character (Napoleon III's policy in 1852–60; the Austro-Prussian War of 1866; France's defeat at Sedan and the development of the German Empire after this event). The bourgeois State thus developed more slowly, and followed a process which has not been seen in many other countries.[8]

Scotland was one of the few other countries.[9] The inter-systemic conflict between England (Britain after 1707) and France, between 1688 and 1763, provided the international aspect for the passive revolution in Scotland, not only because this struggle impacted events in Scotland, through French support for internal counter-revolution, but also because the outcome in Scotland was decisive for resolving the struggle itself.

The second was the key role of a dynamic territorial area as the active core within the process of state formation. Gramsci wrote of the importance of Piedmont in the creation of Italy, over the head of the local bourgeoisie: "This fact is of the greatest importance for the concept of 'passive revolution'—the fact, that is, that what was involved was not a social group which 'led' other groups, but a State which, even though it had limitations as a power, 'led' the group which should have been 'leading' and was able to put at the latter's disposal an army and politico-diplomatic strength."[10] In Scotland the process involved a double movement with two leading areas: England, which drew Scotland as a whole into the emerging British state, and the Lowlands, which unified Scotland itself by overcoming the historic divide with the Highlands.

The third was the formation of a new ruling class involving elements of the old. Gramsci wrote of Italian unification that it involved "the formation of an ever more extensive ruling class": "The formation of this class involved the gradual but continuous absorption, achieved by methods which varied in their effectiveness, of the active elements produced by allied groups—and even those which came from antagonistic groups and seemed irreconcilably hostile."[11] The distinctive nature of the British experience lay in two aspects. First, it had the first capitalist ruling class to be formed in this way. Second, unlike the different regional groupings that combined to form the Italian (or German) ruling classes, the Scottish component retained a separate national consciousness and, despite being the numerically the smaller of the two ruling classes involved, it was the most insistent that integration take place.

The process of passive revolution in Scotland was complex, but can essentially be divided into three major phases. The first, from 1637 to 1692, saw several revolutionary "moments of force," but only one—the Cromwellian occupation of 1651–1660—with the intention, if not the capability, to transform Scottish society.

The second, from 1692–1746, involved the formation of the British state and the decisive reconfiguration of social power within Scotland. It was only during the third, from 1746 to 1815, that the economic transition to capitalism in Scotland was completed, and as a conscious project.

THE PERSISTENCE OF SCOTTISH FEUDALISM

Unlike in England, bourgeois elements in seventeenth-century Scotland were not strong enough to separate out and articulate a program of their own. A political revolution occurred between 1637 and 1641, but by definition this left the social classes standing in the same relation to power as before. Nevertheless, the chaos of civil and national wars did contain a moment of external intervention that both promised change and showed how difficult it would be to achieve at this stage of development. In England, Cromwell and the Independents were challenged from the left by the Levelers and still more radical groups; in Ireland, they were responsible for imposing a colonial regime of notorious savagery; in Scotland, they stepped into a social vacuum and undertook one of the purest examples of bourgeois revolution "from above and outside" until the republics established by the Directory and Napoleon after 1795. This was the Scottish equivalent to the Parthenopean Republic of 1799, from which Vincenzo Cuoco first derived the concept of "passive revolution"; but although the Napoleonic armies that invaded Spain in 1809 were clearly the bearers of a more advanced social system than the Bourbon monarchy they sought to overthrow, the fact that change was being imposed at bayonet point provoked a popular resistance that ultimately aided the reactionary alliance against France. A similar mood, if not actual opposition, was present in Cromwellian Scotland.

In Scotland, the capitalist class was capable of assuming neither political leadership within the state nor economic dominance within society. When Cromwell and his officers displaced the lords from their traditional social dominance, no bourgeoisie arose to replace them, nor did the lords begin to transform themselves into capitalist landowners or manufacturers. The withdrawal of the English military presence between 1660 and 1662 allowed the surviving members of the Scottish ruling class to return to their previous positions. The Act Rescissory, passed on March 28, 1661, by the Scottish Parliament, repealed all legislation enacted since 1633. Nothing better illustrates the distance between Scotland and England in socioeconomic terms than this enactment, which signaled that it was not merely the king who had been restored but the jurisdictional rights of the lords. English absolutism had been like a dead skin sloughed off by a social body that had outgrown it; Scottish feudalism was still like a straitjacket, confining the social body and preventing further growth. In Scotland, the Restoration was therefore a counterrevolution that swept away even the limited gains of the Scottish Revolution and in one respect appeared to go further than simply restoring the status quo ante of 1633, since the Scottish lords appeared to have finally accepted the absolutist form of state, which (the Polish nobility apart) they had successfully resisted longer than any of their European contemporaries, and which they had originally risen in 1637 to oppose.

It was, however, only an appearance necessitated by their temporary weakness, as the outcome of the Glorious Revolution would demonstrate. The nobles did not challenge James VII and II, even as he began constructing the apparatus of the absolutist state with which to overcome them, because the only way to do so would have been a repetition of 1637—with all that implied in terms of possible external conquest and internal insurgency. It took the English Revolution of 1688 to relieve them of that dilemma. The English had broken with their past in the years between 1640 and 1660; the events of 1688 consolidated what had been achieved in those years. No such prior transformation had occurred in Scotland. The religious settlement apart, the verdict thus confirmed was that of the counterrevolution of 1660, minus the absolutist regime. In fact, any attempt to assimilate the revolutionary process in Scotland to that of England because of superficial similarities renders subsequent events incomprehensible. The events of 1688 in Scotland, like those of 1637, represented a political revolution that changed some personnel among the feudal ruling class but left that class as a whole intact. The chessmen were moved around, not swept off the board. What then was the overall balance of social forces within Scotland, by the late seventeenth century? There was as yet no conscious struggle for power between opposing classes, or alliances of classes. Nevertheless, we can discern three broadly aligned congeries of groups within society.

The first consisted of the majority of the established ruling class, the Lowland magnates and Highland chiefs—a class in economic decline, but whose members still possessed greater individual social power than those of any other in Western Europe. They were supported by other social groups whose horizons were limited to maintaining the traditional order, but making it function more effectively and profitably: the vast majority of baronial lairds, clan tacksmen, and traditional east coast merchants. Elements from each of these might have been persuaded to consider new ways of organizing economic and social life—the ways that were so obviously coming to dominate in England—if they could be shown that the potential benefits were worth the risks. But this demonstration would require some form of alternative leadership, which was exactly what Scotland lacked.

The second congeries consisted of those groups that had been part of the existing order but had either been displaced or threatened by the political revolution of 1688. Two in particular stand out: the dispossessed Episcopalian clergy and—more significant in material terms—those Highland clans alienated from the new regime. Both were excluded from the revolution settlement and prepared to act respectively as ideologues and foot soldiers for the Jacobite movement to restore the Stuarts, when it eventually emerged as a serious movement. For it to do so would require a more substantial social base than either of these groups could provide. That would come in due course, but this embryonic movement was already infinitely more ideologically coherent than either the directionless elites at the apex of late feudal Scotland or the fragmented forces groping their separate ways toward a new conception of society.

The third congeries consisted of those actual or potential sources of opposition to the existing order—or rather, to specific aspects of it. The economic independence of bonnet lairds in Fife or the southwest was compromised by the social control that the heritable jurisdictions conferred on the lords within whose superiorities they held their land. The same heritable jurisdictions both rivaled and restricted the functioning of the Edinburgh lawyers who oversaw the central legal system. The ambitions of Glasgow merchants were frustrated by both the privileges that the Scottish state afforded to their traditional east coast rivals and the limitations that the English state imposed on their trade with the Americas. The Church of Scotland was prevented from exercising dominion over the northern territories where Episcopalianism and even Catholicism still held sway. The territorial expansion of the House of Argyll into the west on the basis of new commercial forms of tenure was resisted by hostile clans. But all these groups had different aims, and even where these did not contradict each other, no faction or ideology existed to unite them, let alone to form a pole of attraction for those whose interests were currently served by maintaining the status quo. No group like the Independents, still less the Jacobins, was waiting to meld these disparate groups of the dissatisfied into a coherent opposition.

ECONOMIC CRISIS, STATE RE-FORMATION, AND CIVIL WAR

If Scotland had been isolated from the rest of the world, and the future of Scottish society made entirely dependent on internal social forces, then the most likely outcome would have been an epoch of stagnation similar to the one that affected the northwestern states of mainland Europe, which in most respects Scotland closely resembled. But Scotland was neither isolated nor, consequently, entirely dependent on its own resources. For several of the main players lay outside the borders of Scotland, although they sought to influence or even determine what happened within them. These players were the states—Spain, France, England—locked in competition for hegemony over Europe and, increasingly, its colonial extensions. By 1688, England and, to a much lesser extent, the United Netherlands were the only surviving sources of a systemic alternative to feudal absolutism. But the finality usually ascribed to 1688 is only possible if events in England are treated in complete isolation. It is not possible, however, to separate developments in England, any more than in Scotland, from either the wider struggle with France for European and colonial hegemony, or the impact of that struggle on the other nations of the British Isles, as the English ruling class was only too aware at the time. At the heart of this struggle lay the fundamental difference between the two states, the divine right of kings versus the divine right of property, and it is here that the differences between England and Scotland were of the greatest importance.

Counterrevolution can have both external and internal sources. The external danger to England after 1688 mainly lay in France. The internal threat in the British Isles lay not in England, nor in Ireland, which had been quiescent since the Treaty of Limerick in 1691, but in Scotland. The Scottish and English states were still harnessed together in a multiple kingdom, even though they remained at different stages of socioeconomic development. In general, the English ruling class regarded Scotland as a disruptive element to be contained, rather than a potential ally to be transformed. But as long as Scotland remained untransformed, it was a potential source of counterrevolution. The Scottish feudal classes that had found it convenient to remove James VII and II might, through a further change in their circumstances, wish to return him, or at least his family, to the thrones of the British Isles. But with the Stuarts would come their French backer—the global rival of the English state. Neither the English Revolution nor the new world system that it promised (or threatened) to bring into being would be secure while this possibility remained. The oft-stated desire of the Stuarts to reclaim all of their previous kingdoms, combined with the French need to remove their opponents from the international stage, meant that the English ruling class was potentially faced not only with impoverishment but also with a threat to its continued survival on a capitalist basis.

Within Scotland, the three main congeries of social groups did not align themselves between France and England according to any clear-cut division into progressive or reactionary, feudal or capitalist. The first, comprising the majority of the established ruling class, hoped to avoid the choice if possible, while retaining their freedom of movement within the composite monarchy of the British Isles. The second, comprising those who were excluded (the Episcopalian clergy) or endangered (the Jacobite clans) by the revolution settlement, were willing to contemplate an alliance with France to secure their goal of a second Stuart restoration. The third, comprising the forces who wished to transform Scottish society in various ways, did not counterbalance the second by displaying an equal level of support for an alliance with England. On the contrary, they were hostile to English influence, either because they hoped to protect from it their own sectional interests (the Church of Scotland, Scots Law) or because they were in direct competition with English rivals (the Glasgow tobacco merchants). Social relations remained essentially feudal and, consequently, the economy remained trapped within the twin track of subsistence agriculture and raw material exports. In the 1690s three crises, of appalling social cost, brutally revealed the limits of Scottish development.

The first involved the collapse of foreign trade. The accession of William and the immediate outbreak of the War of the British and Irish Succession would in any event have had a generally disruptive effect, but hostilities led to the cessation of all commercial relations with France, Scotland's major trading partner, which were not restored after the hostilities ended. Between 1697 and 1702 France banned the import of Scottish wool and fish, and imposed heavy duties on coal, as did the Spanish Netherlands. Most serious of all, however, was the decline in trade with England, which had become increasingly significant during the seventeenth century and, unlike trade with the European mainland, was not liable to disruption by France.

The second was a massive failure of subsistence. In August 1695, the Scottish harvest failed for the first time since 1674, and by December it was obvious that the country was on the verge of a famine. It lasted, with peaks in 1696 and 1699, until normal harvests resumed in 1700. The overall population loss cannot, however, have been less than 5 percent and may have been as high as 15 percent; that is to say between fifty thousand and one hundred fifty thousand people. In some areas the collection of rent from tenants who had barely enough on which to survive went on throughout the famine. The main economic effect of the famine was to further retard development by forcing tenants to devote whatever surplus they produced toward paying off rent arrears accumulated during the 1690s.

The third was the failure of an attempt to transcend the developmental impasse by opening up new colonial markets and ultimately a colony in the Isthmus of Panama at Darien, which exposed the underlying weaknesses of the state itself. Darien lay within the overseas territory of the Spanish state, which was guaranteed to be hostile. The project faced malign neglect and, ultimately, conscious obstruction by the English state, which was allied with Spain against France. But the principal reason for the failure of the colony, which cost between one-third and one-half of national GDP, was the fact that neither the state nor civil society in Scotland was resilient enough to sustain the venture.

If the War of the Spanish Succession had resulted in Louis XIV successfully pressing his claim to the Spanish crown, then, whatever the formal terms of the ensuing settlement, the territories of the Spanish monarchy would simply be absorbed by the French, with decisive consequences for future European development. The English ruling class faced the prospect of its greatest rival presiding over a world empire that stretched from the manufactories of Flanders to the gold mines of the Americas and that was positioned to seize the English colonies and so cut off one of the main sources of English ruling-class wealth. Successful prosecution of war against France, temporarily suspended in 1697 at the close of the War of the British and Irish Succession, and shortly to be resumed in 1702 with the opening of the War of the Spanish Succession, was absolutely necessary for the security of the English state. This was the context in which the entire debate over Anglo-Scottish relations took place. It was a strategic necessity for the English ruling class to prevent a Stuart restoration in Scotland, which would almost certainly see that country align itself with France. Their solution was to impose the Hanoverian Succession in Scotland.

By 1707, the Scottish Parliament accepted not only the House of Hanover but an integral union—an alternative that had only a few short years before seemed the least likely of realization. The divisions within Parliament House reflected divisions within the feudal ruling class itself about how best to preserve their existing place within Scottish society. Individual choices were therefore determined not by calculations of short-term financial advantage but by a more long-term assessment of what a union was likely to offer them and what the alternative was likely to be. While Scotland certainly had formal *sovereignty* over its own affairs, what it lacked was the *autonomy* to put its sovereign power into effect. Realizing this, the entire ruling class, with a handful of exceptions, opted to abandon sovereignty altogether for incorporation into a greater power capable of protecting them. The only decision to make was the identity of the state to which they would subordinate themselves: France or England. Why did the majority choose the second?

On the negative side, the return of the Stuarts could only occur under the same terms that Parliament had rebelled against in 1688—at best they would become the comprador nobility of a French satellite, enduring absolutist encroachments on their social power and the imposition of Roman Catholicism on their church—not to speak of the revenge that James might be expected to extract for what he would see as past betrayals of his family. Furthermore, since restoration in Scotland would inevitably mean war with England, the French option also held out the possibility of defeat and an English conquest that would reduce Scotland to the same condition as Ireland. Only the most desperate of the nobility could have contemplated this scenario. It is no accident that the commissioners who gave the most consistent opposition to the treaty were the barons at the bottom of the ruling-class ladder: they had least to lose.

On the positive side, beyond personal bribery, beyond even the specific guarantees of institutional continuity and financial restitution, the treaty contained an overall commitment to preserving the existing structure of Scottish society—with all its contradictions—within the new state. In this respect the key article in the treaty is number twenty, which states: "That all heritable Offices, Superiorities, heritable Jurisdictions, Offices for life, and Jurisdictions for life, be reserved to the Owners thereof, as Rights of Property, in the same manner as they are now enjoyed by the Laws of Scotland, notwithstanding of this Treaty."[12] In this respect the juridical element was infinitely more important than the pedagogic or confessional ones to which it is usually linked, and not as the bearer of some transhistorical "national identity" but as a means of exercising class power. It is a measure of the crisis the lords felt themselves to be in that they consented to its dissolution of Parliament by such a majority. For although their local power was left in place and, indeed, preserved as their private property, they could no longer command national politics in the same way. Reaffirming their power at the socioeconomic base of society, the Union removed it from the political superstructure.

The difference between the period 1692–1707 and the period 1707–45, particularly the years after 1716, can be summarized in this way: In the former, although the obstacles to economic development were recognized by a handful of thinkers, no social force existed that could force the Scottish Parliament to implement the necessary changes or put such legislation as it did implement into practical effect. In the latter, that social force was in the process of formation, but the central institution of the Scottish state no longer existed to be influenced one way or the other, while the British Parliament was unwilling to attack the feudal structures of Scottish society. The Union was a conservative measure for both the English bourgeoisie and the Scottish nobility, but the implications did not remain in neutral for long. Rather than the results of the English Revolution radiating northwards to the benefit of the Scots, the opposite took place; the unfinished business of the Scottish Revolution was instead transferred intact into the new British state, bringing into its territorial framework the very source of counterrevolution itself. This was the paradox that lay at the heart of the Union. The intention of the English regime was to prevent a Stuart restoration in Scotland opening up a second front for France on its northern border through incorporation into a new state. The consequence of incorporation was precisely to increase the chances of such a front being opened, not as a short-term response to the immediate strains of adjusting to Union but as the result of a long-term structural crisis in Scottish society.

The Jacobite risings of 1708, 1715, 1719, and 1745 to restore the exiled House of Stuart to the three kingdoms of the British Isles were all backed by one or another of the two dominant European absolutisms, Spain and France, with an interest in limiting or reversing British expansion. The effects of the military revolution of the seventeenth century had been to force all the major European powers to adopt similar forms of organization and structure in order to compete militarily at all. The main consequence of this transformation was to ensure that where these states were set against each other in conventional battle, the result was almost always inconclusive. The fomenting of internal rebellion was therefore not an optional extra but often the only way in which the balance of forces could be shifted in favor of one of the contending states. The social group internal to Britain that was prepared to take up arms against the state was a section of declining lesser lairds, together with a smaller section of the great magnate families, whose income and indeed survival were threatened by their unwillingness or inability to transform the running of their estates along capitalist lines. The defunct Scottish state apparatus had embodied a transitional society in which feudal economic and military relations, although modified, still prevailed. Since these relationships had been carried directly over into a Union with capitalist England, we might have expected them to disintegrate from within. Instead, the feudal superstructure was artificially preserved with outside support, so that the lords retained a social and political power far greater than their shrinking economic base would otherwise have justified. The Scottish nobility escaped the consequences of successful revolution in England through a combination of their own geographical inaccessibility and the political expediency of all the English regimes from the Restoration onward, but whatever the intentions of the English government in this respect, a mere juridical dictate could not prevent the subtly corrosive influence of "commercial" society from undermining the socioeconomic basis of noble rule.

In these circumstances the lords had three alternatives. The first was to attempt to transform themselves into capitalist landlords. Only the most powerful were secure enough to make this decision confidently, and for these already great lords, the trappings of feudal power became increasingly decorative. For lesser breeds the risk of turning to commercial agriculture was simply too great, for it would involve dispensing with the military linkages and judicial authority that guaranteed them such power, status, and even wealth as they possessed, in favor of the altogether riskier competitive world of the marketplace. The second alternative was therefore to raise funds through greater exactions from their tenants, a process to which there are physical limits. The third alternative, which many of the second group eventually adopted, involved neither changing the means of exploitation nor intensifying the existing means but looking instead for a political solution to the increasing economic pressures they faced. That solution was, of course, the restoration of the Stuarts. A section of the ruling class within Scotland had entered a period of decline—a decline that they assumed restoration would reverse, or at least stabilize more successfully than the Union.

The link between the Stuarts and a section of the Scottish nobility stemmed, on the side of the former, from the absence of any other internal social base capable of conducting the necessarily violent struggle for restoration. The Scottish lords, particularly those north of the River Tay, could raise their tenants to fight; English landlords, even those formally Jacobite in politics, could at best raise their tenants to vote. Even where military tenure was not the dominant form of tenure, the heritable jurisdictions preserved by the Union comprised a set of complex, interlocking territorial domains through which irresistible pressure could be applied to tenants. These territorially dispersed forms of local authority constitute an example of dual power. In the English and the French (although not the Russian) revolutions the centers of dual power opposed to the absolutist state were in territories seized through military onslaught or urban insurrection by forces opposed to the regime. In Scotland the situation was reversed, as feudal enclaves continued to function after the fall of absolutism within the overall territory of a state otherwise dedicated to the accumulation of capital.

Why then did the British state allow the heritable jurisdictions to continue after 1707? If they had originally been preserved as a contingent measure to sell the Union to the Scottish ruling class as a whole, then their continuation was the result of two different and contradictory considerations. First, some of the most committed supporters of the revolution settlement and the Union were themselves beneficiaries of these institutions and in a social crisis would employ them in support of the regime. To alienate these men was to risk depriving the state of their local military apparatus and even pushing them into support for the Stuarts. Second, neither the juridical nor military aspects of the English state had been reproduced in Scotland, partly because it would in any event take time to overcome the uneven level of development between the states, partly because of the suspicion with which the English ruling class continued to regard their new partners. This weak nation-within-a-state was weakest precisely across the area north of the Tay, and successive administrations were prepared—indeed, were forced—to tolerate the continued functioning of local jurisdictions as a form of substitute.

In 1745 the long-expected crisis arrived, in the shape of the last Jacobite rising, making the coexistence of state forms untenable. Louis XV wanted Britain to become a permanent ally of France, but to do so it would have to be turned into a satellite, and this could only be done by replacing the House of Hanover with that of Stuart. Above all, a Stuart restoration would reverse the British rise to world power status that had begun with the War of the Spanish Succession and had been consolidated at the Treaty of Utrecht in 1713. During this period military equivalence among the leading powers made decisive victories difficult and internal revolts necessary. Outright victory was still theoretically possible, however, where the opponent was at so low a level of comparative development that the military techniques and technologies of the more advanced side gave it an overwhelming advantage. In practice, of course, these situations occurred most often in the colonial territories of Asia and the Americas, where the native inhabitants derived a tactical advantage over the metropolitan powers through familiarity with what, to the latter, was unfamiliar and unpredictable terrain. None of these advantages was available to the Jacobites. At the Battle of Culloden, on April 16, 1746, the Hanoverian troops were supported by artillery and equipped with flintlock muskets and bayonets. And even though they outnumbered the Jacobites by something like nine thousand to five thousand, the majority of the government troops did not even have to fight, for to compound the military imbalance still further, the site was flat boggy terrain that deprived the Highland contingent of any element of surprise but provided their opponents with unprotected targets for their mortars and cannon. A comparison of the respective casualty lists tells its own story: sixty Hanoverian dead; over two thousand Jacobite.

To the dominant elements of the Anglo-Scottish ruling class, Scotland seemed to be condemned to an endless series of counterrevolutionary risings as long as the social basis of feudal absolutism remained intact. The measures that were to ensure that the Jacobite Rising of 1745 could never be repeated therefore took the form of a barrage of new laws, which effectively disabled the Old Regime. The Tenures Abolition Act abolished wardholding, whereby personal and, more importantly, military services were performed in exchange for grants of land, and replaced it with nominal cash payments. The Disarming Act reasserted earlier legislation forbidding the possession of arms, and this of course complemented the abolition of military service. Equally significant were two other clauses. The first banned the bagpipes and all outward expression of clan identity, old (the plaid) and new (the kilt), as weapons of war. The only groups exempt from these prohibitions—and they were very important indeed—were the Highland Regiments, some of whom had already seen service against the clans at Culloden. The second struck at the heart of the Episcopalian ideology that had sustained Jacobitism since 1688, by insisting that all tutors, masters, and chaplains in private schools or households publicly take an oath of allegiance to George II and "his heirs and successors" in order to qualify to teach at all. The penalties for unqualified preaching or teaching, or for employing someone unqualified to do so, extended to transportation to a penal colony. The most significant legislation of all, the Heritable Jurisdictions Act of 1747, was significantly titled

"An Act for taking away and abolishing the Heritable Jurisdictions in that part of Great Britain called Scotland ... and for rendering the Union of the Two Kingdoms more complete."[13] The way in which the heritable jurisdictions had been used to mobilize support for the rising meant that their relative usefulness to the British state was well and truly at an end. Now, with some minor exceptions, they were swept away without exception, even for those who had been the most loyal supporters of the Hanoverian regime.

In political and military terms, the American experience, although on a much greater scale than that of Britain, provides the closest parallel to these events. Piedmont and Prussia came to dominance by incorporating smaller formations into new nation-states. The North initially entered the American Civil War to prevent the secession of a major part of the existing nation-state. Of course the Jacobites were not merely involved in an attempt at secession for Scotland, but in overthrowing the existing state throughout the British Isles. Ultimately, however, this was also the goal of the Confederacy in relation to the United States. Once battle was joined the aims of the Confederacy were to expand slave production northward to areas where it had never previously existed, retarding the advance of industrial capitalism and free wage labor, and, as a result, placing the US as a whole under the informal control of the British Empire for whom most of the Southern cotton exports were destined. The analogy cannot be pursued too far—Scotland was itself divided by civil war in a way that the Confederate states never were—but it nevertheless indicates the pattern of "revolution from above" into which the Scottish Revolution falls, or rather, foreshadows.

Even before the French Revolution, the capitalist system had taken on a purely economic momentum that made bourgeois domination unstoppable and irreversible, regardless of the temporary political setbacks suffered by individual revolutions in, for example, 1848–49. Gettysburg in 1863 did not therefore have the same significance as Culloden in 1746. For even if the Confederacy had won that battle and gone on to win the Civil War, the ultimate victory of industrial capitalism across the entire territory of what is now the US would sooner or later have followed, either through a renewed attempt by the North or adaptation by the Confederate plantocracy to the new order, in the manner of the Prussian Junkers or Japanese Samurai. This was not yet the situation in Britain during 1745–46. Had the Jacobites, and through them, absolutist France, been victorious, Britain, the most dynamic economy in the new system and the only significant state geared to capitalist accumulation, would have been severely weakened and its greatest opponent given a further lease of life. The Jacobites would have been incapable of reimposing feudalism over the whole of Britain—the relative economic weight of Scotland was still too slight, and the development of capitalist agriculture elsewhere too great for that to be possible—but they could have established a regime more subservient to French absolutism than even that of Charles II during the previous century. In practical terms this would have removed the main obstacle to French hegemony in Europe, allowed France to inherit British colonial possessions, and, at the very least, reversed the land settlement—particularly in Ireland—that resulted from the revolution. Britain would have necessarily been reduced to a satellite of France; even assuming that the seizure of London had miraculously restored the convictions of wavering Jacobite supporters, their very lack of a firm social base in England would have forced the new regime to rely on the force of French arms for its existence. This violent irruption of the old world into the new finally bestirred the British bourgeoisie into performing its final act as a revolutionary class. The internal victory over the Jacobites in Scotland, together with the external victories over France in Canada and India during the Seven Years' War, ensured the survival and expansion of the capitalist system.

ENLIGHTENMENT THEORY AND AGRARIAN REFORM

The removal of the counterrevolutionary threat posed by the Jacobites had different implications in England and Scotland. In England, it meant safety from forced retrogression for a territory over which capitalism was already established as the dominant mode of production. In Scotland, it meant the removal of institutional or structural obstacles to the process of capitalism becoming the dominant mode of production. Any inventory of these obstacles divides into two distinct sets. One was technical in nature, reflecting quantitative gaps in the Scottish infrastructure: road and water networks by which goods could be transported; markets at which goods could be sold; and clubs and journals whereby means of Improvement—the mechanics of enclosure, drainage, and crop rotation—could be disseminated. More serious, however, is the other set arising from the existing social structure. In Marxist terms, the first contained factors that belong to the forces of production; the second constitute the existing relations of production. In the classic Marxist formulation, gradual, cumulative changes to the forces of production reach a point at which their further development is blocked by the existing relations of production. In Scotland after the '45, everything is reversed. The Scottish economic base (both forces and relations of production) has to be simultaneously brought into line with the British political and legal superstructure established in 1707 and consolidated after the civil war of 1745–46. The technical methods and class structures that had taken centuries to develop in England could be applied immediately in Scotland, in their most advanced form.

The distinctiveness of political economy in Scotland after the '45 was a direct result of the conjunction of certain circumstances: dissatisfaction with existing economic and social conditions; the possibility of changing them with minimum risk as the result of unprecedented political stability; a "higher" motivation for doing so, provided by the emergence of national consciousness (it would be the "nation" that would benefit from their endeavors, not only the reformers themselves) and the availability of an existing set of theoretical concepts that could be developed for their own use. According to the four-stage theory of modes of subsistence, development is characterized as a process in which the backward gradually attain the same level as the more advanced. But if the developmental gap between Scotland and England was to be overcome in the timescale the reformers desired, Scotland would have to overleap several of the stages through which England had passed in moving from the Age of Agriculture to the Age of Commerce. The Scottish path to capitalist agriculture would therefore necessarily diverge from the English, in three main ways. First, the timescale was much shorter. Agrarian capitalist relations in England emerged over a prolonged period stretching from the onset of the Black Death to the passing of the Enclosure Acts. In 1746 Scotland still stood far nearer to the beginning of that process than to the end, but did not have a comparable number of centuries in which to complete it. No other nation would subsequently have the time for a prolonged period of development either, of course, but no nation apart from Scotland possessed social classes with an interest in emulating England in the middle of the eighteenth century. Second, the process was systematically theorized in advance of implementation, rather than proceeding piecemeal on an empirical basis. Third, it was implemented for the most part "from above," rather than, as in the case of England, by a combination of forces from above and below, the latter in the form of large-scale tenant farmers who had emerged through a prolonged process of peasant differentiation. The latter two of these divergences were each associated with one of the two leading elements of the alliance for Improvement.

One group consisted of the social theorists whose names we associate with the Historical School of the Scottish Enlightenment and whose professional lives were generally those of university professors, Church of Scotland ministers, or lawyers. These were the theorists of "commercial society"; they were not, in most cases, the owners of capital. The development of theory was, however, a necessary but insufficient condition for the introduction of capitalist agriculture to Scotland; it still needed to be applied in practice.

The other group of reformers, who would turn the theories into reality, consisted of members of the class whose main source of income was derived from the ownership of land—in other words, the lords, the majority of whom had previously been the greatest obstacle to the introduction of capitalist agriculture. With the project of a second Stuart restoration irrecoverably destroyed, not only the actively Jacobite lords but all those who had hoped to avoid committing themselves to "commercial society" found themselves without alternatives. Scotland saw the first transition to agrarian capitalism carried out almost entirely by an existing class of feudal landowners who realized that the only way to reverse their decline was to adopt the very methods of the capitalist agriculture that they had hitherto resisted. In this way they could at least remain members of a dominant class, albeit within a new set of social relations, using new methods of exploitation. Even after the legislative onslaught of 1746–48, all property in Scotland remained feudal in the technical sense, which is to say it was either held directly from the Crown or indirectly from a Crown vassal. Within this overall framework tenants could still be forced into performing particular actions for the landowner.

Both literati and landowners intermingled in the societies and clubs that were the basic associational forms of the Scottish Enlightenment. But if we were to ask who carried out the majority of the practical reforming measures (as opposed to enabling them through theoretical analysis or changes to tenurial relationships), then the tenants were clearly the most important part of the improving movement. If they were too geographically remote from the major urban centers to participate in their activities, they could still subscribe to the journals in which the new ideas were promoted. And if they could not subscribe to the journals there were other means by which these ideas were disseminated. The societies themselves recognized the need to expand their membership base into the tenant farmer class if they were to succeed in implementing their program of reform.

The program had four essential components, all of which had been proposed long before 1746 but could only now be put into general effect. The first was that all transactions be conducted in cash, rather than in kind (or by the performance of labor service); but the introduction of a fully monetary economy, although necessary, was not a sufficient condition for the establishment of commercial social relations, which is why it had previously been possible for a certain degree of monetization to take place under essentially feudal conditions. The same could also be said of the second essential reform: the division of common lands and—far more significant—of lands held in runrig, under which they were regularly redivided among tenants. The former was considered by reformers to be both an affront to legal conceptions of private property and, on a practical level, a waste of potentially profitable ground. The latter was considered to prevent long-term Improvement (since holdings were regularly changing hands) or a properly competitive attitude (since the work was shared). The elimination of runrig and common land was linked to the third essential reform: reduction of the number of tenants in order to establish commercially viable holdings. Even where runrig did not exist, holdings and farms were often too small to be commercially viable, as a result of the multiple tenancies previously favored by the lords. Alongside the consolidation of tenancies, previously untenanted land was let from the beginning in large units. The fourth and final reform was the introduction of long-term leases. The dominance that the lords had over their tenants was expressed, in the first instance, through the lease itself, both in terms of its duration and the conditions that the tenant was expected to fulfill. Leases were usually awarded for one or perhaps two years, the implication being that they would not be renewed if the lord was unsatisfied with either the tenant's behavior or that of the subtenants for whom the tenant was also held responsible. Short-term leases gave tenants little incentive to improve their yields, since the likely result of so doing would either be a rent increase or eviction and replacement by another tenant who was prepared to pay the difference.

The introduction of long leases gave significance to the other qualitative changes—the transition to a money economy, the abolition of commonly owned or worked land, the consolidation of multiple tenancies—and set the context for quantitative increase in roads, markets, journals, and the rest. The cumulative effect of these changes was that from the late 1740s the value of the landowners' rent rolls had grown dramatically. This sharp upward trajectory of landlord income, which in turn depended on the increased ability of the tenant farmers to pay higher rents, laid the financial basis for the industrialization of the Lowlands and the profits of the tobacco trade, for which both imperial markets and Caribbean slave labor were essential.

The theoretical wing of the improving alliance was always conscious that "commercial society," whatever its ultimate desirability, involved a cost, not least for the majority of the population. The losses associated with commercial society appear, again and again, in the work of the major figures of the Scottish Enlightenment, from which source Hegel and ultimately Marx derived the theoretical basis of the theory of alienation. In addition, many reformers were deeply unhappy that institutions integral to feudal exploitation before 1746 were carried into commercial society afterward. It shadowed their achievements. Behind the complaints of the reformers lay disquiet with the fact that Improvement had not produced the stable commercial society of socially responsible landowners and prosperous tenants they had envisaged. Ironically, given the many ways in which the Scottish path prefigures the Prussian, their model—rarely openly acknowledged, particularly after 1776—was the quite different experience of the American colonies; but developments in Scotland would produce the very opposite of these conditions. Rather than leading to a proliferation of independent farmers, as some had predicted, the dominance of capitalist agriculture now led to a fall in their numbers. The occupiers of the land were increasingly divided between the great landowners and large capitalist farmers, on the one hand, and landless laborers on the other. The main difference between the Scottish and Prussian paths is that Scottish landlords were able to begin reform safe in the knowledge that they would not be met with widespread peasant resistance; their Prussian successors began reform after 1806 in part to prevent peasant revolt from assuming the terrifying proportions that it had already done during the French Revolution.

CONCLUSION

The uniqueness of the situation in Scotland after the failed counterrevolution of 1745–46 was that political power was already in the hands of the bourgeoisie, while feudal social relations still prevailed in the countryside. The situation in Scotland after 1746 was in fact more typical of the aftermath of a proletarian than a bourgeois revolution, in the sense that the economy had to be consciously reconstructed after the conquest of political power. The thinkers of the Scottish Enlightenment were therefore more concerned in their writings with the attainment of economic dominance over society than the conquest of political power within the state. In this respect the Scottish bourgeois experience was therefore richer than any of those that followed it, in that during the latter stages it produced, in the Scottish Enlightenment, a *theorization* of the process, which provides one of the links to Marxism and ultimately to Gramsci himself, not least through the notion of civil society. Unconstrained by feudal lords behind them (since they had been destroyed by the military and juridical apparatus of the British state, or had transformed themselves into capitalists), unafraid of a working class before them (since it had not yet come into existence in significant numbers, and would only do so as a result of their activities), the Scottish bourgeoisie was free, as no other had been before or would ever be again, to reconstruct society in its own image.

5

The French Revolution Is Not Over: Henry Heller on France, 1789–1815

Introduction

Marx and Engels were born into a world shaped by the French Revolution—literally so in the case of Marx, who grew up in the Rhineland where the French occupation between 1807 and 1813 greatly accelerated the dismantling of feudalism in that region. It is unsurprising then that this cataclysmic event should have influenced the formation of their theories. By the mid-1840s the revolution had acquired a threefold significance in their thought.

First, in terms of the past, France provided the clearest example of how capitalism had first emerged within feudalism as a subordinate mode of production, then become dominant across a particular national territory. But this outcome was not simply the inevitable evolutionary triumph of a more dynamic economic system; it also required a successful struggle for political power by the capitalist class against the existing feudal-absolutist order. Because the French Revolution showed this process so clearly, it became possible to retrospectively understand two decisive episodes from previous centuries, the English Civil War and the Dutch Revolt against Spain, as earlier and less developed versions of the same kind of struggle.

Second, in terms of the present, it provided an inspiration for those national bourgeoisies—at this stage the vast majority—who were still excluded from political power. Marx was particularly concerned that the German bourgeoisie should learn the lessons of the French Revolution, although he rightly remained pessimistic about its capacity to do so. He was not so naive as to think, however, that bourgeois leadership involved industrialists and financiers personally mounting the barricades. He was quite aware that the actual fighting had been carried out by classes below the bourgeoisie in the class structure, and on some occasions suggested that without these plebeians the revolution would not have succeeded, or even survived.

Third, in terms of the future, it also provided the emergent proletariat with lessons in the need for revolutionary intransigence on its own behalf, rather than that of a new class of exploiters. But more generally, the mobilizations that characterized the crucial "days" of the revolution involved far greater levels of mass involvement and higher levels of popular initiative than the preceding bourgeois revolutions in the United Netherlands, England, Scotland, or America. Its mass character was therefore paradoxical, making possible the period of bourgeois ascendancy *and* prefiguring the form of the coming proletarian revolutions. As Georg Lukács later noted: "From the Great French Revolution on, all revolutions exhibit the same pattern with increasing intensity."[1] Indeed, the actual pattern of events—the initial unity of the revolutionary forces, their increasing polarization into left and right under pressure from the counterrevolution, the ultimate stabilization on the basis of a conservative reaction within the revolution—seemed to offer a general pattern of development. Russian revolutionaries, particularly the Bolsheviks after October 1917, obsessively drew parallels, often quite misleading ones, between their situation and that of the Jacobins.[2]

For Marx, therefore, the French Revolution involved three key elements: bourgeois leadership that gave the revolution its class character; mass mobilizations of peasants, urban masses, and revolutionary armies that were necessary to take power and defend the new state; and the removal of obstacles to capitalist development that constituted the outcome. In France itself this interpretation gave rise to an extraordinarily rich socialist historiography, from Jean Jaurès to Albert Mathiez, and from Georges Lefebvre to Albert Soboul, much of which can still be read with profit today. But because Marx wrote specifically about the French Revolution and, to a lesser extent, its immediate predecessors, he did not leave behind a general theory of bourgeois revolution. The outline of one did emerge in Engels's later writings and was further developed by Lenin, Trotsky, Lukács, Gramsci, and many other thinkers, although by no means in a systematic way. The underlying theme was that bourgeois revolutions were not the sum total of a checklist of "tasks" that had to be accomplished before they could be declared complete. The only *necessary* component of a bourgeois revolution was not the nature of the process, nor the identity of the class actors, but the outcome: the establishment of a state committed to ensuring the accumulation of capital.

Unfortunately, this approach, like so much else of value in Marxist theory, was suppressed for decades by Stalinism. In its place the orthodoxy became a model of bourgeois revolution based on the French Revolution—or, to be more exact, a particular reading of the first five years of the French Revolution—a model accepted even by people who were not Stalinists, people who were in most other respects opposed to Stalinism. The problem was that the "French model" was a positive obstacle to understanding how the bourgeoisie had come to power on a global scale. By using France as the example against which all other bourgeois revolutions were judged, it was inevitable that even those countries in which the revolutions were structurally quite similar to the French, like England, would be found wanting, while some countries, like Germany, would be found not to have undergone bourgeois revolutions at all, because they had failed to reproduce the French experience. (There was a political subtext to this argument, of course, which was connected to the Stalinist strategy of Popular Fronts and cross-class alliances more generally. If the "tasks" of the bourgeois revolution—usually defined as agrarian reform, national unification, and representative democracy—remained unfulfilled, then it was necessary to form alliances with progressive members of the national bourgeoisie until the bourgeois "stage" had been accomplished.) Opposition to the orthodoxy tended to be framed not in terms of how capitalism actually came to overthrow feudalism across most of the world but in relation to how far the element of "revolution from below" prefigured socialist ideology and organization. But what would become of this conception of bourgeois revolution if even the French Revolution was found not to live up to its image? This was exactly what began to be argued, first in the 1950s and then, with greater confidence and frequency, from the 1970s onward.

THE FRENCH REVOLUTION DID NOT TAKE PLACE

"Revisionism" is the catch-all term for a range of arguments that deny that the French Revolution was a "bourgeois revolution." Some versions go so far as to deny that it can be explained in social terms at all. The arguments have developed in three main phases.

The first, relatively isolated expressions of the case were made over fifty years ago in Britain and Israel. In his inaugural lecture as chair in French history at the University of London, first published in 1955 as "The Myth of the French Revolution," the British historian Alfred Cobban made four points. First, France was no longer a feudal society by 1789. Some dues and services still survived, but these were functionless survivals whose significance may have been deliberately overemphasized by the Constituent Assembly so that their abolition, under pressure from the peasantry, would not set a precedent that could be extended to bourgeois property rights. Second, the main representatives of the Third Estate were not capitalists but lawyers or, more precisely, venal office holders, functionaries, and professional men who used the revolution to ascend the state structure at the expense of the nobility. Third, both the formal abolition of feudal dues and the ascendancy of the bourgeois office holders had been achieved by 1791. The subsequent events were violent but essentially irrelevant, since by 1799 the situation had simply reverted to what it was at the beginning of the decade. Fourth, the impact of the revolution on capitalist development was limited and may even have retarded it until much later in the nineteenth century.[3] What then had led to the Jacobin dictatorship, the September Massacres, the Terror, and all those other supposedly pointless events that Cobban regarded with such fastidious British distaste? The answer had been independently provided, not by a historian but by the political scientist Jacob L. Talmon, then based at the Hebrew University in Jerusalem. His focus was on the Enlightenment beliefs that he claimed had taken on a life of their own and led to the Dictatorship of Virtue, an abstract set of truths that empowered the Jacobins and their supporters to kill in the name of ideological purity.[4] Both Cobban and Talmon were committed cold warriors. Cobban helped ensure that one of his own students, George Rudé, was blacklisted from lecturing in Britain. Talmon contributed toward the "end of ideology" thesis during the 1950s and drew parallels between the "totalitarian democracy" of the Jacobins and that of the supposedly equivalent modern totalitarianisms of Fascism and Communism.[5] I emphasize their contribution because, although the terminology in which Cobban and Talmon expressed their critique has undergone several mutations at the hands of their revisionist successors, and a great deal more research has been undertaken, very little by way of argument has been added to their positions.

What was significant about the second phase of revisionism was where it arose and who was responsible. From the mid-1970s onward, these arguments began to be expressed in France itself by people on the left, or at least people who had been on the left. The most important of these was François Furet, a member of the Communist Party of France. In a history of the revolution written in 1965 with Denis Richet, Furet introduced the idea of "the skidding off-course of the revolution" after 1791.[6] If his first contribution echoed Cobban's claim that the real goals of the revolution had been achieved by 1791, his second, a decade later, recalled Talmon's emphasis on ideology. In this essay, "The French Revolution Is Over," Furet attacks the connections that the French left in particular drew between the French and Russian revolutions. Furet was, however, concerned less with the historical accuracy of this claim than with highlighting what he thought the real connections were, namely the comparable totalitarian systems embodied in the Terror and the Gulag.[7]

Since then, revisionism has tended to fragment into two main camps. One, initiated by Furet but perhaps epitomized by Mona Ozouf, takes a determinedly idealist view, ruling out any social interpretation of events and emphasizing the emergence of a new political culture of deracinated intellectuals, which apparently led to the Terror. For Ozouf, in the beginning there was not even the Word, but only the Thought. (David Bell, an admirer, claims that the revisionists have demonstrated the impossibility of identifying either "a 'bourgeois' social group possessing a distinct relationship to the means of production" or "a group united by a common assertion of 'bourgeois' identity" in 1789.[8]) The other is a more materialist interpretation, found in the work of American historians like Donald Sutherland, but it is equally misleading in different ways. Here the theme is the underlying continuity of peasant life, its imperviousness to new Enlightenment notions, and above all its explosive violence. Sutherland describes peasant land seizures as involving "chiliastic calls for a massive bloodletting . . . more reminiscent of medieval notions of the end of days than of the red dawn of the future." In the end, the shape of the postrevolutionary state was determined by "the vast weight of ancient peasant France," which "imposed itself upon the government, at the expense of many of the ideals of 1789."[9] In accounts like these, continuity is all, the revolution a meaningless surface disturbance eventually becalmed by peasant immobility.

How have Marxists defended the validity of the concept of bourgeois revolution? Benno Teschke has recently claimed that there are "two sharply diverging responses": "One, associated with the orthodoxy, retained the concept while making substantive empirical concessions; the other, associated with political Marxism, dismissed the concept while re-interpreting the empirical on the basis of a new class analysis."[10] The first response, which Teschke calls "consequentialism," is not a response to revisionism at all, and still less is it "associated with the orthodoxy": it is rather a return to the classical Marxist position of the Second and early Third Internationals to which I referred earlier. It was first restated by a trio of very different Trotskyists (Cliff, Deutscher, and Shachtman) in books and articles written in 1948–49, which does somewhat predate the emergence of revisionism.[11] But the second option, which Teschke himself espouses, is not really a response either, but rather a third and, one hopes, final phase of revisionism itself.

Here, as with the influence of Cobban on Furet, there are connections with the preceding phase. George Comninel, for example, makes the apparently curious claim that the "only" bourgeois aspect of the revolution was the fact that the bourgeois led it against their aristocratic opponents. Bourgeois leadership and aristocratic opponents may sound like reasonably decisive criteria, but it is important to understand that Comninel does not regard the "bourgeoisie" as having any necessary connection with capitalism or the "aristocracy" as having any necessary connection with feudalism. In the absence of "a system entirely structured about commodity production as the self-expansion of capital through the reduction of labor to labor-power," capitalism did not exist in France prior to 1789. Rather, the bourgeoisie essentially belonged to the same social class as the aristocracy because both ultimately drew their income through the same method of surplus extraction. The revolution should therefore be seen as "an intra-class conflict" or "civil war" over distribution of the surplus. Unsurprisingly, Comninel does not think that the revolution did anything to promote capitalism either: "The Revolution was not fought by capitalists, and it did not produce capitalist society." If anything, it restricted it further by preserving small-scale peasant production.[12] Virtually the only difference between Comninel and the earlier generations of revisionists is his belief that capitalism, rather than having already surpassed feudalism in France by 1789, did not exist at all.

A NEW SYNTHESIS

From the preceding discussion it should be obvious why a book called *The Bourgeois Revolution in France* should be of interest to readers of *International Socialism*, particularly when the author begins with this assessment: "It seems evident that a connection exists between the predominance of revisionism, the decline of revolutionary movements of the 1960s and 1970s, and the conservative or neoliberal ideological offensive of the last decades. Whether or not the modern world came into being by revolution is more than an academic question. It bears on the present and future as well as on the interpretation of the past."[13] So writes Henry Heller, a Canadian Marxist scholar who, over the last twenty years, has increased our understanding of sixteenth-century France with a series of books reassessing the Gallic experience of Calvinism, the Wars of Religion, and the relationship between economic development and technological change.[14] However, these works focused on the period when revolutionary movements in France failed to emulate the decisive break with feudal absolutism that had occurred in the United Netherlands and, slightly later, in England. It is only now, in his latest book, that Heller broaches the moment in French history during which classical Marxism has traditionally seen the breakthrough to capitalist economy and bourgeois society as finally taking place. And he has a specific purpose in doing so: "This work seeks to reclaim the idea that the French Revolution was a bourgeois revolution."[15] Indeed, it is the first book in English explicitly to defend a Marxist interpretation of the French Revolution since revisionism became entrenched.

Heller seeks "confirmation of the Marxist view" in what he modestly calls "a review of existing scholarly literature."[16] In a relatively short but densely packed book, Heller has synthesized recent work by other historians that is either difficult for non-specialists to obtain or as yet untranslated into English. In the first category are mainly Anglo-American historians who have challenged specific revisionist claims on empirical grounds, without seeking to reject the entire approach. In the second are mainly French Marxists like Michel Vovelle and Guy Lemarchand (but also the Russian Anatoli Ado), who are not only concerned with grounding their work in primary research but also with engaging the revisionists in theoretical terms.[17] Heller assumes that his readers are aware of both the course of events and the main conflicting interpretations. Although the book proceeds through chronological periods, it does not really provide a narrative account, despite claims to this effect by Heller in the preface. Consequently, readers seeking an introduction to the history of the French Revolution should turn instead to the short book written by Albert Soboul during the 1960s (which is also a fine example of the "classic" position) or to the article by Paul McGarr published by *International Socialism* on the bicentenary of 1789.[18] That said, Heller writes simply and accessibly, and conveys a vast amount of information about who was doing what to whom and why. The contrast with more pompous productions, which breathlessly announce supposedly paradigm-shattering theoretical discoveries without actually telling the reader much about anything, could not be more marked. Not that Heller is dismissive of theory, but his own theoretical approach differs from that of most previous historians in three main ways.

First, he does not focus his attention on the popular movements of either the peasants or sans-culottes: "Rather, the focus will be on the step-by-step development of the bourgeoisie as new ruling class."[19] He clearly regards much of the writing about the movements from below as a way of sidestepping discussion of the revolutionary role of the bourgeoisie. But Heller goes further. From Daniel Guérin onward, many historians have stressed the anticapitalist possibilities of working-class power emerging from the activity of the sans-culottes.[20] As far as France is concerned, most of the debate among socialists has not been about the accuracy of this assessment but about how far an anticapitalist program could have succeeded. In a splendidly iconoclastic move Heller rejects the entire premise, writing that "far from being an impediment to capitalism, the popular democratic phase of the revolution was an essential element to the further development of French capitalism."[21] Heller sees "the ideology of the sans-culottes" less as the ideology of a homogenous class of small producers than as an attempt to overcome the economic tensions *between* the classes in the workplace: "Its stress on workplace solidarity and egalitarianism amounted to a new public discourse that could mediate and assuage emergent conflict between labor and capital." Following the work of Richard Mowery Andrews, Heller argues that many of the classic histories of the Revolution "took the egalitarian ideology of the sans-culottes too much at face value," losing sight of "the fact that those who dominated the movement were solid bourgeois, notably the master artisans."[22]

Second, he deals with the revolutionary period as a whole: "This history will make a point of investigating not merely the eighteenth-century background and the most tumultuous years of the revolution, but also the period of its consolidation under the Directory and Napoleon."[23] Just as any serious discussion of the English Revolution has to span the period from the Scottish Covenanters' rebellion of 1637 through to the Restoration of 1660, so too must one of the French Revolution extend from the 1787 Assembly of Notables to the Restoration of 1815. This may seem obvious, but many of the greatest works on the subject—such as the major books by Lefebvre and Soboul—conclude in 1799 with Napoleon's seizure of power, and many finish earlier with Thermidor in 1794.[24] By dealing with the period as a whole Heller affirms that the unheroic later stages are just as central as the years of mass mobilization to the issue of capitalist dominance.

Third, although he foregrounds economic developments in a way that will undoubtedly scandalize the revisionists, Heller does not advocate a crude economic determinism. Rather, "the view advanced here will be one that insists that the economic, political and cultural factors cannot be seen as separate from one another. . . . [S]uch factors will be treated dialectically as coexistent features of a great civilizational transformation."[25] And although he does not use the term, Heller is here invoking the notion of totality: "From a Marxist point of view it is not the primacy of the economic that is the distinguishing feature. Rather it is an insistence on a knowledge of the historical process in its entirety or as a whole."[26] Indeed, his main criticism of the revisionists is their blindness to the inner connections between changes to different aspects of French society. Heller accepts that they may have brought some gains in the study of areas like gender and political culture: "But in the final analysis, the maintenance of a perspective that rejects the idea of the French Revolution as a capitalist Revolution, is only possible by refusing to comprehend these events as part of a unified process or by rejecting the idea that such comprehension is possible."[27]

CAPITALISM AND CRISIS BEFORE 1789

How then does Heller's approach deal with some key themes thrown up by the revisionist debates? If capitalism were already totally dominant in a society, there would be no *need* for a bourgeois revolution, because there would be no forces capable of opposing it. But if capitalism did not exist at all in a society, then there would be no *possibility* of a bourgeois revolution, because there would be no forces capable of supporting it. To what extent had capitalism developed in France by 1789? As Heller writes: "The initial success of the bourgeoisie did not mean that France was a fully developed capitalist economy led by a fully conscious and self-confident capitalist class. It meant only that the bourgeoisie had developed enough economic as well as political strength to get rid of the ancien régime. It would take an extended process over the next twenty-five years for it to mature as a class while further developing its economic underpinnings."[28]

Heller argues that capitalist production existed to varying degrees across the different sectors of the economy in eighteenth-century France. The uneven spatial development of agriculture effectively divided the country into three regions, but only in the north did capitalist agriculture emerge, bringing with it social differentiation between proprietors and large farmers on the one hand, and day laborers and teamsters on the other. Although the point is not original, it is extremely important as a demonstration that the type of productive relations typical of English capitalist agriculture was also present on a geographically more restricted basis in France.[29]

In relation to trade, once the demand for commodities expanded beyond a certain point, it had implications for how production—not simply the division of labor, or the labor process more generally—was organized. Heller shows that there was certainly a massive increase in French trade across the eighteenth century.[30] It is true that much of the production of commodities took place in small workshops and on a seasonal basis, but large factories also began to appear. The greatest of all, the Le Creusot iron and steel factory built during the 1780s, "had a workforce of over 1,300, used the advanced coke reduction process in the manufacture of steel, and operated with the help of at least five steam engines and between twelve and fifteen miles of railway tracking."[31]

And what of the laborers who worked in these enterprises? In many respects they were not fully formed proletarians, completely separated from both the means of production and the means of subsistence. But as Heller points out, people may be driven to work for wages not because they have no access to subsistence production but because it is insufficient to support them. Equally, capitalists are quite content for workers to partially provide for themselves, since this allows the level of wages to be held down.[32] To imagine otherwise is to abandon the possibility of a transitional economy at all: an economy must either be feudal or capitalist or something else altogether, but nothing in between. This is highly unrealistic, to say the least: "The full emergence of abstract labor and value are not capitalist preconditions but the end product of a prolonged historical process in which struggle over the means of production and their further development are primary factors. . . . At a certain stage in the evolution of the economy of the ancien régime, the creation of value began to occur within the structures of the guilds and corporations, institutions that likely facilitated the process."[33]

But capitalist developments were opposed, and from more than one source. Heller cites the example of Jacques de Vaucanson, a mechanic who entered the Academy of Sciences at the insistence of Louis XV because of his inventions, which included "a mechanical silk loom, a draw loom for brocade and figured silk, a silk throwing mill, and a mangle to achieve the effect of moiré or 'clouded silk.'" His entry to the academy was opposed by the aristocratic members who opposed the practical application of scientific theory for the vulgar purposes of commerce. But he was also opposed by the corporate guilds of the artisans, who were themselves already under attack from the merchant capitalists, and who rioted to prevent the introduction of the mechanical loom.[34] The kind of support the absolutist state could give to innovators like de Vaucanson against noble opposition was limited, since the nobility was the ultimate basis of its support.[35]

The absolutist state concentrated power, drawing it away from the local lordships to the centralized state as guarantor of surplus extraction and defense against peasant revolt.[36] Yet centralization did not necessarily mean that the state was all-powerful, despite its propaganda to that effect.[37] As Heller writes: "The absolutist state had deprived the French nobility of much of its ability to control the rural population or to withstand revolt." But it could not always replace that ability with its own power, which mattered in a situation where peasant resistance to the payment of tithes and enforcement of seignorial rights had been increasing since 1775.[38] Heller agrees with most commentators that the fiscal crisis of the state was a major precipitant of the revolution, in particular the increased share of taxation falling on the commoners. Not only were the nobles largely exempt from such taxes, but they increased their own income levels by squeezing greater rents from their tenants. As we have seen, however, Heller also insists that there was an economic as well as a financial crisis. "Economic crisis galvanized the mass of the population to throw its weight behind the political struggle of the bourgeoisie, allowing it to take power."[39] The crisis itself had two aspects. One was in industry and commerce. In relation to the former, Heller follows Lemarchand in arguing that there was a shortage of investment capital in industry and agriculture, "because too much of the economic surplus was drained off in the form of agricultural rents. . . . In the final analysis the paralysis of the leading sectors of an emergent capitalism reflected the ongoing stranglehold of the seignorial class over the economy." The crisis was also agricultural: "The growth in population rendered the holdings of many of the peasants progressively smaller and increasingly fragile." The two were connected by the limitations to French development: "The domestic market was clearly inhibited by growing rural poverty. But the market was also blocked by the persistence of tolls and tariffs, local systems of weights and measures, a lack of adequate means of transport, and the burden of indirect taxes. Such a situation encouraged the persistence of too large a degree of domestic or local subsistence inhibiting urbanization and the commercialization of agriculture." In short, the revolution had three underlying economic causes. Two of these, the crisis of industrial underinvestment in the capitalist manufacturing sector and "a classic Malthusian" crisis of subsistence in feudal agriculture, triggered by the combination of population increase and harvest failure, were primary. They set the context for the third, "the financial insolvency of the state," which in turn "led to an ultimate political crisis." The alignment of the joint crises of capitalism, feudalism, and the absolutist state suggest the transitional, combined nature of the French economy, but also that the transition had reached the point where it would be increasingly difficult for the process to continue without radical political change.[40]

BOTH BOURGEOIS AND CAPITALIST

Who then were the bourgeoisie who took the leadership of the revolution once the crisis had broken? Heller points out that, in terms of social weight, there were simply many more members of that class by the end of the eighteenth century than at the beginning: "It is estimated that the size of the bourgeoisie grew from 700,000 to 800,000 at the beginning of the eighteenth century to perhaps 2.3 million in 1789, vastly outnumbering the 120,000 or so nobles." Partly because of this, from 1720 onward the nobility began to force through measures that excluded the bourgeoisie from joining them, including the ending of ennoblement through office in 1728. The bourgeoisie were opposed to the tax exemptions of the nobility, particularly as taxation increased, although membership in the nobility based on merit was still their goal. As this suggests, the development of their class consciousness was subject to contradictory pressures. On the one hand, their capacity for collective self-organization was limited, for fairly obvious reasons: "Before the onset of the Revolution, the sphere of autonomous political activity was quite circumscribed by the authorities of the ancien régime as a matter of policy." On the other hand, a bourgeois way of life involving distinct forms of dress, manners, speech, and so on began to develop. So too did organizations where new ideas could be discussed and other activities besides. The Freemasons were one such organization: "The meetings of the lodges became sites not only for philosophical discussions, but for the creating and financing of new business partnerships." It was clear to many young bourgeois that certain careers were not open to their talents: "As a result, late eighteenth-century France produced a large stratum of alienated intelligentsia who played an important role in the Revolution."[41]

But what was the relationship of these bourgeois intellectuals to capitalism? As we have seen from the work of Comninel, some Political Marxists claim that capitalists and the bourgeoisie are quite distinct classes, a position that has implications for how we assess revolutions, notably the English and French, which otherwise appear decidedly similar. Benno Teschke, for example, claims that "while the English revolution was not bourgeois, it was capitalist, and while the French Revolution was bourgeois, it was not capitalist."[42] This distinction is completely untenable and relies on a fixation on the etymological origin of the word "bourgeois," as if the fact that it originally meant "town dweller" in the middle ages continued to determine how it was used in the eighteenth century![43] Capitalists are *part* of the bourgeoisie. The latter is a far broader category, but one that could not exist as a class without the centripetal economic core of people committed to capital accumulation. Heller makes two points in this context.

First, there are perfectly good reasons why leadership should be exerted by individuals at the economic periphery. In one of his few direct references to the classical Marxist tradition, Heller notes Gramsci's insistence on the formation of "organic intellectuals" to a revolutionary class: "As a new class develops within the world of economic production, it tends to create from out of itself a stratum of intellectuals that helps to give it a sense of homogeneity and a sense of its economic as well as its social and political functions." In France these included "physicians, journalists, writers and, above all, lawyers." Heller justly remarks that "in this light, to demand why business people and not lawyers were to be found sitting in the Estates General for the third estate in 1789 is to invoke an argument based on a crude reductionism—a position of which Marxists have often been accused."[44]

Second, it is in any case untrue that capitalists in the narrow sense were uninvolved in the revolution. Their direct intervention in government tended to be exercised outwith the capital, something that has often been ignored because of the decisive impact of events in Paris. But as Heller says, "the weight of the economic bourgeoisie made itself felt directly at the level of local rather than national government."[45] Their most obvious impact, however, can be seen in the laws passed by the Legislative Assembly. Take three components of the legislative program of 1791, which clearly embody capitalist interests. Under the Law of Allaire of March 2, feudal guilds were abolished and restrictions on businesses removed. The Le Chapelier Law of June 14–17 banned combinations and industrial action. Finally, the decree on agrarian property rights of June 5, the most important of a series of enactments concerning agriculture, established freedom of ownership, including the right to enclose common land.[46] Because of their dates, these examples may not convince revisionists who believe that the bourgeois content of the revolution ended after 1791. But the majority of the Jacobins saw political dictatorship, economic centralization, the Law of the Maximum, and all the rest as temporary measures made necessary by civil war and invasion. Only at the outer edges of Jacobinism did members see them as being anticapitalist in themselves, and this was the anticapitalism of small producers, not workers. "The creation of the Jacobin state was not simply based on countering the threat of counterrevolution, but on the determination to oppose the threat from economic competition from its English rival by using political means."[47] The arms industry provides a good example of how military necessity contributed to capitalist expansion. In what can retrospectively be seen as early measures of state capitalism, the Committee of Public Safety effectively nationalized the existing armories and organized the building of new ones in Paris and elsewhere. The majority of forges (about a thousand) were confiscated from their noble and ecclesiastical owners and transformed into state property, leased out to the *maîtres de forges* who had previously run them. Under the Directory and Napoleon they were ultimately sold off to the same individuals who, over the entire revolutionary period, began through a process of internal competition to centralize ownership and control: "The stage was set for a future transformation of this industry—key to the development of nineteenth-century industrial capitalism—under the auspices of these *maîtres de forges* who now operated these means of production as their private property." Steel production nearly doubled between 1789 and 1801. And the new owners prospered too: by 1811 more than a dozen of the *maîtres de forges* had assets of between one and three million francs.[48]

In his discussion of the ideology of the revolutionary bourgeoisie Heller focuses on unjustly neglected figures like Pierre-Louis Roederer and Étienne Clavière. The latter was a Genevan financial speculator and banker who "combined fervent idealism and shrewd business calculation," ultimately becoming Minister of Finance briefly in 1792–93. Of this type of individual, Heller writes: "They identified this new regime with the free market."[49] Similar views were unambiguously expressed following the Thermidorian coup of 1794. One member of the new ruling group, Paul-Augustin Lozeau, rejected the Jacobin ideal of universal property ownership and abolition of poverty: "Even if it were possible, how then, asked Lozeau, could the big farmers, the merchants, and the industrialists find the labor power that was indispensable to their enterprises?"[50]

THE NATURE OF POSTREVOLUTIONARY FRANCE

The orthodox view of postrevolutionary France held by virtually everyone from Engels to the revisionists is that a mass of peasant smallholders, left in secure possession of their holdings by the revolution, acted as a brake on the development of capitalism. The assumption here is that only large capitalist farmers can be competitive, but this is not necessarily the case. Following the work of Anatoli Ado, Heller argues that Jacobin encouragement for "petty commodity production as a prelude to primitive accumulation, social polarization and the emergence of a vibrant agrarian and industrial capitalism" was an attempt to reproduce the American version of capitalism rather than that of Britain: "The short-lived Jacobin state may thus be seen as a bold if unsuccessful attempt to install such a capitalism from below." The division of the land would initially have retarded capitalist development: "But under free market conditions it would have speeded primitive accumulation over the medium term by unleashing the path of small-scale commodity production in both town and country." This position was actually theorized under the Directory from 1795 by the proponents of what James Livesey calls "commercial republicanism," who saw it as a conscious alternative to the British path of "enclosure, tenant farming and agricultural innovation": "Comparing Great Britain to France, the commercial republicans argued that Britain could not fulfill the promise of economic liberty, because unlike the republican French, the British under their monarchy did not enjoy full political liberty." But these were a minority. The Thermidorian Reaction refused the demands of the peasants for land and upheld the ownership and dominance of "nobles, bourgeoisie and rich peasants." We therefore may have to revise the traditional view of the agrarian settlement and consider whether it was not "the persistence of large property and the burden of rent, not small peasant property, which inhibited a more rapid development of French capitalism." In turn, this might suggest that "the popular revolution based on the petty producers ought to be seen as an essential element of the capitalist dynamic characteristic of this upheaval."[51]

Heller agrees with Livesey that "revisionist attempts to measure the economic consequences of the Revolution in terms of short-term costs and benefits is historiographically misconceived."[52] This does not mean that there were no benefits. In particular, Heller questions the conventional view that British manufacturing was superior to the French in the immediate aftermath of the revolution. First, Britain was actually less mechanized during this period than was traditionally thought; it was only in the latter half of the nineteenth century that mechanization became dominant. Second, mass production was not the only method of industrialization: "With its higher quality production, France inserted itself differently into the international division of labor . . . [growing] at a rate comparable to that of its neighbors but bas[ing] its secondary sector on small craft and manufacturing enterprises."[53]

THE MISSING INTERNATIONAL DIMENSION

No book can encompass every aspect of a subject, but the one key area where Heller's account is noticeably deficient is in its treatment of the international dimension. This is important because "the international" has become the means of explaining capitalist development outside of England, particularly in the work of Benno Teschke. Now, consideration of the impact of geopolitics on capitalist development is absolutely necessary, providing it is not treated as the demiurge behind the whole of human history since 1688. Clearly a major contributory factor to the territorial expansion of capitalism during the nineteenth century was the competitive pressure that the existing capitalist nation-states, including France, placed on the feudal and absolutist regimes, forcing those that could to establish nation-state structures and capitalist economies. As the theory of uneven and combined development would lead us to expect, once the development of capitalism became a conscious process then obviously changes to the relations of production tended to accompany or even precede changes to the forces of production, precisely because the aspirant capitalists knew what they were trying to achieve, unlike their predecessors in the period when capitalism first emerged as a distinct mode of production.[54] What Teschke is saying, however, is that this happened much earlier and in a completely all-embracing fashion. According to this quite extraordinary theory, *no* country in the world—including France—experienced capitalist development except as a result of the need to emulate Britain, and that in *no* case did this involve building on preexisting capitalist production. Teschke writes that "it was under the pressure of geopolitical competition, especially between France and Britain after the French defeat in the Seven Years' War, that the victorious but financially bankrupt France was eventually forced, in a period of dramatic class conflicts, to violently alter its internal social property relations."[55] The idea that "internal social property relations" might already have begun to change as a result of internal dynamics is inconceivable in this perspective.

At one point Heller notes that the market is scarcely a spontaneous generation in any historical circumstances: "The provision of a more or less trained and disciplined labor force, a reliable currency, law and order, and an infrastructure of roads and bridges are not provided directly through the market but require state intervention." But the main role of the revolutionary French state was in nurturing, not conceiving, French capitalism—a process "made necessary by the ongoing weakness of the capitalist economy in France as compared to, and in competition with, England."[56] As the last sentence suggests, Heller does not ignore the effect on France of competition with Britain. However, he neglects two other aspects of France's situation in the formative world market, one in the period leading up to the revolution, the other in the period flowing out of it.

The first is the extent of capitalist production outside France. Any account of the formative process of French capitalism must include the colonial economy, particularly the slave plantations of the Caribbean. These classically "combined" forms were perhaps the most advanced under French ownership and bore the closest relationship to those of their British rivals. As Robin Blackburn notes: "It would . . . be wrong to propose a sharp contrast between English 'bourgeois' colonization and French 'feudal' colonization, since the social forces involved in both—merchants and colonists—were comparable."[57] As C. L. R. James notes of the slaves, "working and living together in gangs of hundreds on the huge sugar factories which covered the North Plain [of San Domingo], they were closer to a modern proletariat than any group of workers in existence at the time."[58] Extending his focus to the colonial world would have strengthened the argument Heller wants to make about the pre-revolutionary existence of French capitalism.

The second is the international impact of the revolution. Apart from the inspiration that it provided to revolutionaries in other countries, the most obvious aspect is the direct intervention of the French state in the territories that it conquered. Indeed, one of the proofs of the bourgeois nature of the revolution is precisely the way in which it acted to attack feudalism outside its own borders, even after the internal reaction began with Thermidor. Heller's main references are to the extent to which the manufactured commodities of the conquered territories grew or failed to grow under French rule. There are clearly more of the latter than the former (Heller mentions Belgium, the Rhineland, Bavaria, Saxony, and Switzerland), but the issue is surely broader than this.[59] Like the New Model Army in Scotland between 1651 and 1660, the "people's armies" attempted to crush the local nobility, abolish feudal tenures and jurisdictions, and generally rationalize economy and society. Their failure to do so on a permanent basis—for which there are also parallels with the New Model Army in Scotland—was an important factor in determining why capitalist stabilization had to take place on the conservative basis of a restored monarchy. The extent to which the French were able to establish sister republics in conquered Europe depended on whether indigenous forces existed that were willing to be involved in the process of reform, but precisely because of the relative isolation and minority status of these forces, they were not necessarily those with popular followings, as the Spanish rebellion against France and its local supporters after 1808 was to prove. Where there were social forces committed to republican politics, it tended to be in those areas, principally Holland, where bourgeois revolutions had already taken place and consequently where these forces were opposed to the imperial role of the French armies.[60] In Britain, the most advanced of all, the ruling class were violently opposed to France and prepared to ally with absolutist reaction to defeat her, partly because the British bourgeoisie feared—as they had the Dutch in the 1650s—a successful rival, and partly because the very violence of the revolution had acted as an inspiration to nascent working-class forces in England and Scotland, and to bourgeois revolutionaries in Ireland. In some territories, like Hanover and Westphalia in 1807, the French abolished serfdom only for it to be restored after Napoleon withdrew in 1813. In other parts of the German states, notably in the Rhineland, it proved impossible to restore seignorial rights, but these examples were too few to be the basis for a Europe of independent states on the French model.

Perhaps the most important long-term international effect of the French Revolution, however, was the way in which it acted as a stimulus for revolution from above. Even in the short term, French victories led to internal reform. For Prussia, defeat at the hands of the Napoleonic armies at Jena and Auerstadt in 1806, and the subsequent humiliation of the Peace of Tilsit in 1807, seemed to demonstrate the superiority of free peasants over serfs as a source of manpower, while the indemnities imposed by the victorious French demanded an increase in revenues that was unlikely to be produced as long as serfdom endured.[61] The triumph of bourgeois revolution in France now meant that capitalism took on an unstoppable economic force it had not possessed when Britain was the only capitalist power of any size. But the bourgeoisies of Europe were themselves increasingly paralyzed between the conflicting desire to bring about revolutions that would place them in power and fear of the mass mobilizations that seemed necessary to achieve it. Ironically, it was the very grandeur and ferocity of the popular interventions that characterized the French Revolution that ensured it would never be repeated. Other forces, often from sections of the old ruling class, would eventually act in their stead, particularly in Germany, Italy, and Japan.

It is for this reason that I think we have to question some of the formulations that Heller uses here. His work enters a debate over two different if related questions. The first is the specific one of the French Revolution—what caused it, who was involved, what were their motivations, and so on. The other is the general one of whether it is possible to produce a theory of bourgeois revolution that can encompass the French example but also the quite different experiences of countries as distinct Scotland, Mexico, or China. Heller has made a considerable contribution to the first but tends to avoid the second. Indeed, Heller suggests that the French Revolution was bourgeois because it was led by the bourgeoisie.[62] This is certainly true of France, but if direct leadership is the main criterion then there have been precious few other bourgeois revolutions. Heller is surely correct to write: "In Marx's eyes the Revolution in France alongside the English Revolution was the classic form of a bourgeois revolution." "Classic" does not, however, imply that it was typical or characteristic, still less that "it was a model against which the ascent of the bourgeoisie to power elsewhere could be judged."[63] At certain points in his book Heller appears to recognize this, writing of Marx: "His view of the French Revolution as archetypical of bourgeois revolutions may . . . be questioned."[64] Elsewhere, however, he echoes the conventional view of the failure to repeat the French road: "We must acknowledge that transitions to capitalism occurred in Japan and Germany without such a rupture, albeit at an ultimately tragic historical cost in the form of fascism."[65] The view that Fascism arose because of the failure or unfulfilled character of the German Revolution has been subjected to searching Marxist criticism by David Blackbourn and, in particular, Geoff Eley, who have turned the entire argument on its head by arguing that the German Revolution was more authentically "bourgeois" than either the English or French. The tragedy of Fascism arose not because of the form taken by the German bourgeois revolution but as the result of the crisis of the Weimar Republic in the years immediately preceding the Nazi seizure of power.[66]

Conclusion

In many ways, Heller's work resembles that of the late Brian Manning, a writer who defended the bourgeois nature of the English Revolution in his work as vigorously as Heller does that of the French Revolution here. Manning was, however, suspicious of Marxist reappraisals of the bourgeois revolution that downplayed the conscious role of the bourgeoisie, seeing this as moving away from notions of class struggle.[67] I think Manning was wrong about this, since the view that revolutions do not *have* to be carried out by the bourgeoisie does not commit one to the claim that they are *never* carried out by the bourgeoisie, as in their different ways both the English and French revolutions were. It seems quite possible to be able to defend a conception of bourgeois self-emancipation, as Heller so ably does here, while still holding that this was not the only or the most common route to capitalist domination.

It will be interesting to find out what further thoughts Heller has on the subject. For the moment, however, this work is indispensable for anyone interested in a serious Marxist view of the subject. It is a notable demonstration that, contrary to what is claimed by Furet and everyone else who wants to wave goodbye to what Heller calls "the capital event of the modern age," the French Revolution is not yet over.[68]

6 The American Civil War Considered as a Bourgeois Revolution

Introduction

Consideration of any of the great bourgeois revolutions tends to suggest two speculative questions about the outcome: whether it could have been more radical than the one that was actually achieved, and whether it could have been achieved even if the revolution had not taken place. What do these involve in the specific case of the American Civil War? The alternative ending involves a permanent democratization of the former Confederate states, thus preventing the continuing oppression of the black population that in fact took place, albeit in different forms than under slavery. The alternative path to abolition involves a process of gradual, if reluctant, adaptation to capitalist norms of free labor on the part of the South, rather than having them imposed—and even then, incompletely—by military conquest. The point of making these queries is not of course to indulge in the type of "alternative history" most frequently associated with figures of the political right from Winston Churchill to Niall Ferguson, but to explore the balance between the objective limits and subjective possibilities present in this revolutionary situation. These limits and possibilities depended not only on developments internal to the United States of America but also on external pressures exercised by the expansion of capitalist economy on a global scale and the emergence of a states system whose main component parts were increasingly being reconfigured as centers of capital accumulation. In what follows I hope to demonstrate that while the first alternative was at least conceivable, the second was not.

Marxism and the US Civil War

Marxist interpretations of the Civil War fall into two broad historical periods, each with its own characteristic approaches. In the first, which encompassed the overlapping eras of the Second and Third Internationals, the war appeared as an uncomplicated conflict between two opposed and incompatible social systems—although paradoxically, what most distinguished the South as a distinct society, namely chattel slavery, received little attention. As a consequence, discussion of racism was perfunctory at best and the role of slaves or former slaves in achieving their own liberation tended to be dismissed.[1] Whatever other virtues these works possess—and I am not suggesting that these are entirely negligible—they were strongly economistic, often to the point of implying that the outcome of the war was inevitable.

The second period is coextensive with the emergence of the New Left in the US. The main movements of the time, the struggle for black civil rights and opposition to the war in Vietnam, inevitably influenced the attitude of those writing about the Civil War. In the case of the civil rights movement, it helped to refocus attention onto the situation of the slaves themselves, both before and after emancipation. In the case of the anti–Vietnam War movement, opposition to contemporary US imperialism began to influence retrospective judgments on the role of the North. Above all, the fact that the North did not initially enter the war to free the slaves and subsequently abandoned the freed black population after 1877 seemed to confirm the view that the US had always been a self-interested power, and that the motives of its leaders should, throughout history, always be treated with the greatest suspicion. The most important of these interpretations have not, however, dealt so much with the Civil War as with the societies that entered and emerged from it, with perhaps the two single greatest achievements of the historiography dealing respectively with the nature of antebellum Southern slave society and the failure of Reconstruction.[2] So great is the continuing sense that the war was (in the slogan of the time) "a rich man's war but a poor man's fight" that it is still possible to produce books—often excellent on their own terms—dealing solely with the experience of "the people," and in which the actual issues at stake in the outcome are treated merely as which "elite" would emerge victorious from its "center of power."[3]

In both periods the dominant "bourgeois revolution" interpretations of the Civil War were not of Marxist origin, nor did they employ the actual term. The first, dating from the late twenties, was the work of Charles and Mary Beard, historians who explicitly rejected Marxism for a politics that bridged progressivism and moderate reformist socialism while espousing their own brand of economic determinism.[4] Their conceptualization of the Civil War as a "Second American Revolution" that finally allowed the unfettered expansion of capitalism on the basis of industrialization and free farming was—as we shall see—not original to them, but their version became the dominant explanatory framework through which the period was understood by the left. A comparison between the Beards' version of the Civil War in *The Rise of American Civilization* (1927–30) and the nominally Marxist account by Louis Hacker in *The Triumph of American Capitalism* (1940), for example, does not reveal any fundamental differences of approach.[5] The Beards' influence spread far beyond the ranks of orthodox Communism, being accepted by later left-wing professional historians, independent Marxist scholars, and Trotskyists.[6] Followers of the Beards among professional historians also established the theoretical perspective on Reconstruction. Comer Vann Woodward placed the events explicitly in the context of comparable periods in earlier cases, specifically the French, describing Reconstruction as the "final phase of the revolution, the phase the French refer to as Thermidor" and writing that "if the Men of 1787 made the Thermidor of the first American Revolution, the Men of 1877 played a corresponding part in the Second American Revolution."[7] This account too had an influence on the revolutionary left.[8] The other interpretation, dating from the mid-sixties, was produced by Barrington Moore, who belongs to that tradition of radical sociology that is influenced by Marxism but by no means committed to the core doctrines of historical materialism. In *Social Origins of Dictatorship and Democracy* (1966), Moore traced what he called three different roads to "modernity" and expressed skepticism about the concept of bourgeois revolution, at least as it had been conventionally understood for most of the twentieth century.[9] Nevertheless, he wrote that "the American Civil War was the last revolutionary offensive on the part of what one may legitimately call urban or bourgeois capitalist democracy."[10] Moore himself referred back to the Beards, and many writers who had been influenced by them treated his work as a confirmation of or supplement to their earlier analysis, although in many respects Moore is more subtle, allowing—correctly, in my view—the possibility that the South might have won.[11]

John Ashworth's outstanding work on the origins of the Civil War must therefore be welcomed as an important attempt to deal with the sources of the conflict in explicitly Marxist terms. His first volume traces the growing divergence between North and South and concludes by anticipating the outcome of their antagonism: "The result would be war, emancipation, social upheaval—and the consolidation of capitalist relations of production in the United States. In other words the result would be a bourgeois revolution."[12] Yet in his second volume, an element of ambiguity enters. Ashworth shifts his focus from the consequences of the war ("the consolidation of capitalist relations of production") to the motivations of those who defended the Union, highlighting in particular their ideological support for wage labor and opposition to slavery: "Slavery was criticized, condemned, and finally destroyed in the United States essentially because by the norms of northern society it was increasingly unacceptable. These were the norms of northern free-labor society, one characterized by 'bourgeois social relations,' as they are often termed, with wage labor at their core."[13] According to Ashworth, in economic terms the North was not in crisis before the war (although there was a high level of internal class struggle) and the further development of industrial capitalism would not have been constrained by the continued existence of agrarian slavery in the South, however much of an abomination many Northerners found it. Indeed, as far as the South itself was concerned, conditions after the War were scarcely more advantageous to capitalism than before—a situation that would take decades to overcome. The triumph of the bourgeois revolution in the US was therefore coextensive with the ascendancy on a national scale of a hitherto sectional ideology encapsulated in the prewar Republican Party slogan of "free soil, free labor, and free men."

I agree with Ashworth that the American Civil War was a bourgeois revolution—or, more precisely, it constituted a major part of the global process of bourgeois revolution as it unfolded within the US. Where I disagree with him is over why this was so. Different ideologies were clearly important in the Civil War, but if they did not express different means of organizing social relations, then it simply involved two essentially capitalist powers, distinguished by the nature of their political regimes and in conflict because of overlapping territorial claims. Such a situation is quite familiar and can be explained in a number of ways, for example as secessionist nationalism or geopolitical rivalry, but it does not require a concept of bourgeois revolution. An attempt to understand the American Civil War in this way must therefore begin by defining the concept.

The issues at stake were clearly set out back in the sixties by a US academic called Gerald Runkle, in one of the most comprehensive attempts by a non-Marxist to assess the writings of Marx and Engels on the Civil War. Runkle argued that the very validity of historical materialism turned on whether the concept of revolution as understood by Marx and Engels was applicable to events between 1861 and 1865. What did Runkle understand this to involve?

> According to the basic Marxian theory, revolutions occur when the mode of production of a society becomes incompatible with the forces of production of that society. But that this was not so in the South is evident from the almost total absence of bourgeois development there. The "revolution" came from without, not from within. . . . The "class struggle" was indeed an unusual one, for one class was supreme in the South (and virtually non-existent in the North), another was powerful in the North (and virtually non-existent in the South). The great enemies of the privileged class in the South were not the people directly exploited by that class, the Negroes and the "poor whites," but the people in the North! . . . That great changes occurred in the North before, during, and after the war does not mean that the North was spear-heading a revolution in the Marxian sense. Marx's mistake here (and elsewhere) is to mistake the results of the war with the cause of the war. He anticipated very well the results of the war. A more capitalistic America did emerge. The "forces of production" developed rapidly during the war, industry grew, and fortunes were made. The bourgeoisie entered into a period of almost unchallenged supremacy. The economy and society of America were indeed revolutionized. This does not mean, however, that the growing strength of industrial capitalism brought about the war. Many other factors operated with it to bring about the war which was in turn a great causal factor for modern capitalism. In short, the advance of capitalism was a conspicuous, but not the only, result of a war which was brought about by many factors of which bourgeois development was only one.

Consequently, the question of why Marx did not continue to develop his analysis of the Civil War after it concluded presents no great mystery: "One suspects that the

American Civil War did not, therefore, lend itself to the kind of interpretation that would enhance or confirm dialectical materialism. If this is so, then the war constitutes a tacit refutation of basic Marxian theory."[14]

It is true that some care needs to be exercised in trying to extrapolate a general view of the Civil War from Marx's and Engels's contemporary writings. They expressed their views on the subject in three places: personal correspondence between the two men (much of which is taken up with analysis of the military conduct of the war, a subject over which they regularly disagreed until the very final stages); reports for the abolitionist Horace Greeley's paper, the *New York Daily Tribune*, and the Viennese *Die Presse*; and two public pronouncements, in the form of letters to Presidents Lincoln and Johnson, on behalf of the International Working Men's Association (IWMA).[15] Each of these presents its own difficulties. In the private letters, a number of shared assumptions were obviously taken for granted, and this theoretical context has to be recreated by the reader. In the articles, certain complexities were omitted for a general newspaper audience, which tends to give an oversimplified picture of their views. In the open letters, the need to define a working-class position in relation to the conflict inevitably took precedence over the requirements of theory. In addition, the sources on which Marx and Engels based their analysis were limited to often inaccurate newspaper reports and a handful of books on the subject of the South, the two most important of which appeared only during the first year of the War.[16] Their correspondence suggests that they also received updates from German émigrés in the North like August Willich, who fought for the Union. The resulting inconsistencies and flaws in their writings have led to accusations of, among other things, their being over-sympathetic to Lincoln, of neglecting the imperial dimension of Northern war aims on the one hand and the popular character of Southern smallholder resistance to them on the other, of exaggerating working-class opposition to slavery in the North and in Britain, and of succumbing to economic reductionism.[17]

In fact, although much of their work remains of interest, a coherent Marxist analysis is more likely to emerge by starting from first principles rather than from trying to synthesize these fragments. Such an analysis should be able to demonstrate that the elements that Runkle claimed disproved historical materialism—the lack of internal class contradiction within Southern society, the external imposition of revolutionary change, the lack of causal connection between the Northern victory and subsequent capitalist development—do nothing of the kind. Although Marx and Engels did have a very general theory of revolution as resulting from the conflict between the forces and relations of production, they conceived of bourgeois and proletarian revolutions as taking very different forms. In the first part of this article I will therefore offer a general definition of bourgeois revolutions, abstracted from their development down to the 1870s but excluding from consideration at this stage either the American Civil War era or earlier revolutionary periods in US history. In the second I will attempt to show that the real cause of the war, what made it inescapable, was not so much capitalist development in the North as—to use the term used by the slave owners themselves—the "peculiar" nature of class society in the South.

WHAT WERE THE BOURGEOIS REVOLUTIONS?

The "bourgeois revolution" is a concept, a way of identifying historical processes that belong to the same class or category: the difficulty is that there is no agreement about what the essential qualities of the concept are. One solution might be to adopt the procedure Marx outlined in the preface to the first edition of *Capital*—in other words, select the "classic" case where the fundamental characteristics of the concept are most fully developed, as he did in relation to the development of capitalism in England.[18] In one sense this is exactly what Marx and particularly Engels did in relation to bourgeois revolutions, where the "classic" case is taken to be that of France.[19] The French Revolution can indeed yield many insights into the dynamics of subsequent revolutionary movements in which mass mobilizations are central; but the most important of these cases, the Russian Revolution of 1917 and the Iranian Revolution of 1978–79, were not bourgeois revolutions. In other words, the French Revolution illuminates the process of revolution from below in a general sense, but it cannot do so in relation to the underlying nature of the bourgeois revolutions as a specific category, precisely because one of the questions at issue is whether they necessarily involve popular mobilizations.

The key problem, in this context, is the general applicability of the procedure outlined by Marx and Engels. It is certainly appropriate when discussing the capitalist mode of production, which by definition has certain indispensable characteristics, such as generalized commodity production or the self-expansion of capital. It would be equally appropriate in a discussion of any other embodiment of structured social relationships, like the absolutist state, where the French case before 1789 can also be treated as "classic." But the bourgeois revolution is not the embodiment of a structured relationship like that of wage labor to capital or peasants to the tax collector; it is the unfolding of a process. Consequently, to treat the characteristics of the French case as the highest level of bourgeois revolutionary development is to imply that countries that do not display these characteristics have either undergone an incomplete experience or failed to undergo the experience at all.[20]

Perhaps another revolution might be more suitable as a "classic" case then? Geoff Eley has argued that the German experience, in avoiding the "volatile scenario of the English and French Revolutions," is actually a better model.[21] But is Otto von Bismarck any more of a representative figure than Oliver Cromwell or Maximilien Robespierre? In fact, the German experience of territorial expansion by military conquest at the hands of an internally transformed absolutist state has close parallels only with the contemporary events of the Italian Risorgimento.

The problem is irresolvable so long as we treat "bourgeois" as referring to the dominant agency and "revolution" as taking a particular form. An alternative approach would be to place the concept of bourgeois revolution on the terrain of what Andrew Abbott calls "turning point" analysis, in which "neither the beginning nor the end of the turning point can be defined until the whole turning point has passed, since it is the arrival and establishment of a new trajectory . . . that defines the turning point itself." Consequently, "turning point analysis makes sense only after the fact."[22] What would the turning point be in the case of bourgeois revolutions? Alex Callinicos has argued that we should "judge a bourgeois revolution by the degree to which it succeeds in establishing an autonomous center of capital accumulation, even if it fails to democratize the political order, or to eliminate feudal social relations."[23] The test is therefore whether it can be empirically demonstrated that a particular sequence of events ("a bourgeois revolution") led directly to an outcome (the establishment of "an independent center of capital accumulation") that would not otherwise have taken place at that point in history. Since the two characteristics that Callinicos cites as nonessential to the completion of the bourgeois revolution—democratization of the political order and the elimination of feudal and other precapitalist social relations—are central to the American case, their lack of relevance requires some elaboration.

I have dealt with the issue of democracy earlier in this book.[24] The possibility of feudalism in any form surviving a bourgeois revolution is perhaps an even more controversial issue. For if one outcome can be expected of bourgeois revolutions, surely it is to eliminate feudal and other precapitalist modes of production? In fact, this need not be the case. As Geoffrey Ste Croix has pointed out, the key issue in determining the class nature of any society is not necessarily how most labor is performed, but rather how the labor that produced the surplus accruing to the ruling class is performed.[25] It is therefore quite conceivable that a postrevolutionary society might contain precapitalist social relations, perhaps even involving a majority of the direct producers, as long as the ruling class—which by definition includes those in ultimate control of the state—occupied their position through the competitive accumulation of capital based on wage labor. In practice, of course, precapitalist and capitalist modes of production have not coexisted in some dualist fashion, as the former would then be subject to capitalist laws of motion—indeed, another way of defining a bourgeois revolution might be the process by which political obstacles to their unimpeded sway are removed. Jairus Banaji once argued that Marx used the term "mode of production" (*produktionsweise*) in two ways: one to refer to the technical process of production, or the labor process more generally; the other to encompass an entire epoch in the history of the social organization of production. The existence of wage labor, for example, does not necessarily signify the emergence of the capitalist mode of production; wage labor also took place under feudalism, but primarily as a means of meeting the consumption requirements of the lords rather than contributing to the self-expansion of capital. It is rather that the existence of the capitalist mode of production determines that wage labor becomes the central means through which surplus extraction takes place. Equally, however, various types of unfree labor associated with precapitalist modes of production, including slavery itself, can also take place within the context of the capitalist mode of production and, in the terms Marx uses in the *Grundrisse*, both posit and produce capital.[26] The relevance of this argument to our theme is that it perfectly possible for feudal, absolutist, or tributary states to be overthrown, thus removing the last obstacle to establishing "an independent center of capital accumulation," while some social relations remain, initially at least, those associated with precapitalist modes in the purely technical sense.

If the historical role of the bourgeoisie is contingent in an outcome-based definition of bourgeois revolution, then it should be clear from the preceding discussion that the transformation of the state is necessary in each case. The state was central to both the process and the outcome, since the seizure of state power was the goal of the revolutionaries, and—if achieved—it ensured that the territory they controlled could become the site of "an autonomous center of capital accumulation": this theme remained constant across the overlapping periodizations in the overall pattern of development down to the consolidation of the capitalist system. The first period, characterized by revolutions primarily from below, encompasses those in the United Netherlands and England, where economic life was already subject to capitalist laws of motion and only the absolutist state needed to be overthrown to complete the process of transition. The second, still characterized by revolutions primarily from below, begins with the French Revolution and includes all the subsequent, mainly unsuccessful revolutions that followed it down to 1848, where capitalism was still subordinate to feudal laws of motion in addition to the bourgeoisie being politically subordinate to the absolutist state. The third, now characterized by revolutions primarily from above, is compressed into the years between 1859 and 1871, which saw the Italian Risorgimento, German unification, the Japanese Meiji Restoration, Canadian Confederation, and (less decisively) the liberation of the serfs in Russia. In these cases, levels of capitalist development are mixed, extensive in Canada outside of the former French colonies, minimal in Japan and Russia; but the impetus for change comes from a ruling-class fraction within the absolutist state or, in the case of Canada, the colonial state. The central paradox of this shifting trajectory is that as the outcome of capitalist and particularly industrial capitalist development becomes more explicit, the agents of revolution become further and further removed from the capitalist class.

There are, however, two revolutions that do not fit these periodizations. Separated from each other in both scale and time, they are linked by virtue of being the only two examples where a fully conscious bourgeoisie set out to establish capitalism in a part of the sovereign territory of the state from which it had previously been excluded, and in both cases their ability to do so was dependent on prior control of a centralized military and juridical apparatus. One was the Scottish Revolution, during the suppression of the Jacobite Rising of 1745–46 and the transformation of agricultural relations in the decades that followed—a process that seems to have been the first example of the bourgeois revolution from above characteristic of the mid-nineteenth century. Although in no sense a prototype or model for its successors, it did involve the same set of elements that produced them: a favorable geo-political context (the global inter-systemic conflict between Britain and France); a centralizing and expansionist capitalist territory seeking to unify a new nation-state (England and Britain); and the formation of a new ruling class drawn from those of the previously existing nations (England and Scotland).[27] The other was, of course, the American Civil War, to which we can now return.

The first problem for any Marxist analysis of the bourgeois revolutionary process in the United States is to set its chronological parameters. We should not be constrained by the time periods deployed in conventional narratives of national history. The English Revolution does not correspond to the period of the Civil Wars (i.e., 1642–49), but encompasses the entire period from the beginning of Scottish resistance to Charles I in 1637 through to the restoration of the Stuart monarchy in 1660, together with the Glorious Revolution of 1688–89. Similarly, the duration of the American Revolution cannot be restricted to the period of the Civil War, but must include the subsequent period of reconstruction, since it was during the postwar years to 1877 that the form taken by the US as a capitalist nation-state was finally established. Chronologically, then, it falls into the last period, the period of revolutions from above, and has one important characteristic in common with most of them. Prussia, Piedmont, and Upper Canada (i.e., modern Ottawa) successfully incorporated, by a variety of means, a range of smaller, less powerful or less economically developed regions into the new nation-states of Germany, Italy, and Canada. The North played the same role in relation to the US, although here the objective was to prevent the secession of a major part of the existing nation-state, rather than to initiate state formation. Yet in other respects the Civil War era has more in common with earlier periods of bourgeois revolution, in terms of increasing political radicalization and popular involvement, military suppression, and juridical abolition of precapitalist social relations—and a conservative resolution that disappointed radical hopes and failed to complete the liberation of the oppressed.

THE US WAR OF INDEPENDENCE AS A POLITICAL REVOLUTION

What does dating the American Revolution from 1861 to 1877 mean for our assessment of the most important episode in American history prior to the Civil War, the one officially regarded by the US state as "the Revolution"? One approach would be to regard these conflicts as the opening and closing moments of a prolonged period of revolutionary transformation, a view first expressed in the aftermath of the Civil War by several of the participants. Here, for example, is the Northern military commander and twentieth president of the United States, James Garfield: "It will not do to speak of the gigantic revolution through which we have lately passed as a thing to be adjusted and settled by a change in administration. It was cyclical, epochal, century-wide, and to be studied in its broad and grand perspective, a revolution of even wider scope, so far as time is concerned, than the Revolution of 1776."[28]

This conception of a prolonged process has some Marxist support. Mike Davis, for example, writes: "It is possible to see the Revolution of 1776 . . . as very much a civil war against Loyalist *comprador* strata, and the Civil War as a continuing revolution against an informal British imperialism that had incorporated the cotton export economy of the South in an alliance of neo-colonial dependency."[29] More commonly, however, the two wars have been treated as distinct episodes, with the second resolving the issues left unfinished by the first. Although the interpretation of the Civil War as a "Second American Revolution" was made famous by the Beards, it too goes back to the Civil War itself and indeed predates it. "Revolutions never go backward," wrote the abolitionist James Redpath, in the wake of the mini–civil war in Kansas: "The Second American Revolution has begun. Kansas was its Lexington. Texas will be its Bunker Hill, *and South Carolina its Yorktown.*"[30] During postwar reconstruction, the French Radical Georges Clemenceau, who lived and worked in the US between 1866 and 1869, described the leading Radical Republican Thaddeus Stevens as the "Robespierre" of the "Second American Revolution."[31] And as we have seen, the notion has subsequently exercised a wide influence over both professional historians and Marxist revolutionaries. More recently the notion of a "second revolution" has been generalized by Anderson to encompass all the major states that experienced bourgeois revolutions.[32] Nevertheless, there are two difficulties involved in seeing the Civil War as either the culmination of a prolonged process or a "corrective" second revolution.

One is that from referring to decisive turning points that removed obstacles to capitalist development, the concept of bourgeois revolution is stretched to include subsequent alterations in the form of the existing capitalist state that brings it into more perfect alignment with the requirements of competitive accumulation—realignments to which there can be no foreseeable end this side of the socialist revolution. Why then could there not be a third American Revolution in the form of the New Deal, or—given the way in which the Civil War and Reconstruction notoriously failed to achieve equality for the former slave population—a fourth in the form of the civil rights movement? Nor need we stop at this point: some Marxists have referred to the neoliberal ascendancy since the late seventies in general terms as a "bourgeois revolution from above."[33]

The other difficulty, which again has particular resonance for the US, is that it presupposes that the first bourgeois revolution did at least begin to remove barriers to capitalist development, yet this is precisely what is at issue in the case of the War of Independence. The Dutch Revolution and, to a far greater extent, the English Revolution both involved two distinct movements that temporarily converged in opposition to foreign or native absolutism. One successfully consolidated the supremacy of capitalist relations of production; the other failed to achieve equality of condition, a goal that was, implicitly at least, directed as much against the new capitalism as the old feudalism. The American War of Independence was different. It certainly involved the second type of movement, and in this context socialists have rightly emphasized the element of internal class struggle within the independence movement, together with the often contradictory role of minorities. These accounts have provided a necessary corrective to a bourgeois historiography that tends to argue that economic or social issues were largely absent from the war, and that the key motives of the revolutionaries were entirely political and ideological.[34] Marxists have occasionally expressed similar views, albeit linked to different value judgments, where they have allowed their hostility to contemporary US imperialism to overwhelm their historical judgment.[35] This essentially conservative conception has more recently allowed the American Revolution to be celebrated by neoliberal ideologues as providing a model of revolution that, unlike its French and Russian successors, did not involve any utopian attempts at fundamental social transformation.[36] But valuable though alternative accounts are, they do not answer the question of whether or not events between 1776 and 1783 constituted a bourgeois revolution, since popular insurgencies during these years tended to be concerned either with the defense or extension of the franchise, or with resisting the inequalities resulting from existing *capitalist* relations of production.

Unlike the Dutch or the English, the Americans did not have to liberate themselves from a feudal-absolutist state, but rather from the constitutional monarchy that emerged from the settlement of 1688, which they accused of betraying them by behaving in a despotic and tyrannical manner. William Gordon, author of one the first histories of the Revolutionary War, argued in 1776 that property qualifications for voting were "the most hurtful remnant of the Feudal Constitution."[37] The most detailed discussion of the question was however by John Adams, in a series of articles published in the *Boston Gazette* in 1765 and eventually published as "A Dissertation on the Canon and Feudal Law." Adams cited Kames and Rousseau as authorities to prove "the feudal system to be inconsistent with liberty and the rights of mankind." His main point, however, is to demonstrate that the British monarchy was intent on imposing feudalism on the colonies. What he meant by this, however, was mainly the imposition of the Stamp Act.[38] Alas, both restrictions on the franchise and interference with the freedom of the press are compatible with, or even characteristic of, capitalist societies.

It is true that capitalist development was uneven across the colonies. It is also true that there were three genuine attempts to install or "revive" systemic feudalism in the new colonial context, in New York, Maryland, and the Carolinas—the latter with a constitution involving hereditary serfdom drawn up by Mr. Agrarian Capitalism himself, John Locke. All were resisted; all failed. The main feudal mechanism that landlords consistently attempted to impose was the charging of quit rents in lieu of certain kinds of labor service or other obligations. But since these obligations had not, in most cases, been performed by tenants in the first place, this represented less the introduction of feudalism and more a device by absentee capitalist owners to supplement the rent paid by their tenants.[39] The real obstacle to capitalist development in North America was not feudalism but slavery. Slavery is not, of course, necessarily incompatible with capitalism, nor was it in the US, where even in the North many sectors of the economy, such as the New England textile mills, assumed the existence of slavery in the South. But there are definite structural limits to how far capitalist self-expansion can proceed on this basis. More importantly, as we shall see, in the South slavery became the basis of an entire society and ultimately of a short-lived state (the Confederacy), the expansionist aims of which, had they been successful, would have blocked and even rolled back the development of capitalism in the Americas, and perhaps beyond. The continued existence of slavery is therefore the main objection to regarding the War of Independence as a bourgeois revolution, even an incomplete example. For if the definition of a bourgeois revolution is that it allows the unimpeded development of capitalism, then it is difficult to see how a conflict that also strengthened and allowed the extension of a rival, noncapitalist mode of production can be described in this way.

Bourgeois revolutions are a type of social revolution, a struggle to consolidate the transformation of one type of society into another, which involves not merely seizing but transforming the state itself. Historically, social revolutions are extremely rare, and if we leave aside the transition to feudalism as not involving a revolution (except in a metaphorical sense), and the socialist revolution on the grounds that it has not yet been permanently achieved, the bourgeois revolutions are the only successful examples that we have. As this degree of rarity suggests, most revolutions are not social but political.[40] Political revolutions are struggles within society for control of the existing state, but leave the nature of that state, and economy and society, fundamentally intact. They may involve more or less popular participation, may result in more or less improvement in the condition of the majority, but ultimately the class that was in control of the means of production at the beginning will remain so at the end (although individuals and political organizations may have been replaced on the way), and the class that was exploited within the productive process at the beginning will also remain so at the end (although concessions may have been made to secure its acquiescence or participation). The French Revolution of 1848, or in more recent years the Iranian Revolution of 1978, the displays of "people power" in the Philippines, Thailand, and Serbia, and the "color revolutions" in the former republics of the USSR, were all revolutions of this type. Political revolutions sometimes have social aspects and social revolutions always have political implications, but the terms indicate an essential difference. The relation between political revolutions and the bourgeois revolutions is therefore a complex one. Some revolutions that, taken by themselves, appear to be merely political are in fact parts of a more extended bourgeois revolution: the English Revolution of 1688, for example, has this relationship to the Revolution of 1640. By 1688 the overwhelming majority of the English ruling class faced an absolutist regime with virtually no support within the country itself. Consequently the Stuarts had to seek support internally among the more peripheral or colonial areas ruled by the composite monarchy in Scotland and Ireland, as well as externally among the feudal-absolutist rivals to English power in Continental Europe—above all, France. In 1861 the Northern ruling class faced a vibrant and expansive *society* that since secession had established its own rival state. In other words, unlike 1688, 1861 was not the final move in a game where the course of play has already decided the nature, if not the timing, of the outcome; it signaled the opening of the game itself. Interestingly, the Beards themselves seem to have come to this conclusion, writing in their major work not only that "the so-called civil war was in reality a Second American Revolution" but also that it was "in a strict sense, the First."[41]

The War of Independence is therefore best understood as political revolution, more akin to 1688 or 1830 than 1640 or 1789. In the case of the US, the chronological order of importance is reversed: it is the latter period that is decisive. The Civil War did not "complete the unfinished tasks of the War of Independence" because, except for a minority of radicals, the latter was never intended as a means of accomplishing these "tasks" in the first place. Instead, the end of British rule allowed all of the social relations that existed in the US—including small commodity production, capitalism, and slavery—to continue as before, but without the interference of the Crown in Parliament. But of all the different types of social relations it was capitalism that was initially the weakest. As Michael Merrill has pointed out, the principal difference between the Democratic Republicans and the Federalists following the achievement of independence was in their attitude to "commercial society." Adam Smith could be invoked by both sides, of course, but insofar as he was in favor of a stable agrarian society in which the main economic actors were yeoman farmers and landowners (slave owners were a different matter), this could be done with greater credibility by the former. The latter, above all Andrew Hamilton, were interested in developing something closer to what we would now think of as capitalism—although as Merrill notes, this was largely as a means to an end, the end being the elevation of the monied commercial and industrial interest as a base to provide revenue through tax and customs, to construct a viable state power.[42] As one of Hamilton's biographers observes, unlike the other founders of the republic, who "were content merely to effect a political revolution," Hamilton saw the role of Lawgiver differently: "He set out to effect what amounted to a social revolution."[43] In this respect there are interesting parallels with the later careers of Bismarck and Cavour as instigators of revolution from above, but unlike them he did not succeed, as, in the short-term at least, it was the agrarians organized in the Democratic Republican Party who won out, following the victory of Thomas Jefferson in the presidential election of 1800.

THE UNIQUENESS OF THE OLD SOUTH

The "social" nature of the impending conflict was well understood on both sides of the Mason-Dixon Line long before the Confederate attack on Fort Sumter. Southern ideologists were quite aware of the threatening historical precedents. One author,

William Drayton, compared abolitionists to English Puritans during the days of the Commonwealth: "Their columns are almost nasal with cant; and it might be supposed, from the aspect of their publications, that the days of Cromwell were revived, and that his fanatical followers, heated into tenfold fury, were abroad in the land." He argued that if abolitionists succeeded in freeing the slave population it would lead to a repetition of the Haitian Revolution: "Have they studied the history of St. Domingo; and are they prepared to let loose upon the refined and innocent ladies of the South, the savage Negro, incapable of restraint, and wild with ungovernable passions?" Finally, Drayton saw parallels with the French Revolution, claiming that once the opponents of slavery had established equality for blacks, the next stage in their madness would be to establish it for women! Naturally, a quotation from Edmund Burke fell to hand to support his case:

> The French revolutionists, from whom the fanatics derive their notions of abolition, directly undertook to assert the rights of women. The French legislature took up this subject in 1789. "Succeeding Assemblies"; says Burke in his *Regicide Peace*, "went the full length of the principle, and gave a license to divorce at the mere pleasure of either party, and at one month's notice." The reason alleged was "that women had been too long under the tyranny of parents and husbands." To such lengths will these abstractionists carry their insane zeal.[44]

Interestingly, Georgian secessionists actually described the establishment of the Confederacy as a "political revolution," which had been made necessary to forestall the social revolution that the abolitionists would otherwise unleash upon them.[45] The more radical elements in the North were clear that this was exactly what they were planning, although they tended to hold the South responsible for forcing such a course of action upon them. In the debates on confiscation of slaveholder property from the second session of the 37th Congress in 1862, for example, Senator Morrill of Maine offered a robustly materialist explanation for the conflict: "Sir, what we are witnessing and encountering is the old struggle of a class for power and privilege which has so often convulsed the world repeating itself in our history. A class identified with a local and exceptional institution, grown powerful through political representation, demands to govern."[46]

Marx was therefore in the unusual situation, for once, of being in broad agreement with his bourgeois contemporaries in terms of his interpretation of events. Although Marx did not use the term *bourgeois revolution* in relation to the war, he did situate it within his conception of a struggle between two different societies that he first raised in the "Economic and Philosophical Manuscripts" (1844) and first made concrete in "The Bourgeoisie and the Counter-revolution" (1848).[47] In his discussion of the implications of a Confederate victory, Marx wrote:

> What would in fact take place would be not a dissolution of the Union, but a *reorganization* of it, a *reorganization on the basis of slavery,* under the recognized control

of the slaveholding oligarchy. . . . The slave system would infect the whole Union. In the Northern states, where Negro slavery is in practice unworkable, the white working class would gradually be forced down to the level of helotry. This would fully accord with the loudly proclaimed principle that only certain races are capable of freedom, and as the actual labor is the lot of the Negro in the South, so in the North it is the lot of the German and the Irishman, or their direct descendants. The present struggle between the South and North is, therefore, nothing but a struggle between two social systems, the system of slavery and the system of free labor. The struggle has broken out because the two systems can no longer live peacefully side by side on the North American continent. It can only be ended by the victory of one system or the other.[48]

There is little dispute about the capitalist nature of the North; but for Marxists at least, if the Civil War was indeed a struggle between two expansionist social systems, then we need to consider in more detail what kind of economy and society prevailed in the South.

All class societies have involved the ownership of slaves at some point in their history; but very few have been slave societies, societies dominated by the slave mode of production where, in the terms used by Robin Blackburn, slavery is not "ancillary" but "systemic." In effect, there have only been five. Two were in the ancient world: the Greek city-states and parts of the Roman Empire, including Rome itself. Three arose during the transition to capitalism: the South of the United States until 1865, Cuba until 1886, and Brazil until 1888. The proportion of slaves in the South was broadly similar to that in Greece and Rome, at 30–35 percent of the population; in Cuba and Brazil it was higher, nearer 40 percent; yet it was the South that was the most committed to slavery. Why?[49]

I earlier argued that it is possible for a mode of production that was precapitalist in the technical sense to still be subject to capitalist laws of motion: was this true of slavery in the South? Shortly before the Civil War broke out Marx wrote in the notebooks that would become the *Grundrisse*: "*Negro slavery*—a purely industrial slavery—which is besides, incompatible with the development of bourgeois society and disappears with it, *presupposes* wage labor, and if other free states with wage labor did not exist alongside it, if, instead, the Negro states were isolated, then all social conditions there would immediately turn into pre-civilized forms."[50] In a further entry he adds: "The fact that we now not only call the plantation owners in America capitalists, but that they *are* capitalists, is based on their existence as anomalies within a world market based on free labor."[51] Marx is making a number of different claims here, which superficially appear inconsistent, leading many later Marxists to resolve them in unsatisfactory ways. David Roediger, for example, writes that "the form of appropriation makes a vital difference [between North and South]," but "the logic of both systems was, for Marx, capitalist."[52] Why then did Marx argue that the war was intersystemic in nature?

The central issue here is the relationship of the South to capitalism. Marx identified at least one contemporary society, Tokugawa Japan, as being classically feudal.[53] Clearly, the society based on chattel slavery in the South was not of the same order; but neither did it simply involve a variant of capitalism. As was the case in the Americas more generally, slavery in the South began in the seventeenth century as way of resolving the shortage of labor by acquiring and organizing the direct producers in a particular way. As Peter Kolchin has noted, it therefore "had more in common with the serfdom that was emerging in Russia and other parts of Eastern Europe than with many of the premodern slaveries."[54] It is also true that both the Eastern European feudal estates established under the "second serfdom" and American slave plantations produced for the world market; yet this should not blind us to the essential difference between them. The former was originally a response to depopulation that eventually found a market for cereal crops in Western Europe, but did not import manufactured goods in return. The latter existed and expanded entirely because of the Western market for cotton and was mainly dependent on the West for manufactured goods. In short, they were not, as Blackburn puts it, *"equivalently distant from the capitalist mode."*[55] The plantations were therefore integrated into the capitalist world economy, even though they did not correspond to the capitalist mode of production in the purely technical sense, since both involved slave labor. As we have seen, however, this is not the only issue involved: it is also important whether the plantations were "capital positing" and "capital producing," which they were.

A more plausible argument for the noncapitalist nature of the plantations is that they effectively involved a form of merchant capital—that is, one of the two forms of capital (the other being usury) that coexisted with virtually all previous modes of production, where profit is realized through "buying cheap and selling dear" rather than by increasing value in production. On these grounds, it is possible to argue, as Banaji does, that the plantations were not fully subordinate to capitalist laws of motion, because they involved simple reproduction, the formal subsumption of labor, and the production of absolute surplus value through lengthening the working day and intensifying labor. Where expansion took place, it was not through improvements to technological capacity but by extending the territory of the plantation; reproduction of the labor force involved the external supply of slaves through the market.[56] While this is all true, I am not convinced that it proves the noncapitalist nature of the slave plantations. Indeed, it would only do so if they had existed in an environment in which feudal or tributary laws of motion otherwise prevailed, in which case the comparison with, say, medieval merchant capital would be truly apt.

The real issue here is not that some social relations of production in the South had an ambiguous relationship to capitalism; it is that the South had constructed an entire society around these relationships and that, with the secession of the Confederacy, that society had consolidated itself in a new and aggressive state. Although the South was not feudal, it did derive much of its self-image from a particular romantic version of feudal society. Mark Twain was being his usual hyperbolic self when he held Sir Walter Scott responsible for the Civil War in chapter 46 of *Life on the Mis-*

sissippi.[57] There is no doubt that Scott's romanticism contributed to the self-identity of the Southerner, as did the entire mythical heritage of Scottish clanship, not least in the formation of the Ku Klux Klan in December 1865.[58] One young Confederate, the son of a South Carolina planter, wrote to his mother during the war: "I am blessing old Sir Walter Scott daily, for teaching me, when young, how to rate knightly honor, and our noble ancestry for giving me such a State to fight for."[59] There is a double irony here. One is that Scott, for all his conservatism, was a characteristic figure of the Scottish Enlightenment whose novels were intended to demonstrate to his contemporaries that no matter how heroic Scottish feudal society had been, the warlike pursuit of honor was rightly doomed to be replaced by commerce and the peaceful pursuit of money: in the South his elegies were misunderstood as celebrations. The other is that, in due course, the Southern planters were to be destroyed in the way that in history most closely corresponded to the demise of the Highland chiefs and feudal lords traced by Scott in the Waverley novels.

Elizabeth Fox-Genovese and Eugene Genovese claim that the Old South could have gone in two directions: either toward industrialization, which would have meant abandoning slavery and investing capital in expanded reproduction ("qualitative development"); or toward an expansion of slavery where capital is essentially tied up in simple reproduction ("quantitative development").[60] In fact, the ruling class in the South was faced with two related difficulties that did not exist in other societies with widespread slavery, and that meant the latter "choice" was the only real option, as can be seen by contrasting the Old South with other types of society that employed forms of unfree labor. As many historians have noted, even by mid-century, it was the South, rather than the North, that most resembled the rest of the world: free labor was still relatively rare outside of Western Europe and the Northern states. But although unfree labor was still more common, it was also inescapably in retreat: "At the time of the American Revolution, slavery could be found almost everywhere in the New World; on the eve of the Civil War, far more slaves resided in the Southern states than in all the other slave societies combined . . . and—together with Russian serfdom—Southern slavery had come to symbolize for much of the Western world a retrograde system resistant to change."[61] In the same year as the outbreak of the Civil War, the Russian Tsar began what Lenin called "the era of the Russian bourgeois revolution" by liberating the serfs.[62] This was a diluted version of a much more widespread process of "self-transformation" by feudal lords who realized that, subject to the pressures generated by an increasingly capitalist world, the only way to halt their decline, let alone preserve their current position, was to embrace capitalist landownership. In this way they could at least remain members of a dominant class, albeit within a new set of social relations and using new methods of exploitation. Prussia was at the forefront of this process.

Terence Byres has characterized the "Prussian Path" as a form of "capitalism from above" in two senses, not only because the feudal landlord class transformed itself into a capitalist class, but also because they consequently controlled the process, "in a manner which stifled any development of the peasant economy . . . whereby a capitalist agriculture might emerge from an increasingly differentiated peasantry."[63] The top-down nature of the process was then increasingly adopted by other feudal ruling classes, such as those in Hungary and Bohemia, as the nineteenth century progressed.[64] As in the earlier case of Scotland after the Jacobite defeat at Culloden, military defeat precipitated the reform process. In the case of Prussia, it was defeat by the Napoleonic armies at Jena and Auerstadt in 1806, the outcomes of which seemed to demonstrate the superiority of free peasants over serfs as a source of manpower, while the indemnities imposed by the victorious French demanded an increase in revenues that was unlikely to be produced as long as serfdom endured.[65]

Why did the Prussian Junkers and the Southern planters take such different attitudes to the introduction of wage labor? Slavery was widespread in the South but in most cases relatively small-scale. On the eve of war, over 97 percent of slave-holders owned less than fifty slaves, and only 0.1 percent had estates with more than two hundred.[66] But the majority of Southerners were not slave owners, and it is not as if there were no major class differences between the farmers and the slave owners. According to Fox-Genovese and Genovese, the yeoman farmers accepted the system "not because they did not understand their position, or because they were panicked by racial fears, and certainly not because they were stupid, but because they saw them-selves as aspiring slaveholders or as non-slaveholding beneficiaries of a slaveholding world that constituted the only world they knew."[67] The problem for the ruling class was not so much with the yeomen, however, as with the whites below them in the social structure, those who did not own slaves and who had little or no chance of ever owning them. As Theodore Allen has pointed out, it was in order to prevent the emergence of solidarity between this group and black slaves that the condition of racialized slavery had to be absolute: "If the mere presumption of liberty was to serve as a mark of social status for masses of European-Americans without real prospects of upward social mobility, and yet induce them to abandon their opposition to the plantocracy and enlist them actively, or at least passively, in keeping down the Negro bond-laborer with whom they had made common cause in the course of Bacon's Rebellion, the presumption of liberty had to be denied to free African-Americans."[68]

Both Prussian Junkers and the Southern planters understood that commercial success was essential if they were to continue as landed classes, but the Prussian serfs were not a group distinct from the rest of their society, and the Junkers were consequently more vulnerable to the threat of a democratic movement uniting all the oppositional forces against them, perhaps in the form—long hoped for by En-gels—of a repetition of the Peasant War of 1525, alongside an urban insurrection by the modern working class. In one sense, the Southern planters were in a stronger position than their German contemporaries, precisely because the slaves had been absolutely separated from all other subordinate social groups and were not in a po-sition to make common cause with them. But the paradox of this position was that, unlike serfdom, slavery was not a system that could be reformed out of existence, because the entire social structure was based on the position that blacks were racially inferior and incapable of any other role than that of slaves, and could be expected to revert to savagery and exact revenge if freed from the supposedly paternalistic but firm restraints imposed by their masters.[69] There was manufacturing, but it too was constrained by slavery. Firms tended to be smaller and less productive than in the Midwest, and were often operated on a part-time basis, as a supplement to income mainly derived from agriculture. There is no reason to suppose that Southern manufacturers were intrinsically less capable of being successful capitalists than their Northern cousins, but the restricted market characteristic of the Southern economy acted as a barrier to them, both in terms of the limited consumption demands of the large proportion of the workforce who were slaves, and the fact that the larger farms and plantations produced their own small-scale goods for use.[70] As we have already noted, large-scale machinery was imported from Western Europe, and especially Britain. It is not that the Southern slave economy was incapable of either dynamic spurts of growth or adaptation to changing conditions; in fact it displayed both characteristics at different times between 1783 and 1861. It is rather that a system of absolutely racialized slavery tended toward self-imposed limits on expansion. Was there any way for the South to circumvent them?

The fact that social relations of production were based on an absolute connection between skin-color racism and exploitation might have been overcome if the South had been an imperial or colonial outpost of a metropolitan power; but it *was* the metropolitan power. These two factors made reform impossible and consequently made the South different not only from other societies with slaves, but from other slave societies. In the latter, like other societies with unfree labor, slaves were closer to peasant status in that they generally had their own land with which to cultivate crops, this providing for their own subsistence and perhaps even giving them the opportunity to sell any surplus in local markets. In the South, even this was much restricted, as the masters suspected any arrangements that would diminish slave dependence upon them.[71] More importantly, while there was undoubtedly racism toward the black slaves who worked on the sugar plantations in, for example, the British colony of Jamaica, whether or not they remained slaves or became wage laborers and peasants was not crucial to the survival of the British state and society. In the end, slavery was abolished in Jamaica in 1838 as a result of calculations over profitability and the reproduction of the labor force, together with concerns over a repetition of the slave rebellion of 1831.[72] In both of the other slave societies of the Americas, Cuba and Brazil, the state began to lessen the necessity for slave labor by introducing other types of unfree labor, which formed a bridge between slavery and free labor. In Cuba these involved Chinese and even Spanish coolies.[73] In Brazil free blacks and mulattoes could serve in the militia and, crucially, could own slaves themselves.[74] None of this was possible in the South.

The nature of the resulting society was set out, without direct reference to the slaves, in a diatribe by a Southern politician, delivered immediately prewar and recorded by William Howard Russell, a foreign correspondent for the London *Times*. Here, the antibourgeois, anti-urban, and anti-industrial bias of the Southern ruling class is made quite explicit:

> We are an agricultural people; we are a primitive but a civilized people. We have no cities—we don't want them. We have no literature—we don't need any yet. We have no press—we are glad of it. We do not require a press, because we go out and discuss all public questions from the stump with our people. We have no commercial marine, no navy—we don't want them. We are better without them. Your [British] ships carry our produce, and you can protect your own vessels. We want no manufactures: we desire no trading, no mechanical or manufacturing classes. As long as we have our rice, our sugar, our tobacco, and our cotton, we can command wealth to purchase all we want from those nations with which we are in amity, and to lay up money besides. But with the Yankees we will never trade—never. Not one pound of cotton shall ever go from the South to their accursed cities; not one ounce of their steel or their manufactures shall ever cross our border.[75]

Individual plantations could only grow by moving or adding new land; but the same was true of the society that they supported. Slavery in one society was never going to remain viable unless it could be guaranteed further territory. In the North, capital expanded, labor productivity grew, and, potentially at least, both could continue indefinitely. In the South, increased productivity was achieved from moving operations to or extending existing plantations into more fertile soil, but as Richard Ransom and Richard Sutch point out, "there is a natural limit to gains that can be achieved from geographical relocation":

> The South, therefore, grew but did not develop. Slaveholders were capitalists without physical capital. Their wealth was in the form of slaves and land. Slave capital represented 44 percent of all wealth in the major cotton-growing states of the South in 1859, real estate (land and buildings) was more than 25 percent, while physical capital amounted to less than 10 percent of the total. Manufacturing capital amounted to only 1 percent of the total wealth accumulated. . . . [T]he relative shortage of physical capital in the South can be explained by the presence of slavery. In a capitalist society physical capital is owned by private entrepreneurs who are induced to invest in and hold capital by the flow of returns they hope to receive. In the American South slaves were an alternative to physical capital that could satiate the demand for holding wealth. In short, slaves as assets crowded physical capital out of the portfolios of southern capitalists.[76]

Those limits could of course be overcome if the boundaries of Southern slave society were widened, up into the northwest or south and east into the Caribbean and the Americas beyond the US. In a speech made in Mississippi three years before the opening of the war, Southern Congressman Albert Gallatin Brown set out these expansionist aims, which he justified, logically enough, on the grounds that the republic had been founded on the theft of land from the Native Americans: "It may seem strange to you that I thus talk of taking possession of Central America, or any part of it, seeing, as you suppose you do, that it belongs to someone else. Yes, it belonged to someone else, just as this country once belonged to the Choctaws. When we wanted this country we came and took it." After reminding his audience about the biblical endorsement of slavery and of the happy situation of the Negro in the South compared to that of his compatriots in Africa, Brown returned to his main theme:

> I want a footing in Central America for other reasons, or rather for a continuation of the reasons already given. I want Cuba, and I know that sooner or later we must have it. If the worm-eaten throne of Spain is willing to give it up for a fair equivalent, well—if not, we must take it. I want Tamaulipas, Potosi, and one or two other Mexican States; and I want them all for the same reason—for the planting or spreading of slavery. And a footing in Central America will powerfully aid us in acquiring those other states. It will render them less valuable to the other powers of the earth, and thereby diminish competition with us.[77]

Brown was still assuming that the US, rather than an independent South, would carry out these annexations—a reasonable assumption given the way in which the South had dominated national politics, at least until the 1850s and the formation of the Republican Party. Robert Fogel has pointed out that the Confederacy could have dominated Central and South America, and even formed alliances further afield with other slave-trading nations, although this might have brought it into conflict with Britain, which was still applying diplomatic pressure on Brazil and in Africa.[78] But given Britain's reliance on Southern cotton, and her tacit support for the Confederacy during the Civil War, it is very likely that British state managers would have overlooked these transgressions in the spirit of compromise on which they tended to rely when their material interests were in conflict with their moral values. There was, however, a much more serious obstacle to territorial expansion, emblematic of a tension between the individual and collective interests of the slave owners.

Individual slave owners may have wanted to increase cotton production in order to boost their income; but collectively they had an interest in restricting it on the grounds that generalized increased supply would have the effect of lowering prices. Similarly, they did not want the slave population to grow too quickly, as this would have a comparable downward impact on the relatively high price of slaves. As Gavin Wright notes, "these attitudes had roots in their property interest and reflected the kind of economy which that property interest had created": "By slowing the growth of the regional population, both free and slave, that property interest also retarded territorial expansion and political weight. Since this political weight was a factor in secession, and since sheer manpower was a factor in the South's military defeat, in these ways we may say that the economics of slavery contributed to its own demise."[79] As Brown's speech suggests, this was why it was important for the Southern slave owners to move into areas where other crops than cotton could be produced on the basis of slavery; the crucial failure of that class was to delay establishing a state until its Northern opponent was in a position to defeat it.

What then was the nature of the Old South? What mode of production exercised its laws of motion there? The societies over which the slave owners ruled cannot be directly assimilated to those of the ancient world; the insertion of the South into the emergent capitalist world economy meant that the context for the social relations of master and slave was unimaginably different from that of the tribal and tributary formations in which the Greek and Roman city-states developed. But neither can the South simply be regarded as a peculiarly backward variant of the capitalist societies that were consolidating in Western Europe, Australasia, and the rest of North America; the surplus accruing to the landowners did derive from the exploitation of slaves. Perhaps the solution is to regard the South as a society transitional to capitalism, but one in which the transition had never been able to progress beyond a certain point. The South therefore retained a form of production with the accompanying social relations, namely chattel slavery, which elsewhere had been merely one, albeit crucial, element in the primitive accumulation of capital. In other transitional societies the importance of slavery and other forms of unfree labor diminished over time, but in the South it remained and indeed became more central to the economic and social structure rather than less.

Nevertheless, this case of arrested development might simply have led to the South remaining, like the Scottish Highlands or the Italian Mezzogiorno, as the more backward component of a "dual economy," within a nation-state in which the laws of motion were set by the capitalist mode of production. It did not. In order to survive, the Southern ruling class established, on the basis of this retarded early stage in the transition to capitalism, a new and expansionist state, the Confederate States of America, and it did so with the support of the overwhelming majority of the inhabitants who were not themselves slaves. In most societies where the economy was transitional from precapitalist modes of production to the capitalist mode, states remained under the control of the precapitalist ruling class, although they adapted to the new conditions, most typically in the emergence of absolutism: society became increasingly opposed to the state. As we have seen, these tensions were resolved either by a direct external challenge to the state from the new social classes created by capitalism or, in order to avoid this outcome while enabling the ability to compete in geopolitical terms, by internal challenge from sections of the existing ruling class who themselves undertook the process of transforming the state—or some combination of these two paths, with one predominating. None of these options was possible in the South. There was no alternative ruling class capable of overthrowing the plantocracy, but, because of the unbreakable divisions associated with racialized slavery, neither could the slave owners engage in self-transformation without unleashing the very social conflicts that, in Europe, the process had been undertaken to avoid.

Strictly speaking, the South is therefore sui generis, and its ideologues were more justified than they knew in referring to the "peculiarity" of Southern institutions. The

South was exceptional; very few other societies—effectively only Cuba and Brazil—were so absolutely dependent on one particular transitional form of labor exploitation, and no other society became both developmentally "frozen" at such a fundamental level while embodying that stage of development in the state form. The South was exceptional; but it is not therefore inexplicable in Marxist terms—providing we reject the assumption that all immediately precapitalist states have to map tidily and conveniently onto our categories of tributary, feudal estates, or feudal absolutist monarchy.

DUAL POWER AND THE NORTHERN BOURGEOISIE

To summarize the argument so far: if slavery had been dispersed throughout the US, then the combined pressure of abolitionist campaigning on the one hand, and of slavery's comparative economic inefficiencies on the other, would have led to its supersession, perhaps through a series of staged transitions to free labor, without the type of violence that ultimately ensued. But because it was territorially concentrated and the basis of a distinct society in which labor was defined in racial terms, this solution was not available. Instead, the Civil War acted as the resolution to a situation that Marxists would, in other contexts, immediately understand as one of dual power, involving a geographically based form of class opposition to the existing nation-state.

The concept of dual power was of course first used after the Russian Revolution of February 1917 to describe how the councils of workers—and later those of the peasantry and armed forces—came to constitute an alternative source of economic, social, and political organization to that of the state headed by the Provisional Government. "Two powers *cannot exist* in a state," wrote Lenin shortly before one overthrew the other.[80] Trotsky also discerned similar experiences—involving different social classes and institutions—in earlier revolutions, such as the English and the French: "the two-power regime arises only out of irreconcilable conflicts—is possible, therefore, only in a revolutionary epoch, and constitutes one of its fundamental elements."[81] He was careful to add, however, that this situation does not arise merely where there are divisions of interest within a ruling class, and he cited as an example the conflict between the Junkers and the bourgeoisie in Germany under both the Hohenzollern Empire of 1871 and the Republic of 1918. He might have added to this the struggle between Whig and Tory in England during the first half of the eighteenth century. In the English and the French (although not the Russian) revolutions, the centers of dual power opposed to the absolutist state were in territories seized through military onslaught or urban insurrection by forces opposed to the regime.

In the US two territorially bounded societies, within the same state, were in competition to determine the direction taken by a third, the West. Once battle was joined the aims of the Confederacy were to expand slave production northward to areas where it had never previously existed, retarding the advance of industrial capitalism and free wage labor. One unintended result would have been to place the US as a whole under the informal control of the British Empire, for whom most of the Southern cotton exports were destined. The Northern bourgeoisie were not the initiators of the struggle, but had to respond to the act of secession and declaration of war by their enemy; yet they were ultimately compelled to fight to a decisive conclusion. Moore's famous claim that the Civil War was "the last capitalist revolution" involves a rather restricted notion of capitalism, but it was certainly the last to directly involve the bourgeoisie, and virtually the only one to involve actual industrial capitalists. "Unpalatable as it is to many," writes Andrew Dawson of this class in Pennsylvania, "manufacturers constituted the revolutionary class and not their workforce":

> Industrialists threw themselves wholeheartedly into preserving the Union. They reserved jobs for volunteers, supported widows and orphans, sponsored the Great Sanitary Fair and organized factory militias in case of invasion. Their finest political achievement, though, came in 1862 with the foundation of the Union League. The League represented the demise of the merchant class and the ascent of manufacturing. Tirelessly publicizing the northern cause, the League raised regiments of soldiers, called for the end of slavery, and supported black civil rights in Pennsylvania.[82]

The level of revolutionary commitment displayed by the bourgeoisie was extremely unusual by this date. The Northern bourgeoisie were faced by a factory proletariat that had already demonstrated its militancy. After the experience of the German Revolution of 1848–49, Marx tended to believe that the bourgeoisie were incapable of fighting on their own behalf. The half-hearted conduct of Northern politicians and their military commanders for the first two years of the war only seemed to offer a further confirmation of this tendency. In 1862 Engels wrote to Marx complaining about the "indolence" and "indifference" displayed in the North: "Where, amongst the people, is there any sign of revolutionary vigor?" So bad was the situation that Engels added the most insulting comparison of which he was capable: "I've never encountered the like of it before, not even in Germany at the worst of times."[83] Marx even argued that the Northern bourgeoisie would have to be rescued by "a slave revolution."[84] In the end, some elements of this did occur in the formation and intervention of the black regiments, which involved a quarter of a million former slaves and signaled the long-delayed adoption of decisive revolutionary tactics by Lincoln. Indeed, one of the reasons for the somewhat exaggerated praise with which Marx and Engels regularly lauded Lincoln after the Emancipation Declaration may have simply been their relief at this development.[85] How was it possible?

Within the North as a whole the dominant reason for opposition to slavery was the perception that its citizens were potentially or actually oppressed by what they called the "slave power," an attitude that involved hostility to the slave owners without necessarily displaying any sympathy for the slaves. Accordingly, attitudes within the working class were complex, dividing between those who supported the war on abolitionist grounds, those who supported it on antisecessionist grounds (which could be quite compatible with racism toward the slaves), those who opposed it on grounds of opposition to the draft or the economic hardships it caused ("a poor man's fight"), and those who opposed it on straightforwardly racist grounds. What the bourgeoisie did not face was a revolutionary working class attempting to drive the revolution forward *in the North* in a more radical direction, in the manner of the "permanent revolution" envisaged by Marx in 1850. Indeed, the biggest upheavals were directed against the war and the free black population in the shape of the New York anti-draft riots of 1863. It is in this context that the territorial dimension assumes great importance. The fact that revolutionary violence could be directed outward to a now effectively external enemy, through the mechanism of disciplined state power, meant that a far greater degree of radicalism could be attempted than if the struggle had been a purely internal one, conducted, as it were, by civilians. In other words, the Northern bourgeoisie were ultimately prepared to embrace the logic of total war rather than face defeat, even if this meant emancipating the slaves and harnessing the freedmen against their former masters as part of the Union's military apparatus.

But these enabling conditions for the overthrow of the Confederacy also indicate reasons for the retreat from radicalism once the war was won. "Nothing renders society more restless than a social revolution but half accomplished," wrote Carl Schurz, a veteran of the German Revolution of 1848 and a Northern commander and politician, at the end of the war: "The South will have to suffer the evil of anarchical disorder until means are found to effect a final settlement of the labor question in accordance with the logic of the great revolution."[86] Yet the Northern politicians, including figures like Schurz himself, are usually seen as "leaving the social revolution unfinished," and in some cases the Republican Party is accused of "betraying" the former slaves.[87] As I suggested above, this seems to rest on a misunderstanding of what bourgeois revolutions in general and this one in particular involve. Once the Confederacy had been defeated; once the coherence of the South as a society had been shattered and its potential to dominate the US ended; once actual slavery had been dismantled and the threat of subjugation to the former British colonial power removed—then the majority of the Northern ruling class, many of whom were themselves racists, had no particular interest in ensuring equal rights and democratic participation for the black population. In the end, the "anarchy" invoked by Schurz—or the process of black liberation, as we would see it—could not be endured when it was no longer absolutely necessary for the security of US capitalism, particularly if the possibility existed of black radicalism in the former South coinciding, or even overlapping, with renewed worker militancy in the North. "The North's conversion to emancipation and equal rights was primarily a conversion of expediency rather than conviction," writes James McPherson. "It became expedient for Northern political and business interests to conciliate Southern whites and to end federal enforcement of Negro equality in the South was part of the price of that conciliation."[88] The necessary importance given by socialists to the question of racism has perhaps obscured the way in which this outcome was absolutely typical of the bourgeois revolutions from above, to which the American Revolution in most respects belongs. The fate of the rural masses in the Italian Mezzogiorno, for example, remained unchanged after the Risorgimento, as they continued to labor on the same latifundia for the same landowners. Racism added another, deeper level of oppression to the black population of the South, but their abandonment by a triumphant bourgeoisie, now safely in command of state power, was entirely typical. Free labor as conceived in the ideology of the prewar Republican Party was very distant from the types of labor into which blacks were now forced, such as sharecropping, let alone a prison system in which inmates were forcibly conscripted into production; but the latter were perfectly compatible with capitalism—as, indeed, were several other identity-based restrictions on the freedom of labor. As Lisa Lowe notes: "In the history of the US, capital has maximized its profits not through rendering labor 'abstract' but precisely through the social production of 'difference,' restrictive particularity and illegitimacy marked by race, nation, geographical origins and gender. The law of value has operated, instead, by creating, preserving and reproducing the specifically racialized and gendered character of labor power."[89] And in that sense, the actual outcome of Reconstruction foreshadowed how US capitalism has developed ever since.

Conclusion

We can now return to the question of alternatives with which I began this essay. First, the potential for a more democratic outcome to radical Reconstruction existed: we are not dealing with a situation in which the objective was literally impossible of realization, like Anabaptist or Digger attempts to achieve Communism in sixteenth-century Germany or seventeenth-century England. The issue is rather one of balance between objective and subjective conditions. Those who refer to "betrayal" by Northern politicians have to accept the implication of this position, which is that the achievement of equality was dependent on the actions of the reunified state and its military and juridical apparatus. For the reasons given in the preceding section, the Northern bourgeoisie was always collectively going to be more influenced by the necessity for social stability than by the desirable but, from its point of view, optional quest for political equality. This is virtually an objective condition. In these circumstances the decisive issue was whether the former slaves could form an alliance with the majority of non–ruling class whites, both groups then allying with the organized working class in the North and forcing through a democratic (i.e., political) revolution "from below." Obviously the Southern ruling class did everything they could to prevent such an outcome. The question—and this still seems to me to be an open question—is whether its success in doing so was preordained by the strength of a racism that was impossible to dislodge in the decade following Lee's surrender, or whether a different strategy on the part of the Radicals could have overcome it. This at least introduces the possibility that the subjective element might have been determinate here.

The question of whether the war was necessary is, I think, more straightforward. By some point in the second half of the eighteenth century—let us say from the conclusion of the Seven Years' War in 1763—the capitalist system took on a purely economic momentum that made bourgeois domination ultimately unstoppable and irreversible, regardless of the temporary political setbacks suffered by individual revolutions such as, for example, those of 1848–49. For most historians, therefore, Gettysburg in 1863 does not have the same significance as, for example, Culloden in 1746. According to the Beards: "The main economic results of the Second American Revolution would have been attained had there been no armed conflict, for the census returns with rhythmic beats were recording the tale of the fates."[90] McPherson concludes perhaps the greatest single-volume history of the Civil War with essentially the same argument: "Of course the northern states, along with Britain and a few countries in northwest Europe, were cutting a new channel in world history that would doubtless have become the mainstream even if the American Civil War had never happened. Russia had abolished serfdom in 1861 to complete the dissolution of ancient institutions of bound labor in Europe."[91] What McPherson ignores here is that it took the Russian Revolution of 1917 to complete the liberation of the serfs. The assumption, which I used to accept, is that, even if the Confederacy had won that battle and gone on to win the Civil War, the ultimate victory of industrial capitalism across the entire territory of what is now the US would sooner or later have followed, either through a renewed attempt by the North or adaptation by the Confederate plantocracy to the new order, in the manner of the Prussian Junkers or Japanese Samurai.[92] But this view ignores the fact that a Confederate victory or—what amounts to the same thing—a Northern refusal to oppose the expansionist drive of the South in the first place would have altered the conditions under which capitalism would then have developed, on a continental and ultimately global scale. The Confederacy, after all, was not intent on preserving a compromise with the North but on imposing a new and—in the literal sense of the word—reactionary settlement on the US as a whole. We should therefore recognize that the American Revolution was probably the most decisive and significant of all the nineteenth-century bourgeois revolutions. The issues that it left unresolved could not have been resolved by the bourgeoisie and cannot now: they will have to be accomplished by a genuine second American Revolution that can only be socialist in nature.

7

When History Failed to Turn: Pierre Broué on the German Revolution

Introduction

"This not a German event. There no longer are any 'German events.'"[1] With these words to the founding conference of the Communist Party of Germany in December 1920, its president, Paul Levi, declared the inseparability of the German Revolution from the global struggle for socialism. There had, of course, been many events in Germany during the preceding three years. And what events they were. Apart from Russia, no other country could boast of a comparable succession of revolutionary episodes in such a relatively short period of time. But Germany was not just inseparable from the world revolution in the years following 1917, it was also central to its ultimate success or failure. In October 1923, only three years after Levi had optimistically greeted the formation of the Communist Party of Germany as the harbinger of the working class's ascent to power, the party proved itself incapable of seizing the opportunities presented by the capitalist crisis. That defeat, that refusal to even seriously engage in battle, was a decisive precondition for the rise of Stalinism in Russia and Nazism in Germany itself.

An understanding of this moment in German history is therefore of considerable importance to contemporary socialists. Where should we turn to gain such an understanding? In his own book on the German Revolution, first published in 1982, Chris Harman noted that he had written it for "all those who are—like myself before I began work on the book—frustrated by the need to pull together a fragmentary knowledge of the German Revolution out of a plethora of different sources, some out of print and many of the best only available in German or French."[2] Thankfully, one of the French works to which Harman alludes, perhaps the best of all, Pierre Broué's *The German Revolution*, has at last been published in English.[3]

Broué's achievement

Broué does full justice to the importance of his subject. This is a work conceived on an epic scale, comprising nine hundred pages of carefully researched text, plus a chronological table and biographical notes. The editors are particularly to be congratulated for giving up-to-date English references for Broué's original Russian and German sources wherever these were available. The main problem with this excellent edition is that the publishers have neglected to provide an index—a quite extraordinary omission in a book of this size and one that is likely to prove the biggest obstacle to anyone trying to negotiate their way through it. Those prepared to try will, however, find it worth the effort.

Revolutions—even failed revolutions like the German—occupy definite periods of time, starting from the moment at which the victory of the contending class becomes possible and ending in either victory or defeat, but one way or the other with the passing of the "revolutionary situation," at least for the immediate future. The periodization of even successful revolutions has posed significant problems for historians; with unconsummated "revolutionary situations" these difficulties are multiplied.[4] Prior to Broué's book first appearing in 1971, most discussions of Germany focused either on the few months between November 1918 and May 1919, when the most obvious "revolutionary" activity took place (insurrection in Berlin, civil war in the Ruhr, the short-lived Bavarian Soviet Republic), or on the entire period from the end of the First World War to the triumph of Hitler in 1933. Broué's focus on the six years between the strike by revolutionary metalworkers in April 1917 and the aborted insurrection of October 1923 is wider than the first timescale, but narrower than the second.

Broué was one of the first modern Marxist historians to fully explore the decisive significance of the latter date. The British historian A. J. P. Taylor once famously wrote of the failed bourgeois revolution of 1848 that "German history reached its turning-point and failed to turn."[5] Taylor makes too many untenable assumptions about the nature of "normal" capitalist development for this to be true of 1848, but for the year 1923 the notion of a "turning point at which history failed to turn" is apt. Broué notes that "even today, the international Communist movement has not devoted to this unprecedented disaster the minimum attention which it affords to victories or even to defeats of less importance."[6] Only two writers at the time seriously attempted to understand the significance of what had happened, Trotsky in *The Lessons of October* and Levi—by then writing from a left Social-Democratic perspective—in his introduction to the German edition of the same work.[7] Since then, outside of the ranks of the revolutionary left, only a handful of books have approached a comparable level of understanding.[8] At the heart of Broué's account therefore is the question of why the revolution failed. He recognizes that Germany (and the West more generally) was not identical to Russia, but rightly does not see this as decisive. Neither was it because of any lack of revolutionary capacity on the part of the German working class. His answer is ultimately that the collective hero of his book, the Communist Party of Germany (Kommunistische Partei Deutschlands, or KPD), the organization that should have provided the necessary leadership to workers, was unable to play the same role in Germany as the Bolshevik Party had played in Russia.

THE CENTRALITY OF THE KPD

The founding of the KPD was inspired in equal parts by rage at the betrayals of a Social Democracy that had led the German working class into the disasters of war, and admiration for what the Bolsheviks had achieved in Russia. But it was born in the very course of the revolution itself. Only a handful of leaders had any serious prior experience in the movement, and many of them—above all, Rosa Luxemburg—were to die at the hands of the counterrevolution before the party or the revolution were more than months old. The neglect of socialists to build a revolutionary party prior to the outbreak of revolution was not, of course, some special failure on the part of the Germans: *no one* outside of Russia fully understood the need to build such a party before the October Revolution. Nevertheless, this fact meant that the KPD had to develop in conditions that called for a party already schooled in the class struggle.

The problems and dangers this late birth bequeathed were perfectly well understood and articulated by Levi at the founding conference of the Communist Party of Germany in 1920.[9] Unfortunately, he and those who thought like him were unable to prevail. On the one hand the party carried out policies that were wildly ultraleft. In some cases this led to abstention: it initially refused to participate in the general strike of March 1920 to stop the right-wing Kapp Putsch—possibly the greatest moment in the entire history of the German working class—because the moment, apparently, was not yet right for socialist revolution. In other cases it led to attempts to force the pace of struggle without support from even a large minority of the broader class: in "the March Action" of 1921 the KPD attempted an insurrectionary movement that involved, among other things, sending unemployed comrades into the factories to attack workers who refused to go on strike at its behest. But in reaction to these absurdities, the party just as often pulled so far back that it committed the opposite error of accommodating to the existing reformist structures of the labor movement. Of these twin errors, Broué writes: "The logic of both of them alike would lead the Party to disaster, either as a sect isolated by the policy of putchism, the theory of the offensive—or in dissolution within a general unity, the price of conceding too much in order to forge a united front at any price."[10] The consequence was a cumulative loss of self-belief by the leadership: "Convinced by the leadership of the International of the magnitude of their blunder [in March 1921], they lost confidence in their own ability to think, and often failed to defend their viewpoint, so that they systematically accepted that of the Bolsheviks, who had at least been able to win their revolutionary struggle."[11]

There were, of course, members of the KPD who attempted to change its direction. Two individuals dominate Broué's book. The first is Levi himself—the only significant leader that the KPD had after the annihilation of the original leadership in 1919. If Broué's book does nothing else, then it restores Levi—whatever his faults—to the historical memory of the left as one of the few figures involved in the Communist International outside of Russia who was capable of independent thought. The second is Karl Radek, the Bolshevik leader most involved in German affairs. As Broué writes: "They had been the most important leaders of the party between 1918 and 1923, and were as completely eliminated from Bolshevik history as Trotsky had been, and whenever it was deemed necessary to mention their names, they were merely branded with the traditional epithets of 'enemies of the people,' 'traitors' or 'renegades.'"[12] But their reputation suffered even among the ranks of the revolutionary left: Levi because of his expulsion from the KPD in 1921 for breaching discipline and his subsequent retreat to reformist politics, Radek because of his capitulation to Stalin during the late 1920s. Broué devotes two chapters (45 and 46) to reassessing their contribution, not in order to exculpate them from their mistakes, but simply to treat them with the seriousness they deserve.

What emerges from Broué's account is that many of the political positions we tend to associate with the individual geniuses of Lenin or Gramsci were in fact much more widespread and originated during the strategic debates within the KPD: "Lenin, in 'Left-Wing' Communism: An Infantile Disorder, did no more than to systematize the themes which Radek and Levi had developed against the German opposition and the KAPD, although, no doubt, with wider vision and less rancor."[13] Similarly, in The Development of the World Revolution and the Tactics of the Communist Parties in the Struggle for the Dictatorship of the Proletariat (1919)—one of the texts that anticipate "Left-Wing" Communism—Radek also argues for the difference between Russia and the West in ways that clearly anticipate those of Gramsci in his prison notebooks. Radek notes that, as the result of the absence of a revolutionary peasantry combined with the presence of a more confident, experienced bourgeoisie and the greater strength of reformism, "the illusion of a quick victory arose from the incorrect interpretation of the lessons of the Russian Revolution, the conditions of which, although within an identical historical framework, were by no means the same as those of the European revolution."[14]

This a work of committed socialist scholarship, but it never reads—as many socialist histories unfortunately do—as Political Journalism with Historical Examples, where the subject has merely been chosen to illustrate a point the author wants to make ("the need for the revolutionary party," or whatever). There are lessons for us here, not least about the pointlessness of small groups of revolutionaries trying to force the working class into struggle through their own "exemplary" actions. But these arise from Broué's narrative and analysis, and rarely appear as prepackaged programmatic points superimposed on the text. Nevertheless, it would be unrealistic to expect a work of this size and scope to be flawless, and indeed there are some problems and omissions here.

Some involve relatively minor theoretical issues. Broué too easily accepts that the German bourgeois revolution was "incomplete" prior to November 1918, which brings with it the inevitable corollary that the November Revolution was in some sense its completion.[15] This position is a strange one for a Trotskyist like Broué to hold, given that (as he himself notes) it was the official position of the Stalinist regime in the German Democratic Republic. Trotsky himself provided a more realistic assessment: "As to the German Revolution of 1918, it was no democratic completion of the bourgeois revolution, it was proletarian revolution decapitated by the Social Democrats; more correctly, it was a bourgeois counter-revolution, which was compelled to preserve pseudo-democratic forms after its victory over the proletariat."[16]

Some important episodes pass by with far less attention than they merit. The short-lived Bavarian Soviet Republic, for example, is dealt with in a handful of pages.[17] Yet this debacle demonstrates in microcosm the reasons why the failure to build a revolutionary party in advance was disastrous. Harman's shorter book spends proportionally far more space discussing this episode and, in this respect, is stronger as a result.[18]

PARTY OVER CLASS?

By far the greatest weakness, however, is the obverse of the book's greatest strength: its minute reconstruction of the political and theoretical life within the KPD and the relationship of its various factions with the Communist International. Now, these are important issues. The role played (and in the end, not played) by the KPD is absolutely central to the outcome of the revolution; the influence of the Communist International, for good or bad, was inescapable. But Broué's relentless focus on these themes is undertaken—for the most part—at the expense of the society that the KPD sought to transform. Perry Anderson once wrote: "Any decent history of a communist party must take seriously the Gramscian maxim, that to write a history of a political party is to write the history of the society of which it is a component from a particular monographic standpoint." Such a history, writes Anderson, "must be constantly related to the national balance of forces of which the party is only one moment, and which forms the context in which it must operate."[19] Broué fails to do this and indeed almost tends to reverse Anderson's formulation, so that the history of Germany is seen through the filter of the KPD—and Broué's book is ostensibly a history of the revolution, not the party.

In the end, revolutions are made by social classes, not organizations, and what is missing here is a sense of the changing condition of the German working class, of its consciousness, its readiness or otherwise to fight, and so on. However, the working class does at least appear in motion from time to time: the ruling class does not, at least in any serious sense. But without a sense of who the revolution was being made against—a class whose representatives were very far from being passive during these events—the picture we receive is misleadingly partial. In fairness to Broué, this approach was quite common in the late '60s and early '70s; it identifies the book as belonging to its time far more than, say, the failure to discuss the role of women of which Eric Weitz complains in the foreword.[20]

The greatest problem, however, is not one that Broué or perhaps anyone could have dealt with. It is the issue of what would have needed to happen for the German Revolution to be successful. This raises issues of historical causation too vast to be adequately discussed here, but the outlines of an answer can be suggested. The deaths of Rosa Luxemburg and the other capable leaders, notably Jogiches and Leviné (not the heroic but politically inept Liebknecht, with whom Luxemburg broke shortly before their assassination) removed the possibility of the KPD developing an understanding of how to operate within the short time available to it. If they had survived, then it is just possible that the KPD might have seen the possibilities of the strike in response to the Kapp Putsch, would not have committed the absurdities of the March Action, would have taken a decisive lead in October 1923—and of course a different response to each of these would have changed the conditions under which the subsequent events took place. The role of the individual in history was as crucial in a negative sense in Germany as it was in a positive sense in Russia. But we have to have the courage to accept the implications of this: after January 1919, the chances of the German Revolution succeeding were greatly reduced. After the expulsion of Paul Levi in 1921 they were virtually nonexistent. And this was not only a problem in Germany but for the entire International: "After Leibknecht and Luxemburg were killed, and after Paul Levi left the movement, there was no person in the international Communist movement, and in particular in Germany, comparable to the Bolshevik leaders."[21]

CONCLUSION

The working-class response to the Kapp Putsch still offers us a tantalizing glimpse of what might have been, as Broué recounts in some of his most gripping pages:

> But the German workers did not hear [the KPD's] appeal for passivity. On 14 March, a Sunday, it was possible to judge the ardor and the scope of their resistance. One after another the trains ceased to move. By five o'clock in the evening there were in Berlin no trams, no water and no electricity. . . . In Chemnitz, the workers' organizations decided immediately to recruit 3,000 men to the workers' militia. . . . The reality was that by the 15th, the Kapp-Lüttwitz government was completely paralyzed. The Belgian socialist Louis De Brouckère wrote: "The General Strike now grips them with its terrible silent power."[22]

In spite of the problems that I have sketched out here, Broué's magnificent work is imbued with the spirit of this moment. It is in the same spirit that we should read it today.

8

FROM UNEVEN
TO COMBINED DEVELOPMENT

INTRODUCTION

Results and Prospects introduced Trotsky's two most original contributions to Marxist theory, although it was only later that they received the names under which they have passed into history: the strategy of "permanent revolution" and—in a much more embryonic way—the theory of "uneven and combined development." Both terms are equally important, yet they have not received comparable levels of scrutiny. In particular, the radical *novelty* of what Trotsky meant by uneven and combined development is often underestimated. The most common mistake is to reduce it to, or confuse it with, the long-standing theory of uneven development. This is partly because the theory of uneven and combined development has not yet received comparable levels of scrutiny to what has been visited on the strategy of permanent revolution. Perhaps the most accurate and detailed exposition ever made of the latter devotes precisely three out of two hundred and thirty-one pages to the subject whose political implications it seeks to discuss.[1] Those works that do attempt to discuss uneven and combined development tend to do so only in relation to "the advantages of backwardness" and "the disadvantages of priority."[2] In a recent exchange with Justin Rosenberg, Alex Callinicos cites Robert Brenner's comparison between English and French feudalism in a passage that concludes: "The development of the mechanisms of feudal accumulation tended to be not only 'uneven' but also 'combined,' in the sense that later developers could build on previous advances made elsewhere in feudal class organization."[3] Giovanni Arrighi summarizes this conception of "combination" for the contemporary period as "the process whereby laggards in capitalist development seek to catch up, and eventually succeed in catching up, with the leaders of that development."[4] But what exactly is being "combined" in such cases? As we shall see, what is being discussed in these passages remains uneven development.

The theory of uneven development is by no means irrelevant today. As Callinicos's reference to Lenin suggests, it was also a component of the classical Marxist tradition. Trotsky himself stressed that the concept, if not the term, was present in the work of Marx and Engels, despite claims to the contrary by Stalin.[5] More recently, it has also informed such memorable analyses as Robert Brenner's delineation of competition between the core economies of global capitalism after the Second World War, Doreen Massey's construction of a general explanatory model of regional inequality more comprehensive than those of either the neoclassical equilibrium or cumulative causation schools, and Neil Smith's depiction of the "see-saw" reproduction of capital that leads to both spatial differentiation and equalization on the urban, nation-state, and global scales.[6] These are important themes, but they fall within the province of uneven development as such. In order to demonstrate the innovation that combined development represents in social theory, it might therefore be useful to briefly trace the prior development of uneven development.

The Enlightenment

Enlightenment thinkers developed a theory of staged development through a series of four increasingly complex modes of subsistence. In the initial formulations at least, most peoples or nations could be expected to traverse these stages, albeit at different historical times, until they finally reached the fourth or commercial stage. There were, however, two exceptions to the universalism of Enlightenment thought on this question.

One was concerned with the socioeconomic distinctions between different geographical areas. Eastern societies (principally Turkey, Persia, India, and China) were classified by Montesquieu as "Asiatic" or "Oriental" Despotisms, terms that implied two characteristics. On the one hand, they referred to the political regime, which bore an uncomfortable resemblance to European absolutism. On the other, they referred to those aspects of the socioeconomic order distinct from the West: the absence of hereditary nobility, a legal system subject to the will of the ruler, state ownership of land, and more generally an overall stagnation made all the more obvious when contrasted with the dynamism of the new capitalist system. It was Adam Smith who decisively shifted Enlightenment views of the East in the latter direction, arguing that the political differences between East and West were based on underlying economic differences. If the West was characterized by private property, manufactures, and foreign trade, then the East (which for Smith was typified by China) was characterized by state property, agriculture, and a localized internal market.

The other exception was concerned with biological distinctions between different human groups, or "races." Enlightenment thinkers were deeply divided on this issue. One trend, represented by John Millar, Denis Diderot, and Johann Herder, broke with the racist ideology that had been used to justify the conquest of Native Americans and enslavement of Africans by both the absolutist and early capitalist empires after 1492. Another, expressed by David Hume, Montesquieu, and Immanuel Kant, doubted whether people with black skins could even be regarded as fully human. But the universality of the former, "progressive" aspect of Enlightenment thought, and consequently the optimism that it displayed down to the French Revolution, could not survive the experience of colonialism and the racism that the possession of colonies engendered—not, at any rate, without turning Enlightenment values against the system that required colonies in the first place.

A small minority of Enlightenment thinkers allowed not only for exceptions to staged development but also for nations and peoples compressing or bypassing certain stages. In many cases these alternatives appeared in the margins of work by individuals who otherwise adhered to the classic stages theory of development by successive modes of subsistence. The first example occurred, appropriately enough, in relation to Russia. During the reign of Peter the Great (1672–1725), Russia was forced by pressure from the more advanced absolutisms of Western Europe, particularly that of Sweden, to develop naval and military forces of comparable strength. This led in turn to the need for an indigenous manufacturing sector capable at least of producing ships and cannon. In the short term, Peter imported not only the technology and technicians but also intellectuals who could advise him on the type of educational system capable of training Russians in engineering and other skills. Many of these were Germans who may have seen in the Tsar a monarch of the type necessary to unite the divided German-speaking principalities. One of these hired savants was Gottfried Leibniz. He wrote to Peter in 1712, claiming that from a position of backwardness, even blankness ("tabula rasa"), Russia could borrow what it needed from Europe and Asia but discard in the process what was unnecessary or contingent.[7] This may be the first reference to what would eventually be called uneven development, although it would find no echo for nearly forty years. Then, during the 1750s, Anne-Robert-Jacques Turgot opined that France, "whom Spain and England have already outstripped in the glory of poetry," might benefit from her current economic position behind England: "France, whose genius finishes forming itself only when the philosophical spirit begins to spread, will owe perhaps to this very backwardness the exactitude, the method, and the austere taste of her writers."[8] But the suggestion was made only in passing and specifically in relation to culture, not society.

Ironically, it was in Scotland, where the four-stage theory was first formulated, that the alternative was elaborated in the greatest detail. Having helped to establish the organic metaphor of development (childhood, maturity, and decline) in theory, the reformers simultaneously set about subverting it in practice. In the successful attempts to overleap several of the stages that England had passed through in moving from the Age of Agriculture to the Age of Commerce, we see for perhaps the first time the brute fact of unevenness being the basis for a developmental strategy.[9] But even the astonishing speed of Scottish development could not overcome the legacy of feudal backwardness overnight. For over half a century, therefore, Scotland was the site—perhaps the first site—of what Trotsky would call *combined* development. It did not last. By the second decade of the nineteenth century writers were reflecting, with some astonishment, how far they had progressed in a matter of decades. By 1815 an anonymous supplement to Lord Kames's *The Gentleman Farmer* could observe

> that there never were greater agricultural improvements carried on in any country than there have been in Scotland during the last thirty years; that the progress of the most correct systems of husbandry has been rapid and extensive beyond what the most sanguine could have anticipated; and that, in short, when we contrast the present state of agriculture in the south-eastern counties with what must have been its state about the middle of the last century . . . the efforts of several centuries would seem to have been concentrated in the intermediate period.[10]

Nor was it only in agriculture that effects were registered. During the previous year, Walter Scott published his first novel, *Waverley*, which recounts the adventures of the eponymous hero during the '45. Near the end, the omnipresent narrator looks back from his vantage point in 1805 at the changes that had taken place in Scotland over the preceding sixty years:

> There is no European nation, which, within the course of half a century, or little more, has undergone so complete a change as the kingdom of Scotland. The effects of the insurrection of 1745,—the destruction of the patriarchal power of the Highland chiefs, the abolition of the heritable jurisdictions of the Lowland nobility and barons,—the total eradication of the Jacobite party, which, averse to intermingle with the English, or adopt their customs, long continued to pride themselves upon maintaining ancient Scottish manners and customs,—commenced this innovation. The gradual influx of wealth, and extension of commerce, have since united to render the present people of Scotland a class of beings as different from their grandfathers, as the existing English are from those of Queen Elizabeth's time.[11]

The astonishing claim in the final sentence was entirely justified. Because Scotland could draw on what England had already accomplished, it was able to make up the same ground in a much shorter period of time. But it was so overwhelmingly successful in doing so that—with the exception of the Highlands—the socioeconomic differences between Scotland and England had been overcome by 1815 and the political differences by 1832. No other country would ever complete the transition from feudal agriculture to capitalist industrialization so quickly or completely. The moment was too brief, the result too uniquely decisive, for any theoretical generalization from this experience to be possible.

Marx and Engels

There are several differences between the Enlightenment concept of a mode of subsistence and the concept of a mode of production introduced by Marx and Engels. For our purposes the most important is that Marx and Engels were not proposing a universal succession of stages. Those modes of production that they listed in various places—primitive communism, slavery, feudalism, capitalism, socialism, and Communism—were chronological only in two senses. One is that, as Eric Hobsbawm puts it, "each of these systems is in crucial respects further removed from the primitive state of man."[12] The other sense is that these lists indicate the order in which the modes of production arose historically; they do not suggest that every social formation is fated to pass under the dominance of each of them in succession. In fact, Marx and Engels seem to have regarded only one transition as universal, that from primitive communism to different types of class society (Asiatic, slave, tributary, and feudal). Beyond that, they seem to have regarded the transition from feudalism to capitalism as a possible outcome that was in fact occurring during their lifetime, which in turn opened up the possibility for another, final transition from capitalism to socialism. But neither of these two transitions was automatic or inevitable.

What level of capitalist development was necessary for socialism? At one point in *The German Ideology* (unfinished and unpublished during their lifetime) Marx and Engels seem to suggest that the forces of production would need to exist at a globally even level of development before socialism was possible.[13] During the later 1840s their attention became focused on Europe and its colonial-settler extensions in North America, which they saw as decisive and where the situation was relatively straightforward. Capitalism was the dominant mode of production only in parts of Western Europe and the eastern seaboard of the United States, and industrialization was still more narrowly focused. Elsewhere the bourgeoisie were still politically and socially subordinate to the Old Regime. The task for Communists was therefore to encourage the revolutions that would overthrow the feudal-absolutist states, remove the structural obstacles to capitalist development, and thus create the material basis for the international working class that would make socialism a possibility. During the 1840s they assumed that only a short period of time would be necessary for capitalism to develop to the point where the socialist revolution was possible. However, as early as 1858 Marx wrote to Engels admitting that capitalism had a much longer future ahead of it than either man had thought possible in 1848, and that consequently socialism might be a more distant prospect than they had initially hoped.[14]

In the meantime, what were the implications of what Marx called "this little corner of the earth" bringing the rest of the world under colonial domination? In the preface to *Capital* he wrote that "the country that is more developed industrially only shows, to the less developed, the image of its own future."[15] He was not suggesting that all countries would take the same length of time to reach the future as the original metropolitan powers, nor that arriving there would have the same implications for late developers, but neither was he suggesting that they could bypass sections of the road. Marx and Engels seem to have taken the view that it was necessary for the European bourgeoisie to introduce capitalism into Asia and Africa because the nature of these societies acted as a block to its indigenous development. Neither man had any illusions as to the means by which that bourgeoisie would accomplish this revolution.[16]

Were Marx and Engels right that India, China, and the other colonial and semicolonial countries could only be dragged from their stagnation by colonial conquest? They certainly exaggerated the lack of socioeconomic development prior to colonization, particularly with relation to India. In this respect they retained the Enlightenment view of the East as immobile and subject to Asiatic despotism. It is possible that, with sufficient time and freedom from external interference, at least some of these countries might have seen the indigenous emergence of capitalism. But given the existence of the capitalist powers and their need to secure territories for raw materials, markets, and investments, they were not to be given that time or that freedom. What might have been possible had India and the rest been situated in a dimension unreachable by the British navy is a question for science fiction, not historical materialism. Once colonization had taken place, Marx and Engels needed to take an attitude toward it. Their assumption was that whatever atrocities the colonial powers committed on the way, they would ultimately develop the countries over which they ruled, to the point where they would produce their own gravedigger as they had in the existing capitalist countries. This was their real error. The colonial powers had no intentions of hastening their own demise by developing the economies of the subject peoples, at least not in any systematic way. The implications of this for revolution in the colonial and semicolonial world only become apparent after their deaths.

Only once did either Marx or Engels suggest that capitalist development could be circumvented altogether. This was not in relation to the colonial world, however, but to Russia, the most backward of the great European powers. In 1877 Marx argued that Russia did not need to undergo capitalist development but could move directly to socialism through the institution of the peasant commune or mir. If not, then Russia would be condemned to suffer all that the peasant populations of the West had suffered. In response, Marx makes two points. First, although the Russian peasant commune may provide the launching pad for the advance to Communism in Russia, the advance of capitalism outside of Russia is already undermining the possibility of that happening. Second, even if capitalist development in Russia does come to fruition, it will not replicate exactly the earlier process in Western Europe.[17] Under what conditions might the peasant commune play the role that Marx has suggested for it? These were outlined the following year in a preface, published under the names of both men, for the second Russian edition of the "Manifesto." Here, revolution in Russia may act as the spark, but success is still dependent on the victory of the proletariat in the West.[18] That the victory of a revolutionary movement in the West could establish a socialist context for Russian development and thus avoid the fate of capitalism was in their view a possibility, but by no means a certainty. By the early 1890s it had become clear which direction events had taken, and Engels changed his position accordingly. In his last writings, he drew up a balance sheet that is clearly loaded against those who still expected the peasant commune to act as the social basis of the Russian revolution. In the absence of revolution in the West and the beginning of capitalist development in Russia, the opportunity to bypass bourgeois society had passed.[19] Beyond the Russian question, only two anticipations of uneven development appear in the work of Marx and Engels.

The first consists of a cluster of references to a particular form of unevenness arising from colonial settlement. In *The German Ideology*, they reflected on how these settlements could be established on the basis of a purer, more advanced version of the dominant mode of production than the societies the settlers left behind. On the one hand, where the settled territory was uninhabited: "Thus they begin with the most advanced individuals of the old countries, and, therefore, with the correspondingly most advanced form of intercourse, even before this form of intercourse has been able to establish itself in the old countries." On the other hand, where the colonized territory was inhabited by peoples at a much lower level of development: "A similar relation issues from conquest, when a form of intercourse which has evolved on another soil is brought over complete to the conquered country: whereas in its home it was still encumbered with interests and relations left over from earlier periods, here it can and must be established completely and without hindrance, if only to assure the conqueror's lasting power, when they received the most perfect form of feudal organisation."[20] The examples on which they tended to draw later in their careers were from the feudal period.[21] They do not seem to have specifically considered that capitalism might also develop in this way.

The second is a single passage in a review of Friedrich List written during 1845. List had argued that Germany should seek to follow the same path of economic development as England.[22] Marx, on the other hand, rejected the idea that every nation had to repeat the same experience and argues instead that it might be possible for nations to draw on what other nations had accomplished in the specific areas where they were most advanced.[23] There is the embryo of an idea here, but it never achieved full term—unsurprisingly, since it would be contrary to Marx and Engels's own method to suppose that their thought could run ahead of actual developments. By the time of the foundation of the Second International in 1889, those developments had begun to unfold.

THE SECOND INTERNATIONAL

The second generation of Marxists took as their text on development a passage from the same work by Marx in which he identified the different epochs of human history, the "Preface" to *A Contribution to the Critique of Political Economy*: "No social order is ever destroyed before all the productive forces for which it is sufficient have been developed, and new and superior relations of production never replace older ones before the material conditions for their existence have matured within the framework of the old society."[24] Marx by no means regarded the role of socialists as playing a waiting game until the conditions were universally "mature," yet this was the lesson that the theoretical leaders of the Second International drew.

The nation in which this position was articulated and upheld more rigorously than any other was, appropriately enough, Russia, in whose future Marx and Engels had briefly glimpsed a possible alternative before dismissing it. Ironically, it was no

Marxist but the Russian populist Alexander Herzen in the 1850s who became the first thinker since the Scottish Enlightenment to notice a decisive fact about late development: "Human development is a form of chronological unfairness, since late comers are able to profit by the labors of their predecessors without paying the same price."[25] But for Herzen (and contemporaries like Chernyshevsky) this meant that Russia could avoid the traumas of the capitalist transition completely. It was only in the early years of the twentieth century that the insight was properly theorized in a more realistic basis. The key figure in this respect on the Russian Marxist left was Georgi Plekhanov.

Given the opposition that Plekhanov showed for the Russian Revolution toward the end of his life, it is important not to read back later positions onto those of an earlier period, for Plekhanov was perhaps the most sophisticated thinker of his entire generational cohort. His recognition of the necessity for capitalism in Russia was accompanied by an insistence that the working class, which it was bringing into being, had to struggle against the new bourgeoisie as hard as it did against the feudal-absolutist state to which both classes were ostensibly opposed. Indeed, he was initially prepared to echo Marx's more unorthodox pronouncements concerning the prospects for Russian development.[26] But this element of his thought was quickly submerged by the need to emphasize the necessity of capitalist development against the populists. The ultimate outcome of the revolution in Russia, given the preponderance of land-hungry peasantry, could only be the more extensive implantation of capitalist economy in the countryside, not the agrarian Communism predicted by the populists.[27] If this was true for Russia, then it was even more so for those states, like China, which were further east in geographical terms and further behind in developmental terms: "The West European revolution will be mighty, but not almighty. To have a decisive influence on other countries, the socialist countries of the West will need some kind of vehicle for that influence. 'International exchange' is a powerful vehicle, but it is not almighty either."[28] This is a more pessimistic perspective than that of Engels. It is important to note that, for Plekhanov at least, this was not a racist or paternalist discourse. He maintained essentially the same position in relation to the history of Western Europe: "Everywhere there has been imitation; but the imitator is separated from his model by all the distance which exists between the society which gave him, the *imitator*, birth and the society in which the *model* lived." Plekhanov correctly notes that Locke was the greatest influence on French philosophers of the eighteenth century: "Yet, between Locke and his French pupils there is precisely that same distance, which separated English society at the time of the 'Glorious Revolution' from French society as it was several decades before the 'Great Rebellion' of the French people." His conclusion? "*Thus the influence of the literature of one country on the literature of another is directly proportional to the similarity of the social relations of those countries. It does not exist at all when that similarity is near to zero.*"[29]

In cruder hands than those of Plekhanov, the perspective simply became one of a socialist West continuing colonialism until the "backward races" had developed sufficiently to rule themselves. The debate on colonial policy that took place at the Stuttgart Conference of the Second International in 1907 raised some of these issues in stark relief. A Dutch delegate, Hendrick van Kol, supported by Eduard Bernstein among others, argued unashamedly that the colonies were necessary for the continuation of modern industry and as a place of emigration from "overpopulated" Europe. In the end an anti-imperialist position was adopted by the conference, but opposition to van Kol and his supporters, while stressing that Marx did not propose a universal linear path of development, had little positive to say with respect to how the colonial world could contribute to the struggle for socialism. Julian Marchlewski argued on relativist grounds that non-Western societies also possessed important cultures; Karl Kautsky argued that free trade would allow development to take place; but these positions either celebrated the culture of a precolonial past or saw socialism as a prospect for the long-term future.[30] What of the present?

The previous year, Kautsky had identified the disproportionately advanced role that Russian workers were playing in the Revolution of 1905, despite the paradoxical backwardness of Russian capital.[31] But here, as in the work of Marx and Engels—and his contemporaries like Rosa Luxemburg and Franz Mehring—Russia is seen as an exception in Europe, not a model for Asia or Africa. What Trotsky would later call "the peculiarities of Russia's development" had been noted by other Marxists, notably Antonio Labriola in 1896, who was a major influence on Trotsky's thought.[32] In other words, several writers had noted and commented on the peculiar militancy of the Russian working class, just as several more had noted the variety of different forms characteristic of the Russian economy. No one, however, had drawn the connection between them.

The problem lay in the conception of unevenness that emerged from the center and left of the Second International. Until the First World War uneven development had been a largely descriptive concept, without specific political implications. As Neil Smith notes, it "was first examined in any depth by Lenin, who tried to sketch some of the economic and geographical outlines of the process."[33] In *Imperialism: The Highest Stage of Capitalism* (1916), Lenin wrote that "the uneven and spasmodic development of individual enterprises, individual branches of industry and individual countries is inevitable under the capitalist system."[34] Essentially, he argued that by the beginning of the twentieth century uneven development had acquired three main aspects.

The *first* was the process by which the advanced states had reached their leading positions within the structured inequality of the world system. During the late nineteenth century the "skipping of stages" had been the experience of several states, notably Germany, Italy, and Japan. The pressure of military and commercial competition between the actual or aspirant great powers forced those that were still absolutist states based on the feudal mode of production—at least, the ones that were capable of doing so—to adopt the current stage of development achieved by their capitalist rivals, if they were to have any chance not only of successfully competing but of surviving at the summit of the world order. In very compressed timescales they had been able to adopt the socioeconomic achievements of Britain to the extent that they became recognizably the same kind of societies, without necessarily reproducing every characteristic of the Anglo-Saxon pioneer: where backwardness remained it tended to be in the nature of the political regimes led by monarchs or emperors supported by a landowning aristocracy.

By the outbreak of the First World War membership of the dominant states was essentially fixed. What remained was the *second* aspect of uneven development: the ongoing rivalry between the great powers that involved them constantly trying to "catch up and overtake" each other in a contest for supremacy that would continue as long as capitalism itself. This rivalry led in turn to a *third* aspect: the developed imperialist states collectively but competitively asserting their dominance over two other types, described by Lenin as "the colonies themselves" and "the diverse forms of dependent countries which, politically, are formally independent, but in fact are enmeshed in the net of financial and diplomatic dependence," like Argentina and Portugal.[35] Colonial expansion prevented some of the societies subject to it from developing at all, and in the case of the least developed, the peoples involved suffered near or complete extermination, and their lands were taken by settlers. More often the peoples survived, but their social systems were immobilized by imperial powers interested in strategic advantage or plunder, or both.

Trotsky, writing in 1907–09, was one of a group of Marxist thinkers (including Rudolf Hilferding in 1910 and Antonio Gramsci in 1917) who noted the way in which backward states did not recapitulate the entire history of capitalist development again, but began at the most advanced forms of technology and the labor process.[36] The insight was not restricted to Marxists. In 1915 the radical American economist Thorstein Veblen claimed—with some exaggeration—that in both economic and political terms Germany in 1870 had been two hundred and fifty years behind England. By the time of the First World War Germany had overcome this lag, but only in some respects. Veblen argued that, as in the case of Japan, these technologies that arrived "ready-made" would not necessarily overcome ideological or political backwardness, with which they could coexist for a period at least.[37] As we shall see, Trotsky's position was subtly different from this.

By the First World War, then, a group of politically diverse thinkers had arrived at broadly similar conclusions about how capitalism had developed since the first epoch of bourgeois revolutions from above had ended in 1871. Specifically, they recognized that there were advantages in starting from a relatively backward position. It was possible to begin industrialization with the most advanced forms of technology and industrial organization, rather than work through all the stages of development that their predecessors had experienced. Indeed, it was impossible for them to avoid doing so if they wished to enter the competitive struggle between national capitals with any hope of success.

TROTSKY

We can now return to Trotsky and to the new element that he introduced into the debate. In *Results and Prospects* Trotsky acknowledged the influence of Kautsky on his argument that the working class would be the dominant force in the Russian Revolution, and that the peasantry would only play a subordinate role. Where he went beyond Kautsky—and indeed everyone else who took this position—was in suggesting that the Russian Revolution could lead not only to the overthrow of absolutism but to socialism, provided it was joined by the revolutionary movement in the advanced West.[38] What was missing from Trotsky's account of permanent revolution was any explanation for the *origin* of the revolutionary process—for the revolutionary militancy of the Russian working class and, by extension, at least some of the other working classes in the underdeveloped world.

The most famous (and certainly the most often quoted) passage in Trotsky's *The History of the Russian Revolution* is an expression of this position: "The privilege of historic backwardness—and such a privilege exists—permits, or rather compels, the adoption of whatever is ready in advance of any specified date, skipping a whole series of intermediate stages."[39] But if all that Trotsky had proposed was a schema in which the "advantages of backwardness" allowed less developed nation-states to adopt the most modern available technologies, he would have remained within the established limits of unevenness and, indeed, would not have distinguished himself from Stalinist usage of the same concept. Indeed, the position was standard in Stalinist textbooks for several decades after the Second World War.[40] As Ernest Mandel once wrote, part of the "magnificent theoretical achievement" represented by the law of uneven and combined development is precisely that it is "quite distinct from the law of uneven development familiar to all Marxists."[41] Why was the distinction necessary?

Trotsky certainly took uneven development in the three senses outlined above as his starting point—as is suggested by the word order in the title of his own theory: "I would put *uneven* before *combined*, because the second grows out of the first and completes it."[42] How then does the concept of uneven and combined development differ from uneven development as such? The main difference is that it is takes account of the internal *effects* of uneven development.[43] To explain the link between the advanced nature of Russian industry on the one hand, and the militancy of Russian workers on the other, Trotsky had to transcend the theory of uneven development, a process he did not complete until the early 1930s. The inability of uneven development to fully encapsulate these phenomena is what appears to have made Trotsky search for a new concept with which to supplement it. It took a political crisis to provoke this conceptualization.

During the Chinese Revolution of 1925–27 the emergent Stalinist regime in Russia ordered the local Communist party to subordinate its own organization and demands to those of the bourgeois nationalists in the Kuomintang. The ultimately disastrous outcome for the Chinese working-class movement was the catalyst for Trotsky to generalize the strategy of permanent revolution from Russia to sections of the colonial and semicolonial world, not indiscriminately—since some were still untouched by capitalist development and had no working class of any size—but where conditions similar to those in Russia prevailed. Due to a common set of circumstances, the working classes in these countries had far greater levels of both consciousness and organization than the proletariat in the more developed countries, where Marxists had traditionally expected the socialist revolution to begin. Trotsky claimed that "the prediction that historically backward Russia could arrive at the proletarian revolution sooner than advanced Britain rests almost entirely upon the law of uneven development."[44] But uneven development was not the sole basis for this prediction, as we can see by contrasting actual Russian development with two possible alternatives.

One was the path of the advanced capitalist states. The pace of development was relatively faster in most of the countries that followed Holland and England, partly because of the urgency of acquiring the attributes of capitalist modernity and partly because the long period of experiment and evolution, characteristic of the two pioneers, could be dispensed with. In the case of Scotland in the eighteenth century or Prussia in the nineteenth century, this led to enormous tensions that resolved themselves in moments of class struggle foreshadowing the process of permanent revolution, above all in the 1820 general strike in the former and the 1848 revolution in the latter. But because these societies did make the transition to the ranks of the advanced societies, either as the center (Prussia/Germany) or a component part of another national formation (Scotland/Britain), these moments passed with the tensions that caused them.

The other was the path of the colonies or semicolonies. What Peter Curtin calls "defensive modernization" was not enough to protect these societies from Western incursions. In the case of the Merina monarchs of Madagascar, for example: "They not only failed to modernize beyond adopting Christianity and superficial European fashions, they failed to build a kind of society and government administration that would perpetuate their own power."[45] Colonial rule could even throw societies backward, as in the case of British-occupied Iraq. Ruling through the Hashemite monarchy after 1920, the regime deliberately rejected any attempts at modernization, except in the oil industry. Instead, it reinforced disintegrating tribal loyalties and semifeudal tenurial relationships over the peasantry. Peter Gowan describes the British initiatives as "the creation of *new* foundational institutions of landownership in order to *revive* dying traditional authority relations, resulting in economically and socially regressive consequences, undertaken for thoroughly modern imperialist political purposes—namely, to create a ruling class dependent upon British military power and therefore committed to imperial interests in the region."[46]

A further group of states embodied "combination." These were unable to reproduce the level of development attained by the advanced capitalist states, but were nevertheless able to "unblock" themselves to the extent of making partial advances in specific areas. There were essentially three subsets in this group. The first were feudal-absolutist or tributary states, like Russia or Turkey, which, under pressure from the Western powers, were forced for reasons of military competition to introduce limited industrialization and partial agrarian reform. The second were still more backward states like China or regions like the post-Ottoman Arab Middle East, which had been broken by imperialist pressure but which, instead of being colonized, were allowed to disintegrate while the agents of foreign capital established areas of industrialization under the protection of either their own governments or local warlords. The third were colonial states like British India, and to a lesser extent French Algeria, where the metropolitan power was unwilling to allow full-scale industrialization in case it produced competition for its own commodities, but was prepared to sanction it in specific circumstances for reasons of military supply or where goods were not intended for home markets. Tsarist Russia neither emulated the process of "catch up and overtake" among the advanced countries nor suffered that of "blocked development" with the backward, but instead experienced a collision between the two.

It was in relation to developments in China that Trotsky finally moved beyond uneven development. He continued to employ the term between 1928 and 1930, most importantly in the articles collected in *The Third International after Lenin* and in *Permanent Revolution* and its various prefaces. In these texts his main emphasis is still distinguishing his use of uneven development from that of Stalin, for whom countries developed at different tempos and therefore had to advance through a series of stages—including that of socialism—at their own individual pace. Trotsky highlighted instead the "unity" of the world economy and the "interdependence" of the imperial powers and the colonial and semicolonial world. Unevenness in this sense means simultaneously that individual countries could leap over the capitalist stage of development, as Russia had done and as China might have done, but would still be unable to complete the transition to socialism while the world economy as a whole remained dominated by the capitalist mode of production: the international system was both a spur at one moment and a block at another.[47] Yet these important insights still did not address the question of how the first part of this process, the revolutionary moment, was possible; Trotsky needed a new concept, incorporating uneven development but deepening its content.

It was in the first volume of *The History of the Russian Revolution* (1932) that he first outlined this new concept: "From the universal law of unevenness thus derives another law which for want of a better name, we may call the law of combined development—by which we mean a drawing together of the different stages of the journey, a combining of separate steps, an amalgam of archaic with more contemporary forms."[48] The precise forms that combination took obviously varied depending on whether the country involved was a formal colony controlled by a single imperial power, like India, or one nominally independent but actually subdivided between several warlords and imperial powers, like China. Clearly there were differences.

Unlike tsarist Russia, neither imperial nor republican China was in a position to stimulate capitalist industrial growth. Where similarities did exist was in the role of foreign capital and imported technology, and in the limited geographical implantation of capitalist industry. Nevertheless it was possible to generalize in relation to the effects: "Historical backwardness does not imply a simple reproduction of the development of advanced countries, like England or France, with a delay of one, two, or three centuries. It engenders an entirely new 'combined' social formation in which the latest conquests of capitalist technique and structure root themselves into relations of feudal or pre-feudal barbarism, transforming and subjecting them and creating peculiar relations of classes."[49]

Uneven and combined development affects the totality of a national society, not merely the economy. Trotsky was not saying that forms characteristic of different stages of development simply coexist alongside each other in striking or dramatic contrasts, although that could be true. Nor was he just emphasizing the existence of transitional modes of production, although he recognized that these could exist. Uneven and combined development usually involves what Michael Burawoy calls "the combination of the capitalist mode of production with pre-existing modes."[50] Jamie Allinson and Alex Anievas, too, have written of how the "logics of different modes of production interact with one another in consequential ways in backward countries."[51] But a process that permeates every aspect of society, ideology as much as economy, must involve more than this. The "articulation" of capitalist and precapitalist modes had, after all, been progressing slowly in the Russian countryside since the abolition of serfdom in 1861 and had led to many complex transitional forms, as Lenin documented.[52] None by themselves led to the type of situation Trotsky was seeking to explain: "At the same time that peasant land-cultivation as a whole remained, right up to the revolution, at the level of the seventeenth century, Russian industry in its technique and capitalist structure stood at the level of the advanced countries, and in certain respects even outstripped them."[53]

The detonation of the process requires sudden, intensive industrialization and urbanization, regardless of whether the preexisting agrarian economy was based on feudal or capitalist relations. Burawoy is therefore right to describe uneven and combined development as a product of "the timing of industrialisation in relation to the history of world capitalism."[54] Here too the Chinese experience was important. Trotsky was quite insistent—perhaps overly insistent—on which mode dominated the Chinese social formation. He rejected Communist International claims that feudalism predominated in the Chinese economic base and political superstructure: "Of course, matters would be quite hopeless if feudal survivals did really *dominate* in Chinese economic life," he wrote in 1929. "But fortunately, survivals in general cannot dominate." Instead he emphasized the extent of market relations and influence of different forms of mercantile and banking capital. Rural social relations "stem in part from the days of feudalism; and in part they constitute a new formation," but within this formation, "it is capitalist relations that *dominate* and not 'feudal' (more correctly, serf and, generally, pre-capitalist) relations. Only thanks to this dominant role of capitalist relations can we speak seriously of the prospects of proletarian hegemony in a national revolution."[55]

Whatever the extent of Trotsky's exaggerations here, it is important—not least in relation to modern China—that uneven and combined development can take place where the capitalist mode was already dominant.[56] The archaic and the modern, the settled and the disruptive, overlap, fuse, and merge in all aspects of the social formations concerned, from the organization of arms production to the structure of religious observance, in entirely new and unstable ways, generating socially explosive situations in which revolution became what Georg Lukács termed "actual."[57] It is tempting to describe these as mutations, except that the inadequacy of the language led Trotsky to reject the biological metaphors in which stages of development had been described from the Enlightenment to the Third International in its Stalinist phase: "The absorptive and flexible psyche, as a necessary condition for historical progress, confers on the so-called social 'organisms,' as distinguished from the real, that is, biological organisms, an exceptional variability of internal structure."[58]

These new combined formations gave rise to conflicts unknown in earlier historical periods. On the one hand: "The [backward] nation . . . not infrequently debases the achievements borrowed from outside in the process of adapting them to its own more primitive culture."[59] From 1861 tsarism established factories using manufacturing technology characteristic of monopoly capitalism in order to produce arms with which to defend a feudal-absolutist state.[60] On the other hand, by doing so they brought into being a class more skilled, more politically conscious, than that faced by any previous absolutist or early capitalist states.[61] All subsequent non-Marxist theories of "the advantages of backwardness" assumed that technological transfers had a limited, or at least delayed, impact on other aspects of social life.[62] Against this, Trotsky argued that these transfers could in fact quicken the pace of change more generally, so that they attained higher levels of development than their established rivals. As an example of this he drew attention to the greater implantation of Marxist theory among the working classes of Russia and, later, China than in that of Britain. Thus, for Trotsky, the most important consequence of uneven and combined development was the enhanced capacity it gave the working classes for political and industrial organization, theoretical understanding, and revolutionary activity:

> When the productive forces of the metropolis, of a country of classical capitalism . . . find ingress into more backward countries, like Germany in the first half of the nineteenth century, and Russia at the merging of the nineteenth and twentieth centuries, and in the present day in Asia; when the economic factors burst in a revolutionary manner, breaking up the old order; when development is no longer gradual and "organic" but assumes the form of terrible convulsions and drastic changes of former conceptions, then it becomes easier for critical thought to find revolutionary expression, provided that the necessary theoretical prerequisites exist in the given country.[63]

But uneven and combined development can also work, as it were, in reverse: "debased adaptation" is not only a feature of backward societies. Here too the opening of the age of imperialism is decisive. Between 1870 and 1914, for example, imperial Britain, Germany, and Japan all consciously emphasized the role of their monarch-emperors; in each case, the preexisting symbolism of the Crown was used to represent national unity against two main challenges: external imperial rivalry and internal class divisions.[64] But Trotsky saw this as a much more general phenomenon, one necessarily caused by the need to maintain bourgeois hegemony over the exploited and oppressed in an era of revolution, and which reached its apogee in the US: "It is considered unquestionable that technology and science undermine superstition. But the class character of society sets substantial limits here too. Take America. There, church sermons are broadcast by radio, which means that the radio is serving as a means of spreading prejudices."[65]

Trotsky's argument suggests two questions about the character of uneven and combined development. One is whether it applies to all periods in human history. Trotsky himself tended to think that it did. His claim that "the entire history of mankind is governed by the law of uneven development" can certainly be defended.[66] He later extended this, writing in *The Revolution Betrayed* (1937): "The law of *uneven* development is supplemented throughout the whole course of history by the law of *combined* development."[67] Whether this is equally defensible is, however, another matter.[68] Trotsky did not attempt to demonstrate his claims for the transhistoricity of uneven and combined development, but Justin Rosenberg has attempted to do so with examples from the Russian state after 800 AD, which he claims show three aspects of combination. First, "the course of Russian development was 'combined' in the sense that at every point it was causally integrated with a wider social field of interacting patterns of development."[69] By this he means that Russia was subject to "inter-societal causality," an environment in which the endless interplay of other states or social forces shaped her internal structure in a way that could never be completed. Second, combination also involved "structures" that "extended beyond Russia itself." Among such structures Rosenberg includes "regional political orders, cultural systems and material divisions of labour." The third, "yet deeper" dimension is the consequence of the first two, the creation of a "hybrid" social formation, "a changing amalgam of pre-existent 'internal' structures of social life with external sociopolitical and cultural influences." Consequently, there "never existed a 'pre-combination' Russia"; at every point its existence was traversed by these influences: "combined development identifies the inter-societal, relational texture of the historical processes within which the shifting meanings of the term 'Russia' crystallized and accumulated." In general terms, Rosenberg invites us to "abandon at the deepest theoretical level any notion of the constitution of society as analytically prior to its interaction with other societies."[70]

The inseparability of the international from the social is, however, inscribed in historical materialism from the moment of its formation, notably in *The German*

Ideology. But in this moment, Marx and Engels were also clear that "history becomes world history" only as a result of capitalism.[71] Why? Before capitalism all class societies, with the exception of those based on slavery, were based on variations of the same mode of production, involving surplus extraction from a class of peasants and taking either a "feudal" or "tributary" form depending on whether the main agent of exploitation was a class of local landlords or the state bureaucracy.[72] There were important differences between them, particularly in terms of how the ruling classes organized, but most precapitalist societies seem to have involved elements of both, with one or the other achieving dominance at different times. Those cases that were the purest examples of one variant or the other (for example, feudal England or tributary China) had quite different possibilities for capitalist development. Until that development took place, however, societies could borrow from each other, influence one another—particularly in the field of culture and philosophy—but were not sufficiently differentiated from each other for elements to "combine" to any effect. The very terms that Trotsky uses in describing combination—"archaic and more contemporary forms"—were unthinkable until capitalism defined what it meant to be "archaic."[73]

We therefore need to draw a distinction between Trotsky's general account of Russian development, which, as Rosenberg correctly says, was always subject to external influence, and the specific moment at which these influences were not merely successfully absorbed into an endlessly mutating social form, but also set up a series of tensions that threatened to, and eventually did, tear the fabric of Russian society apart in 1917. The moment of uneven and combined development, in other words, only arrived with capitalist industrialization and the historically unique society to which it gave rise. The immense difference between industrial capitalism and previous modes of production meant that, from the moment the former was introduced, combination became *possible* in a way that it had not been hitherto; but the structural dynamism of industrial capitalism compared to previous modes of production also meant that combination became *inescapable*, as all aspects of existing society registered the impact on them, to differing degrees, of this radically new means of exploitation. "In contrast to the economic systems that preceded it," wrote Trotsky, "capitalism inherently and constantly aims at economic expansion, at the penetration of new territories, the conversion of self-sufficient provincial and national economies into a system of financial interrelationships."[74] Rosenberg himself notes that "for Trotsky, capitalism did not just change the world: it actually changed the overall nature of historical change itself."[75] I think he has insufficiently incorporated this insight into his own work.

The second question is whether uneven and combined development is a process necessarily confined to individual states. Rosenberg argues that, for Trotsky, "'combined development' was a phenomenon not of individual societies alone, but of the evolving international social formation as a whole."[76] In a discussion of Marx's original plan for the structure of *Capital*, he further claims that if we "neglect the significance of uneven and combined development" at the level of those determinants that apply to all societies, then the result will ultimately be either economic reductionism or a version of Realist International Relations theory in which states appear as sovereign actors seeking—insofar as they are able—advantage and security within the global system.[77] Colin Barker has reached similar conclusions to those of Rosenberg, suggesting that an "extended" concept of uneven and combined development is implicit in Trotsky's own work: "Only from the angle of world economy, of the *combined development* of the different countries within it, do words like 'advanced' and 'archaic' have any meaning, as measures of *coercive comparison* within a larger system of competitive transactions."[78]

I have more sympathy with these arguments, since, as I have argued above, uneven and combined development is produced by the impact of different aspects of the international capitalist system (economic competition, military rivalry, and colonial rule) on the societies constitutive of it. It is important, however, not to confuse the *sources* of a particular historical process with the process itself. Trotsky famously wrote that "Marxism takes its point of departure from world economy, not as a sum of national parts, but as a mighty and independent reality which has been created by the international division of labour and the world market, and which in our epoch imperiously dominates the national markets."[79] Uneven and combined development is a consequence of the world economy, but it is played out within the component parts of the states system: the territorial confines of these states are where the specific combinations take place. Indeed, it is difficult to see how any analysis of a "concrete situation" can be undertaken while remaining at the level of "the international." If the writers quoted in the previous paragraph are right, and what happened in Russia was merely an example of a universal process, then what remains of the "peculiarities" of Russian development, which Trotsky took as the basis of his theory, and which he later extended to other areas of the colonial and semicolonial world? If everywhere is subject to uneven and combined development then it clearly explains nothing in particular about Russia, or anywhere else for that matter, and we must search for another theory to achieve what Trotsky sought to do.

Uneven and combined development is a feature of certain societies: unlike the world economy of which Trotsky spoke, or the states system, whose interaction gave it birth, it does not constitute "an independent reality" greater than its component parts. Uneven development occurs at the international level, but it is meaningless to talk about combined development in this respect. The significance of the process is precisely the tensions and conflicts to which it gives rise within the territorial boundaries of particular states, not least because the state itself is a combined formation. In Russia after 1861, for example, the state apparatus remained staffed by members of the landed aristocracy; but these were not, as in England after 1688 and Germany after 1871, essentially agrarian capitalists but rather feudal landlords presiding over a complex set of class relationships in various early stages of the transition to capitalism. The absolutist state nevertheless needed to industrialize in order to remain in a position of military parity with its rivals, but the reliance that it placed on the landlord class meant that industrialization could not be financed through taxation or by using the appropriation of agricultural surpluses. This in turn compelled the state to borrow foreign capital, above all from France, with contradictory effect. Industrialization took place rapidly and intensively, but without leading to the creation of a powerful native bourgeoisie. In order to sustain it the state needed to export grain in order to service its foreign debt repayments, leading, as prices for the commodity fell, to greater pressure on the peasantry to deliver more without the means to increase productivity, which led in turn to growing peasant unrest. And since industrialization effectively coincided with the transition to capitalism, the proletariat was formed without intermediary stages, making it more volatile from the start, in a situation where the state could afford less in terms of making concessions over wages, conditions, or political rights.[80]

CONCLUSION

We can now summarize the argument. The theory of uneven development was a major theoretical breakthrough in two respects, by identifying both the relative changes in position between the advanced capitalist powers and the structural inequalities between these powers and the colonial and neocolonial world that they dominated. It further showed, with regard to the first set of relationships, how in the competitive struggle, national capitals could attain temporary economic advantage, but their rivals could appropriate in completed form the technologies, skills, or organizations that had given this advantage, without having to repeat the entire developmental process. This applied in the cases of those undertaking capitalist industrialization and of those already engaged in industrial competition. What the theory omitted, particularly as it became codified under Stalinism, was how this process applied in the case of the colonial and neocolonial world. Indeed, it was assumed that it was irrelevant: unevenness was seen as a dynamic process *within* the advanced capitalist world, but essentially as static *between* the advanced capitalist world and the colonial or neocolonial world. The theory of uneven *and* combined development explained what occurs when the same "overleaping" process takes place in the colonial or neocolonial world, where it is impossible to fully "catch up" with, let alone "overtake," the developed West, and developing states must do so instead in a fragmentary or partial way. But the resulting combined forms, because of their inbuilt social instability, paradoxically made revolutionary outbreaks more likely than in the developed world, with its greater levels of stability and reformist traditions. In other words, combined and uneven development made it possible for a strategy of permanent revolution to be pursued.

There is a particular irony in the fact that Trotsky, who emphasized more than any of his contemporaries the reality of the world economy, was also the thinker who refocused attention from "the international" in general to its impact on individual nation-states. He never faltered in his belief that the socialist revolution could only ever be accomplished on a global basis, but was equally forceful in arguing that the strategies adopted by revolutionaries outside the developed West had to be based on an assessment of the extent of combined development and the specific forms that it took.

CHINA: UNEVENNESS, COMBINATION, REVOLUTION?

INTRODUCTION

The pace of change in contemporary China is so intense that discussions of it intended for publication are often overtaken by events before they appear in print—a fate from which contributions to collections of essays are not exempt. It would therefore be futile to try to register every episode down to the one that happens to be current as I write (the impact of Chinese textiles on European markets), the historical significance of which is in any case unlikely to be apparent immediately. I want instead to situate recent Chinese developments, particularly since 1978, within the framework of uneven and combined development. If there is one place in the world where the *process* is unmistakable, it is China, but what should the *theory* lead us to expect from the process?

THE FIRST PHASE OF UNEVEN AND COMBINED DEVELOPMENT[1]

China was the first country outside Russia for which Trotsky argued that a strategy of permanent revolution was applicable; and, although he did not formulate the law of uneven and combined development until after the revolutionary crisis of the 1920s had ended in disaster for the working class, it clearly lay behind his political conception. Combination emerges from unevenness where a backward country attempts to "catch up" with the advanced in terms of capitalist development, but is unable to complete the process fully in the way that Scotland did in the eighteenth century or that Japan did in the nineteenth. These countries are then in a contradictory position. They may have adopted the most modern forms of technology, industrial organization, and scientific thought in certain areas, but most of society remains at a much lower level. The decisive point, however, is that the archaic and modern do not simply sit side by side, offering a picturesque or appalling contrast according to personal taste, but interpenetrate to produce new hybrid forms of explosive instability. The importance of China in relation to Trotsky's theorization of the process was that it clarified two important issues that the Russian experience did not.

First, it made clear that the process of uneven and combined development was not confined to countries, like Russia, that were either politically independent of imperialism or themselves imperial powers. The precise forms that combination took in these countries obviously varied depending on whether the country involved was a formal colony controlled by a single imperial power, like India, or one nominally independent but actually subdivided between several warlords and imperial powers, like China. Clearly there were differences. Unlike tsarist Russia, neither imperial nor republican China was in a position to stimulate capitalist industrial growth. Where similarities did exist was in the role of foreign capital and imported technology, and in the limited geographical implantation of capitalist industry.

Second, it demonstrates that "combination" does not necessarily involve two different modes of production. Where industrial capitalism was established in China, the changes it involved for the working class were dramatic. After 1918, these workers were mainly former peasants or rural laborers, who were now subject to the very different and unaccustomed rhythms of industrial urban life without any intervening stage. Jean Chesneaux writes that the main characteristics of the Chinese proletariat were "its youth, its instability, its swollen lower ranks and its lack of a developed labor elite."[2] And in this the Chinese working class closely resembled its Russian forerunner, not least in the openness to Marxism that these conditions tended to produce.

Combined development was not only experienced in the workplace, of course, but in the entire texture of urban life where capitalism took hold. Shanghai was in the vanguard in terms of both production and consumption. It had textile mills before anywhere in the southern states of the US and by 1930 was home to the largest mill in the world; the first cinema in Shanghai opened only five years after the first large cinema opened in San Francisco.[3] But important though it was, Shanghai was not the only site of these transformations. By the 1920s Lanzhou, the capital of Gansu province, was "a study in contrasts weighted towards the pre-industrial": "A few official buildings, banks and hospitals in Lanzhou were modern style and of two or three stories. But most residences and shops had dirt floors, mud roofs and old-style paper windows. Self-consciously conservative Lanzhou residents described their community as one in which 'women's feet are small [bound] and heads [hair-styles] are big.' But more recently, the number of women with natural feet and bobbed hair had seemed to increase day by day."[4]

The parallels between the 1920s and what is currently happening in China are striking. Harold Isaacs opened his classic account of the Chinese Revolution of the former decade with this evocative picture:

> On the fringes of big Chinese cities the shadows of lofty factory chimneys fall across fields still tilled with wooden ploughs. On the wharves of seaports modern liners unload goods carried away on the backs of men or shipped inland on primitive barges. In the streets great trucks and jangling trams roar past carts drawn by men harnessed like animals to their loads. Automobiles toot angrily at man-drawn rickshaws and barrows which thread their way through the lanes of traffic. Streets are lined with shops where men and women and children still fashion their wares

with bare hands and simple tools. On some of these streets are huge mills run by humming dynamos. Airplanes and railroads cut across vast regions linked otherwise only by footpaths and canals a thousand years old.[5]

Yet a recent account of China found different, but equally evocative, contrasts in the rapidly growing cities of the 1990s:

> We find, at one end of the economic scale, international hotels, shopping malls, housing developments, nightclubs, gold shops, modern factories funded largely by foreign investment, Development Zones, new roads and airfields. . . . At the other end of the urban spectrum, we find serious overcrowding in colorful but unmodernized lanes, alleys, sweatshops and back-street factories which are frequently ill-lit and unsafe, an array of small peddlers and street stalls reflecting considerable underemployment, and a new underclass composed of part-time or professional criminals, beggars and even street-children (now estimated to total at least 200,000 throughout China).[6]

The same process has obviously not persisted uninterruptedly over the intervening period of eighty years. What has happened?

DECADES OF REVERSAL

In effect, the components of the Chinese social formation separated out as the process of combined development went into reverse toward the end of the 1920s. The defeat of the working-class movement by the Kuomintang alone would not in itself have achieved this result. More significant was the devastation caused by civil war between the Kuomintang and the People's Army, and, overlapping with it, the subsequent national war between the Japanese and both Chinese forces. "In Shanghai, which had been the center of the textile industry and of working class formation, the war essentially wiped out the working class as factories closed and workers retreated to the countryside to survive."[7] What is interesting is that the process of uneven and combined development did not resume with the advent of the Maoist regime in 1949.

After the Second World War almost every developing nation pursued a strategy of urbanization, in addition to one of industrialization, whatever the ostensible nature of the regime. In some cases the cities expanded regardless of whether a conscious strategy of growth had been pursued or not. Many former country dwellers found even the dangerous uncertainties of life in the shanty towns that circle all the great Third World conurbations more attractive than the unchanging, unending toil of peasant life. China was the major exception. From the launch of the First Five-Year Plan in 1952, investment was concentrated into production for heavy industry, not consumption. In this respect the Chinese path resembled that of Russia after 1928 and Eastern Europe after 1948. However, it diverged from them in that the growth of urban population was far more tightly controlled. Labor requirements were met through the "temporary worker system," which conferred no rights on incomers and was widely criticized when state control temporarily slackened during the Cultural Revolution.[8] It was successful enough, as R. Bin Wong puts it, to have "effectively created distinct economic worlds in China's cities and the far vaster countryside."[9] Consequently, although industrial output grew 17 times between 1952 and 1978, the urban population in 1978 was only 2.4 times larger than it had been in 1949.[10]

One of the main sites of combined development is the industrial city, the breeding ground in which new mutations are born. The Maoist regime seems to have consciously aimed at preventing China's cities from playing this role. In part, this was because the cities could not have accommodated migration from the countryside, and any influx would have threatened social order. But the regime had no intention of expanding the urban area to house potential migrants: "Communist bureaucrats feared urban growth, because they recognized the peril in population concentrations that weighed too heavily on public infrastructures, with some people enjoying secure jobs in state run enterprises and bureaucracies while others scrambled at the margins of society."[11] The Chinese Communist Party (CCP), it seems, was not only opposed to Trotsky but to the social process that he identified and sought to theorize. In effect, it sought to compartmentalize all sections of Chinese society in a process that one is tempted to call "uneven and separate development": "In the years of 1954–1956, a constellation of policies created a great divide between the state and the collective sectors, between city and the countryside, and between industry and agriculture. These multifaceted processes formalized sectoral divisions, gave local and political sanction to lifetime (and even intergenerational) positions, and permanently froze individuals and households in sectoral jobs and residential pigeonholes."[12] Unevenness remained and grew. Ajit Bhalla notes that there was a conflict between the twin strategies of "self-reliance" and "balanced regional development": "The strategy of self-reliance and self-sufficiency seems to have reinforced regional inequalities and may in practice have neutralized the egalitarian effects of redistributive measures. The promotion of rural industry, within the framework of a local self-reliant strategy, seems to have widened regional inequalities."[13]

In addition to preventing the social combustion of unfettered development, the regime also tried to bind the new working class materially to the state. Raymond Lau has noted that "the workers were tied to the enterprise's exploitative and hierarchical relations by means of a form of lifelong personal (and family) dependence on its leaders who, inter alia, took care of them as a 'parental authority' by means of collectivist practices." He argues that in the enterprise or "work unit," "hierarchical relations were a modified form of the organization of socio-political life in the traditional village, and recogniz[ed] the predominant peasant origins of the CCP and the newly created working class." Exploited though they obviously were, workers were therefore spared full exposure to the accompanying effects of industrialization and urban modernity.[14]

UNEVEN AND COMBINED DEVELOPMENT RESUMED

It was the break with Maoist economic and social policy initiated in 1978 that allowed the process of uneven and combined development to resume. Harvey has argued that the reforms (the "Four Modernizations") initiated by Deng have to be seen as an early episode in the global turn to neoliberalism.[15] The inclusion of China within this trend is apt, perhaps even more so than Harvey supposes. If we regard the Chinese system after 1949 as a form of bureaucratic state capitalism (as I do), then events after 1978 are best seen as shifts within an already dominant capitalist mode of production—more extreme than those in the West, of course, because of the almost total level of state ownership and control in China, but essentially of the same type. It is the social impact of neoliberalism, rather than the policies themselves, that distinguishes China from the rest of the world, even the rest of the developing world.

The outcome has by no means been entirely negative for the mass of the population. In 2000 over 1.2 billion people in the world were living on less than one dollar a day and 2.8 billion on less than two dollars a day. The fact that by 2002 the number of those living on a dollar a day had fallen from 30 percent to 23 percent is almost entirely due to economic growth in one country—China.[16] Behind these social changes were the so-called third and fourth waves of industrialization. The first fell between the First World War and the Japanese invasion of 1937. The second began with the First Five-Year Plan (1953–57) and collapsed in the chaos of the Cultural Revolution (1965–68). The third resumed with the rural industrialization projects launched in 1978. But the fourth, from the mid-1980s, has been the most far-reaching and sustained: "Chinese industrialization in the last two decades of the century took place at a speed and on a scale unequalled anywhere in the world." The economy grew by an annual average of 10 percent and per capita income doubled twice over.[17] In 1981 only 53 percent of Chinese exports were manufactures; by 2001, 90 percent were.[18] Only the prior experiences of Lowland Scotland (1760–1820) and Stalinist Russia (1928–41) come anywhere near to matching the speed and intensity of Chinese growth.

Internal unevenness has been exacerbated by post-1978 developments. "While China as a whole is in the middle range of human development, by global standards, some individual regions, such as Shanghai and Beijing, score well above that and would separately rank as high as 25th and 27th in the world; while poor and minority nationality regions such as Tibet and Qinghai belong in the lower range of human development and would rank 147th and 135th respectively."[19] "First World and Third World coexist in China," write Shaoguang Wang and Angang Hu; but First and Third World also coexist *within* regions, not only between them.[20] This is important for two reasons.

First, taken as a whole, it is possible to underestimate the extent of Chinese economic achievement. Andrew Glyn notes that "China is still as far behind the

USA as Korea and Taiwan were before their three decades of rapid catch-up beginning in the late 1960s; its percentage GDP is still well below that from which Japan started its spectacular growth climb in the mid-1950s."[21] But the regional figures give quite a different picture. The most extreme example, Shanghai, has seen the most spectacular growth, with a GDP twice that of the capital Beijing and 5 percent of the national total. It had an average annual growth of 9.5 percent over 1999–2000 and attracted 10 percent of foreign investment in China. The population is over 20 million (although this is still only 1.6 percent of the national total), but of these, only 13.5 million people are permanent residents. The remainder are temporary workers and their families who join them for at least part of the year. Many earn only a fifth of the average income of employed permanent residents ($4,300), although even that is far greater than they would have been able to earn in the countryside where 90 cents a day is common.[22] In the four years between 1994 and 1997 total office space rose from 500,000 square meters to 3.5 million square meters: "Shanghai is achieving in one decade what it took Hong Kong the best part of four decades to do."[23] As an economic actor Shanghai would outperform many Western national capitals.

Second, the mass of the Chinese are becoming aware of the inequalities associated with unevenness in a way that they were not previously:

> Before 1978, China was a closed society. Not only did the country close its doors to the outside world, but localities within the country were also largely cut off from one another. . . . At that time, peasants had little chance of leaving their villages. To them, regional disparities were nothing but differences between production brigades or among different communes. Nor did urban dwellers have much chance of travelling. They knew that there were regional gaps, but without travel and access to television, it was hard for them to imagine how serious regional inequality really was. Quite possibly, perceived regional gaps were smaller than objective ones during the pre-reform years. . . . No longer comparing their localities to neighboring communities, people may now use what they know of the most advanced regions in the country as the benchmark for comparison.[24]

The difference in attitude has been caused by access to media and, more importantly, the freedom—in practice, if not fully in law—to migrate. By the early 1980s there were around two million rural migrants, but by the mid-1990s the figure had risen to around eighty million.[25] In the countryside this has led to enormous pressures as the young in particular are drawn to the cities. In part they are pulled by the possibilities of different experiences, new skills, and higher incomes. In part they are pushed by the rural economic crisis generated by market Stalinism, in which peasants have high and rising production costs but low and falling sales prices; many of the young are consequently surplus in the sense that their families can no longer afford to keep them. The resulting fault line runs throughout Chinese society. Within the family itself it threatens the collectivist approach to intergenerational division of income that both preceded and continued under the Stalinist regime. Hitherto children had contributed to the familial income according to their abilities, and this had been redistributed throughout the family. But with the flight to the cities many children no longer feel the need to assist their siblings who earn less or are simply unable to afford to contribute to the family income because of their own requirements. The regime remains unwilling to encourage permanent urban settlement, although it is prepared tacitly to encourage temporary migration as long as conditions are made so bad that workers are unwilling to consider relocating. This seems to correspond to the wishes of many—particularly the less well educated—of the migrants them-selves, the majority of whom retain some links with the countryside and wish to return there someday. On the other hand, the employers of migrant labor are unwill-ing to train workers only to see them leave and have to be replaced by a new wave of unskilled ones.[26]

It was estimated that in the mid-1990s there were over seventy million farm-ers "floating" in cities throughout China. These urban nomads are not permitted household registration and are consequently excluded from access to free education, subsidized housing, and pensions. "Rural to urban migrants could only find housing in the flourishing private-rental sector and it is not unusual to find several rural migrants crowded into one room in the suburban areas of large cities."[27] The floating population does not simply apply pressure on the urban infrastructure: "Further spatially detached from their home villages, rural migrants could no longer be di-rectly reached by the rural authority in their places of origin. But at the same time, migrants, considered outsiders by local officials, were not effectively brought within the local control system."[28] And the comparisons they draw with their rural situa-tion are exactly the ones that the regime struggled to deny them the opportunity to make: "The peasants and semi-peasants who winter in the city feel comparatively deprived by the tightly locked city walls. Peasants coming in want to enjoy this fat meat with city people. When in the countryside, they feel that everyone is poor, so [their poverty] can be tolerated. But differences in wealth become obvious after entering the city."[29]

Unevenness therefore possesses its own potential for social unrest. But it is es-pecially with reference to the experience of the cities that we see the particular form taken by *combination*. In 1949 there were only six cities in China with more than a million inhabitants; by 2000 there were twenty-three. Yet the greatest growth in both population size and levels of urbanization has come in the last twenty years: between 1949 and 1978 the number of cities of all sizes only grew from 135 to 192, but by 2000 there were nearly 400.[30] There were no cities in the southwestern province of Yunnan in 1949, and the urban population (meaning those who lived in towns not big enough to be called cities) was only 5 percent of the provincial total. By 1989 there were four cities and an urban population of 12 percent, and by 1999 there were fifteen cities and an urban population of 45 percent. In 1994 the urban section of Xuanwei County comprised no more than 7 square kilometers; by 1999 it had nearly doubled to 13 square kilometers. While "the growing urban population and expanded business activities put increasingly high demands on public sanitation and energy supply," it also led to an increased demand for educational provision, which was extracted from the peasants of the rural hinterland through the levy of an "educational surcharge" to pay for what, in China as in Britain, is referred to as "modernization."[31]

Behind the statistics it is the experience of the city, particularly for the recent rural migrant, that offers new forms of consciousness and perception. Rowe has written of the "strange new world" effect experienced by migrants to the cities:

> Many if not most have practically no prior urban experience, given the persistence and strong enforcement of China's household registration system. Although the effect of this sudden change of living environment is also difficult to gauge fully, it will surely be palpable in the future majority's perception and appreciation of life and the manner in which they lay claim to issues on the national agenda. It was often said of Shanghai during its heyday in the 1930s that it was like no other place in China. The effect of this "otherworldliness" now seems likely to spread both widely and rapidly and, when it becomes more fully familiar, the impact on Chinese society will likely be considerable.[32]

But the city is not only a postmodern wonderland of sensory overload: for the majority of urban Chinese, it is a site of intense social struggle. Neoliberalism has brought with it the inevitable increase in sectional unemployment. The official rate in 1997 was 6 million, or 3.2 percent of the urban labor force, although most sources regard this as a massive underestimate. In 1998–2000, 21 million workers in State-Owned Enterprises (SOEs) were sacked, although the regime claims that 13 million of these have since found other jobs. If we add to this number perhaps 15 million workers not formally sacked but "stood down" or suspended from their jobs, and the "floating" population, the true level of unemployment may be nearer 20 percent, or 150 million people.[33]

Even those who are still in work are faced with attacks on their living conditions while they see vast and ostentatious displays of wealth by the "little princes and princesses," the offspring of the bureaucracy and—increasingly—the bourgeoisie proper:

> Today one senses the presence of the new rich throughout the coastal region and larger cities. One not only notes the prevalence of luxury vehicles, four and five star hotels, golf courses, exclusive gyms and clubs, but in many places (such as Shanghai) there are even posh housing complexes that rival the residences of top government officials, surrounded by forbidding gates and separated from ordinary society. . . . [T]his middle class makes up less than 1 percent of the population, but controls at least half of the gross national income.[34]

The balance of employment is shifting from the state sector to that of new private capital. Between 1995 and 1997 the number of workers in the industrial state sectors fell by four million and those in the private sector rose by ten million. The latter figure therefore does not simply represent transfers from one sector to the other but involves the proletarianization of new generations of workers. As Henderson writes: "The benefits of the iron rice bowl were psychological as much as they were real." For a hundred million state workers, "the smashing of the iron rice bowl is a deeply traumatic message, as well as representing a threat to their financial well-being": "Difficult working conditions which were taken for granted in the past when Chinese society was in fact relatively egalitarian (in its misery if nothing else!), are now less tolerated in a time when the official mantra is 'to get rich is glorious.' The perception of widening income gaps reminds the 'proletariat' first and foremost of their stifling working conditions on the factory floor, where advantage is gained by whom one knows rather than what."[35]

The differences between workers in the SOEs and those set up by foreign private capitalists are extreme. And it is not only in terms of wages that the divisions are enormous. Workers in the Reebok factories are expected to work an average of eighty-six hours a month in compulsory overtime. They receive no compensation for dismissal and are "represented" by business unions whose officials are appointed by the factory management. The workforces are almost exclusively female because of the assumption that they will be more docile than ones that are male.[36]

Toward the next Chinese revolution?

The resistance to restructuring has been spectacular. Between 1992 and 1997 an estimated 1.26 million workers were involved in disputes, with this figure rising to 3.6 million in 1998 alone.[37] In one center for foreign capitalists, Xiamen, incomplete strike figures show that there were 50 disputes in 1991, rising to 450 by 1993.[38] Yet it was only in the spring of 2002 that what Leung calls the "third wave" of post-Mao labor movements began to emerge. The first coalesced around the Workers' Autonomous Federations that were set up during the democracy movement of 1989, initially to support the students, who were also allowed to join. After Tiananmen Square and the repression that followed (in which working-class spokesmen for the movement were treated with particular brutality), the second movement took shape between 1990 and 1994 as a series of mostly short-lived underground organizations (such as the League for the Protection of Working People). These were often led by intellectuals and not necessarily involved with the actual, if inchoate, struggles taking place against liberalization. Nevertheless, they were focused on particular issues of concern to the working class, rather than democracy in general. The third wave emerged in the northwest of China in the provinces of Daqing and Liaoyang, where between eighty and one hundred thousand workers, mainly from the oil and metal industries, were involved in strikes, occupations, demonstrations, and road blockades against retrenchment, the absence of social security, and official corruption. The name of one organization, the Daqing Provisional Union of Retrenched Workers, gives some idea of the defensive nature of the movement. Nevertheless, the demands made by workers show an opposition to the bureaucracy that is based on its failure to be sufficiently socialist and supportive of the working class. As Trini Leung writes:

> The 2002 spring protests are still a far cry from mass strikes waged by hundreds
> of thousands of dock and railway workers in Canton, Shanghai and Beijing in the
> 1920s and 1930s, which delivered the first Chinese labor movement. But these
> early labor struggles of the 20th century were primarily nationalist struggles. The
> 21st century labor movement takes shape as a defensive and class-specific struggle.
> In their struggle for the rights to defend their work and livelihoods in the face of
> privatization and globalization, the Chinese labor movement has at last found com-
> mon ground with the democratic labor movements around the world.[39]

It would not be the first time in history that an attack on established terms and
conditions of skilled workers has detonated a more general struggle, spreading out
beyond the groups initially involved. The most immediate comparison here is the
generalized assault on skilled metalworkers across Europe during the First World
War.[40] What will be crucial in China is the link between threatened or displaced
workers from the SOEs and the new workers in foreign and privately owned enterprises—and beyond these, with the vast incendiary countryside.[41] As one reformist
intellectual, Li Minqi, said in a recent roundtable discussion:

> The situation will be different [from 1989] in years to come. For the first time in
> Chinese history the modern working class will soon make up a majority of the pop-
> ulation. This is going to make a decisive contribution to the victory of democracy
> in the future. . . . In the West, the historic strength of the labor movement forced
> the bourgeoisie to make major concessions to the working class, including political
> democracy and the welfare state. . . . But in the case of China, where capitalism de-
> pends so much on the abundance of cheap labor, is there any comparable room for
> the Chinese bourgeoisie to make similar concessions—to grant political democracy
> or social welfare—and at the same time maintain competitiveness in the world
> market and a rapid rate of accumulation? It seems rather questionable.[42]

As Li suggests, the so-called Fourth Generation leaders (i.e., since the Revolution
of 1949) have no intention of moving toward bourgeois democracy. Andrew Nathan
and Bruce Gilley report from their study of internal party documents: "Some of
them want to soften authoritarian rule, make it more responsive, and use the media
and some political institutions, such as elections and courts, as tools to discipline the
lower bureaucracy. But they think that their society is too complex and turbulent to
be governable by a truly open, competitive form of democracy."[43]

Leaving aside appearances, the current discontent has been met by ferocious
levels of repression. An internal investigation report on Lu Gan, the politburo member responsible for law and order, notes that more than sixty thousand people were
either executed or killed by the police between 1998 and 2001—an unsurprising
result given that China currently has sixty-eight capital offenses on the statute book
including "bribery, pimping, selling harmful foodstuffs and stealing gasoline." If these

figures are correct—they are far higher than the Amnesty International estimates—then in 2002 the Chinese state was responsible for approximately 97 percent of all executions committed in the world.[44] This is slaughter on a truly eighteenth-century British scale, what Peter Linebaugh once called "capital punishment as the punishment of capital."[45] Western governments and media offered token protestations—epitomized by Rupert Murdoch in this respect as in many others—but they have no real objection to the repression: "They need the authoritarian rule of the Party to safeguard their billions of dollars of investments, and for this reason are prepared to shut their eyes to any number of crimes it may commit against its own people, first delinking human-rights violations from trade and now keeping silent about the numerous bans on critical works and the suppression of the Fa Lun Gong."[46] In fact the CCP today plays a similar role to that previously played by the Russian tsar or Chinese emperor as the bearer of pure parental authority, no matter what the crimes and corruptions of its representatives in the factory: "Despite widespread corruption, among both SOE leaders and government officials, and notwithstanding the victimization of workers in the state's drive towards reforms, one should not underestimate the extent to which the populace in general, and workers in particular, remain attached to the CCP in the absence of an alternative."[47] Feng has argued that there are parallels here with the moral economy displayed by eighteenth-century British crowds in protecting traditions or established practices and norms in the face of encroaching market relations.[48]

Here we can see aspects of the downside of uneven and combined development, the "debasing of achievements" of which Trotsky spoke in *The History of the Russian Revolution*.[49] In particular, the resumption of the process has left social movements in China at an ideological level below that of the 1920s. Given the way in which the exploitation of the Chinese workers and peasants has been carried out under the banner of Marxism, it is unsurprising that historical materialism has not instantly become the theoretical guide to forces seeking to challenge the regime. Instead many have turned to religion. "The desire for a better life has also seen a religious revival in the country, and for most Chinese the desire for property and material things is complemented by an appeal to the supernatural for aid in that quest."[50] For a large minority this led to support for the Falun Gong, certainly the best known of Chinese religious movements, but it is not alone.

Balong is a hamlet of ninety households in the village of Landu, in the (to Western ears) evocatively named county of Shangri-La. The population was originally Muslim, but increasing religious repression after 1949, climaxing during the Cultural Revolution, led to a situation where virtually no one even recalled what their belief system had involved, except for the prohibition on eating pork. However, during the period of market reforms the hamlet experienced a resurgence of Islamic belief: "Balong's story is not atypical in contemporary China. Across the country there are an increasing number of examples of rural communities that are inventing a heritage, be it through religion or lineage, to promote group identity, rebuild solidarity and safeguard the interests of the community."[51] Or take Sipsongpanna in the southwestern border region of Yunnan, where "hills have been levelled to make way for new roads, power lines have replaced the canopy of the rain forest, and new migrants from the coast are building cities in place of villages." The Buddhist religion practiced by the Tai population has been repressed since 1953, but has recently experienced a revival as monks operating across the national borders of Thailand, Laos, Burma, and China have attempted to introduce these religious beliefs to a new audience, "though today they carry it not on palm leaves but on floppy disks, videos and CDs." As Deborah Davis says: "Thus we should attend not just to the video itself but to the person who carries the video, who puts it in the machine and presses 'play,' who explains the images that appear in terms a village teenager can understand."[52] Religion represents a consolation or defense against the intrusion of capitalist modernity, but religion is also communicated and celebrated using the techniques and technologies that capitalist modernity has provided. State repression of religion may in time drive its adherents to more secular ideologies of resistance, a possibility that is made more likely by the spectacular level of resistance to neoliberal restructuring that is already taking place.

Stanley Rosen has argued that "as the economy continues to grow at a reasonably high rate, the state and society is not likely to produce an unmanageable crisis for the regime in the near term."[53] But this assumes that a crisis will only emerge as the result of economic downturn. However, this survey suggests that it is the very success of the Chinese economy that has produced the internal strains and tensions that threaten to explode. From Tocqueville on, serious students and practitioners of revolution, of whom Trotsky himself was perhaps the most eminent, have argued that revolutions are more likely to occur when social classes see the possibility of improving conditions, rather than when they are in the depths of economic depression or the grip of political repression.[54] In China, conditions for many have improved, and repression is not consistently applied. At Nanchong in Sichuan province, twenty thousand workers besieged the town hall for thirty hours demanding unpaid wages, until officials were forced to organize loans and partial back payments.[55] As one commentator has noted:

> Workers may soon begin to demand more of the benefits that market globalization is bringing to some Chinese. Like workers elsewhere, Chinese laborers may not be satisfied with the line that their wages and benefits must be kept low so as to maintain Chinese "competitiveness" in a global market. In Shekou we saw a rise in worker solidarity as factory laborers described workmates as their closest friends, even across regional and linguistic lines. If these feelings become more widespread, they may give workers the social cohesion to challenge the state and system more forthrightly.[56]

The competitive struggle within the world system led the Chinese ruling class to unleash social forces that for thirty years they had, more or less successfully, prevented from forming. To say, therefore, that China is entering a revolutionary situation, is not to utter a truism about the general objective readiness of the world for socialist revolution, it is to say that quite specific conditions are pushing China in that direction. Although China develops more dramatically than any of the other countries, like India, with which it is usually bracketed, it is unlikely in any remotely foreseeable scenario to "catch up" with the West overall. The tensions that uneven and combined development has brought therefore remain, awaiting release. It may be that China does indeed show us the future, but not quite in the way that those who look to it to save the world capitalist system imagine.

10

THIRD WORLD REVOLUTION

INTRODUCTION

At the beginning of the last century, a series of revolutions in Russia (1905), Turkey (1906), Persia (1909), Mexico (1910), China (1911), and Ireland (1916) announced that the inhabitants of the colonial and semicolonial world were not prepared to be passive spectators of the historical process. Yet beyond freeing themselves from the direct or indirect control of the great powers, the goals of these revolutionary movements were ambiguous, even contradictory. Were they to enable the newly liberated states to enter the world capitalist system? Or were they to achieve a more fundamental freedom for the mass of their populations—in other words, were they to bring about socialism?

At the time most people, including most Marxists, believed that only the former goal was possible: socialism would have to wait until colonial and precapitalist domination had been overthrown. However, from 1905 Leon Trotsky began to develop two concepts that suggested socialism might be a more immediate prospect. One was the theory of "uneven and combined development," which I have discussed in the preceding chapters. To recapitulate: starting from the imperialist stage of capitalism, which opened during the last third of the nineteenth century, advanced forms of capitalist production were introduced into otherwise precapitalist societies, causing new tensions. In particular, capitalist industrialization gave rise to working-class movements that, because of the intensity with which they were formed, had the potential to rise to higher levels of theoretical understanding and industrial militancy than those in the dominant imperialist countries. These new working-class movements often found themselves in conflict with state machines that were much weaker than those of the older capitalist countries.

The other concept was the strategy of permanent revolution made possible by uneven and combined development. The working classes in the developing world, although a minority of the population, have a social weight greater than their numbers. This, Trotsky argued, made them potentially capable of leading the other oppressed classes directly toward socialism.[1] This strategy only gained majority support within the working-class movement during the Russian Revolution of 1917. In every other situation where it has been applicable, alternative strategies have been followed that

189

have led, at worst, to total defeat (China in the 1920s) or, at best, to partial victories that gained considerably less than was possible (South Africa in the 1990s). A crucial factor in these failures has been the absence of a sizeable revolutionary party capable of successfully arguing for permanent revolution.

Colonial rule had not yet achieved its full geographical extent in 1917, and precapitalist regimes still existed. Most of these have long since ended, swept away by a series of revolutions. In China in 1949, Cuba in 1959, and a host of other countries, the transformations masqueraded as Communist in content but in effect acted as the handmaidens of state-capitalist development. Indeed, the Chinese state is now one of the most dynamic sectors in the global capitalist economy. The working class in the Third World has risen time and time again during the same period but has nowhere succeeded in taking power on its own behalf. Does this mean that Trotsky's claims for its revolutionary role have been proved wrong?

Does the Third World still exist?[2]

The first thing we need to establish is that the Third World—in the sense of a group of countries sharing a common position of underdevelopment within the capitalist world system—still exists. For some Marxists this is an unnecessary question. In an interview conducted toward the end of the 1970s, the late Ernest Mandel asked: "Is there a dependent capitalist country, or an ex-colony, that has undergone sufficient socio-economic transformation that the tasks now facing the proletariat in that country are substantially identical to the tasks facing the proletariat of countries such as Germany, France, Britain, or the United States? Once we pose the question in this manner, the answer becomes evident. There is no such country, and there is no reason to expect that there will be one."[3] Against this kind of dogmatism many people, on both sides of the globalization debate, claim that even if the ex-colonies have not achieved Western European levels of development, the situation is considerably more complex than allowed for by Mandel's certainties, for three main reasons.

First, there is the increasingly differentiated pattern of socioeconomic development across Third World countries. Even a hundred years ago, there were difficulties with including in the same category such different states as imperial China, which was disintegrating and increasingly under the control of the great powers; and tsarist Russia, unified and itself an imperial power across two continents. But at least China and Russia were comparable in terms of population and territory. Nevertheless, in the ensuing decades even more disparate countries were grouped together, ultimately under the designation of the "Third World," despite what Eric Hobsbawm calls "the evident absurdity of treating Egypt and Gabon, India and Papua New Guinea as societies of the same type."[4] Indeed, the states that lie outside the core of the system now occupy such different and unequal places that any attempt to continue classifying them under a single heading is completely misleading. As Gilbert Rist writes, "the 'Third World' broke up in the mid-seventies":

At the very moment when it was vigorously expressing its collective demands, it ceased to exist as an entity with a common destiny: now there were ultra-rich countries living off oil-rent, "least developed countries" (LDCs) sunk in extreme poverty, and between the two, the "newly industrialising countries" (NICs). The "common interest" between these groups—an interest anyway based more on their colonial past than on a collective project for the future—has totally disappeared and could no longer sustain any kind of mobilization.[5]

Nor are the differences simply between individual states, but between regions, even between entire continents. There is grotesque poverty in East Asia, but even this is relative, as a comparison with Africa shows:

TABLE I: PERCENTAGES AND NUMBERS OF PEOPLE LIVING IN EXTREME POVERTY[6]

	East Asia (including China)			Sub-Saharan Africa
1987	26.6%	417.5 million	46.6 %	217.2 million
1998	15.3%	278.3 million	46.3 %	290.9 million

What possible comparison can there be between "failed states" like Haiti and Liberia, where the state has essentially collapsed and society reverted to the proverbial war of all against all, and giants like India and—especially—China, which are beginning to challenge the West in economic and even military terms?

The second argument is based not on increasing disparities within the less developed countries but on the increasing homogenization across the world as a whole. In *Empire*, perhaps the most original and certainly the most idiosyncratic contribution to the literature of anticapitalist globalization, Michael Hardt and Antonio Negri argue: "The spatial divisions of the three Worlds (First, Second and Third) have been scrambled so that we continually find the First World in the Third, the Third in the First, and the Second almost nowhere at all." Hardt and Negri do not, however, claim that there are no differences: "If the First World and the Third World, centre and periphery, North and South, were ever really separated along national lines, today they clearly infuse one another, distributing inequalities along multiple and fractured lines. This is not to say that the United States and Brazil, Britain and India are now identical territories in terms of capitalist production and circulation, but rather that between them there are no differences in nature, only degrees."[7]

The third reason follows from the second and is based on the needs of international solidarity in a world entirely dominated by capital. Contemporary activists who advocate globalization from below are understandably reluctant to differentiate between regions of the world, not least because globalization from above is increasingly binding all populations to the same machine. As Roger Burbach writes: "The labouring classes in the North and the South have begun to realise that their struggles against the adverse effects of globalisation must take on a transnational perspective and that they even need to engage in transnational organising."[8] Since 1999 the movements against capitalist globalization and imperialist war have spread from the metropolitan centers in which they first emerged to Latin America, Asia, and Africa, as can been seen from the cities associated with the great forums and demonstrations. Mumbai has contributed as much as Florence in debating resistance to the neoliberal agenda. Representatives of the G8 find themselves as unwelcome in Cancun as they were in Edinburgh. Cairo has been as important as London in opposing the invasion and occupation of Iraq. The international solidarities expressed by this geographical spread are relatively new and absolutely precious. As one Egyptian opponent of the war on Iraq said: "Demonstrations against US and British aggression which take place in London or New York show that the war is not about Christians versus Muslims. It shows that millions in the West disagree with the war—that it's not a new crusade, as the Islamists say."[9] Do we want to jeopardize this unity by focusing on what distinguishes, for example, Egypt from Britain?

CHARACTERISTICS OF THE THIRD WORLD TODAY

And yet, even when the vast disparities between the less developed nations are taken into account, even when the interpenetration of the global economy as a whole is registered, even when the need for unity among the oppressed and exploited on a global scale has been reaffirmed, we are left with the fact that the less developed still share certain defining characteristics that qualitatively distinguish them from the more developed. Four of these characteristics are particularly important. It could be argued that all of these are also present in the more developed countries, but, as we shall see, there are qualitative differences in each case.

First, the majority of the population tends to be poor in absolute rather than relative terms, and this has dramatically increased since the last third of the nineteenth century: "From 1870 to 1990, the average absolute gap in incomes of all countries from the leader has grown by an order of magnitude from $1,286 to $12,662." The ratio of GDP from richest to poorest has increased over the same period from 8.7 to 45.2.[10] The richest 5 percent of the people in the world receive 114 times the income of the poorest 5 percent. The richest 1 percent receive as much as the lowest 57 percent.[11] The poorest tenth of people living in the US have average incomes higher than two-thirds of the world population. The richest tenth of people living in the US have a combined (aggregate) income equal to that of 43 percent of the world population; in other words, twenty-five million Americans have incomes equal to that of two billion other people.[12]

The key distinction is between those less developed countries that have experienced sufficient economic growth for them to compete with the more developed in the market for particular goods and services (the "newly developing countries") and those that have not. Between 1960 and 1981 the percentage of manufacturing output produced in the North American and Western European core of the system fell from 78 percent to 59 percent, while that of the newly industrializing countries (NICs) rose from 22 percent to 42 percent.[13] The greatest increases were in Asia. "By 1990, non-Japanese (non-OPEC) Asia held 13.1 percent of world goods exports, a greater proportion than the US (11.7 percent), Germany (12.7 percent), or Japan (8.5 percent)."[14] As Neil Smith notes, "by the early twenty-first century, five of the largest thirteen economies in the world are Asian or Latin American countries that in 1965 would have been called, unequivocally, 'Third World': China (6th), Mexico (10th), India (11th), South Korea (12th), and Brazil (13th). The economies of the Netherlands, Australia, Russia, Belgium, and Sweden all rank lower."[15]

This does not mean, of course, that everyone in the less developed world is poor: "In Angola's capital Luanda, innumerable street children, amputees and destitute people sleep on the broken pavement amid heaps of rubbish, while the latest models of Mercedes Benz, BMW and Porsche zoom by, their cell phone–holding drivers nattily dressed in French and Brazilian couture."[16] The 2005 *World Wealth Report*, prepared by investment bankers Merrill Lynch and the consultancy firm Capgemini, found that the number of "high net-worth individuals" (i.e., with liquid assets of more than $1m) had increased by 6.5 percent from the previous year to 8.7 million, but the greatest increases had occurred in the developing world, with increase of 21 percent in South Korea, 19 percent in India and 17 percent in Russia.[17] Mike Davis notes: "Even the most egalitarian country in Latin America, Uruguay, has a more unequal distribution of income than any European country."[18] As even Nigel Harris, a born-again supporter of capitalist globalization, notes: "The numbers who are poor have increased and seem to be increasing, even though the proportion of the world's population that is poor is decreasing."[19] The change is largely due to the decrease of extreme poverty in the largest Asian countries like China, India, and Indonesia; those that stay poor are those that remain the least integrated into the world economy. But if we probe beneath the figures even for the new Asian giants, a more complex picture emerges. Peasants working at close to subsistence level may have little or no income as such. Once they have been pushed or pulled from their villages into the cities for work, their income will almost certainly be higher in cash terms, but they will now have to pay for goods and services as commodities that they would once have provided for themselves.[20]

Poverty is also growing in the West. It was always there, of course, even in the golden age of the welfare state. As Harris once expressed it, in the days when he took a less benevolent view of capitalism: "The poor of the United States were defined out of existence. The rich of India were carefully concealed from view."[21] The US is second only to Russia in the extent to which its social structure is polarized, with 27 percent poor or near-poor (below 50 percent median income and between 50 and 62.5 percent median income), 46 percent middle-income (between 62.5 and 150 percent of median income) and 27 percent well-to-do (over 150 percent of median income).[22] Richard Wilkinson reports that data from twenty-three rich and poor areas of the US found:

> White women who had reached the age of sixteen and were living in the richest areas could expect to live until they were eighty-six years old, compared to seventy for black women in the poorest areas of New York, Chicago, and Los Angeles—a difference of sixteen years. Similarly sixteen-year-old white men living in rich areas could expect to live until they were seventy-four or seventy-five, whereas black men in the poorest areas could expect to live to only about fifty-nine. . . . the poorest areas of the United States, such as Harlem in New York or the South Side of Chicago, have death rates that are higher at most ages than in Bangladesh—one of the poorest countries in the world.

As Wilkinson comments: "What would we think of a ruthless government that arbitrarily imprisoned all less well-off people for a number of years equal to the average shortening of life suffered by the less privileged in our own societies? Given that higher death rates are more like arbitrary execution than imprisonment, perhaps we should liken the injustice of health inequalities to that of a government that executed a significant proportion of its population each year without cause."[23] But the swollen bellies of the poor in Galveston are the signs of the malnourishment and obesity associated with the consumption of highly processed and artificially flavored food, not the absence of food altogether that this would indicate in Gujarat.[24] Both are social evils, but the respective urgency with which the second requires to be tackled is much the greater.

The second characteristic, partly as a result of scarcity conditions, is a state that tends to be unstable and consequently prone to both internal police repression and external military adventures: elementary democratic rights freely to assemble, organize, or elect representatives therefore remain basic demands. As Sophie Bessis writes: "Making the construction of industrial cathedrals and more or less totalitarian state apparatuses the alpha and omega of progress, they treated any demands for individual liberty or a redefinition of gender roles as deadly threats to the very foundations of identity." Bessis calls the activities of these regimes "modernization without modernity" and argues that "reduced to its material dimension, that which was called modernity also helped to ensure the survival of regimes on the point of exhaustion."[25] It is, of course, the antidemocratic, repressive nature of these regimes that has provided the Western powers with an excuse for their highly selective military interventions from the Gulf War of 1991 onward.

In the developed world, many rights were imperfect in the first place, and in some areas minorities had very limited access even to formal democratic procedures (blacks in the southern states of the US, Catholics in Northern Ireland). Furthermore, whatever their imperfections, these rights are now under attack across the West, often under the guise of a response to the atrocity of 9/11, precisely because their attainment restricts the power of the state to do what it will with its citizens. In most parts of the developing world, however, they have yet to be won in the first place.

The third characteristic, as the increased level of direct Western intervention suggests, is that the economies and societies of the majority of the less developed states will continue to be influenced or even completely determined by imperialism as a system. Some radicals have seen the wars against Iraq, Serbia, Afghanistan, and Iraq again as "a new round of conquest and colonisation," citing "the overtly 'colonial' character of the war in the Middle East" as evidence.[26] But with the long-term exception of occupied Palestine, colonialism in its classic form no longer exists, nor is it likely to return. Neither those enthusiastic for the US to formally recognize its imperial role nor those anxious for the supposedly "postmodern" West as a whole to take up its responsibilities for maintaining world order argue that territorial empires on the nineteenth-century European model are either desirable or, more importantly, feasible.[27]

The apostles of capitalist globalization have a simple answer. "What we want," said Stephen Krasner, head of policy planning at the US State Department, "is a world of democratic, market-oriented countries."[28] In economics these countries must adopt the neoliberal agenda of privatization, deregulation, and free trade: this will lead to economic development. In politics, they must conform to the norms of representative democracy: this will lead to political stability. It might appear that acceptance of the former effectively minimizes the significance of the latter. As one neoliberal ideologue, Johan Norberg, notes of the Indian turn to "welcoming trade and foreign investments and encouraging competition and enterprise": "The economy was freed from numerous restrictions by three consecutive governments, even though the governments represented different party constellations."[29] Stefan Andreasson calls this "virtual democracy": "Virtual democracy comes at the expense of inclusive, participatory democracy and of any possibility of the extension of public welfare provision that social democratic projects elsewhere have entailed."[30] Supporters of the system believe—or at any rate pretend to believe—that there are no structural obstacles to them becoming Western-style societies. And if these measures are introduced with sufficient ruthlessness then in due course backwardness can be overcome and the Indians become like us in the advanced West. "It is possible, even probable," writes Bill Emmott, then-editor of *The Economist*, "that the very long-term trends will again be positive and powerful: that democracy will spread further; that China, India and the other now-poor nations will develop and emerge as modern, richer, industrialised societies."[31]

Neoliberal policies have not only failed to increase economic growth but have actually reduced it. Median per capita growth in the developing world fell from 2.5 percent between 1960 and 1979 to zero between 1980 and 1999—a fact that has been registered as a "puzzle" even by officials of the World Bank, without however bringing any change to policy.[32] Analysis by region gives a more nuanced picture, but not one that is any more favorable to the claims of globalization. As John Weeks writes: "the country groups that introduced the globalisation policies to the greatest degree fared least well in the 1990s relative to previous decades (the OECD, the Latin American and the sub-Saharan countries); the best performing group since

1960, East and South-East Asia, entered into a severe recession in the 1990s; and the group whose growth improved in the 1990s without recession, South Asia, was that which least adopted policies of deregulation, trade liberalisation and decontrol of the capital account."[33] So "why the IMF and the US Treasury continue to insist on neoliberalisation is an apparent mystery," writes David Harvey. But the mystery is more apparent than real, for, as Harvey points out, the real goals of the policy are not economic growth but "the restoration or reconstitution of naked class power, locally as well as transnationally, but most particularly in the main financial centres of global capitalism."[34]

The unintended consequences have been disastrous. As Amy Chua has written, "in the numerous countries around the world with a market-dominant minority, the simultaneous pursuit of free markets and democracy has led not to widespread peace and prosperity, but to confiscation, autocracy, and mass slaughter."[35] In his own more scholarly if equally somber account of the historical patterns of ethnic cleansing Michael Mann has described "Chua's attempts to trace genocide and murderous cleansing in Rwanda and Yugoslavia to market exploitation" as "rather far-fetched."[36] Yet he also notes: "International institutions seek to free capital from the 'dead hand' of regulation and economies are given the 'shock therapy' of market freedom, almost regardless of the consequences in terms of unemployment, wage levels, worker protections, and political reactions. Where inequalities acquire ethnic overtones, they encourage ethnic conflict between proletarian and imperial ethnic groups."[37] Harvey gives the example of the fate of the ethnic Chinese in Indonesia, after the East Asian financial collapse of 1997–98: "While the wealthiest Chinese business elite decamped to Singapore, a wave of revenge killings and attacks on property engulfed the rest of the Chinese minority, as ethnonationalism reared its ugly head in search of a scapegoat for the social collapse."[38] And for those countries unwilling or unable to do so, there are arrays of pressures that can be brought, ranging from the denial of aid all the way up to military action.

Despite their increasing frequency since 1989, aggressive wars are still relatively rare, still at the most extreme end of a spectrum of means by which imperialist goals can be achieved. Peter Gowan has listed some of the means employed in what he calls the "exploitation of power by the US and EU in order to extract every possible useful advantage through re-engineering societies outside the core; or, to put it the other way round, to expel as many problems as can be expelled outwards from the core societies":

> Financial crises in the South, dependencies on US and EU markets, inherited debt burdens, inabilities to steer economies in the face of bewildering changes in the international economic environment—all these factors have been seized upon by the Atlantic powers as instruments for gaining positions in the countries concerned: for seizing control of product markets, for buying local company assets to centralise capital under Atlantic control, for exploiting huge pools of cheap labour (shut out by ever-stronger immigration barriers from access to core economies), for taking effective control of financial systems for speculative purposes, gaining higher mar-

ginal yields for the pension funds of the populations of the North and for engaging in orgies of speculation and frequently corrupt and criminal activities.[39]

The notion of "blowback," popularized by Chalmers Johnson, was first developed by analysts in the CIA to describe "the unintended consequences of policies that were kept secret from the American people."[40] Johnson used the term before the crimes of 9/11, but he subsequently noted that the effects on the US population were not restricted to terrorist attacks, however spectacular and destructive: "In its extended sense it also includes the hollowing out of key American industries because of the export-led economic policies of our satellites, the militarism and arrogance of power that inevitably accompany the role of global hegemon, and the distortions to our culture and basic values as we are increasingly required to glorify warrior roles."[41] Smith writes of "front page news about terrorists 'over there'... cowing people from Wyoming to Arkansas into believing they are in mortal danger from a foreign or home-grown fifth column unless they lie down, do what the good President tells them, and spy patriotically on their neighbours. Conversely, ratcheted-up fear at home rationalises the suspension of civil rights from New York to Abu Ghraib."[42]

The fourth characteristic is that the main source of hope for overcoming these obstacles, the working class, is still a minority, albeit a growing minority, of the population. This is true even in China, the biggest and most rapidly industrializing of all the less developed countries, where peasants constitute 70 percent of a total population of 1.2 billion.[43] The existence of large numbers of not only peasants but independent producers and small businesses means that the working class has insufficient social weight to take and exercise power alone. Populations have shifted away from the countryside without being proletarianized. Class alliances of some sort—the precise nature of which we can leave to one side for the moment—therefore remain necessary.

There is however a new problem, unknown to Trotsky. In its original formulation, permanent revolution involved the working class leading other oppressed groups, the largest of which was the peasantry. The peasantry has not vanished, but its importance is diminishing because of the emergence and expansion of massive urban slum areas on the peripheries of the great Third World cities. The number of cities with populations of over one million has risen from eighty-six in 1950 to four hundred in 2004, and these are expected to account for all future population growth from 2020, until the anticipated peak is reached with a global population of ten billion in 2050, of which 95 percent will live in urban areas in the developing world. Yet these urban areas are unlike the ones that arose during the original process of industrialization in the West. Mike Davis writes of "urbanization-without-growth," which has become "radically decoupled from industrialization, even from development per se": "The global forces 'pushing' people from the countryside—mechanization in Java and India, food imports in Mexico, Haiti and Kenya, civil war and drought throughout Africa, and everywhere the consolidation of small into large holdings and the competition of industrial-scale agribusiness—seem to sustain urbanization even when the 'pull' of the city is drastically weakened by debt and depression."[44] About two-thirds of Mexico City's population of eight million live in the colonias populares. While these are not all slums, the irregular settlements, often built by the inhabitants themselves and consequently precarious, are at risk from landslides and floods, and always underprovided with services.[45] Larissa Lomnitz writes of one such area on the periphery of Mexico City:

> The residents of Cerrada del Cóndor have little contact with city-wide or national organizations. Articulation with Mexican urban culture occurs mainly through mass media such as radio and television. Adult reading is limited to sports sheets, comics, and photo-romance magazines. Only about one-tenth of the men belong to the social-security system. About 5 percent are union members. In general, extremely few people belong to any organized group on a national level, such as political parties, religious organizations, and so on . . .

And as Lomnitz emphasizes, it is only "'reciprocal exchange' among relatives and neighbours in the shanty-town which ensures their survival during the frequent and lengthy spells of joblessness."[46]

The vast, improvised repositories of semi-surplus population such as those around Mexico City are explosively volatile. Involved in work mainly through what is politely referred to as the informal sector, the relationship of these populations to organized labor tends to be minimal. Yet potentially they could be an extraordinary revolutionary force (we have seen the possibilities of this in Bolivia)—or the foot soldiers of right-wing demagoguery. The question of leadership therefore remains essential.

But surely the working class is also a minority of the population in the West? Even if this were true the situations would be different, since in the West the working class is supposed to be shrinking in relation to the new middle class, while in the East it has simply failed to yet grow sufficiently to overtake the old peasantry. It is not the case, however, that the Western working class is disappearing. A change is certainly occurring, as has occurred several times before, to the types of occupation in which members of the working class are likely to find themselves. Most recently these have been in the information technology sector where Ursula Huws has detected the birth of a "cybertariat," which is at least as likely to turn to class struggle as its predecessors:

> If low-level office work is perceived as the bottom rung of a ladder that can be scaled successfully by keeping on the right side of the boss, then hard work, keeping one's nose clean, and sycophancy will offer the best route to advancement. If, on the other hand, no promotion prospects seem likely—for instance, because the higher levels are located on another site halfway across the globe, or because only men, or only white people, or only people of a certain nationality or caste ever get promoted—then the best way to better one's income may well seem to lie with making common cause with one's fellow workers.[47]

The size of the new middle class varies across the developed world, and is probably largest in the US, but nowhere constitutes more than 15–20 percent of the population. Given its intermediary position, individual members will likely take different political positions in any crisis, so the role of the working-class movement will be to win those who can be won to socialist politics and neutralize the rest; but this is scarcely an alliance of the sort that will be necessary in Indonesia, India, or China.

The presence of absolute levels of poverty, the absence of representative democracy, the susceptibility to imperialist intervention, and a population in which the working class is a minority—the relative weight of these characteristics varies from country to country and from region to region, but some combination of the four is present in them all. I think, therefore, that it is still necessary to retain a distinction between the more and less developed countries. The latter countries should, however, not be seen as belonging to an undifferentiated category but as occupying a range of different positions along a spectrum in which, say, Venezuela is near the top and Burkina Faso near the bottom. What then does the future hold for these countries?

The New Third Worldism

Faced with the enormous human costs that capitalist globalization has imposed and will continue to impose, sections of the left have turned to the struggle by the indigenous peoples of the developing countries to retain their way of life against development in either its market or state-capitalist form. "What greater transgression, in this context," writes Katherine Moseley, "than the primitive, not only the idea but the real-existing primitive, refusing incorporation, occupying the last bastions of free space, and providing a coherent, living example of self-reliance, equality, and the subjection of the economic to an autonomous conception of needs?"[48] Where the New Third Worldists diverge from their predecessors is in arguing not that peasants are the vanguard of socialist revolution but that they already live in socialist (or at any rate nonexploitative) communities, which have lessons for us: "On the one hand, it constitutes a mute but radical transgression of the hegemonic orders of the present, which, once understood, can be linked to other elements of resistance, autonomy, and critique. On the other hand, it is a source of practical economic lessons that may help modern civilization to survive in recognizable forms. In both cases, sacrifices would have to be made in the areas of self-image and ideology and in forms of production and of growth."[49]

For John McMurtry: "In the Third World subsistence economies and in the larger non-monetary economies across the world, peoples and societies can stick to the life economies of sustenance farming and mutual provision of each other's needs, and be infinitely better off without any relationship to foreign money lenders or export-crop schemes driven by leveraged money-sequences expelling them from their lands, homogenising their food crops for foreign markets, and debt-enslaving them." Here too is where the forces for change are to be found: "The emerging liberative agent in the Third World is the unwaged force of women who are not yet disconnected from the life economy in their work. They serve life, not commodity production."[50]

According to Burbach, an early supporter of the Zapatista Army of National Liberation (EZLN), like other movements of indigenous peoples, it "seeks to end the victimisation of Indians by centuries of western modernisation." "Their demands for change," the same enthusiast informs us, "have become postmodern in that they want a new social and economic order that goes beyond capitalism and even 'formally existing socialism.'"[51] These are certainly admirable goals, but elsewhere Burbach makes clear that this is a movement for preservation rather than innovation: "They [i.e., the EZLN] want to build new equitable societies that will enable their Indian cultures and families to survive while they till the lands communally, using ecologically sound and sustainable practices. This is what makes them postmodernists."[52] The enthusiasm for Zapatismo can scarcely be because anyone expects a return to precapitalist communal farming in Kansas or East Anglia. Nor is it just because of the enormously attractive personality of Subcomandante Marcos, as conveyed in his communiqués. It is, in fact, because three aspects of EZLN theory and practice appear to confirm the preexisting politics of the Western academic left.

The first is that Zapatismo does not seek to overthrow the state, but rather to build an alternative to it from among the different groups that constitute civil society.[53] Some individuals on the Western left can hardly believe that the Zapatistas are implementing a strategy that they have been advocating for so long: "I want them to be right when they say that they want to change the world without taking state power," writes John Holloway. What is their aim, then, if not state power? Dignity. "Dignity is to live in the present the Not Yet for which we struggle." Holloway contrasts this with what has hitherto been the goal of the left: Power. "Power is not that which is, but that which is not, that which is Not Yet (as Bloch would put it)."[54] I trust that is clear.

The second is that Zapatismo does not believe in the necessity for development. Marcos has criticized the Marxism-Leninism of the Latin American left for viewing the indigenous peoples "as a backward sector preventing the forces of production ... blah, blah, blah." "From developing" is the phrase Marcos thinks it unnecessary to complete. These attitudes had strategic implications: "so what was required was to clean out these elements, imprisoning or re-educating some, and assimilating others into the process of production, to transform them into skilled labour—proletarians, to put it in those terms."[55] In other words, the industrialization strategies pursued by Stalin in Russia and then by his followers in the Third World—above all by Mao in China—are identified by Marcos as socialist.

The other aspect of postmodern left politics, which Zapatismo seems to confirm, is the rejection not only of vanguard party organization but also of the working class itself. Here again Holloway is characteristic:

> Through the process of being integrated into the communities of the Lacandon Jungle, the original group of revolutionaries were forced to listen in order to communicate, they were forced to abandon the great revolutionary tradition of talking, of telling people what to think. Revolutionary politics then becomes the articula-

tion of Dignity's struggle, rather than the bringing of class consciousness to the people from outside. . . . The concept of the proletariat is particularly problematic. As it is usually understood, it refers to a particular group of people defined by a particular type of subjection to capital. As such, it privileges the struggles of certain people over others and certain types of struggle over others. The Zapatista concept of ¡Ya Basta! [i.e. Enough!], on the other hand, can be seen as based on the idea that class antagonism runs through all of us, although in different ways, and as allowing a much richer concept of struggle as embracing all aspects of human activity.[56]

Unfortunately, the New Third Worldism is even less likely to disturb the calculations of imperialism than the old, if only because of its essentially defensive nature. Any sober assessment of what has practically been achieved by the Zapatistas would make rather less exhilarating reading than the elaborate fantasies of their Western admirers. As one report on the eve of the tenth anniversary of the Chiapas uprising noted: "The Zapatistas have little to show for their years of struggle. After their initial success putting indigenous demands on Mexico's political agenda, they have failed to secure the legal reforms to answer them. Many indigenous villagers sympathetic to the Zapatistas still live in the abject poverty that prompted the rebellion, banned by the leadership from using the schools, clinics and other development projects lavished on Chiapas state after the uprising."[57] As one Chiapanecan activist told Judith Hellman:

This concept of autonomy is illusionary because it suggests that *caciquismo*, the divisive forces of class, religion, political affiliation, and all the corrupt and violent people are external to indigenous communities and can be shut out once the communities gain autonomous control over their affairs. But these forces don't lie *outside* of indigenous communities. They are already deeply rooted *inside* these communities, and autonomous administration will only reinforce the divisions and the dominance of the powerful over the weak, of rich over poor, of men over women.

Another activist, Juan Pedro Viqueira, said: "What I think is needed is not autonomy but a serious redistribution policy."[58]

Many of those who dismiss the idea of the working class making a revolution in the Third World focus elsewhere in Latin America and celebrate the electoral successes of Hugo Chávez in Venezuela and Evo Morales in Bolivia as an alternative strategy. But again this is to miss the point. Welcome though the success of these leaders is, they were only elected and sustained in office because of mass mobilizations at the heart of which were working-class movements. In Bolivia, for example, the previous government planned to sell off natural gas supplies to the US through Chile and Peru as part of an overall neoliberal strategy to join the free-trade area of the Americas and introduced repressive laws to prevent opposition. After months of blockades and occupations by the rural campesinos, often organized by the Landless Movement, the Bolivian Workers' Central called a general strike on September 29 in their support. Two aspects of this intervention were particularly important. First, that it gave a focus to the rural unrest and pulled the peasants in behind the working-class movement. Second, that it succeeded in bringing down the government and reversing the neoliberal agenda.

CONCLUSION

For nearly fifty years Stalinism and varieties of secular nationalism dominated the politics of the Third World, using organized labor as a stage army when popular mobilization was required. The pretensions of both have been exploded, above all in the Middle East. The space vacated by the collapse of Stalinism and secular nationalism means that millions of people who want to be part of a movement against both imperialism and poverty are looking for ideas that can take the struggle further than simply the establishment of bourgeois-democratic regimes. We can be sure that the working class will continue to fight to improve its conditions—by which I mean increasing democracy as much as improving living standards—as we have seen in Iran, Egypt, and China over the last year. What is still an open question is whether it can go beyond this to challenge for state power.

11

FROM DEFLECTED PERMANENT REVOLUTION TO THE LAW OF UNEVEN AND COMBINED DEVELOPMENT

INTRODUCTION

"Trotsky is the one for whom there is no room either in pre-1990 Really Existing Socialism or in post-1990 Really Existing Capitalism, in which even those who are nostalgic for Communism do not know what to do with Trotsky's permanent revolution."[1] Slavoj Žižek wrote these words at the beginning of the millennium and, in this case, he expresses a sentiment with which readers of *International Socialism* are likely to agree. The question of "what to do" with the concept of permanent revolution is one that this journal first addressed in a systematic way with the publication of Tony Cliff's major reappraisal of 1963, in which he augmented Trotsky's original concept with that of "deflected permanent revolution."[2] Cliff's article was part of a wider revisionist project. In the two years before his assassination in 1940, Trotsky made a number of claims about the world system and committed himself to a series of predictions about its future development. These included: that global capitalism had entered a period of permanent and irreversible decline, that the Russian Stalinist regime was an inherently unstable and historically unique formation that was doomed to collapse, and that the coming revolutions in the colonial and semicolonial world would be led by the working class, as the Russian Revolution had been in 1917. In fact, following the Second World War, capitalism entered the greatest period of growth in its history; Stalinist Russia expanded territorially through conquest, and its basic structures were independently replicated by Stalinist parties in the Third World; and—as this outcome suggests—the revolutions that occurred there were led not by the working class but by elements of the middle class, who then became the managers of a new bureaucratic state. Given these outcomes, some revision of Trotsky's final perspectives was inescapable, but short of abandoning them altogether, this could be done in one of two ways.

One way, ultimately adopted by adherents of what Isaac Deutscher called Orthodox Trotskyism, was effectively to revise reality so that it corresponded with the theory—a necessary consequence of treating particular judgments by Trotsky as beyond falsification. In Alasdair MacIntyre's words, "It transformed into abstract dogma what Trotsky thought in concrete terms at one moment in his life and canonized this."[3] Canonization involved two strategies of reality avoidance. The first was the recategorization of social classes: a party led by petty-bourgeois intellectuals and consisting of militarized ex-peasants could, for example, be described as representing "the Chinese working class" and its victory in 1949 hailed as a socialist revolution. But even those Trotskyists who treated Marxist class theory with greater seriousness than this could still avert their gaze from the truth with a second strategy, namely the adoption of an arbitrary formal definition of a "workers' state," where state ownership of the means of production became the only deciding factor, although the working class had neither led nor even participated in the revolution, did not in any sense control the new state, and was subjected to a ruthless police dictatorship.

The second way, taken by Cliff and his initially small band of followers, was to revise the theory in the light of reality. Cliff held fast not to specific judgments by Trotsky but to the central tenets and methods of historical materialism that underpinned the latter's greatest achievements. Above all, Cliff cleaved to the self-activity of the working class, not as an optional if desirable extra, but as the indispensable core of Marxism as a theory of socialist revolution. In his autobiography, Cliff recounted how, starting from this perspective, he "devoted a lot of time and effort to developing three interlinked theories to deal with the three areas of the world" where Trotsky's predictions had proved false, "Russia and Eastern Europe, advanced capitalist countries, and the Third World": "The three theories were: state capitalism, the permanent arms economy, and deflected permanent revolution." This "troika," Cliff writes, "make a unity, a totality, grasping the changes in the situation of humanity after the Second World War."[4]

Cliff was therefore responding to changes in the world capitalist system that Orthodox Trotskyism refused to recognize; but there have been similarly dramatic shifts since Cliff concluded his reconsideration of the Trotskyist legacy. State capitalism still exists as a policy option for governments, as the quasi- nationalization of banks during the financial crisis of 2007–08 has shown, but the era of state capitalism as a general tendency within the system ended between the emergence of neoliberalism in the mid-1970s and the fall of the Stalinist regimes in 1989–91. Vast sums are still wasted (in economic as well as moral terms) on arms, but military expenditure no longer acts to stabilize the system.[5] What then of the third component of "the troika"? Has deflected permanent revolution also become an essentially historical category?

In *International Socialism* 126, Leo Zeilig argued that deflected permanent revolution remains relevant today, despite the declining significance of the other component of the troika most closely related to it: "While the central role of the intelligentsia in the absence of a self-conscious working class subject is an absolute law in Cliff's theory, the importance of state capitalism for the deflected permanent revolution is neither absolute nor a requirement."[6] Zeilig applies the concept to Africa, a continent that, with the partial exception of Egypt, Cliff himself did not discuss, but the individual countries Zeilig considers do fall into one of Cliff's categories, that of "deviations from the norm" of deflected permanent revolution.[7] The "norm" was established by those revolutions that had resulted in the most complete state-capitalist outcomes under Stalinist leadership independently of Russia, particularly those in China and Cuba, although at the time when Cliff was writing in the early 1960s he could also have referred to North Vietnam, Albania, or Yugoslavia. The "deviations" were those— actually the majority of cases—where the outcome was a mixture of state and private capitalism under radical nationalist leadership that may have been influenced by Stalinist ideas and organizational methods, but that often—as in the cases of Egypt or Iraq—oscillated between trying to incorporate the local Communist Party and trying to suppress it. With the very important exception of India, the most typical examples of the "deviations" were to be found in North Africa and the Middle East. Zeilig's use of the concept is illuminating in relation to those African states in which liberation movements were either completed (Ghana) or at least begun (Zimbabwe) within the postwar period of decolonization that formed the context of Cliff's argument; but is it also the case that the theory can be applied to contemporary Africa and, by extension, the rest of the global South?

I remain unconvinced. Not because I disagree with, for example, Zeilig's analysis of the recent events in the Democratic Republic of Congo—quite the contrary— but rather because these seem to me to have little to do with permanent revolution, deflected or otherwise. Trotsky saw permanent revolution as a strategy that would enable the less developed countries to decisively break with feudal, tributary, or colonial rule under working-class leadership and move directly to socialism as components of an international revolutionary movement. Cliff saw deflected permanent revolution as the process that ensues when the working class does not carry through that strategy and another social force takes on the role of leadership, enabling the break with precapitalist modes of production or foreign domination to take place, but only in order for the countries in question to become parts of the capitalist world system. Although Cliff did not use the term, he effectively treated deflected permanent revolution as the modern version or functional equivalent of the bourgeois revolution.[8] Both the original and the revised concept therefore involved fundamental social transformations leading to either socialism (permanent revolution) or state capitalism (deflected permanent revolution).

Yet the term now tends to be used, as in Zeilig's article, to mean political events of far less significance. That this can be done without undue conceptual stretching suggests, at the very least, that there was always an ambiguity in Cliff's revision of Trotsky, which I think has two sources. One, which Cliff directly inherited from Trotsky, is the presence of an outstanding set of bourgeois revolutionary "tasks" that can be carried out by either the working class (permanent revolution) or by the middle class "intelligentsia" (deflected permanent revolution). Much of the continued validity of both concepts therefore depends on how these tasks are defined and whether they are still outstanding. The other is the absence of any discussion of the relationship between permanent revolution and the prior process of uneven and combined development, which was central to Trotsky's original conception. Nor did Cliff deal with the subject in later writings. Despite describing uneven and combined development as "the essence of the permanent revolution" in the first volume of his biography of Trotsky, the discussion is confined to a mere five pages across that work as a whole, all relating solely to Russia.[9] Yet, as we shall see, reintegrating the law of uneven and combined development with the strategy of permanent revolution will help answer many of the unresolved questions raised by its "deflection."

FROM BOURGEOIS TO PERMANENT REVOLUTION

Trotsky was not alone in arguing that, by the beginning of the twentieth century, the bourgeoisie was no longer capable of carrying out the revolution that bore its name.[10] Where he went far beyond his fellow revolutionaries was in claiming that the Russian Revolution could lead not only to the overthrow of absolutism, the establishment of representative government, and the capitalist development of the productive forces, but to socialism itself. This was conditional, however, on the Russian Revolution being assisted by the revolutionary movement in the advanced West, whose own success could provide the material resources for socialist development that Russia lacked as an individual state. Trotsky was later to generalize this conception of permanent revolution, describing it as "the general trend of revolutionary development in all backward countries."[11] He also made what seemed at the time to be minor qualifications in relation to the two main social classes, but these contained possibilities, the realization of which formed the background to Cliff's article.

On the one hand, Trotsky thought that even where foreign dominance was "concealed by the fiction of State independence," the ruling bourgeoisie was capable of resisting imperialism, at least up to a certain point.[12] This tended to be the case in countries that had never been formal colonies, or that ceased to be such during the era of classic bourgeois revolutions. The most obvious examples were the first and last destinations of his final exile: Turkey and Mexico. In this context he described the period of the 1930s as generally being one "in which the national bourgeoisie searches for a bit more independence from the foreign imperialists" and in which revolutionaries were "in permanent competition with the national bourgeoisie as the one leadership which is capable of assuring the victory of the masses in the fight against the foreign imperialists." As the notion of "competition" suggests, although the organizations of the national bourgeoisie were in some senses "the Popular Front in the form of a party," they played a different role from the entirely reactionary Popular Fronts in Europe and North America: "It can have a reactionary character insofar as it is directed against the worker; it can have an aggressive attitude insofar as it is directed against imperialism."[13] Trotsky had written off the possibility of decolonization without permanent revolution, seeing the relative freedom of states like Turkey or Mexico as exceptional; but what were the implications of states with a similar relationship to the world system (i.e., backward capitalism) multiplying, as they did from 1947 onward with the creation of India and Pakistan?

On the other hand, Trotsky was also aware that the level of capitalist economic development, "the hierarchy of backwardness," varied enormously across what we now call the global South.[14] As a result, the size of the working class and its ability to influence events was also subject to massive differentiation. Trotsky was the opposite of a utopian voluntarist, and he accepted that a certain degree of social weight was necessary on the part of a working class before it could aspire to taking power; what was possible in India and China would not necessarily be possible in equatorial Africa or Afghanistan. It was always necessary to establish working-class organizational and political independence, but "the relative weight of the individual and transitional demands in the proletariat's struggle, their mutual ties and their order of presentation, is determined by the peculiarities and specific conditions of each backward country and—to a considerable extent—by the *degree* of its backwardness."[15] However, even in those countries where the working class was much smaller than the Russian in relative terms, the global nature of the socialist project would enable them to overcome this obstacle.

SOCIAL OR POLITICAL REVOLUTION?

What then were the "tasks" that Trotsky thought had to be accomplished in the process of passing from the bourgeois to the proletarian revolution? In Cliff's summary, the bourgeoisie is "incapable of carrying out the thoroughgoing destruction of feudalism, the achievement of real national independence and political democracy," which he treats as the main tasks of the bourgeois revolution: "A consistent solution to the agrarian question, of the national question, a break-up of the social and imperial fetters preventing speedy economic advance, will necessitate moving beyond the bounds of bourgeois private property."[16] A more orthodox Trotskyist, Michael Löwy, similarly concluded from a study of Trotsky's works that what he calls the "democratic tasks" of the bourgeois revolution are "the agrarian democratic revolution," "national liberation," and "democracy."[17] These are potentially very demanding criteria indeed, many of which remain unmet throughout the entire global South and indeed beyond today. In some places Trotsky seemed to realize that this was a problem. He was reluctant to describe the Japanese Meiji Restoration of 1868, for example, as a bourgeois revolution, referring to it instead as "a bureaucratic attempt to buy off such a revolution," while at the same time acknowledging that the Meiji regime had accomplished in a matter of decades what it had taken Russia three hundred years to achieve.[18] But if the notion of "tasks" were taken seriously in the case of Japan, then this would mean that the bourgeois revolution was only consummated when agrarian reform and representative democracy were imposed by the US occupiers between 1945 and 1955. Unfortunately this introduces further problems, since the American Revolution itself was presumably unfinished until the black population achieved full and formal civil rights with the passing of the 1965 Voting Rights Amendment Act, the 1967 judgment in the case of *Loving v. Virginia* allowing "mixed" marriages, and so on.

The question of democracy is particularly important here, since with the partial exception of France, even the classic bourgeois revolutions did not lead to the installation of representative democracy. In fact, if we take bourgeois democracy to involve, at a minimum, a representative government elected by the adult population, where votes have equal weight and can be cast without intimidation by the state, then it is a relatively recent development in the history of capitalism. Far from being intrinsic to bourgeois society, representative democracy has largely been introduced by pressure from the working class, often involving the threat of revolution, and extended by pressure from the oppressed.[19] To insist that countries in the global South are only completely capitalist when they have achieved stable representative democracy, apart from committing a category mistake (capitalism=economy; democracy=polity), is to expect a more complete outcome there than was achieved in the countries of the developed world. There are still important unresolved democratic issues in many countries, but they have nothing to do with the accomplishment or consolidation of capitalism.

This is what Cliff seems to have been implying in an important article from 1950 where he wrote of German unification "from above" during the 1860s: "The 'Bismarckian' path was not the exception for the bourgeoisie, but the rule; the exception was the French revolution."[20] The general conclusion was drawn by Alex Callinicos in a 1982 review article of Löwy's book for *International Socialism*, when he noted the problem of making "an identification of bourgeois-democratic revolution with merely one of its cases," which is of course the French, "and making its specific features . . . necessary components of any 'genuine' bourgeois revolution": "Surely it is more sensible, rather than invoke the metaphysical concept of a 'complete and genuine solution' [to the tasks of the bourgeois revolution], to judge a bourgeois revolution by the degree to which it succeeds in establishing an autonomous centre of capital accumulation, even if it fails to democratize the political order, or to eliminate feudal social relations."[21] I agree with these conclusions; but they have certain implications for the theory of deflected permanent revolution that we have not considered. "Deflection" originally involved shifting from proletarian to bourgeois revolutionary objectives, but what can it mean if the real task of the bourgeois revolution has largely been accomplished on a global scale? In any case, "establishing an autonomous centre of capital accumulation" is scarcely an outcome that the working class can be expected to accomplish in the absence of the bourgeoisie!

The root of the problem is illustrated by the two main cases that Cliff discusses: China and Cuba. From the evidence of Cliff's autobiography, China seems to have been the main model for deflected permanent revolution; indeed he describes the 1963 article as being a "distillation" of his earlier book *Mao's China* (1957), with additional material on Cuba, which, at that time, was the most recent addition to the roster of state-capitalist regimes.[22] Before 1949 China stood historically before the completion of the bourgeois revolution: there was effectively no central state, the agrarian sector still contained tributary and feudal relations, and it was subject to oppression by several competing imperialist powers. Cuba by 1959, on the other hand, was a bourgeois state—a very weak one, of course, overawed by the US state and penetrated by organized crime, but it seems to be an abuse of language to say that it was in any sense precapitalist, nor was the working class striving for power in the 1950s in the way that the Chinese working class had in the 1920s. In order to understand the difference between these two revolutions, we need to establish an important distinction first made by Marx in 1840s and later adopted by Trotsky: that between social and political revolutions.[23]

Political revolutions sometimes have social aspects and social revolutions always have political implications, but the terms nevertheless indicate an essential difference. Political revolutions are struggles within society for control of the existing state, but they leave the social and economic structure intact. These revolutions have been relatively frequent in history, from the Roman civil wars, which led to the abandonment of republican rule for the principate in 27 BCE, to the Eastern European revolutions of 1989–91, which swept away the Stalinist regimes and began what Chris Harman called the "sideways" movement from Eastern state capitalism to an approximation of the Western trans-state model.[24] They may involve more or less popular participation, may result in more or less improvement in the condition of the majority, but ultimately the class that was in control of the means of production at the beginning will remain so at the end (although individuals and political organizations may have been replaced on the way). The class that was exploited within the productive process at the beginning will also remain so at the end (although concessions may have been made to secure its acquiescence or participation). Social revolutions, however, are not merely struggles within existing society but result in the transformation of one type of society into another and, as such, are extremely rare—so rare that we only know of two, and one of these has not yet succeeded: the bourgeois revolution and the socialist revolution.

The relation between these two types of revolution is complex. Some revolutions that, taken by themselves, appear to be merely political revolutions are in fact part of a more extended social revolution. In relation to the bourgeois revolution, the English Revolution of 1688 has this relationship to the Revolution of 1640; similar cases could be made for the French Revolution of 1830 in relation to that of 1789 or, reversing the chronological order of importance, the American Revolution of 1776 in relation to the Civil War of 1861–65. More importantly in the context of this discussion, some revolutions end up as political revolutions because they are failed social revolutions. In relation to the socialist revolution, this is clearly the case with the German Revolution of 1918.[25] A similar case could also be made for the Portuguese Revolution of 1974—and indeed most of the so-called democratic revolutions to have taken place since, above all, that of Iran in 1978–79.

China experienced a social revolution in 1949: it could have been the socialist revolution, if the movements of the mid-twenties had succeeded, but ended up instead as the functional equivalent of the bourgeois revolution instead—a lesser but still decisive systemic shift. Cuba only experienced a political revolution, which did not fundamentally change the nature of the economic system and represented—using Harman's term, but reversing the direction of movement—a sideways shift from a highly corrupt market-capitalist economy to one on the state-capitalist model. This would have been more obvious if US paranoia about encroaching "Communism" had not effectively forced the new Cuban regime to ally with Russia and adopt state-capitalist forms of organization—which was certainly not Castro's original intention. There were, in other words, two different types of revolution encompassed by the term "deflected permanent revolution" from the very beginning. As capital increasingly sweeps away even the remnants of previous modes of production and the social formations that included them, the pattern of revolutions has increasingly tended toward the "political" rather than the "social" type: the revolutions of 1989 in Eastern Europe; the subsequent displays of "people power" in the Philippines, Thailand, and Serbia; and the "color revolutions" in the former republics of the USSR. Capitalism endlessly reproduces differences in power and autonomy—the "unevenness" that I discuss below. Except in a handful of cases (Afghanistan, Nepal, Tibet) the unstable but structured inequality that results is not an unresolved issue from an earlier period, not a remnant of feudalism or colonialism, but a result of the normal operation of competitive accumulation expressed at the level of the states system.

At least one leading thinker in the International Socialist (IS) tradition did argue that none of the cases of deflected permanent revolution involved social revolutions, although without using the latter term. Discussing the same examples as Cliff in an article for *International Socialism* written during the collapse of the Stalinist regimes, Harman noted:

> In none of these cases was there a shift from one mode of production to another. In each case those who had control of the exiting state apparatus used it to reorganize industry, reducing internal competition to a minimum to accumulate in the face of external pressures. That does not mean that there was never any opposition to such a move—"police" actions of various sorts were often taken against old, "private" capitalist interests who resisted the changes. But these were possible without any mobilization of the mass of the population for full blooded social revolution, indeed in some cases without any mobilization of the mass of the population at all.[26]

This perhaps goes too far, not only in respect of the Chinese Revolution of 1949 but a minority of the revolutions that followed it. Before the Ethiopian Revolution of 1974, for example, feudal social relations were still dominant and the state was the nearest to the European absolutist model of any remaining in the world.[27] Neverthe-less, Harman's central point about the nonsocial nature of the revolution is correct; but it does raise the question of whether retaining the term "deflected permanent revolution" has any benefits other than providing the consolations of familiarity. It is possible, of course, to explicitly detach it from the "tasks" of the bourgeois revolution, real or imagined, and instead relate it to the possibility of working-class leadership in accomplishing democratic tasks (as in Thailand) or to anti-imperialist struggle (as in Iraq) on the road to socialism—and this is more or less how the term tends to be used; but this has the danger of obscuring what is at stake.

Political revolutions, changes of regime by nonconstitutional methods, are a fact of life in the global South and likely to remain so, but these can take place without involving any independent working-class intervention. If one Russian-backed gang of scoundrels replaces another US-supported collection of villains (or vice versa) in, say, Kyrgyzstan, and some working-class people take part in accompanying demon-strations, this is not an example of deflected permanent revolution. There are of course very important recent examples where the working class has irrupted into what would otherwise been an internal ruling-class dispute, thus opening up the possibility of social(ist) revolution, and again Iran in 1978–79 is the key example; but their failure to seize power meant that the revolutions *remained* at the political level. Again, this is not an example of deflected permanent revolution: Iran was a capitalist state, the working class was defeated, and one wing of the bourgeoisie emerged triumphant over another on the basis of a different strategy for accumula-tion. This struggle between two alternatives (social revolution based on the working class versus political revolution that involves the ascendancy of a different section of the bourgeoisie and is organized by political Islamists) still obtains in Iran and also in Egypt, the two areas of the Middle East where new upheavals are most clearly being prepared. As we shall see in due course, they are not alone. Before turning to the question of what is generating these potentially revolutionary situations, how-ever, we need to address the nature of the class (or class fraction) that Cliff argued had replaced the working class, allowing the process of "deflection" to take place.

THE INCAPACITIES OF THE BOURGEOISIE

Cliff identified the "revolutionary intelligentsia" as a substitute for the revolutionary bourgeoisie in the global South. No summary can substitute for actually reading his exemplary analysis of this group, but the main characteristics that he ascribed to it are important to note here. As nonspecialists, members of the intelligentsia can offer to represent the "nation" against other, merely sectoral groups. The backwardness of their nation offends them, not simply as a matter of civic pride but because in mate-rial terms it means they are unable to find work—at least, work in the state apparatus at a level appropriate to their education. As the traditional aspects of their society are increasingly destabilized by the irruption of capitalist development, they find it hard to maintain its values, looking instead to those of efficiency, modernization, and industrialization, all of which are apparently embodied in the USSR. They claim to love "the people" but simultaneously feel guilty at their relative privilege and distrustful of those less educated or intelligent than themselves. Above all, they are hostile to democracy and strive to exclude the masses from their strategies of transformation, except in a subordinate or supportive role, which is why their preferred method is one of military struggle on a guerrilla or even conventional basis.[28] Harman subsequently extended the argument in an important article on political Islam. Although Cliff's category was originally used with reference to "Stalinism, Maoism and Castroism," Harman now claimed that it was equally applicable to "the Islamist intelligentsia around Khomeini in Iran," who "undertook a revolutionary reorganisation of ownership and control of capital within Iran while leaving capitalist relations of production intact."[29]

The brilliance of this collective portrait is not in doubt, but was the class fraction it describes really a new development in the history of capitalism? The classical Marxist tradition was more skeptical than is generally thought about the extent to which the bourgeoisie had been at the forefront of revolutionary struggle, even in 1640 or 1789.[30] Trotsky tended to regard the petty bourgeoisie as the driving force behind successful bourgeois revolutions up to and including the French.[31] He also recognized, however, that other social groups had also played this role, including feudal landlords in Prussia during the 1860s and—potentially at least—the working class in the Chinese Revolution of the 1920s. He did not, of course, claim that the bourgeoisie had never played a revolutionary role: simply that this was not a necessary condition for a revolution to qualify as bourgeois.[32] But in the cases where the bourgeoisie did lead, it is important to understand which sections were involved.

The bourgeoisie does not only consist of capitalists, in the literal sense of those who own or control capital. Further, it is historically demonstrable that, down to 1848 at least, the most decisive leaderships tended to emerge from those sections of the bourgeoisie without direct material interests in the process of production, who were simultaneously less concerned with the destructive effects of revolutionary violence and more able to overcome the competitive economic divisions within their class.[33] Are the leaders of the "deflected" revolutions so very different from those who led them between 1789 and 1848? Guevara trained as a doctor, but Robespierre was a lawyer, Danton a journalist, Roux a priest; only a very few, of whom Roederer was the most important, could seriously be described as capitalists. In some respects the parallels are exact. As Eric Hobsbawm notes of the radicalism of students and intellectuals in 1848: "It was largely based on the (as it turned out temporary) inability of the new bourgeois society before 1848 to provide enough posts of adequate status for the educated whom it produced in unprecedented numbers, and whose rewards were so much more modest than their ambitions."[34] John Rees once observed that the intelligentsia "had, in an earlier incarnation, often been a crucial element of the practical leadership of the classical bourgeois revolutions," without however drawing any conclusions.[35] But if the above argument is correct, then the bourgeoisie's supposed abdication of its revolutionary role after 1848 was in fact simply an expression of the hostility that the core membership of this class had always displayed toward plebeian intervention, now heightened by the even greater threat posed by the working class.

The two real changes after 1848 lay elsewhere. One was that the noncapitalist sections of the bourgeoisie, which had previously given revolutionary leadership and which might have been less paralyzed by fear of the working class, were increasingly integrated into a society in which their former frustrations and humiliations were rapidly becoming things of the past. The other was that sections of the existing ruling classes of Europe and Japan (such as the Prussian landlords to whom Trotsky refers) that had previously resisted revolution now embraced a top-down version in order to make their states capable of military competition with their rivals—or, in the case of Japan, to avoid the fate of colonization and dismemberment that had befallen China. In the colonial world after 1945, the core bourgeoisie had inherited the traditional fear of revolution from their predecessors, but the "revolutionary intelligentsia" were not in the position of their European equivalents after 1848; in fact they far more closely resembled them before 1789. In other words, they could not look forward to wealth, power, and recognition without a revolution. In some cases they did not need to take action for themselves because the process of transformation was initiated by an army coup.

This type of event, distantly related to the "revolutions from above" in Germany, Italy, and Japan in the 1860s, had of course begun before the advent of Stalinism with the Turkish Revolution of 1919, led by groups that Ellen Kay Trimberger calls "autonomous military bureaucrats."[36] This is one area in which Cliff's account needs to be qualified, as it is not entirely clear that "intelligentsia" is sufficiently broad a category to include the leading social forces involved in these revolutions, at least two of which (those led by Nasser in Egypt and by Mengistu in Ethiopia) were among the most important of the "deviations from the norm" of deflected permanent revolution. These military leaders, who are quite often junior officers, do of course have one important characteristic in common with members of the intelligentsia in that they can also claim to represent "the nation" beyond mere factional interests. In the majority of cases where a military solution was not available, however, the intelligentsia needed to mobilize themselves. What was new in these situations was not therefore the existence or activity of a "revolutionary intelligentsia" hitherto unknown: both were already familiar from the history of the nineteenth century. It was rather that this class fraction felt able to take action in the knowledge that they did not need to fear the working class. Why not?

Cliff offers a number of reasons why the working class in the global South did not play the role envisaged by Trotsky, down to the early 1960s. Of these, the general influence of ruling-class ideas and the illiteracy and inexperience of the workers are clearly relevant, but they were also factors in the situations of Russia in 1917 and China in the 1920s; they are not in themselves an explanation. Other reasons have genuine explanatory power and remain extremely pertinent even today. Many workers in urban industry retain links to small holdings in the countryside, to which they return in times of unemployment, making the permanent formation of class consciousness and organization difficult. Conversely, those workers who are in stable employment can have relatively higher living standards than the rural masses, making the possibility of alliances with them less likely. Those trade unions or community groups that do exist are often led by non-working-class elements—"outsiders," with different interests and political goals—and are heavily reliant on support from the developmental state, which tends to impose an apolitical agenda acceptable to the regime. Both these leaderships and the personnel who run the state apparatus are influenced by Stalinist politics, the key subjective element in controlling and lowering the aspirations of the working class.[37] But many of these characteristics were also present in prerevolutionary Russia: workers with links to the countryside; trade unions established by agents of the state; and industries where trade unions did not exist, even before the ban that followed the Revolution of 1905.[38] Some deeper level of explanation is required.

The absence of a revolutionary party is clearly part of the explanation, but parties themselves can only have a meaningful existence where certain determinate conditions allow them to form and grow. Lack of revolutionary leadership can explain the outcome in China during the 1920s or in Iran in 1978–79, where major upheavals took place and Cliff's other inhibiting conditions were overcome, but not where such situations did not arise. At the end of his discussion of workers in the global South, Cliff writes: "An automatic correlation between economic backwardness and revolutionary political militancy does not exist."[39] But Trotsky never argued that such an automatic correlation did exist; for him it was conditional, and Cliff does not refer to, let alone discuss, the enabling condition that Trotsky saw as fundamental to its establishment: uneven and combined development.[40]

This was the central absence in Cliff's revision of Trotsky. The theory of uneven and combined development explained what occurs when the process of overleaping takes place in the colonial or neocolonial world, where it is not possible to *fully* catch up with, let alone overtake, the developed West, but only to do so in a fragmentary or partial way. The resulting combined formations, because of their inbuilt social instability, paradoxically made revolutionary outbreaks more likely than in the developed world with its greater levels of stability and reformist traditions. In other words, the presence of combined and uneven development made it possible for a strategy of permanent revolution to be pursued with greater likelihood of success; its absence made it, not inevitable, but less likely that such a strategy would be pursued in the first place, leading to the process of "deflection" highlighted by Cliff.

Permanent revolution, and consequently deflected permanent revolution, may now be historical concepts, but uneven and combined development is not, with important implications for the possibility of socialist revolution beginning in the global

South. Following Trotsky, Tim McDaniel argues that there were four reasons why what he calls the "autocratic capitalism" of tsarist Russia tended to produce a revolutionary labor movement. First, it eliminated or reduced the distinction between economic and political issues. Second, it generated opposition for both traditional and modern reasons. Third, it reduced the fragmentation of the working class but also prevented the formation of a stable conservative bureaucracy, thus leading to more radical attitudes. Fourth, it forced a degree of interdependence between the mass of the working class, class-conscious workers, and revolutionary intellectuals.[41] McDaniel claims that a comparable situation has since arisen only in Iran, but this seems to unnecessarily restrict the applicability of the model to situations that resemble prerevolutionary Russia closely in formal terms.[42] In fact, the relentless expansion of neoliberal globalization and the consequent irruption of industrialization and urbanization into areas they had previously bypassed, often under conditions of intense state repression, mean that the responses identified by McDaniel are being reproduced in places as distinct as China and Dubai.[43] But these are only the most extreme examples of a general trend that is characteristic of the current phase of capitalist development. Two points need to be made in relation to the process.

One is that it is not limited to the global South but extends to the less developed parts of the First and former Second Worlds. As Beverly Silver writes:

> Strong new working-class movements had been created as a combined result of the spatial fixes pursued by multinational corporate capital and the import substitution industrialization efforts of modernizing states. In some cases, like Brazil's automobile workers, labor militancy was rooted in the newly expanding mass production consumer durable industries. In other cases, like the rise of *Solidarnosc* in Poland's shipyards, militancy was centered in gigantic establishments providing capital goods. In still other cases, like Iran's oil workers, labor militancy was centered in critical natural resource export industries.[44]

The second point to be made is that, in the global South proper at least, the process is still unable completely to transform those societies. The state "containers" within which uneven and combined development unfolds, including China, will never achieve the type of total transformation characteristic of the states that formed the original core of the capitalist world system, at least in any foreseeable timescale. One intelligent conservative commentator, Edward Luttwak, has referred to "the perils of incomplete imitation" whereby developing-world ruling classes "have been importing a dangerously unstable version of American turbo-capitalism, because the formula is incomplete." What is missing? On the one hand, the legal regulation to control what he calls "the overpowering strength of big business," and on the other internal humility on the part of the winners and acceptance of the essential justice of their personal situation by the losers within the system.[46] Uneven and combined development is therefore likely to be an ongoing process, which will only be resolved by either revolution or disintegration. In the meantime, China and other states like India and Brazil where growth has been less dramatic remain both inherently unstable in their internal social relations and expansive in their external search for markets, raw materials, and investment opportunities. It is in this inherent instability that the possibilities for permanent revolution lie. This does not mean that wherever uneven and combined development exists today the working-class movement will automatically adopt what Trotsky called the "boldest conclusions of revolutionary thought." In circumstances where Marxist ideas (and those of secular radicalism more generally) are either unavailable or discredited after the experience of Stalinism, movements will reach for whatever ideas seem to assist them in their struggle, regardless of their antiquity—but they will transform them in the process, contrary to what is asserted by reactionaries in the West.

CONCLUSION

The late Fred Halliday once expressed his own disillusionment after the fall of the Soviet empire, rejecting the revolutionary possibilities of uneven and combined development:

> The insight of Trotsky was that of locating the history and revolution of any one country in a broader, contradictory context, in seeing how ideas and forms of conflict, like forms of technology or economic activity, could be transposed to contexts very different from that in which they originated. The mistake of the Marxist approach was to conclude that, in the end, the combination would prevail over the unevenness. The unevenness, evident above all in the widening income gaps between rich and poor on a world scale, has continued to grow, and is replicated dramatically in an era of capitalist globalization. But because of the fragmentary character of states, the spatial and political distributor of that unevenness, the combination, *the world revolutionary cataclysm*, did not occur.[47]

To this we reply: combination is not "the world revolutionary cataclysm," it is the objective enabling condition for it to take place. And if the cataclysm has not yet occurred, this is largely because of the absence of the missing subjective condition that Trotsky recognized in 1917 and that Cliff highlighted back in the 1960s: the revolutionary organization capable of giving focus to the social explosions that the process of uneven and combined development brings in its wake. Whatever else may have changed since both men wrote, the necessity for the party remains, if the incredible energies unleashed by uneven and combined development are not to be wasted yet again, with terrible consequences for the world and those who live in it.

12

REVOLUTIONS BETWEEN THEORY AND HISTORY: A RESPONSE TO ALEX CALLINICOS AND DONNY GLUCKSTEIN

INTRODUCTION

Any author who attempts to reappraise a fundamental concept in historical materialism, in this case bourgeois revolution, can at the very least expect their work to receive close scrutiny from fellow Marxists. If, more specifically, that author is prepared to express doubt about the continued relevance of the most original aspect of Leon Trotsky's Marxism, the related concept of permanent revolution, then this scrutiny is likely to be tinged with suspicion, at least from those who trace their political lineage back to the Left Opposition and the Fourth International. And if they are further prepared to extend these doubts to an important revision of Trotsky that has been central to the politics of the SWP and its predecessors, namely deflected permanent revolution, then suspicion is likely to be colored with outright hostility, at least from others who stand in the IS tradition. Since I was foolish enough to attempt all three risk-bearing endeavors in *How Revolutionary Were the Bourgeois Revolutions?* (*HRWTBR*), it is scarcely an occasion for surprise, let alone for complaint, to find the book subject to criticism by Alex Callinicos and Donny Gluckstein in previous issues of this journal.

Indeed, authors should only complain about reviews on three grounds. One is when the reviewer has not actually read the book.[1] In socialist publications this usually happens because the reviewer already "knows" what the author's position is on the basis of his or her party or factional affiliation and therefore needs not waste time with what he or she has actually written, except perhaps for the purposes of extracting a few choice quotes to demonstrate the author's unprincipled abandonment of Leninism, or whatever. Another is where an author has criticized a particular position supported by the reviewer, but the latter, instead of responding to these criticisms, merely repeats the original position with added emphasis. Another still—of which I have some recent experience—is where reviewers deliberately misrepresent what authors have written, often by ascribing to them views that are easier or more convenient to criticize than the positions they actually hold, which is a splendid strategy for taking the difficulty out of political debate but also for rendering it completely valueless. Happily—although I expected nothing less—neither Alex nor Donny has committed any of these sins against the conduct of intellectual debate. Although I think that in some respects they have misunderstood what I was attempting to do, their objections largely correspond to real theoretical disagreements. In this reply I will address the issues raised by Alex in the same order as they appear in his review, referring to Donny's subsequent comments where appropriate.

Before turning to these matters, however, I will comment on the factual and theoretical errors that Alex has identified and listed in a footnote.[2] Alex was not alone in spotting a number of factual errors in the book; so too did a number of other comrades, although they were courteous enough to communicate these to me in private rather than listing them in a public forum. Most were due to lapses of attention on my part, of the sort that tend to occur in the early hours of the morning with the end of yet another deadline extension looming. Most books contain mistakes, and a book of this size will almost inevitably contain a higher than average number—a problem exacerbated by my publisher's understandable desire to have the book in print for sale at the International Socialist Organization's Socialism 2012 event in Chicago and the Socialist Workers Party's Marxism 2012 in London, which meant the time allowed for proofing was shorter than usual. And since Haymarket's blameless proofreaders are, like the vast majority these days, nonspecialists who tend to check for punctuation, layout, and sense rather than factual accuracy, authorial lapses of the latter type often stand uncorrected.

Nevertheless, irritating though Alex's catalog of shame has been to readers, and embarrassing though it is to me and Haymarket, I'm not convinced that it deserves even a footnote. I am, after all, quite aware that the Communist Party of Great Britain's official historian did not spend his twilight years acting as a coroner in a US prime-time TV drama, although I am undoubtedly impressed that someone of Alex's mandarin demeanor is actually aware of the existence of *Quincy*; nor does mistyping the first name of James Klugmann—or indeed, Klugman, as he tended to drop the second "n" in later life—invalidate my views on the influence of the Popular Front on British Marxist historiography. In academic reviewing this type of point-scoring is done partly to show off but mainly to cast doubt on the arguments of the person being reviewed, the logic being: if he can't even get Cornelius Castoriadis's name right, how seriously can we take his views on the transition to capitalism? Realizing this, most academic journals now ask contributing reviewers not to list mistakes unless they reveal a degree of ignorance that brings the integrity of the work into question. This is one of the few areas in which we might sensibly follow them, since these mistakes and others will be corrected in the forthcoming edition of *HRWTBR* without altering its content.

Alex occupies more solid ground in relation to what he calls my "most serious theoretical mistake not pertinent to the main argument," concerning Karl Marx's distinction between the formal and real subsumption of labor in *Capital*.[3] He is correct to point out that I wrongly elide Marx's distinction between those forms transitional to wage labor and the formal subsumption of labor. The latter involves integration into the wage-labor-capital relationship, after which real subsumption follows when competition between industrial capitals begins to drive successive technological transformations. Now, Alex's authority with respect to *Capital* is clearly far greater than mine, but there is more at stake here than correctly ascribing Marx's categories to different stages in the development of the labor process.

Marx's tripartite distinction between a) transitional forms of labor, b) formal subsumption of labor and c) real subsumption of labor is valid in terms of the abstract model of capitalism described in *Capital*. Marx might also have reasonably assumed that transitional forms, including the various forms of unfree labor, would in due course be transformed into wage labor subject first to formal then real subsumption. The American Civil War was, after all, the backdrop to the composition of *Capital*, and Northern victory both abolished slavery and seemed to foreshadow a more general end to unfree labor on a global scale.[4] Unfortunately, forms of unfree labor, far from being legacies or anomalies, have proved to be extraordinarily resilient in the subsequent history of capitalism. Is noting this, as Alex says, offering Political Marxism "a huge hostage to fortune"? Quite the contrary: it is simply to acknowledge that, although wage labor—where the direct producers are subject to market compulsion rather than physical coercion—is part of what defines capitalism, to argue that capitalism can *only* exist where every direct producer is "free" in this sense is to be subject to a formalism that can lead to quite absurd conclusions, such as George Comninel's assertion that capitalism only became the dominant mode of production in France in 1959. Rather, free labor acts as a kind of norm, beyond which there are many gradations of formal freedom, but all subject to what Jairus Banaji calls "capitalist laws of motion."[5]

This has nothing to do with endorsing "Marcel van der Linden's proposal to submerge wage workers in the much broader category of 'subaltern workers.'"[6] It is true that I cite an article by van der Linden and Shahid Amin, along with others by Stanley Engerman and Banaji, in my discussion about wage labor.[7] But the former piece does not mention "subaltern workers," a term van der Linden began to use much later in a book that, contrary to what Alex implies, I do not cite and had not actually read when I completed *HRWTBR*.[8] The concept of the subaltern worker is in any case both wrong and unnecessary. On the one hand there are actual wage laborers subject to varying degrees of unfreedom. On the other there are direct producers, subject to capitalist laws of motion, who are not necessarily wage laborers at all. As Banaji writes in relation to the latter group: "The argument is not that *all* sharecroppers, labour-tenants and bonded labourers are wage-workers, but that these 'forms' may reflect the subsumption of labour into capital in ways where the 'sale' of labour-power for wages is mediated and possibly disguised in more complex arrangements."[9] Here Alex has allowed his polemical zeal (and his antipathy toward van der Linden's work) to ascribe views to me that I do not hold.

SUBJECT AND STRUCTURE

In different ways both Alex and Donny express the wish that I had written a different book from the one they are actually discussing. Alex writes: "the book's form as an intellectual history . . . means that there is no compact narrative or analysis of the bourgeois revolutions themselves. Discussions of particular problems or episodes there are aplenty, but they are dispersed through the book."[10] Donny similarly complains that I do "not give a sense of the upheavals on the ground with which to judge 'how revolutionary' the bourgeois revolutions actually were. One has the sensation of eavesdropping on swimmers at a pool side discussing the temperature of the water. The only way to find out is to plunge in."[11] It is possible that Donny's expectations may have been shaped too much by the title rather than by what I actually intended to do. It might therefore be useful to begin by explaining my original conception of the book.

The plan involved a tripartite structure. Part one was to have traced the development of the theory of bourgeois revolution, including the emergence of the distinct theory of proletarian revolution, against the backdrop of the actual history that the different versions of these theories were intended to explain or influence. Part two was to have synthesized this discussion to present a general theory of revolution, distinguishing first between political and social revolutions and then different types of social revolution ("feudal," bourgeois, and socialist), before establishing the preconditions for the era of bourgeois revolution and the outcomes that would allow us to say when both the individual instances of bourgeois revolution and "the" bourgeois revolution as a whole had been consummated. Part three was to have revisited the historical trajectory overviewed in part one, now foregrounding the actual events themselves. In other words, this third part would have been the history of the bourgeois revolutions that both of my critics would have preferred me to have written.

In the end, this plan was simply impossible to achieve as a single project. Leaving aside the likely response of my long-suffering publisher had I actually submitted a work of the envisaged size, sticking to my original conception would have meant the book languishing unfinished even now. Horrifying though it may be for those concerned with global deforestation, I do eventually intend to write the history of the bourgeois revolutions, but this was not the occasion. Once it became apparent that the main focus would have to be on the history of the theory, I revised the proposed structure, and what remains of the final part is now concentrated, in very broad outline, in chapter 22.[12] The results raise two questions.

The first is whether it is possible adequately to account for theoretical developments without previously or simultaneously writing the history of the period in which they emerge. Donny thinks not, writing: "Without grounding the history of ideas in a close study of the events they deal with, the impression is unintentionally given that one idea leads to the next, or that the ideas can be properly understood as independent entities. The strength of an idea (and in this case that idea is a description of a social or political process) depends on how closely it reflects or explains reality rather than how it compares with other ideas."[13] Now there is a historical school that does attempt to discuss ideas in terms of how "one . . . leads to the next"; it is the so-called Cambridge School, whose chief representatives are J. G. A. Pocock and Quentin Skinner.[14] However, despite its many achievements in delineating the history of ideas—some of which I draw on in *HRWTBR*—I do not identify with this school, since it is methodologically incompatible with historical materialism.

Donny is obviously right that ideas cannot be understood in isolation from their social context, but it is necessary to retain a sense of proportion here. One way of looking at *HRWTBR* is as an account of political thought since Machiavelli, refracted through the prism of the concept of revolution. To say that I needed to write the history of the world since the Reformation in order to make sense of the concept is to set a standard virtually impossible of accomplishment—total history reduced to the point of absurdity—or else Donny's position merely means establishing a series of vulgar one-to-one correspondences between events and the ideas they are supposed to have inspired, like the legendary apple falling on Newton's head and inspiring the concept of gravity. But theoretical positions can rarely be traced back to individual moments; Lenin's change of position as to the nature of the Russian Revolution in April 1917 is one of the rare occasions where we can follow this happening in some detail, as I attempt to show in *HRWTBR*.[15]

The second question is whether I have *actually* written a decontextualized history of ideas, as Alex and Donny claim. In fact, even within the more restricted final scope of the work, I would never have attempted anything so alien to our tradition. At every point, including the discussion of Lenin in 1917 mentioned in the previous paragraph, I try to show how social change enabled certain theoretical positions, which had hitherto been literally "unthinkable," to emerge. The book begins by establishing how aspects of the development of capitalism enabled revolution in general to be understood as a progressive rather than cyclical process. It then shows how a specific theory (or prototheory) of bourgeois revolution was formulated as the result of certain conjunctures within this context, not in the Netherlands, where capitalism first developed on a "national" basis, but in England, which followed it. The determining factor here is that the struggle against absolutism in the former was directed against an external enemy (the Spanish Habsburg empire), while in the latter it was directed against one that had its basis in internal social relations (the absolutist regime of the Stuarts), thus allowing the nature of the contending classes to be more clearly understood, initially by James Harrington.[16] And so the book goes on. What I have tried to do is establish the mediations between historical process, direct experience, and theoretical production on a basis that can be defended. A detailed history of the bourgeois revolutions is no doubt still required; but it is not a prerequisite for understanding how they have been theorized.

In addition to my subject matter, Alex also has objections to the structure of the book, describing *HRWTBR* as "a book of extended ruminations, not a focused theoretical or historical analysis."[17] While I am, of course, delighted to be compared to that great protomodernist Laurence Sterne (and, indeed, to Hegel), I think this is one of the occasions where Alex has misunderstood my method, which is not—OK, not *primarily*—one of digression. One of my two starting points was the need to respond to the Political Marxist dismissal of the concept of bourgeois revolution, not only as an attempt to theorize a supposedly nonexistent process but as an alien, liberal materialist intrusion into Marxism. What I was attempting to demonstrate was that the concept is in fact absolutely central to the entire structure of historical materialism. Its centrality can, however, only be demonstrated by showing the linkages between it and other constitutive elements of that tradition. In some cases these elements are the wider processes and institutions to whose transformation the bourgeois revolutions were essential, particularly the transition from feudalism to capitalism and the construction of territorially bounded states capable of acting as centers of competitive accumulation. But in other cases bourgeois revolution is central because of the need for a comparator, a standpoint from which to comprehend other great transformations, either fixed in the distant past or possible in a still uncertain future: long-term shifts in the balance between base and superstructure, between social revolution and economic transition, between conscious agency and unintended consequences, and between the different structural capacities of oppressed and exploited classes. Let me take two examples, both raised by Alex at different points in his review.

First, as a specific example of my supposed propensity for discursiveness, Alex cites my discussion of the absolutist state, which, he claims, "leads to quite an extensive discussion of the tributary mode of production, where peasants are exploited by a state independent of the landowning class: there's a connection between the two topics, but dealing with one doesn't demand discussing the other."[18] Actually, it does. In order to explain why capitalism initially became *dominant* in parts of Western Europe, one also has to explain why it did not do so anywhere else, even though it certainly *existed* at various times in parts of the (in many respects more advanced) Ottoman, Mughal, and Chinese empires. I am not simply attempting to minimize the inevitable accusations of Eurocentrism with which anyone daring to point out the priority of Western capitalism tends to be confronted these days, but to make a point about states that I consider of central importance. The emergence of a capitalist world system was dependent on a number of conditions of possibility, one of which was the *absence* of a state with the centralized bureaucratic power of the tributary empires. The connection with absolutist states is that I regard their creation as an attempt, not necessarily conscious, to establish some of the characteristics of the tributary states in a European context, above all the subordination of the emergent capitalist class as bankers and bureaucrats for a regime that had centralized the individual powers of the lords. The extent to which the various absolutist regimes were successful in doing so depended on how far capitalist development had reached: too far to be halted in the Netherlands and England; far less so in France and, above all, in Russia, where the revolutions were consequently delayed until later historical periods.[19] The subject of the tributary state is scarcely a digression, then.

In the second and far more general example Alex writes that my title "invites us to reflect on the nature of revolution in general, as well as that of bourgeois revolutions." He acknowledges that "to some extent this is unavoidable," because of the need to distinguish between bourgeois and proletarian revolutions, but my "exploration of the general topic of revolution extends much more broadly than this. The very first chapter concerns the early modern transformation of the concept of revolution from a cyclical movement to a progressive transformation. More general reflections recur throughout the book."[20] The reasons for this are quite simple.

First, in order to define bourgeois revolution as a specific category you need to have previously defined revolution as a general one. Indeed, from Harrington in the 1640s to François Guizot in the 1820s, the idea of a social revolution and what came to be called bourgeois revolution were inevitably coterminous, since any other kind of social revolution was as yet unimaginable. It was only when the possibility—however distant—of one based on the working class became visible that the notion of a specifically bourgeois revolution could even be named, as it was by Louis Blanc in 1839.[21]

Second, with the exception of the Russian Revolution and a handful of even shorter-lived socialist successes, mainly in individual cities—Paris in 1871, Barcelona in 1936–37, Budapest in 1956—the *only* successful modern social revolutions have been bourgeois revolutions, even though they may have been disguised in "Communist coloration." To point this out is not to succumb to the myth of congenital proletarian incapacity spread by Georges Bataille and his current followers, in which every revolution is bourgeois because socialist revolution is simply impossible.[22] It is, however, to understand that the structures, organizations, agencies, and ideologies of the bourgeois revolutions have an enormous significance for us, if only because they can alert us to how different our own must be, if we are to emulate the success of the bourgeoisie as a revolutionary class.

"Consequentialism"

Alex and I broadly agree about the need for a consequentialist definition of bourgeois revolution—unsurprisingly, since (as I am happy to acknowledge once again) his own discussion in this journal was very influential on my own views.[23] What I have tried to do in *HRWTBR* is not only elaborate the position but also establish its intellectual lineage from Friedrich Engels's writings on German unification onward. I have some minor issues with Alex's original presentation of the argument, namely his use of Perry Anderson's "moment of convulsive transformation" formula to describe bourgeois revolution and the related fact that most capitalist states have not undergone anything that could remotely be described in this way.[24] Alex describes these as "pettifogging" objections.[25] They are certainly not decisive objections, but neither are they negligible. My reluctance to follow his reliance on Anderson, leaving aside the fact that the latter is describing socialist and not bourgeois revolution, is less about the length of a process as opposed to an event and more about the nature of the process. I can see where this "moment" was in relation to, say, the Meiji Restoration, but not in relation to Italian or German unification. These largely military-diplomatic struggles centered on Piedmont and Prussia respectively, but when were *their* prior "moments" of revolution? There appears rather to have been a prolonged process of internal reform, starting in the German states during the Napoleonic Wars and intensifying after 1848–49, followed by episodes of externalized violence in order to create an expanded territorial nation-state. My point was really that, while the German "moment"—understood as a period of decisive change in the nature of the state rather than one of specific duration—can certainly be confined to the years between 1862 and 1871, there must have been a prior and much more extended moment in the history of Prussia's own state that enabled it to play the role of unifier in the first place. This in turn suggests that, in the areas immediately adjacent to revolutionary France at least, the process of "accelerated reform" actually started much earlier in the nineteenth century than is usually supposed. It is true that Alex doesn't claim that every nation-state had to undergo a bourgeois revolution: he doesn't say anything about the subject at all. Here I was simply trying to fill in a gap in the argument: I certainly wasn't trying to manufacture an artificial difference between us in order to distinguish my own position from his.

Donny's conception of "consequentialism," however, is markedly different from both Alex's and mine. Donny claims that I call

> the connection between the early bourgeois revolutions and the very different processes that came later (spreading capitalism across the world) consequentialism. So the various national processes whereby capitalism triumphed around the globe were a consequence of unique early bourgeois revolutions without being a copy of these ... the consequentialist argument should not just be applied to changes in the mode of production or the accumulation of capital. It extends to the continuing ideological impact of the early bourgeois revolutions, which are continually replenished and reinvigorated through new struggles (whether successful or not), and through the operation of market relations themselves.[26]

I'll return to why Donny wants to emphasize "the continuing ideological impact of the early bourgeois revolutions" below, but it is important to understand that the definition offered in the first half of this quote is not what I, at any rate, understand by consequentialism.

The term was originally associated with moral philosophy and for that reason is not perhaps the happiest to use in this context, although it flows more readily off the tongue than "outcome-ism," which might nevertheless be more exact. Either way, it does not refer to the way that "the various national processes whereby capitalism triumphed around the globe were a consequence of unique early bourgeois revolutions." It refers instead to the way in which individual bourgeois revolutions, early or late, can be identified: not by the structural forms that they took, nor by the social forces that brought them about, but by their consequences, their outcomes. Decisive among these consequences is the transformation of the state into one that—depending on where in the overall cycle a particular bourgeois revolution took place—either initiates or consolidates the period of capitalist dominance. This definition does not commit us to a position that holds that the bourgeoisie have never been a revolutionary class; only that they are not required to be for the theory of bourgeois revolution to be coherent. In fact, I was concerned to defend the historical role of the bourgeoisie where it had played this role, against the endless disparagement of revisionists and Political Marxists alike.

According to Donny I do not "explore the specific nature of bourgeois freedom and bourgeois democracy in any depth. In relationship to previous times these were, and in the many instances of dictatorship today still are, revolutionary."[27] Far from being intrinsic to bourgeois society, representative democracy has largely been introduced by pressure from the working class and extended by pressure from the oppressed. This is one of the few points on which I agree with Political Marxists, in particular Charles Post: far from being integral to capitalism, democracy was in many respects its opponent.[28] The authors of an important study of the relationship between capitalism and democracy are therefore right to reject any automatic correspondence between the two: "It was not the capitalist market nor capitalists as the new dominant force, but the contradictions of capitalism that advanced the cause of democracy":

> The relationship between working class strength and democracy may be summarised in the following way: a diachronic analysis within each of the Western European countries reveals that the growth of working-class organisational strength led to increased pressure for the introduction of democracy; a synchronic analysis reveals that these pressures led to the development of stable democratic regimes where the working class found allies in other social groups. If the pro-democratic alliance was strong, the bourgeoisie was not able to act to move the country in an authoritarian direction even where it perceived a threat from the working class movement, as it surely did in Norway and Sweden.

These authors conclude that "the optimal configuration of working class organisation for the development of democracy would be one in which the class was well organised, in both unions and a party, but that these organisations were not radical."[29] The reason why democracy is such a relatively recent development is therefore because the bourgeoisie resisted it for as long as possible, particularly where the working class and oppressed groups pressed their claims for suffrage in militant terms—although that same militancy was often what ensured the establishment of democracy.

The ruling classes assumed that if the working classes had the vote, they would surely use it to deprive them, their masters, of their property. Marx and Engels initially thought so too—that is the meaning of the "battle for democracy" referred to in the "Manifesto of the Communist Party."[30] They were wrong. Both the bourgeoisie and its greatest opponents initially underestimated the way in which capitalism tended to generate a reformist rather than revolutionary consciousness within the working class. It was only after this became apparent during the late nineteenth century that the attitude of the more intelligent representatives of the former changed from outright opposition to democracy to grudging tolerance of it. Even so, actual implementation was rarely achieved without a struggle. Other than where democracy has been imposed as the result of defeat in war—for example in Japan after 1945—national bourgeoisies have only accepted it as a necessary concession to forestall what were, for them, still more dangerous outcomes.

In other words, none of this has very much to do with the influence of the French Revolution. Furthermore, harking back to the bourgeois revolutions as inspiration has positive dangers, not least in depriving the concept of democracy of any class content. More generally, it blurs the distinction between bourgeois and proletarian revolutions by establishing imaginary continuities between them on the basis of a "radical tradition," the critique of which was my second starting point. Alex questions my inclusion of Walter Benjamin in chapter 14 (which focused on the attempts to maintain the classical Marxist tradition in the face of Stalinism) on the grounds that the latter did not develop the theory of bourgeois revolution to anything like the extent that Antonio Gramsci or Trotsky did.[31] I actually agree that Benjamin's contribution was of a different and lesser order of magnitude, but he did nevertheless make a contribution that I regard as essential to any integrated Marxist approach to the subject. This has less to do with the theory of bourgeois revolutions and more to do with his challenge to their role as constitutive events in the collective historical memory of the socialist movement, as a pre-Marxist, often presocialist notion of "the people's story," which was absorbed by Social Democracy after the establishment of the Second International (on the centenary of the Great French Revolution) and transmitted more or less intact into Stalinism. By counterposing "the tradition of the oppressed" to "the tradition of the victors" (i.e., the victors in the bourgeois revolutions), Benjamin disrupted the uncritical assumptions about continuities and suggested that we may have to look to other places and times entirely for what may be useful to us, quite separate from the lineage that supposedly flows from Cromwell to Robespierre to Lincoln ... to Lenin.[32]

POLITICAL AND SOCIAL REVOLUTION

If there are matters of detail that distinguish my position from that of Alex in relation to consequentialism, there are more serious disagreements over the relationship between political and social revolutions. Alex summarizes some of the issues in the following passage:

> There are two puzzles here. First, a page after differentiating social revolutions from transitions between modes of production, he includes in his list . . . a transition between modes of production. Neil's discussion of the end of classical antiquity

focuses on the change in mode of production without any consideration of the political transformations meticulously studied by Chris Wickham in *Framing the Early Middle Ages*. Secondly, why so few social revolutions? When Neil writes that the transition from slavery to feudalism is "the first direct passage in history from one exploitative mode of production to another" one is inclined to ask: what about the shift from tributary palace bureaucracies to city states based on heavy citizen infantry and increasingly reliant on slavery in Greece during the early centuries of the first millennium BC, or the formation of the Chinese empire a few centuries later? No doubt others could add more to this list of candidates.[33]

As far as the number of social revolutions is concerned, I argue (here using Alex's preferred terminology) that there have been three *kinds*: "feudal," bourgeois, and socialist. It should be obvious to all but the deliberately obtuse that I think there have been more than three *instances* of social revolution, since I refer to over a dozen in the course of the book. But the relationship between kinds and instances is different depending on the nature of the former. The transition from slavery to feudalism in Western Europe occurred across the former Roman Empire, in which distinct territorial states were only in the process of formation. It is therefore difficult to identify individual instances, since the process involves a centuries-long shifting of borders and jurisdictions across the landmass as a whole, which only takes shape as a coherent state system at the end—the point usually identified as the "feudal revolution" by French Marxists like Guy Bois and Georges Duby. In the field of bourgeois revolutions, there are certainly many individual instances, but even here—as suggested in the discussion above—there comes a point, roughly between 1871 and 1918, when the cumulative impact of the successful bourgeois revolutions have brought into being a world system in which individual revolutionary instances are no longer necessary, except in the colonial or semicolonial world, simply a more or less prolonged process of adaptation. The socialist revolution will be similar, in the sense that it will also involve a number of instances—but almost certainly more, since, unlike capitalism, socialism will not have an economic dynamic independent of the nation-states in which it has triumphed and will require to be consciously established everywhere, although after a certain point we might hope that remaining capitalists will simply give up. These comparisons should give some idea of what I was trying to do in chapter 20 of *HRWTBR*, namely to identify the main characteristics of the great transition that preceded the bourgeois revolution and the one that might still follow it, in order better to understand the specificity of the bourgeois revolution itself.

Does this mean that I think there were no social revolutions prior to the transition from slavery to feudalism? Not in the terms in which I define social revolution. I take a traditional view that there are only a limited number of precapitalist modes of production—slave, tributary, and feudal—although small commodity production based on the peasant household is a constant feature in all of them. Social revolutions are the means of accomplishing the transition from a society based on one mode to that based on another. These do not follow each other in succession, as is often assumed from a misreading of Marx's 1859 "Preface" to *A Contribution to the Critique of Political Economy*, but emerged in uneven and staggered ways from nonclass society, a process that took several millennia to accomplish. In other words, slave, tributary, and feudal societies are all specific expressions of the general transition to class society. In this process, different societies oscillated from variations of one nascent mode to another, often combining aspects of more than one, until they began to emerge as states where one was clearly dominant in developed form, as in the case of the Chinese tributary state to which Alex refers. Clearly this involved class struggles, even political revolution, but not social revolution. In some places, notably Scandinavia and the British Isles, feudalism was the direct passage out of nonclass society, but in the Western Roman Empire it arose as the result of a transition from one fully fledged exploitative mode to another. This too was accompanied by class struggles, as Wickham has described so vividly.[34] But class struggle is *normal* in class societies. It only leads to social revolution in cases where the exploited or oppressed classes have the structural capacity to achieve it, which is precisely what I deny was the case for slaves and peasants in this period.[35]

All this has taken us some way back in time from the bourgeois revolutions, but there is a modern context for Alex's unhappiness about a too-rigid distinction between political and social revolutions: "Neil's unwillingness to see the potential for permanent revolution that may be present in political upheavals in capitalist states sometimes leads to some strange choices: thus he virtually ignores the Mexican Revolution of 1910–20, one of the greatest upheavals of the 20th century and the subject of a major study by the Trotskyist historian Adolfo Gilly, apparently on the grounds that the Mexican state was already capitalist, and devotes more space to colonial Canada's mid-19th century reorganisations."[36] In fact, I have no doubts at all about the potential for revolution "present in political upheavals in capitalist states"; it is simply that in the current period, I don't think these have anything to do with permanent revolution, at least as I understand the term. I will return to the question of whether this is more than a terminological dispute below. But, as far as my neglect of the Mexican Revolution is concerned—is this really so strange? We have already established that in a book about the theory of bourgeois revolution I do not discuss *any* revolution in great detail (I devote three paragraphs to Canadian Confederation). Far from being ignorant of Gilly's work, I actually quote his view that the transition to capitalism was completed in Mexico by 1860, so the Mexican Revolution of 1910–20 clearly falls outside my remit.[37] It may have had the potential to turn into a socialist revolution—I think this is unlikely, although not impossible—but it was not in any sense a bourgeois revolution, so why would I discuss it in even summary terms?

There is however a real problem here: some revolutions that end up as being merely "political" actually involve far greater "social" upheavals and far more mass involvement than successful social revolutions. The Iranian Revolution—a political revolution in my terms—confused many analysts for precisely this reason.[38] Egypt is a more immediately relevant case in point. Alex rightly criticizes Aijaz Ahmad for "preferring the July 1952 military coup that brought Gamal Abdel Nasser to power and enabled him to carry out a state capitalist restructuring of Egypt's political economy to what he concedes were 'two massive popular risings of historically unprecedented scale.'"[39] But there is a sense in which July 1952 *was* a decisive instance of social revolution in Egypt, while the process that began with Hosni Mubarak's resignation on February 11, 2011—from the perspective of revolutionary socialists, infinitely more significant—has not yet even achieved the outcome of a political revolution, since the coup of July 3, 2013, restored the military to power.[40]

Alex quotes Colin Sparks to the effect that permanent revolution is a theory of alternatives.[41] True, but surely all revolutions pose a set of alternatives? One outcome, the victory of the working class, has not yet been achieved anywhere, but there are three others, all of which are present in the Arab Spring: outright defeat; "the common ruin of the contending classes," or at any rate partial social collapse; and victory for a new or different fraction of the existing ruling class ("political revolution"): Bahrain, Libya, or Tunisia. There is a sense then in which it is not only the historical bourgeois revolutions that have to be judged by their outcomes, but *all* modern revolutions.

DEMOCRACY AND PERMANENT REVOLUTION

Inevitably then, we (re)turn to the question of permanent revolution, which I have already discussed at length in *International Socialism*, *HRWTBR*, and a shortly-to-be-published book on this subject and related issues.[42] I will therefore pass on the opportunity to respond to all of Alex's comments and restrict myself to two points, one concerning ideology and the other uneven and combined development—although, as we shall see, these have a significant degree of overlap.

Leaving aside for the moment the question of whether permanent revolution is relevant where the bourgeois revolution has been accomplished, one of my other arguments for the historical nature of the former is that the strategic position to which it formed the alternative—Stalinist stages theory—has itself been overtaken by history. In other words the argument revolutionaries now need to make is for socialist revolution as such against a reformism that, even at its most radical in South Africa and Bolivia, no longer talks in terms of socialism as an end goal at all, or if it does, then only as one achievable at such a distance in time that it is effectively unattainable. Alex underplays the contemporary consequences of the collapse of Stalinism and concentrates instead on my historical point concerning the attitude of Stalinists toward their own position. Alex comments that I display "a remarkable approach to the critique of ideology, relying as it does on the idea that we can ignore theories if we think their exponents are fibbing and what they propose isn't feasible. . . . Stages strategy was *never* practicable (that was the point of Trotsky's critique), but that doesn't mean that as an ideology it can't still exercise a hold because of the social needs it serves."[43]

On reflection, I think my original position *was* wrong, but not for the reasons that Alex gives. Actually, I don't think the Stalinists were "fibbing"—they sincerely believed that the stages theory was correct, for example in the case of the "democratic stage" in Eastern Europe, supposedly between 1944 and 1949. Furthermore—and contrary to what Trotsky believed—it was also "practicable," but from the point of view of establishing state capitalism, not socialism. The problem was that Trotsky regarded the degeneration of the USSR as a historically unique event, and he could not imagine, except as a very tentative hypothesis in his last writings, that similar societies could be created as a conscious project. He was wrong. The Stalinists were perfectly sincere state capitalists, a position they—in my view genuinely, for the most part—regarded as socialism. The point, however, is that they quite correctly no longer think state capitalism ("socialism") is achievable and consequently have now reverted to a reformism that treats capitalism as the limit of human development. Capitalism may be subject to greater democratization, but there is no longer any further stage beyond it—and maybe there never was.

What is the relationship of the collapse of Stalinism to uneven and combined development? Alex writes of my attitude toward this subject: "By removing its political moorings in the theory of permanent revolution, he can unintentionally reinforce this unwelcome tendency [toward ahistorical abstraction]. In his concluding remarks to Part Four he underlines the destabilising potential of uneven and combined development, but fails to notice that this makes it hard to counterpose social and political revolutions as starkly as he does."[44] The term "permanent revolution" describes both a possible outcome of a revolutionary situation and a strategic orientation that attempts to make that outcome more likely. For me, it is best understood as the violent intersection of two social facts. On the one hand, there is a precapitalist state, whether absolutist, tributary, or colonial (the latter usually coexisted with or incorporated local precapitalist state formations): in other words, a situation where the fundamental task, the only real task of the bourgeois revolution, has still to be achieved. On the other hand is uneven and combined development, where an economy and society combine elements of the most archaic and the most modern forms, not merely in technology but also in politics, culture, and ideology. It was the explosive dynamic caused by the latter running up against the immovable bounds of the former that produced the possibility of permanent revolution. But what happens if one of these social facts is removed? What happens if you still have uneven and combined development, but not the possibility of bourgeois revolution because the latter has been achieved—and in ways Trotsky himself never envisaged? A new situation needs new terms, if only to prevent the assumption that the dynamics at play are the same as in 1906, or even 1963.

Against this notion, Alex (and, implicitly, Donny) argue that it is still possible to use the term because the absence of democracy in large areas of the global South means that something analogous to the tensions that originally produced permanent revolution still exist. They argue, correctly, that Trotsky himself believed that permanent revolution was a possibility in capitalist states that had not yet achieved all of the supposed 'tasks" of the bourgeois revolution, of which democracy was preeminent. I think Trotsky was wrong to discuss two distinct situations under a single rubric, but leave that aside; the real question is whether—bearing in mind my earlier comments on the ambiguities of the concept—democracy can play the role required of it: "To detect the presence of the dynamic of permanent revolution in cases such as these is not merely to assert the universal truth that socialist revolution represents the solution to every society's problems. It is to recognise the peculiar fluidity of political and social struggles that uneven and combined development induces in some but not all situations. One index of the presence of this dynamic is the centrality of democratic demands ... Democratic demands [in Egypt] have a unifying character absent in the British case."[45] Well, events in Egypt prior to the coup of July 2013 would suggest that democratic demands also have the potential to *disunify* in ways that have badly misdirected the mass movement. The main point, however, is this: precapitalist states, at least those that existed in Trotsky's lifetime and for several decades after his death, were not susceptible to reform and had either to be overthrown by revolution or destroyed in war. This is not true of contemporary capitalist states, even those in the global South. However backward they may be in many respects, they have a far greater capacity for absorption and renovation under pressure, which means that revolutions simply about nonspecific—but actually bourgeois—"democracy" are far more likely to result in political revolutionary outcomes than was the case in Russia in 1917 or even Ethiopia in 1974. We have already seen this in the Philippines, in Indonesia, in Thailand, and in South Africa. We may now be seeing a similar process unfold in the Ukraine, where the level of struggle has been extraordinarily high over a prolonged period, but without the slightest suggestion of left-wing influence among the demonstrators in Independence Square; if anything, it is the far right that has provided political leadership.

And so we return to the question of ideology or, more precisely, of revolutionary socialist politics and how this has been absent from almost all the great struggles of recent decades, although South Africa and Bolivia present partial exceptions (which is also why "old-style" reformism remains relatively strong in those countries). Despite the way in which the IS tradition has been shaped by opposition both to Stalinism and to orthodox Trotskyist concessions to it, there was a way in which we failed to understand that its demise, at the moment of neoliberal ascendancy, would not automatically encourage the struggle for genuine liberation but would cast doubt in the minds of many of the exploited and oppressed about the possibility of any systemic alternative to capitalism at all. Stalinism was like a drug that both poisoned and preserved the body of its victim, namely the idea of socialism. Across the world it has variously been replaced by any number of populist, Islamist, or autonomist alternatives; but the most common has been "democracy." In other words, the demand for democracy is not necessarily the gateway to revolution but can remain an end in itself—although a dead end in relation to the problems it is intended to address. But this discussion takes us into contemporary problems of organization, strategy, and consciousness, and far from the era of the bourgeois revolutions.

CONCLUSION

How serious are the differences to which I have attempted to respond here? It is not clear to me that they involve alternative strategies for revolution in the global South, although they may involve different conceptions, or at least differences in emphasis, about the difficulties revolutionaries there face. The real difference, I suspect, is less tangible and has more to do with an attitude toward tradition, both the Marxist tradition in general and the IS tradition in particular. Alex himself was once concerned about the possibility of stagnation in both: "We cannot simply 'return' to the classics. . . . Classical Marxism is not a monolith, a seamless robe. Its gaps, aporias, too-hasty answers created the space in which vulgar Marxism emerged. . . . Classical Marxism requires conceptual development as well as application in concrete analyses and embodiment in revolutionary organisation."[46] This quote is taken from the preface to Alex's 1982 book *Is There a Future for Marxism?* The desire to retain certain concepts come what may is an example of the type of conservatism that I criticized in a recent issue of *International Socialism*: once there was a need for theoretical innovation to understand a changing world, but apparently now there is no longer any, even though the world has not ceased changing.[47] Paradoxically, one of the effects of this kind of conservatism—where every initiative has to be legitimated by reference to a text written in 1906 or a strategy codified in 1921—is that the genuine innovations of the Socialist Workers Party are never recognized as such, because we have to pretend that they are already present in the works of the classical Marxists.

In 1983, Alex responded in the pages of this journal to severe—if almost entirely misplaced—criticism of his book by then-editor Peter Binns. Alex noted that "the basis on which debates of this nature should be conducted is a common acceptance of the fact that we are all pursuing the same goal of working-class self-emancipation, and seeking to clarify the revolutionary Marxism we share, not merely to knock down each other's positions." He then went on to express his "great disappointment" at the "entirely negative response" to his book from comrades, which he regarded as symptomatic of a wider problem: "It is especially a danger at a time such as the present that revolutionaries will simply retreat into the stronghold of orthodoxy, pulling up the drawbridge behind them." Binns, he thought, was guilty of precisely this type of intellectual retreat, of a "defensive attitude, a refusal to admit that Marxism requires anything except reiteration": an attitude alien to the IS tradition, which, on the contrary, "has been marked by its intellectual daring, its willingness to question the accepted truths. It would be sad, even disastrous if that ceased to be true of us now."[48] Alex and Donny have been far more positive in their responses to my book than the party was to Alex's in 1982, but I detect some of that same defensiveness. It would be equally sad, equally tragic, if that attitude were to influence our approach to the challenges of the twenty-first century.

Afterword: We Cannot Escape History

1

Anyone ignorant of the source of the phrase "we cannot escape history" might be forgiven for thinking that it expresses a profoundly pessimistic worldview. History must be a prison like the Château d'If where Edmond Dantès is confined in Alexander Dumas's *The Count of Monte Cristo*, from which prisoners cannot exit except in a burial sack. Or perhaps it is an implacable pursuer like Inspector Javert in Victor Hugo's *Les Misérables*, whose reach cannot be evaded except, again, by death. But the best metaphor for this perspective may still be the one given by Stephen Daedalus early in James Joyce's *Ulysses*: "History, Stephen said, is a nightmare from which I am trying to awake."[1] The words "we cannot escape history" were not, however, uttered in a spirit of defeat at all, and when Abraham Lincoln addressed them to his "fellow-citizens" in Congress on December 1, 1862, he did not feel himself to be incarcerated, persecuted, or haunted by unrelenting nighttime visions.[2]

On September 22, 1862, Lincoln had issued a preliminary Emancipation Proclamation warning that from New Year's Day, 1863, all slaves held in the states then in rebellion against the United States would be regarded as free by the federal government. Many historians argue that this was the moment at which the Civil War became a social revolution, or perhaps the moment when Lincoln and his allies came to realize, as Karl Marx had done from the start, that it had always been a social revolution.[3] There have been several attempts to compare the attitudes of the sixteenth president of the United States and those of Marx toward slavery, and toward the civil war that brought it to an end; Lincoln's second annual State of the Union address does not, however, tend to figure among the evidence.[4] Perhaps it should, for the opening sentence of Lincoln's concluding remarks was a remarkably Marxist statement for this most consummately bourgeois of politicians to have made. It is not my intention here to subject the entire speech to the kind of detailed scrutiny to which, for example, Garry Wills has subjected the Gettysburg Address; but the earlier speech, if inferior to the later one as rhetoric, nevertheless represents a more significant shift in his thinking.[5]

233

As David Bromwich notes, at the beginning of the US Civil War, Lincoln made a number of speeches that revealed him to be in several respects "more traditionalist than the upholders of tradition in the South."[6] The irony is palpable, but not historically unprecedented. In previous bourgeois revolutions, notably those in seventeenth-century England, their outbreak was triggered by the attempted imposition of innovations in the state and religion by a monarchy with absolutist aspirations. The parallels with the US experience are not exact, of course, but in the South we are also confronted with the spectacle of precapitalist conservatives claiming to uphold tradition—in this case the Constitution—while actually breaking with it in the most radical way possible, in order to maintain and strengthen their social power. Against this, Lincoln's original stance, expressed in his famous 1854 speech in Peoria, was genuinely conservative, seeking to defend the original principles of the Constitution with all the tensions it contained between the respective rights of freedom and slavery:

> Our republican robe is soiled, and trailed in the dust. Let us repurify it. Let us turn and wash it white, in the spirit, if not the blood, of the Revolution. Let us turn slavery from its claims of "moral right," back upon its existing legal rights, and its arguments of "necessity." Let us return it to the position our fathers gave it; and there let it rest in peace. Let us re-adopt the Declaration of Independence, and with it, the practices, and policy, which harmonize with it.[7]

Yet later in the same speech, in a phrase foreshadowing his changed position, Lincoln refers to "giving up the old for the new faith." Then, eight years later and eighteen months into the war, this: "As our case is new, so we must think anew and act anew," he told the assembled congressmen: "We must disenthrall ourselves, and then we shall save our country."[8] What is new here? Marx noted at the time that the Emancipation Proclamation was "tantamount to the tearing up of the old American Constitution," but Lincoln was now, as it were, theorizing what had occurred.[9] As Bromwich writes: "It may be the first time in American writing that *history* is used in quite this way, to denote a force outside human volition, and partly alien to it: not a question of mere heritage or the accretion of practices, and not the same, either, as a destiny projected from the past to the future. History is imagined rather as a force in the present that makes demands without parallel on those who would have any future at all."[10] History was neither "mere heritage" nor "a destiny projected," but a "force," *inherited* from the past, which could be deployed in the creation of the new. Wills has pointed out that Lincoln was not only a revolutionary in the obvious sense; in the Gettysburg Address "he not only put the Declaration [of Independence] in a new light as a matter of founding law, but put its central proposition, equality, in a newly favored position as a principle of the Constitution (which, as the Chicago *Times* noticed, never uses the word). What had been a mere theory . . . that the nation preceded the states in time and importance—now became a lived reality of the American tradition."[11] The United States was *a* nation-state; its citizens were *one* people; they always had been.

To understand the radical implications of what Lincoln had said, we have to turn to one of the founding texts of conservative political thought. In his *Reflections on the Revolution in France* (1790), Edmund Burke expressed a fear that the French revolutionaries were not only intent on changing the present but also on *changing the past*, or at least our understanding of the past. Take, for example, the principle that the people should be able to choose their monarch:

> Once such an unwarrantable maxim is established, that no throne is lawful but the elective, no one act of the princes who preceded their era of fictitious election can be valid. Do these theorists mean to imitate some of their predecessors, who dragged the bodies of our ancient sovereigns out of the quiet of their tombs? Do they mean to attaint and disable backwards all the kings that have reigned before the Revolution, and consequently to stain the throne of England with the blot of a continual usurpation?[12]

Now, in the US, as Burke had feared was going to happen in England, the past was actually being changed by revolution. As Wills notes: "The Gettysburg Address has become an authoritative expression of the American spirit—as authoritative as the Declaration itself, and perhaps even more influential, since it determines how we read the Declaration. For most people now, the Declaration means what Lincoln told us it means, as a way of correcting the Constitution itself without overthrowing it. It is this correction of the spirit, this intellectual revolution, that makes attempts to go back beyond Lincoln to some earlier version so feckless."[13] Have any other historical figures undertaken such a revision of their own position and been responsible for a comparable shift in perception? Perhaps there is one.

2

Among the pantheon of revolutionary leaders it is difficult to think of one more personally unlike Lincoln than Vladimir Ilyich Lenin; but dissimilarity of character is not the only factor marking them off from each other. Several of the essays in this book have been concerned with establishing the *differences* between kinds of revolution—political or social and, among the latter, bourgeois and socialist: it therefore follows that an examination of bourgeois and working-class revolutionary leaders is likely to yield more contrasts than comparisons.[14] Hal Draper once mischievously traced the activities of Thomas Jefferson during the War of Independence as if he were describing those of Lenin during the Russian Civil War. Draper's point was that the same type of policies for which Lenin is regularly denounced as a totalitarian by US liberals were also pursued by Jefferson, and in the case of the latter were in many respects less justified. Draper, however, also concluded: "Jeffersonianism is no model for Marxists, not because it is too good but, on the contrary, because not even the best of bourgeois-democratic paladins have ever risen to the level demanded by socialist democracy."[15] The US Civil War was a far more decisive event than the

War of Independence and Lincoln a greater figure than Jefferson; but can we draw any useful comparisons between this bourgeois revolution and the Russian socialist revolution, or between their respective leaders?

A comparison of the two revolutions is possible because of the distinctive position that the Civil War holds within the historical pattern of bourgeois revolutions. The earliest, in the Netherlands, England, and France, were led by noncapitalist sections of the bourgeoisie who did not consciously seek to establish capitalist states; later bourgeois revolutions, in Italy, Germany, and Japan, were led by sections of the existing feudal ruling class and, while they did consciously seek to establish capitalist states, it was primarily for reasons of geopolitical self-preservation or advantage. However, the Northern side in the US Civil War *was* led by representatives of the capitalist bourgeoisie who *did* consciously seek to establish a unified capitalist state on the ruins of the precapitalist society of the South. As Charles Post writes, "the social origins of the US Civil War indicates that it, almost alone among the 'bourgeois revolutions' identified by the historical-materialist tradition, actually fits the classical schema . . . a 'classic' bourgeois revolution led by a self-conscious class of capitalist manufacturers and commercial farmers struggling to remove the obstacle posed by the geographical expansion of plantation-slavery."[16] The element of revolutionary-class self-emancipation, albeit on a very different basis and in very different forms, therefore provides a link between the US Civil War and the Russian Revolution.

A comparison of the two leaders is possible because both men were prepared to overturn long-established positions at a moment of crisis. Marx described Lincoln as a "*sui generis* figure in the annals of history" with "no initiative, no idealistic impetus, no cothurnus, no historical trappings": "The new world has never achieved a greater triumph than this demonstration that, given its political and social organization, ordinary people of good will can accomplish feats which only heroes could accomplish in the old world!"[17] Lincoln did not enter politics in order to lead a revolution, and his greatness in this role was achieved by responding to events that were out of his control.[18] He moved from a position of defending the preexisting notion of the US to one of recognizing that the Civil War had revealed the irreconcilable antagonism between two societies, both of which could legitimately claim descent from the founding moment of the state, but only one of which would inherit it. By contrast, Lenin knew that a revolution was coming to Russia and always intended his organization to play a part in determining the outcome. He moved from a position of defending a preexisting conception of the Russian Revolution as a bourgeois revolution, albeit one led by the working class ("the democratic dictatorship of the proletariat and the peasantry") to one of recognizing that it could only survive, let alone achieve its goals, as the founding moment of the international socialist revolution.

Lenin's achievement is in some respects the more remarkable, given his initial isolation and the greater speed with which he changed his position. Lincoln was encouraged and supported, not to say pushed, into his new position by an array of forces that had arrived at it before him—in some cases long before him. As Robin

Blackburn points out: "The emancipationist policy was impressed on the president by the unrelenting pressure of the Radicals in Congress, by the growing influence of abolitionists, black and white, on Northern public opinion, and, last, but not least, by the emergence of military abolitionism."[19] It nevertheless took him a year and a half from the beginning of the Civil War to make the shift. Lenin, on the other hand, was virtually alone among Marxists in registering the changed nature of the Russian Revolution and did so in a matter of months, famously producing shocked reactions among not only his political opponents but a majority of his own party.[20] To acknowledge this is not to succumb to the Stalinist legend of Lenin's individual genius, but rather to understand that Lenin, unlike Lincoln, was able to draw on a theoretical tradition that enabled him to recognize the significance of new social facts—above all the Soviets—that suggested previously undreamt-of possibilities inherent in the present.

3

The reality of Lenin's change of position has been challenged by Lars Lih: "The so-called 'April Theses' announced by Lenin as soon as he arrived in Petrograd have traditionally been regarded as the expression of a major shift in Lenin's outlook, yet identifying exactly what is new in these theses is quite difficult." Lih, here as in his work more generally, wants to argue for the continuity of Lenin's thought across all stages of his career, conceding only that "in an unpublished draft written on 8 April . . . we find for the first time the idea of 'steps toward socialism' in Russia itself."[21] In fact, Lenin's position changed at least twice.

His initial view of the Russian Revolution was that it would be both *bourgeois*, in the sense that it would liberate capitalism from the confines of feudalism, and *democratic*, in the sense that it would overthrow the absolutist state, enfranchise the working class, and legalize the socialist parties:

> Marxists are absolutely convinced of the bourgeois character of the Russian revolution. What does this mean? It means that the democratic reforms in the political system and the social and economic reforms, which have become a necessity for Russia, do not in themselves imply the undermining of capitalism, the undermining of bourgeois rule; on the contrary, they will, for the first time, really clear the ground for a wide and rapid, European, and not Asiatic, development of capitalism; they will, for the first time, make it possible for the bourgeoisie to rule as a class.... The idea of seeking salvation for the working class in anything save the further development of capitalism is *reactionary*. In countries like Russia, the working class suffers not so much from capitalism as from the insufficient development of capitalism. The working class is therefore *decidedly interested* in the broadest, freest and most rapid development of capitalism. The removal of all the remnants of the old order which are hampering the broad, free and rapid development of capitalism is of decided advantage to the working class.[22]

Although Lenin expected this revolution to inspire working-class movements to the west of Russia (as the 1905 revolution did), he did not think that it would necessarily initiate the transition to socialism on a global scale—indeed, his very insistence on the need for a prolonged period of capitalist development in Russia suggests otherwise.

As in many other respects, it was the outbreak of the First World War, and what it demonstrated about both the destructive capacity of imperialism and the capitulation of the parties of the Second International to "their" nation-states, that prompted a shift in perspective. It is difficult to overestimate the impact of the war on Lenin's thought:

> The war of 1914–15 is such a great turn in history that the attitude towards opportunism cannot remain the same as it has been. What has happened *cannot* be erased. It is impossible to obliterate from the minds of the workers, or from the experience of the bourgeoisie, or from the political lessons of our epoch in general, the fact that, at a moment of crisis, the opportunists proved to be the nucleus of those elements within the workers' parties that deserted to the bourgeoisie. Opportunism—to speak on a European scale—was in its adolescent stage, as it were, before the war. With the outbreak of the war it grew to manhood and its "innocence" and youth cannot be restored. An entire social stratum, consisting of parliamentarians, journalists, labour officials, privileged office personnel, and certain strata of the proletariat, has sprung up and has become *amalgamated* with its own national bourgeoisie, which has proved fully capable of appreciating and "adapting" it. The course of history cannot be turned back or checked—we can and must go fearlessly onward, from the preparatory legal working-class organizations, which are in the grip of opportunism, to revolutionary organizations that know how *not* to confine themselves to legality and are capable of safeguarding themselves against opportunist treachery, organizations of a proletariat that is beginning a "struggle for power," a struggle for the overthrow of the bourgeoisie.[23]

The first shift in Lenin's position was that he now saw a revolution in Russia as triggering socialist revolutions in the West, while still holding to his original conception of the nature of the revolution within Russia itself: "Only a revolutionary-democratic dictatorship of the proletariat and the peasantry can form the social content of the impending revolution in Russia. . . . The task confronting the proletariat of Russia is the consummation of the bourgeois-democratic revolution in Russia *in order* to kindle the socialist revolution in Europe."[24] And Lenin retained this conception even after the revolution began, although he remained unbending in his stress on the need for the political independence of the working class: "Ours is a bourgeois revolution, we Marxists say, *therefore* the workers must open the eyes of the people to the deception practised by the bourgeois politicians, teach them to put no faith in words, to depend entirely on their *own* strength, their *own* organisation, their *own* unity, and their own *weapons*."[25]

We can see the beginning of a second shift of position in the last piece Lenin published before returning to Russia, dated April 8, where he stresses the contingent nature of the circumstances that have placed Russian workers in the European vanguard, but—more importantly—now treats the socialist revolution as an international event that also encompasses Russia itself. Lenin had, in other words, moved beyond the conceptualization of the Russian Revolution as bourgeois in outcome: "Single-handed, the Russian proletariat cannot bring the socialist revolution to a *victorious conclusion*. But it can give the Russian revolution a mighty sweep that would create the most favorable conditions for a socialist revolution, and would, in a sense, *start* it. It can facilitate the rise of a situation in which its *chief*, its most trustworthy and most reliable collaborator, the *European* and American *socialist* proletariat, could join the decisive battles."[26]

The twofold shift in Lenin's position was a response to two developments. One was the way in which the imperialist stage of capitalism had both unified the world, by enmeshing every corner of the globe in the circuits of capital, and threatened to destroy it through war. In this context, the Russian Revolution could not have a purely "bourgeois" significance, but in any case neither was the prospect of a prolonged period of internal capitalist development an attractive one, even under democratic conditions, given the way in which the descent into barbarism had removed any element of progressiveness from the capitalist system. The other was the organizational innovation represented by the Soviets. The relative absence of the possibility for opportunism meant the Russian working class was always more revolutionary than those in the West, but this had always been the case; the re-emergence of Soviets in 1917 did not simply indicate a new level of working-class democracy but an alternative form of social organization to that of the capitalist state.[27] It was the existence of this alternative that seems to have been the main impetus behind Lenin abandoning his former position on the nature of the Russian Revolution:

> Not a parliamentary republic—to return to a parliamentary republic from the Soviets of Workers' Deputies would be a retrograde step—but a republic of Soviets of Workers', Agricultural Laborers' and Peasants' Deputies throughout the country, from top to bottom. . . . It is not our immediate task to "introduce" socialism, but only to bring social production and the distribution of products at once under the control of the Soviets of Workers' Deputies.[28]

What allows Lih to claim that Lenin's position went fundamentally unchanged is the statement that socialism will not be the "immediate task" of a Soviet government, the implication being that if socialism is not on the agenda then capitalism must of necessity still be the only realistic horizon of the revolution. This, however, is to confuse politics and economics. Lenin was perfectly aware that socialism could not be fully achieved overnight, that it would never be achieved by Russia in isolation, and that, post-revolution, it contained at least five different socioeconomic structures: natural peasant economy, small commodity production, private capitalism, state capitalism, and socialism. His claim was rather that Russia now had a state in which the working class, and the oppressed and exploited more generally, held political power and were moving toward socialism to the degree this was possible in the absence of further successful revolutions in the more developed world.[29] The point at which the Russian working class ceased to exercise power in any real sense is of course one of the great debates in the history of the revolution, but the criteria used by Lenin are perfectly clear and enable us to make that judgment. John Marot has summarized the likely outcome if Lenin had not changed position on the nature of the Russian Revolution and persuaded the Bolsheviks to do likewise:

> Had Old Bolshevism remained intact in every salient respect, as Lih holds, it would have remained indistinguishable from Menshevism. The revolution would have halted at its bourgeois democratic stage—and then been thrown back. A reunited, Menshevik-led RSDLP would have called on workers to yield Soviet Power to the Assembly. Had Soviet Power self-dissolved, little could have stopped the Right-SRs and their allies from following up on this victory by continuing the war, re-establishing the authority of the Tsarist officer corps, reversing peasant land seizures and dismantling the factory committees. In brief, they would have rewound the film of history back to February 1917 and beyond—all the while writing up the most democratic constitution in the world for the most democratic republic in the world. . . . Had the Bolsheviks not adopted a radically new conception of the Russian Revolution, they could not have fought for it. Had the Bolsheviks rejected the April Theses and maintained continuity with Old Bolshevism, the October Revolution would never have taken place.[30]

4

During the phase of the Russian Revolution that we know as the July Days, at the opposite end of Europe the British Tank Corps were investigating the condition of the Flemish countryside over which the opening attack of the Battle of Passchendaele was to be made. They discovered that any bombardment—such as would inevitably precede the infantry advance—would destroy the system of underground drainage, leading to flooding that would in turn make tank mobility impossible. Tank Corps staff even prepared a series of maps, which were duly forwarded to General Headquarters, showing where water was likely to gather. According to Lloyd George, "the only reply vouchsafed to this effort to save the Army from disaster was a peremptory order that they were to 'send no more of these ridiculous maps.' Maps must conform to plans and not plans to maps. Facts that interfered with plans were impertinence."[31]

Marxists have long used analogies drawn from warfare to illuminate the forms taken by the class struggle: Gramsci's distinction between "war of position" and "war of maneuver" was itself based on alternative strategies pursued during the First World War.[32] In this case, a coincidence of dates suggests a deeper connection. The various general headquarters of the contemporary revolutionary socialist left have for several decades now been working on plans drawn up in 1917 and ignoring maps that suggest these might have to be changed. The example of Lenin is often invoked in these plans, but the difference between our world and the one in which Lenin developed his politics is far greater than the difference between his world and that of Lincoln. This is one reason why faithfulness to Lenin is best demonstrated by adherence to his method rather than reiteration of his positions. And in a sense this has always been true. As early as 1924, the year of Lenin's death, in what is still the best introduction to his thought, Georg Lukács warned: "Those who think that they can find in his decisions 'formulas' and 'precepts' for correct and practical action applicable everywhere misunderstand him. . . . Lenin never laid down 'general rules' which could be 'applied' in a number of different cases. His 'truths' grow from a concrete analysis of the concrete situation based on a dialectical approach to history."[33]

One of the Marxists who did concern themselves with drawing more accurate maps, the late and badly missed Daniel Bensaïd, noted how "fidelity can itself become a banally conservative routine, preventing one from being astonished by the present."[34] His own interpretation of Lenin started from the necessity for astonishment: not to succumb to paralysis in the face of the new, but to recognize it and deploy the necessary means to respond:

> Hence two practical conclusions of great importance: first, that the revolutionary class must, in order to carry out its task, be able to take possession of all forms and all aspects of social activity without the slightest exception; secondly, the revolutionary class must be ready to replace one form by another rapidly and without warning. From this Lenin deduces the need to respond to unexpected events where often the hidden truth of social relations is suddenly revealed. . . . Stir up all spheres! Be on the watch for the most unpredictable solutions! Remain ready for the sudden change of forms! Know how to employ all weapons! These are the maxims of a politics conceived as the art of unexpected events and of the effective possibilities of a determinate conjuncture.[35]

On this point we can also find some level of commonality between Lincoln and Lenin. As we have seen, the former wrote of how "our republican robe is soiled, and trailed in the dust" and of the need to "repurify it." The latter, in the struggle against "routinism," "inertia," and "stagnation," took the metaphor a stage further, suggesting that some garments are beyond purification:

> We are out to rebuild the world. We are out to put an end to the imperialist world war into which hundreds of millions of people have been drawn and in which the interests of billions and billions of capital are involved, a war which cannot end in a truly democratic peace without the greatest proletarian revolution in the history of mankind.
>
> Yet we are afraid of our own selves. We are loth to cast off the "dear old" soiled shirt. . . .
>
> But it is time to cast off the soiled shirt and to put on clean linen.[36]

Lincoln was right: we cannot escape history, nor should we seek to do so. History has brought us here, and however inconvenient it may be for our plans, it is nevertheless from here that we must begin, and not from 1917, or 1968, or 1999. For Lenin too was right: the course of history cannot be turned back or checked—we can and must go fearlessly onward.

Notes

Preface

1. Neil Davidson, preface to *Holding Fast to an Image of the Past: Explorations in the Marxist Tradition* (Chicago: Haymarket Books, 2014), ix.
2. Johanna Brenner and Robert Brenner, "Reagan, the Right and the Working Class," *Against the Current*, first series 2:2 (Winter 1981); Robert Brenner, "The Paradox of Social Democracy: The American Case," in *The Year Left 1985*, edited by Mike Davis, Fred Pfeil, and Mike Sprinkler (London: Verso, 1985); Ellen Meiksins Wood, *The Retreat from Class: A New "True Socialism"* (London: Verso, 1986).
3. Neil Davidson, *Discovering the Scottish Revolution, 1692–1746* (London: Pluto Press, 2003), 40 and 312, note 8.
4. Some leading figures, like Brenner himself or Charles Post, are revolutionaries, but as I have written elsewhere: "One of the difficulties with Political Marxism . . . is its political *indeterminacy*. Not all proponents are revolutionaries: Wood inhabits a centrist position close to that of Ralph Miliband and his successors on the editorial board of *The Socialist Register*, although she too has made important theoretical contributions, above all in relation to the nature of democracy under capitalism. Other Political Marxists, however, inhabit an almost exclusively scholastic universe in which ferocious declarations of adherence to what they take to be the Marxist method are completely detached from any socialist practice." See Neil Davidson, "Is There Anything to Defend in Political Marxism?" *International Socialist Review* 91 (Winter 2013/14), 48–49.
5. Compare Benno Teschke, *The Myth of 1648: Class, Geopolitics and the Making of Modern International Relations* (London: Verso, 2003), 262–63, and Neil Davidson, *How Revolutionary Were the Bourgeois Revolutions?* (Chicago: Haymarket Books, 2012), 580–86.
6. See, for example, Michael S. Kimmel, *Revolution: A Sociological Interpretation* (Philadelphia: Temple University Press, 1990) 4–7, although in most other respects this is a serious study.
7. See Neil Davidson, "Enlightenment and Anti-capitalism," *International Socialism* 2:110 (Spring 2006); my original version will be printed in *Nation-States: Consciousness and Competition*.
8. See Ursula Huws [2006], "Begging and Bragging: The Self and the Commodification of Intellectual Activity," in *Labor in the Digital Economy* (New York: Monthly Review Press, 2015), 80–83.
9. Examples include [1981] "The Summer of 1981: A Post Riots Analysis"; [1984] "Women's Liberation and Revolutionary Socialism"; and [1994] "The Prophet and the Proletariat," all reprinted in Chris Harman, *Selected Writings* (London: Bookmarks Publications, 2010).
10. See Chris Harman, "Theorizing Neoliberalism," *International Socialism* 2:117 (Winter 2008), especially pages 92–99, and my comments in Neil Davidson, "The Neoliberal Era in Britain: Historical Developments and Current Perspectives," *International Socialism* 2:139 (Summer 2013), 173–78. Harman was of course scarcely alone in taking this position: for a more recent version of the argument that neoliberalism is essentially an ideology, see Kean Birch, *We Have*

Never Been Neoliberal: A Manifesto for Doomed Youth (Winchester, UK: Zero Books, 2015).

11. Tom Nairn [1980], "Internationalism: A Critique," in *Faces of Nationalism: Janus Revisited* (London: Verso, 1997), 36.

12. Robert Brenner [1999], *The Economics of Global Turbulence: The Advanced Capitalist Economies from Long Boom to Long Downturn, 1945–2005* (London: Verso, 2006), 25.

13. See, for example, Pierre Broué [1971], *The German Revolution, 1917–1923*, edited by Ian Birchall and Brian Pearce (Leiden: E. J. Brill, 2005), chapter 32, "The 'Mass Communist Party.'" The point was made in the second "general principle" of the Communist International's 1921 organizational theses: "There is no absolute form of organization which is correct for all Communist Parties at all times." Amen to that. See [1921], "The Organizational Structure of the Communist Parties, the Methods and Content of their Work: Theses," in *Theses, Resolutions and Manifestos of the Third International*, edited by Alan Adler (London: Ink Links, 1980), 234.

14. Justin Rosenberg, "Isaac Deutscher and the Lost History of International Relations," *New Left Review* 1: 215 (January/February 1996). Rosenberg's position has evolved since this starting point; for a brief critical discussion of his work see Alexander Anievas, *Capital, the State and War: Class Conflict and Geopolitics in the Thirty Years' Crisis, 1014–1945* (Ann Arbor: University of Michigan Press, 2014), 49–56.

15. For a useful corrective to exaggerated claims about forthcoming Chinese global dominance, by way of a review of Martin Jacques's *When China Rules the World*, see Perry Anderson, "Sinomania," *London Review of Books* 32, no. 2 (January 28, 2010).

16. The analogy with the Three Whales of Bolshevism is inexact, since these—the eight-hour day, land reform, and a constituent assembly—were agitational demands rather than theoretical positions. See, for example, Paul Le Blanc [1995], "One for the Encyclopaedias," in *Unfinished Leninism: The Rise and Return of a Revolutionary Doctrine* (Chicago: Haymarket Books, 2014), 30. As far as the IS/SWP tradition is concerned, a fourth "whale" is sometimes invoked in the form of postwar "do-it-yourself reformism" driven by shop stewards' organization in engineering and the auto industry, but as an observation that allowed militants to orient themselves in working-class activity rather than as a theory, and this type of shop-steward activity was in any case largely confined to the UK and its former Dominions.

17. See, for example, Chris Harman, "The Storm Breaks," *International Socialism* 2:46 (Spring 1990), 36–38.

18. Michael Kidron, "Two Insights Don't Make a Theory," *International Socialism* 1:100 (July 1977).

19. Chris Harman, "Better a Valid Insight Than a Wrong Theory," *International Socialism* 1:100 (July 1977), 11.

20. For an initial and very sketchy attempt to identify positive contributory factors behind the long boom, see Davidson, *How Revolutionary Were the Bourgeois Revolutions?*, 447–48.

21. The following three paragraphs draw on ibid., 305–15.

22. "In its mental purity, this mental construct cannot be found empirically anywhere in reality. It is a *utopia*." Max Weber [1904], *On the Methodology of the Social Sciences*, edited by Edward A. Shils and Henry A. Finch (Glencoe: The Free Press, 1949), 90.

23. John Rees, "The Socialist Revolution and the Democratic Revolution," *International Socialism* 2:83 (Summer 1999), 67. I find myself in the odd position of agreeing with Rees's historical analysis while taking the diametrically opposite view of what it means for permanent revolution, since he—implicitly at least—adopts the position which I criticize below. For areas of agreement, compare, for example, ibid., 27–30, with Davidson, *How Revolutionary Were the Bourgeois Revolutions?*, 463, 618–21.

24. For an extended discussion of this point, see Alex Callinicos, "The Limits of Passive Revolution," *Capital and Class* 34, no. 3, special issue, *Approaching Passive Revolutions*, edited by Adam David Morton (October 2010), 4.

25. Joseph Choonara, "The Relevance of Permanent Revolution: A Reply to Neil Davidson," *International Socialism* 2:131 (Summer 2011).

26. Davidson, *How Revolutionary Were the Bourgeois Revolutions?*, 492–93, 621–29.

27. Neil Davidson and Donny Gluckstein, "Nationalism and the Class Struggle in Scotland," *International Socialism* 2:48 (Autumn 1990).

28. I therefore agree with Alasdair MacIntyre when he writes that "there is no way to do the history of ideas adequately without doing genuine history and, more particularly, that the treatment of social and political ideas in abstraction from those contexts from which they derive life is doomed to failure." See "Review of Baruch Knei-Paz, *The Social and Political Thought of Leon Trotsky*," *American Historical Review* 84, no. 1 (February 1979), 114. But there are limits to this, beyond which the distinctions between different types of history break down. Any history of ideas has to contain enough "genuine" history to explain why it became possible for certain theories or positions to be formulated or expressed at a particular historical juncture and not before. How much history this involves in any particular case is always a matter of judgment, but it is unlikely to include reconstructing the entire epoch in which the formulation or expression took place. As I point out in perhaps too-exasperated terms in chapter 12, adherence to the notion of total history does not mean writing "a history of everything" every time one sits down to explore a set of ideas; it means always seeing those ideas as part of a greater whole rather than as autonomous moments.

29. See, in particular, Alex Callinicos, "Trotsky's Theory of 'Permanent Revolution' and Its Relevance to the Third World Today," *International Socialism* 2:16 (Spring 1982); *Making History: Agency, Structure and Change in Social Theory* (Cambridge: Polity Press, 2007), 205–33; "Bourgeois Revolutions and Historical Materialism," *International Socialism* 2:43 (Summer 1989); and *The Revenge of History: Marxism and the East European Revolutions* (Cambridge: Polity Press, 1991), chapter 2, especially 50–66.

30. Alex Callinicos, "Continuing the Discussion," *International Socialism* 2:142 (Spring 2014), 200.

CHAPTER 1: HOW REVOLUTIONARY WERE THE BOURGEOIS REVOLUTIONS?

1. Neil Davidson [2004], "The Prophet, His Biographer, and the Watchtower: Isaac Deutscher's Biography of Leon Trotsky," in *Holding Fast to an Image of the Past: Explorations in the Marxist Tradition* (Chicago: Haymarket Books, 2014).

2. Isaac Deutscher [1965], "Marxism in Our Time," in *Marxism in Our Time*, edited by Tamara Deutscher (London: Jonathan Cape, 1972), 17–20.

3. Arno Mayer, *The Persistence of the Old Regime: Europe to the Great War* (London: Croom Helm, 1981), 3–4, 11; *Why Did the Heavens Not Darken? The "Final Solution" in History* (London: Verso, 1990), 3, 32.

4. Perry Anderson, "The Figures of Descent," *New Left Review* I/161 (January/February 1987), 26, 27, 47–48.

5. Tom Nairn, *The Enchanted Glass: Britain and Its Monarchy* (Second edition, London: Vintage, 1994), 375.

6. Neil Davidson, *Discovering the Scottish Revolution, 1692–1746* (London: Pluto Press, 2003), 5.

7. Christopher Hitchens, *Regime Change* (Harmondsworth: Penguin Books, 2003), 32–33, 48.

8. See, for example, Edward P. Thompson, "The Peculiarities of the English," in *The Socialist Register 1965*, edited by Ralph Miliband and John Saville (London: Merlin Press, 1965), 321.

9. Davidson, *Discovering the Scottish Revolution*, 10.

10. See, for example, Gary Teeple, *Globalization and the Decline of Social Reform* (Second edition, Toronto: Prometheus Books, 2000), chapter 7, "Globalization as the Second Bourgeois Revolution."

11. Nigel Harris, *The Return of Cosmopolitan Capital: Globalization, the State and War* (London: I. B. Tauris, 2003), 89, 264.

12. Immanuel Wallerstein, "The Rise and Future Demise of the World Capitalist System: Concepts for Competitive Analysis," *Comparative Studies in Society and History* 16 (1974), 398.

13. For example, on the differences between English and French agriculture, see Max Weber [1919–20], *General Economic History* (London: Collier-Macmillan, 1961), 69–70, 72, 76–77, 85–86; on the specificity of economic rationality under feudalism, see Witfold Kula [1962], *An Economic Theory of the Feudal System: Towards a Model of the Polish Economy, 1500–1800* (London: New Left Books, 1976), 165–75; on the uniqueness of English economic development, see Harold Perkin, "The Social Causes of the Industrial Revolution," *Transactions of the Royal Historical Society*, fifth series 18 (1968), 135–36; on the initial development of capitalism by English landlords see R. S. Neale, "'The Bourgeoisie, Historically, Has Played a Most Revolutionary Part,'" in *Feudalism, Capitalism and Beyond*, edited by Eugene Kamenka and R. S. Neale (London: Edward Arnold, 1975), 92–102; on both the integration of the towns into the feudal economy and, more generally, on the misidentification of markets for capitalism, see John Merrington, "Town and Country in the Transition to Capitalism," in *The Transition from Feudalism to Capitalism*, edited by Rodney H. Hilton (London: New Left Books, 1976), 173–87.

14. Robert Brenner, "Bourgeois Revolution and Transition to Capitalism," in *The First Modern Society: Essays in English History in Honor of Lawrence Stone*, edited by A. L. Beier, David Cannadine, and J. M. Rosenheim (Cambridge: Cambridge University Press, 1989), 281.

15. Robert Brenner, "Property Relations and the Growth of Agricultural Productivity in Late Medieval and Early Modern Europe," in *Economic Development and Agricultural Productivity*, edited by Amit Bhaduri and Rune Skarstein (Cheltenham: Edward Elgar, 1997), 23.

16. Ibid., 25.

17. Robert Brenner, "The Social Basis of Economic Development," in *Analytical Marxism*, edited by John Roemer (Cambridge: Cambridge University Press, 1986), 53.

18. Brenner, "Bourgeois Revolution and Transition to Capitalism," 300–301.

19. Robert Brenner [1976], "Agrarian Class Structure and Economic Development in Pre-industrial Europe," in *The Brenner Debate: Agrarian Class Structure and Economic Development in Pre-industrial Europe*, edited by T. H. Aston and C. H. E. Philpin (Cambridge: Cambridge University Press, 1985), 38–40; Robert Brenner, "Dobb on the Transition from Feudalism to Capitalism," *Cambridge Journal of Economics* 2 (June 1978), 130.

20. Brenner, "Agrarian Class Structure and Economic Development in Pre-industrial Europe," 40–41.

21. Ibid., 36.

22. Robert Brenner [1982], "The Agrarian Roots of European Capitalism," in *The Brenner Debate*, 293.

23. Brenner, "Agrarian Class Structure and Economic Development in Pre-industrial Europe," 55.

24. James Holstun, *Ehud's Dagger: Class Struggle in the English Revolution* (London: Verso, 2000), 119.

25. See, for example, Karl Marx [1857–58], *Grundrisse: Foundations of the Critique of Political*

Economy (Rough Draft) (Harmondsworth: Penguin Books/New Left Review, 1973), 510–11, and Karl Marx [1867], *Capital: A Critique of Political Economy*, vol. 1 (Harmondsworth: Penguin Books/New Left Review, 1976), 876, 915–16, note 1. When confronted with those sections of Marx's writings that contradict their views, Political Marxists either, like Wood, pretend that they mean something else or, like Comninel, issue disapproving admonitions about Marx's failure to understand his own theory. See, for example, Ellen Meiksins Wood, "Horizontal Relations: A Note on Brenner's Heresy," *Historical Materialism* 4 (Summer 1999), 175, and George C. Comninel, *Rethinking the French Revolution: Marxism and the Revisionist Challenge* (London: Verso, 1987), 92. Rather than speculate on what Marx really meant, would it not be simpler to accept that Marx meant exactly what he said, and that, consequently, they and their co-thinkers have a theory of capitalism that is different from his?

26. See, for example, Marx, *Grundrisse*, 278, and Marx, *Capital*, vol. 1, 875.

27. Stephen H. Rigby, *Marxism and History: A Critical Introduction* (Second edition, Manchester: Manchester University Press, 1998), xii.

28. Guy Bois [1978], "Against the Neo-Malthusian Orthodoxy," in *The Brenner Debate*, 115.

29. Marx, *Grundrisse*, 508, where he also refers to the tenants of the landed proprietors as "already semi-capitalists," albeit "still very hemmed in ones."

30. Karl Marx [1850], "Review of Guizot's Book on the English Revolution," in *Political Writings*, vol. 2, *Surveys from Exile*, edited by David Fernbach (Harmondsworth: Penguin Books/New Left Review, 1973), 252–55.

31. John Maynard Keynes [1931], "A Pure Theory of Money: A Reply to Dr Hayek," in *Collected Works*, vol. 13, part 1, *The General Theory and After: Preparation*, edited by Donald E. Moggridge (London: Macmillan, 1972), 243.

32. Marx, *Capital*, vol. 1, 874, 975. See also Marx, *Grundrisse*, 505.

33. Wood, "Horizontal Relations," 176, 177. See also Benno Teschke, *The Myth of 1648: Class, Geopolitics and the Making of Modern International Relations* (London: Verso, 2003), 140–41.

34. Davidson, *Discovering the Scottish Revolution*, 25–26.

35. Wood, "Horizontal Relations," 171.

36. Nikolai I. Bukharin [1920], "The Economics of the Transition Period," in *The Politics and Economics of the Transition Period*, edited with an introduction by Kenneth J. Tarbuck (London: Routledge and Kegan Paul, 1979), 78.

37. Friedrich von Hayek, *The Fatal Conceit: The Errors of Socialism*, in *Collected Works*, vol. 1, edited by W. W. Bartley (London: Routledge 1988), 7.

38. In Freudian terms, capitalism is the triumph of the market superego over the collectivist id.

39. Ricardo Duchesne, "Remarx: On *The Origins of Capitalism*," *Rethinking Marxism* 14, no. 3 (Fall 2002), 135.

40. Adam Ferguson [1767], *An Essay on the History of Civil Society*, edited by Duncan Forbes (Edinburgh: Edinburgh University Press, 1966), 8.

41. [Robert Wedderburn] [1549], *The Complaynt of Scotland wyth ane Exortatione to the Three Estaits to Be Vigilante in the Deffens of their Public Veil, with an appendix of contemporary English tracts*, re-edited from the originals by J. A. H. Murray (London: Scottish Text Society, 1822), 123.

42. Jane Whittle, *The Development of Agrarian Capitalism: Land and Labor in Norfolk, 1450–1550* (Oxford: Clarendon Press, 2000), 310.

43. Fernand Braudel, *Capitalism and Civilization, 15th–18th Centuries*, vol. 3, *The Perspective of the World* (London: Fontana, 1985), 63.

44. Brenner, "Bourgeois Revolution and Transition to Capitalism," 280.

45. Brenner, "Dobb on the Transition from Feudalism to Capitalism," 139, note.

46. Teschke, *The Myth of 1648*, 12.

47. Comninel, *Rethinking the French Revolution*, 151.

48. James Harrington [1659], "The Prerogative of Popular Government," in *The Political Works of James Harrington*, edited by J. G. A. Pocock (Cambridge: Cambridge University Press, 1977), 405–06; Edward Hyde, Earl of Clarendon [1646–74], *Selections from* The History of the Rebellion *and* The Life by Himself, edited by Gertrude Huehns (Oxford: Oxford University Press, 1978), 229–30.

49. Both quoted in Brian Manning, *Revolution and Counter-revolution in England, Ireland and Scotland, 1658–1660* (London: Bookmarks, 2003), 10, 60.

50. James Dalrymple, *An Essay Towards a General History of Feudal Property in Great Britain* (London: A. Millar, 1757), 338–39.

51. Neil Davidson, "The Scottish Path to Capitalist Agriculture 2: The Capitalist Offensive (1747–1815)," *Journal of Agrarian Change* 4, no. 4 (October 2004); "The Scottish Path to Capitalist Agriculture 3: The Enlightenment as the Theory and Practice of Improvement," *Journal of Agrarian Change* 5, no. 1 (January 2005).

52. Adam Smith [1762–63, 1766], *Lectures on Jurisprudence*, edited by Ronald L. Meek, David D. Raphael, and Peter G. Stein (Oxford: Oxford University Press, 1978), 264.

53. See chapter 5 in this volume.

54. Quoted in William Sewell, *A Rhetoric of Bourgeois Revolution: The Abbe Sieyès and* What Is the Third Estate? (Durham: Duke University Press, 1994), 72.

55. Monsieur B-de, *Reflections on the Causes and Probable Consequences of the Late Revolution in France, with a View of the Ecclesiastical and Civil Constitution of Scotland, and of the Progress of Its Agriculture and Commerce* (Dublin: W. Wilson et al., 1790), 44, 100, 103–04, 116.

56. Antoine-Pierre-Joseph-Marie Barnave [1792–93], "Introduction to the French Revolution," in *Power, Property, and History: Barnave's Introduction to the French Revolution and Other Writings*, edited by Emanuel Chill (New York: Harper Torchbooks, 1971), 122.

57. Marx, *Capital*, vol. 1, 174.

58. François P. G. Guizot [1826], preface to *History of Charles the First and the English Revolution from the Accession of Charles the First to His Execution* (London: David Bogue, 1846), xvi, xviii, xix. My emphasis.

59. Brenner, "Bourgeois Revolution and Transition to Capitalism," 280–85; Comninel, *Rethinking the French Revolution*, chapter 3; Ellen Meiksins Wood, *The Pristine Culture of Capitalism: An Essay on Old Regimes and Modern States* (London: Verso, 1991), 2–8; Teschke, *The Myth of 1648*, 165–67.

60. Karl Marx and Friedrich Engels [1845–46], *The German Ideology: Critique of Modern German Philosophy according to Its Representatives Feuerbach, B. Bauer and Stirner, and of German Socialism according to Its Various Prophets*, in *Collected Works*, vol. 5 (London: Lawrence and Wishart, 1976), 32.

61. Karl Marx [1847], *The Poverty of Philosophy: Answer to the* Philosophy of Poverty *by M. Proudhon*, in *Collected Works*, vol. 6 (London: Lawrence and Wishart, 1976), 166; Karl Marx [1847–49], "Wage Labor and Capital," in *Collected Works*, vol. 9 (London: Lawrence and Wishart, 1977), 211; Karl Marx and Friedrich Engels [1848], "Manifesto of the Communist Party," in *Political Writings*, vol. 1, *The Revolutions of 1848*, edited by David Fernbach (Harmondsworth: Penguin Books/New Left Review, 1973), 72; Marx, *Grundrisse*, 277; Karl Marx [1859], "Preface to *A Contribution to the Critique of Political Economy*," in *Early Writings* (Harmondsworth: Penguin Books/New Left Review,), 425; Marx, *Capital*, vol. 1, 175, note 35; Friedrich Engels [1886], *Ludwig Feuerbach and the End of Classical German Philosophy*,

in *Collected Works*, vol. 26 (London: Lawrence and Wishart, 1990), 390; Karl Marx [1894], *Capital: A Critique of Political Economy*, vol. 3 (Harmondsworth: Penguin Books/New Left Review, 1981), 927–28, 1024.

62. Marx, *Capital*, vol. 1, 183.

63. Marx to Weydemeyer, March 5, 1852, in *Collected Works*, vol. 39 (London: Lawrence and Wishart, 1983), 60.

64. Georg Lukács [1923], "Towards a Methodology of the Problem of Organization," in *History and Class Consciousness: Studies in Marxist Dialectics* (London: Merlin Press, 1971), 308.

65. Pierre-Louis Roederer [1815], "The Spirit of the Revolution of 1789," in *The Spirit of the Revolution of 1789 and Other Writings of the Revolutionary Epoch*, edited by Murray G. Forsyth (Aldershot: Scolar, 1989), 4–7.

66. Marx and Engels, "Manifesto of the Communist Party," 80, 98. Indeed, some writers seem to believe that the "Manifesto" does not refer to the bourgeois revolution at all. See Perry Anderson [1976], "The Notion of a Bourgeois Revolution," in *English Questions* (London: Verso, 1992), 107.

67. Marx and Engels, "Manifesto of the Communist Party," 69, 70, 72.

68. Marx [1848], "The Bourgeoisie and the Counter-revolution," in *The Revolutions of 1848*, 193.

69. Michael Löwy, "'The Poetry of the Past': Marx and the French Revolution," *New Left Review*I/177 (September/October 1989), 115.

70. Karl Marx [1847], "Moralizing Criticism and Critical Morality: A Contribution to German Cultural History *Contra* Karl Heinzen," in *Collected Works*, vol. 6, 319; Marx, "The Bourgeoisie and the Counter-revolution," 192.

71. Friedrich Engels [1892], "Introduction to the English Edition (1892) of *Socialism: Utopian and Scientific*," in *Collected Works*, vol. 27 (London: Lawrence and Wishart, 1990), 291–92.

72. Marx, *Capital*, vol. 1, 875.

73. Friedrich Engels [1865], "The Prussian Military Question and the German Workers' Party [Extract]," in *Political Writings*, vol. 3, *The First International and After*, edited by David Fernbach (Harmondsworth: Penguin Books/New Left Review, 1974), 122.

74. Friedrich Engels [1849–50], "The Campaign for the German Imperial Constitution," in *Collected Works*, vol. 10 (London: Lawrence and Wishart, 1978), 155.

75. Friedrich Engels [1887], "The Role of Force in History," in *Collected Works*, vol. 26, 464–66.

76. Friedrich Engels [1895], "Introduction to Karl Marx's 'The Class Struggles in France: 1848 to 1850,'" in *Collected Works*, vol. 27, 513.

77. Friedrich Engels [1885], "England in 1845 and in 1885," in *Collected Works*, vol. 26, 297.

78. Vladimir I. Lenin [1905], "Two Tactics of Social-Democracy in the Democratic Revolution," in *Collected Works*, vol. 9, *June–November 1905* (Moscow: Foreign Languages Publishing House, 1962), 42.

79. Vladimir I. Lenin [1911], "The 'Peasant Reform' and the Proletarian-Peasant Revolution," in *Collected Works*, vol. 17, *December 1910–April 1912* (Moscow: Foreign Languages Publishing House, 1963), 120–22, 125, 128.

80. Vladimir I. Lenin [1899], *The Development of Capitalism in Russia: The Process of the Formation of Home Market for Large Scale Industry*, in *Collected Works*, vol. 3, *1899* (Moscow: Foreign Languages Publishing House, 1960), 239.

81. Vladimir I. Lenin [1907], "The Agrarian Question and the Forces of the Revolution," in *Collected Works*, vol. 12, *January–June 1907* (Moscow: Foreign Languages Publishing House, 1962), 334–35. See also Lenin, "Two Tactics of Social-Democracy in the Democratic Revolution," 49–51.

82. Leon D. Trotsky [1906], "Results and Prospects," in *The Permanent Revolution & Results and Prospects* (New York: Pathfinder Press, 1969), 67, 77.

83. Leon D. Trotsky [1923], "Can a Counter-revolution or a Revolution Be Made on Schedule?," in *The First Five Years of the Communist International*, vol. 2 (London: New Park, 1974), 348.

84. Georg Lukács [1923], "Critical Observations on Rosa Luxemburg's 'Critique of the Russian Revolution,'" in *History and Class Consciousness*, 282.

85. Georg Lukács [1924], *Lenin: A Study in the Unity of His Thought* (London: New Left Books, 1970), 20.

86. Lukács, "Towards a Methodology of the Problem of Organization," 307.

87. Antonio Gramsci [1929–34], "Notes on Italian History," in *Selections from the Prison Notebooks of Antonio Gramsci*, edited by Quintin Hoare and Geoffrey Nowell-Smith (London: Lawrence and Wishart, 1971), 82–83, Q10§24; 105, Q15§59.

88. Quoted in Julia Mikhailova, "Soviet Japanese Studies on the Problem of the Meiji Ishin and Development of Capitalism in Japan," in *War, Revolution and Japan*, edited by Ian Neary (Folkestone: Curzon Press, 1993), 33–34.

89. Reproduced in Eric J. Hobsbawm, *Echoes of the Marseillaise: Two Centuries Look Back on the French Revolution* (London: Verso, 1990), 133.

90. Trotsky, "Results and Prospects," 54.

91. Leon D. Trotsky [1925], "Where is Britain Going?," in *Collected Writings and Speeches on Britain*, edited by R. Chappell and A. Clinton, vol. 2 (London: New Park, 1974), 86.

92. Marx and Engels, "Manifesto of the Communist Party," 67.

93. Geoffrey de Ste Croix, *The Class Struggle in the Ancient Greek World: From the Archaic Age to the Arab Conquests* (London: Duckworth, 1981), 66.

94. Marx and Engels, "Manifesto of the Communist Party," 68.

95. The bourgeoisie were included in an earlier version of this list. See Marx and Engels, *The German Ideology*, 432.

96. Marx, "Preface to *A Contribution to the Critique of Political Economy*," 426.

97. Eric J. Hobsbawm, introduction to Karl Marx, *Pre-capitalist Economic Formations* (New York: International Publishers, 1965), 38.

98. Peter Linebaugh and Marcus Rediker, *The Many-Headed Hydra: The Hidden History of the Revolutionary Atlantic* (London: Verso, 2000), 352.

99. John R. Green, *A Short History of the English People* (Revised edition, London: Macmillan and Company, 1888), xviii.

100. Marx and Engels, "Manifesto of the Communist Party," 86.

101. Geoff Eley, *Forging Democracy: The History of the Left in Europe, 1850–2000* (Oxford: Oxford University Press, 2002), 109.

102. Vladimir I. Lenin [1920], "Fourth Session," in *Second Congress of the Communist International: Minutes of the Proceedings*, vol. 1 (London: New Park, 1977), 110–11.

103. Leon D. Trotsky [1933], "Japan Heads for Disaster," in *Writings of Leon Trotsky [1932–33]*, edited by George Breitman and Sarah Lovell (New York: Pathfinder Press, 1972), 291. Compare two writers from the Stalinist tradition: Eric J. Hobsbawm, *The Age of Capital: 1848–1875* (London: Weidenfeld and Nicolson, 1975), 151, and Albert Soboul, *A Short History of the French Revolution, 1789–1799* (Berkeley: University of California Press, 1977), 167–68.

104. Alex Callinicos, "Trotsky's Theory of 'Permanent Revolution' and Its Relevance to the Third World Today," *International Socialism* 2:16 (Spring 1982), 110.

105. See Davidson, "The Prophet, His Biographer, and the Watchtower."

106. Isaac Deutscher, *Stalin: A Political Biography* (Oxford: Oxford University Press, 1949), 554–55.

107. Isaac Deutscher, *The Unfinished Revolution, 1917–1967* (Oxford: Oxford University Press, 1967), 27–28; "The Unfinished Revolution, 1917–1967," *New Left Review* I/43 (May/June 1967), 21–22.

108. Tony Cliff [1949], "The Class Nature of the People's Democracies," in *Neither Washington Nor Moscow: Essays on Revolutionary Socialism* (London: Bookmarks, 1984), 66.

109. Max Shachtman [1949], "Isaac Deutscher's Stalin," in *The Bureaucratic Revolution: The Rise of the Stalinist State* (New York: The Donald Press, 1962), 230–31.

110. Thompson, "The Peculiarities of the English," 325.

111. Christopher Hill, "The Theory of Revolutions," in *Isaac Deutscher: The Man and His Work*, edited by David Horowitz (London: Macdonald and Company, 1971), 124–25, 127–28.

112. Christopher Hill, *Change and Continuity in Seventeenth-Century England* (London: Weidenfeld and Nicolson, 1974), 279–80.

113. Christopher Hill, "A Bourgeois Revolution?," in *Three English Revolutions: 1640, 1688, 1776*, edited by J. G. A. Pocock (Princeton: Princeton University Press, 1980), 110, 131.

114. Ellen Meiksins Wood [1999], *The Origin of Capitalism: A Longer View* (London: Verso, 2002), 118.

115. Imre Lakatos, "Falsification and the Methodology of Scientific Research Programs," in *Criticism and the Growth of Knowledge*, edited by Imre Lakatos and Alan Musgrave (Cambridge: Cambridge University Press, 1970), 117–18.

116. Indeed, the problem with even the most important recent discussions of the theory—and an indication of how far the insights of the classical Marxist tradition have been lost in this respect—is their failure to recognize the extent to which they are revisiting positions that had been established and lost in an earlier period. This is indicated by the absence of any systematic discussion of these antecedents in the post-Hill works most responsible for establishing the validity of a consequentialist position. See, for example, David Blackbourn and Geoff Eley, *The Peculiarities of German History: Bourgeois Society and Politics in Nineteenth-Century Germany* (Oxford: Oxford University Press, 1984); Alex Callinicos, "Bourgeois Revolutions and Historical Materialism," *International Socialism* 2:43 (Summer 1989); and Anderson, "The Notion of a Bourgeois Revolution."

117. Karl Marx [1850], "The Class Struggles in France: 1848 to 1850," in *Surveys from Exile*, 131.

118. Marx, "Preface to *A Contribution to the Critique of Political Economy*," 426.

119. Daniel Bensaïd, *Marx for Our Times: Adventures and Misadventures of a Critique* (London: Verso, 2002), 282.

120. Marx was anxious to make his work available to workers in the German states, where he still considered his main audience to be, particularly since his rival Ferdinand Lassalle appeared to be gaining support there. In order to guarantee that *A Contribution to the Critique of Political Economy* would reach them, however, he had to ensure that it would not be banned from publication by the censors, hence the absence of reference to the class struggle in the somewhat mechanistic formulations of the preface. See Arthur M. Prinz, "Background and Alternative Motive of Marx's 'Preface' of 1859," *Journal of the History of Ideas* 30, no. 3 (July/September 1969).

121. Cornelius Castoriadis [1964–65], "Marxism and Revolutionary Theory," in *The Imaginary Institution of Society* (Cambridge: Polity, 1987), 18–19.

122. Perry Anderson [1983], "Geoffrey de Ste Croix and the Ancient World," in *A Zone of Engagement* (London: Verso, 1992), 17. See also Perry Anderson, *Arguments within English Marxism* (London: Verso, 1980), 55–56.

123. Alex Callinicos, *Making History: Agency, Structure, and Change in Social Theory* (Cambridge:

Polity, 1987), 93–94.

124. Callinicos, "Bourgeois Revolutions and Historical Materialism," 124–27; Gareth Stedman Jones, "Society and Politics at the Beginning of the World Economy," *Cambridge Journal of Economics* 1 (1977), 86.

125. Claudio Katz, *From Feudalism to Capitalism: Marxian Theories of Class Struggle and Social Change* (New York: Greenwood Press, 1989), 181.

126. Pierre Bonnassie [1984], "The Survival and Extinction of the Slave System in the Early Medieval West (Fourth to Eleventh Centuries)," in *From Slavery to Feudalism in Southwest Europe* (Cambridge and Paris: Cambridge University Press and Éditions de la Maison des sciences de l'homme, 1991), 38–46.

127. Leon D. Trotsky [1923], "The Lessons of October," in *The Challenge of the Left Opposition (1923–25)*, edited with an introduction by Naomi Allen (New York: Pathfinder Press, 1975), 252.

128. Lukács, "Critical Observations on Rosa Luxemburg's 'Critique of the Russian Revolution,'" 283.

129. Vladimir I. Lenin [1918], "'Left Wing' Childishness and the Petty Bourgeois Mentality," in *Collected Works*, vol. 27, *February–July 1918* (Moscow: Foreign Languages Publishing House, 1965), 335–36. It was of course Trotsky who first changed the definition of a workers' state from one in which the working class held power to one in which property was nationalized. For an account that is rightly critical but sensitive to the pressures that pushed him in this direction, see Tony Cliff [1948], "The Nature of Stalinist Russia," in *Selected Writings*, vol. 3, *Marxist Theory after Trotsky* (London: Bookmarks, 2003), 3–4.

130. Michael Mann, *The Sources of Social Power*, vol. 2, *The Rise of Classes and Nation-States, 1760–1914* (Cambridge: Cambridge University Press, 1993), 229. Mann claims to have discovered this concept in the work of Lucien Goldmann, but his discussion of leadership is more specific to the Jansenist movement in seventeenth-century France than to the bourgeoisie as a whole. See *The Hidden God: A Study of Tragic Vision in the Pensées of Pascal and the Tragedies of Racine* (London: Routledge and Kegan Paul, 1964), 117.

131. Hal Draper, *Karl Marx's Theory of Revolution*, vol. 2, *The Politics of Social Classes* (New York: Monthly Review Press, 1978), 169.

132. Anderson, "The Notion of a Bourgeois Revolution," 112.

133. Jones, "Society and Politics at the Beginning of the World Economy," 87.

134. Callinicos, *Making History*, 229.

135. Wood, *The Origin of Capitalism*, 118.

136. See chapter 2 in this volume.

137. Alexander Chistozvonov, "The Concept and Criteria of Reversibility and Irreversibility of a Historical Process," *Our History* 63 (Summer 1975), 9–10.

138. Linebaugh and Rediker, *The Many-Headed Hydra*, 24–26. See also Holstun, *Ehud's Dagger*, 432–33.

139. Davidson, *Discovering the Scottish Revolution*, 290–94.

140. Lukács, "The Change in Function of Historical Materialism," in *History and Class Consciousness*, 225.

141. William Morris, "A Dream of John Ball," in *A Dream of John Ball and A King's Lesson* (London: Reeves and Turner, 1888), 31.

Chapter 2: Asiatic, Tributary, or Absolutist?

1. Chris Harman, "From Feudalism to Capitalism," *International Socialism* 2:45 (Winter 1989), 44–46.

2.   Curiously, for a writer whose own political roots lie in the Trotskyist tradition, Brenner's position is close to Althusserianism in this respect, although he is considerably more comprehensible and actually discusses specific historical examples. Compare Robert Brenner, "The Social Basis of Economic Development," in *Analytical Marxism*, edited by John Roemer (Cambridge: Cambridge University Press, 1986), 53, with Etienne Balibar [1965], "The Basic Concepts of Historical Materialism," in Louis Althusser and Etienne Balibar, *Reading Capital* (London: New Left Books, 1970), 292.

3.   Brenner is actually less dogmatic on this point than some of his followers, particularly Ellen Meiksins Wood, and has conceded that the capitalist mode of production was established in both Catalonia and the United Provinces at approximately the same time as in England, although without acknowledging how this damages his overall case. See Robert Brenner, "Agrarian Class Structure and Economic Development in Pre-industrial Europe," in *The Brenner Debate: Agrarian Class Structure and Economic Development in Pre-industrial Europe*, edited by T. H. Aston and C. H. E. Philpin (Cambridge: Cambridge University Press, 1985), 49, note 81, and "The Low Countries and the Transition to Capitalism," *Journal of Agrarian Change* 1, no. 2 (April 2001). For Wood's more-royalist-than-the-king response, see "The Question of Market Dependence," *Journal of Agrarian Change* 2, no. 1 (January 2002).

4.   Chris Harman, "The Rise of Capitalism," *International Socialism* 2:102 (Spring 2004), 74–77. See also the footnotes to pages 85–86, particularly note 57. Responding to a footnote—even a long one, as in this case—may seem somewhat excessive, but we have Chris's own authority for their significance. See Chris Harman, "Footnotes and Fallacies: A Comment on Brenner's 'The Economics of Global Turbulence,'" *Historical Materialism* 4 (Summer 1999), 95.

5.   Chris Wickham, "The Uniqueness of the East," *Journal of Peasant Studies* 12, nos. 2–3 (January/April 1985), 167.

6.   Karl Marx [1859], "Preface to *A Contribution to the Critique of Political Economy*," in *Early Writings* (Harmondsworth: Penguin Books/New Left Review, 1975), 426.

7.   Chris Harman, *A People's History of the World* (London: Bookmarks, 1999), 27.

8.   Harman, "The Rise of Capitalism," 74.

9.   For the early debates, see Marian Sawer, "The Soviet Discussion of the Asiatic Mode of Production," *Survey* 24, no. 3 (Summer 1979), and for the later ones, see Ernest Gellner, "Soviets against Wittfogel: Or, the Anthropological Preconditions of Mature Marxism," in *States in History*, edited by John A. Hall (Oxford: Basil Blackwell, 1986).

10. Engels writes: "Slavery was the first form of exploitation, peculiar to the world of antiquity; it was followed by serfdom in the Middle Ages, and by wage labour in modern times." Friedrich Engels, *The Origins of the Family, Private Property and the State: In the Light of the Recent Researches of Lewis H. Morgan*, in *Collected Works*, vol. 26 (London: Lawrence and Wishart, 1990), 274. Engels was at this point under the influence of Morgan, whose *Ancient Society* posits a direct transition from primitive communism to class society without any intervening "Asiatic" stage. See Maurice Godelier, "The Concept of the 'Asiatic Mode of Production' and Marxist Models of Social Evolution," *Relations of Production: Marxist Approaches to Economic Anthropology*, edited by David D. Seddon (London: Frank Cass, 1978), 231–35. Lenin followed Engels in referring to "these great periods in the history of mankind, slave-owning, feudal and capitalist." In a lecture to students at Sverdlov University in 1919, Lenin states four times in the space of one page of the printed version that mankind has passed or is passing through slavery to feudalism to capitalism. He also emphasizes that each period includes "such a mass of political forms, such a variety of political doctrines, opinions and revolutions"

that it was vital for students to retain the fundamental centrality of class divisions to history and of the role of the state in representing the dominant classes throughout. Vladimir I. Lenin, "The State," in *Collected Works*, vol. 29, *March–August 1919* (Moscow: Foreign Languages Publishing House, 1965), 477. For his reliance on Engels, see ibid., 473.

11. Karl A. Wittfogel, *Oriental Despotism: A Comparative Study of Total Power* (New Haven: Yale University Press, 1957), 387, 389. Hal Draper decisively disposes of this line of argument in *Karl Marx's Theory of Revolution*, vol. 1, *State and Bureaucracy* (New York: Monthly Review Press, 1978), 629–38, 657–60.

12. Geoffrey de Ste Croix, *The Class Struggle in the Ancient Greek World: From the Archaic Age to the Arab Conquests* (London: Duckworth, 1981), 52.

13. Harman, "The Rise of Capitalism," 74.

14. Perry Anderson, *Lineages of the Absolutist State* (London: New Left Books, 1974), 485–86.

15. Karl Marx, *Grundrisse: Foundations of the Critique of Political Economy (Rough Draft)* (Harmondsworth: Penguin Books/New Left Review, 1973), 479, 495.

16. Godelier, "The Concept of the 'Asiatic Mode of Production' and Marxist Models of Social Evolution," 241.

17. Barry Hindess and Paul Q. Hirst, *Pre-capitalist Modes of Production* (London: Routledge and Kegan Paul, 1975), 335–36.

18. Draper, *State and Bureaucracy*, 537. See also his similar comments on page 535.

19. Eric J. Hobsbawm, introduction to Karl Marx, *Pre-capitalist Modes of Production* (New York: International Books, 1965), 32, 35.

20. Ernest Mandel, *The Formation of the Economic Thought of Karl Marx* (New York: Monthly Review Press, 1971), 124–25.

21. Anderson criticizes Godelier on precisely this point. See Anderson, *Lineages of the Absolutist State*, 486, note 3.

22. Marx, *Grundrisse*, 443.

23. See Samir Amin, *Class and Nation Historically and in the Current Crisis* (New York: Monthly Review Press, 1980), 68.

24. Samir Amin, *Unequal Development* (London: Hassocks ,1976), 15–16. For an overview of Amin's life and opinions, see David Renton, "Samir Amin: Theorizing Underdevelopment," in *Dissident Marxism* (London: Zed Books, 2004), chapter 9.

25. Wickham, "The Uniqueness of the East," 170–71.

26. Ibid., 182, 187.

27. Eric R. Wolf, *Europe and the People without History* (Berkeley: University of California Press, 1982), 243 and 247 (the quote is from the latter page). Engels made essentially the same point in 1890. See Engels to Danielson, June 10, 1890, in *Collected Works*, vol. 48 (London: Lawrence and Wishart, 2001), 507.

28. Alex Callinicos, *Theories and Narratives: Reflections on the Philosophy of History* (Cambridge: Polity Press, 1995), 171–76. The other major analysis of a tributary society from within the International Socialist tradition is Colin Barker's 1982 study of Japan, "The Background and Significance of the Meiji Restoration of 1868," available at www.marxists.de.

29. Karl Marx [1894], *Capital: A Critique of Political Economy*, vol. 3 (Harmondsworth: Penguin Books/New Left Review, 1981), 925–27. My emphasis.

30. Harman, "The Rise of Capitalism," 85, note 57.

31. Brenner, "Agrarian Class Structure and Economic Development in Pre-industrial Europe," 55.

32. Benno Teschke, *The Myth of 1648: Class, Geopolitics and the Making of Modern International Relations* (London: Verso, 2003), 191.

33. Ellen Meiksins Wood, *The Pristine Culture of Capitalism* (London: Verso, 1991), 159.

34. Ellen Meiksins Wood, *The Origin of Capitalism: A Longer View* (London: Verso, 2002), 184.

35. Harman, "The Rise of Capitalism," 86.

36. John Haldon, *The State and the Tributary Mode of Production* (London: Verso, 1993), 67, 84, and 75–87 more generally.

37. Amin, *Class and Nation Historically and in the Current Crisis*, 88.

38. Anderson, *Lineages of the Absolutist State*, 428–30.

Chapter 3: Centuries of Transition

1. Chris Wickham, *Framing the Early Middle Ages: Europe and the Mediterranean, 400–800* (Oxford: Oxford University Press, 2005), 9.

2. Ibid., 6, note 6.

3. Ibid., 728–41, 759–80.

4. For some preliminary comparisons and contrasts between three great revolutionary transitions, see chapter 1 in this volume, although the purpose of the discussion there is to identify the specificity of the bourgeois revolution rather than that of its predecessor.

5. Michael Mann, *The Sources of Social Power*, vol. 1, *A History of Power from the Beginning to A.D. 1760* (Cambridge: Cambridge University Press, 1986), 295–98, 371–76. In a review article, Wickham criticized Mann's assumption that capitalism was already implicit in developments within medieval Europe, but does not broach his failure to discuss the emergence of feudalism in the first place. See "Historical Materialism, Historical Sociology," *New Left Review* I/171 (September/October 1988), 73–75.

6. Compare Chris Harman, *A People's History of the World* (London: Bookmarks, 1999), 85–86, 104–05 (on the transition to feudalism) and 161–374 (on the transition to capitalism).

7. Friedrich Engels [1884], *The Origins of the Family, Private Property and the State: In the Light of the Recent Researches of Lewis H. Morgan*, in *Collected Works*, vol. 26 (London: Lawrence and Wishart, 1990), 245–56.

8. Max Weber [1896], "The Social Causes of the Decline of Ancient Civilization," in *The Agrarian Sociology of Ancient Civilizations* (London: New Left Books, 1976), 397–408.

9. Marc Bloch [1947], "How Ancient Slavery Came to an End," in *Slavery and Serfdom in the Middle Ages* (Berkeley: University of California Press, 1975), 1–31.

10. Richard Southern, *The Making of the Middle Ages* (London: Hutchison, 1953), 15.

11. Perry Anderson, *Passages from Antiquity to Feudalism* (London: New Left Books, 1974), 128.

12. Perry Anderson, *Lineages of the Absolutist State* (London: New Left Books, 1974), 154–55.

13. Karl Marx, *Grundrisse: Foundations of the Critique of Political Economy (Rough Draft)* (Harmondsworth: Penguin Books/New Left Review, 1973), 97–98.

14. John Haldon, "The Feudalism Debate Once More: The Case of Byzantium," *Journal of Peasant Studies* 17, no. 1 (October 1989), 7; *The State and the Tributary Mode of Production* (London: Verso, 1993), 73–74. Anderson expresses disagreement with Shtaerman in several contexts, but does refer to her work in relation to the transition itself. See Anderson, *Passages from Antiquity to Feudalism*, 61, note 9; 83, note 43; and 85, note 48.

15. Moses Finley [1973], *The Ancient Economy* (Second edition, Harmondsworth: Penguin Books, 1985), 180.

16. Geoffrey de Ste Croix, *The Class Struggle in the Ancient Greek World: From the Archaic Age to the Arab Conquests* (London: Duckworth, 1981), 136, 138, 267–69.

17. Anderson, *Lineages of the Absolutist State*, 420–29

18. Ibid., 403–10. His definition of feudalism can be found on 407.
19. Guy Bois [1989], *Transformations of the Year One Thousand: The Village of Lournard from Antiquity to Feudalism* (Manchester: Manchester University Press, 1991), 135.
20. Ibid., 152.
21. Georges Duby [1978], *The Three Orders: Feudal Society Imagined* (Chicago: Chicago University Press, 1980), 147–66, and Pierre Bonnassie [1978], "From the Rhône to Galicia: Origins and Modalities of the Feudal Order," in *From Slavery to Feudalism in South-Western Europe* (Cambridge: Cambridge University Press, 1991), 104–31. Although the term is not used, the same concept and chronology can also be found in Jean-Pierre Poly and Eric Bournazel [1984], *The Feudal Transformation: 900–1200* (New York: Holmes and Meier, 1991), 2–3, 118–40, 351–57, and Pierre Dockes [1979], *Medieval Slavery and Liberation* (London: Methuen, 1982), 105–10.
22. Georges Duby [1987], *France: The Middle Ages, 987–1460: From Hugh Capet to Joan of Arc* (Oxford: Oxford University Press, 1991).
23. Adriaan Verhulst, "The Decline of Slavery and the Economic Expansion of the Early Middle Ages," *Past and Present* 133 (November 1991), 200–202.
24. Bois himself admits that he might be "reproached for an excessive legalism," but claims that "the social condition of the slave changed without slavery disappearing, just as workers' conditions have changed since the nineteenth century without it therefore being possible to assume the definitive disappearance of this class." See *Transformations of the Year One Thousand*, 17, 18.
25. Robert Moore is clearly unhappy about the Marxist connotations of the term "revolution" but nevertheless argues that a "new social order" came about, dominated by "the *clerici* who became the power elite of the new Europe" and who "constituted a class in all but name." See *The First European Revolution, c. 970–1215* (Oxford: Blackwell, 2000), 6.
26. Chris Wickham [1984], "The Other Transition: From the Ancient World to Feudalism," in *Land and Power: Studies in Italian and European Social History, 400–1200* (London: The British School at Rome, 1994), 29.
27. Ibid., 26.
28. Ibid., 20.
29. Ibid., 23.
30. Ibid., 28.
31. Ibid., 33.
32. Ibid., 36–40; Chris Wickham [1985], "The Uniqueness of the East," in *Land and Power*, 43–50, 73–74.
33. Halil Berktay, "The Feudalism Debate: The Turkish End—Is 'Tax-versus-Rent' Necessarily the Product and Sign of a Modal Difference?," *Journal of Peasant Studies* 14, no. 3 (April 1987), 301–10; Haldon, "The Feudalism Debate Once More," 9–15; Haldon, *The State and the Tributary Mode of Production*, 63–69, 87–109.
34. Wickham, "The Uniqueness of the East," 75.
35. Eric J. Hobsbawm, introduction to Karl Marx, *Pre-capitalist Modes of Production* (New York: International Books, 1965), 28. See also 32.
36. Marx, *Grundrisse*, 443. See also Samir Amin, *Unequal Development* (London: Hassocks, 1976), 15–16.
37. Chris Wickham, "Debate: The 'Feudal Revolution,'" *Past and Present* 155 (May 1997), 207–08.
38. Ste Croix, *The Class Struggle in the Ancient Greek World*, 19–98
39. Chris Wickham, introduction to *Land and Power*, 1.

40. Wickham, *Framing the Early Middle Ages*, 822. And see, more recently, Chris Wickham, "Memories of Underdevelopment: What Has Marxism Done for Medieval History, and What Can It Still Do?," in *Marxist History Writing for the Twenty-First Century*, edited by Chris Wickham (Oxford: published for the British Academy by Oxford University Press, 2007), 20.

41. In Robert Brenner's recent summary: "Feudalism had emerged, as they saw it, as a result of exogenous shocks, when a series of invasions—by the so-called barbarians, then the Muslims, and finally the Vikings—disrupted the great trans-Mediterranean trade routes that had long nourished the European economy going back to Roman and Greek times." See "Property and Progress: Where Adam Smith Went Wrong," in *Marxist History Writing for the Twenty-First Century*, 49.

42. Wickham, *Framing the Early Middle Ages*, 302. See also 819, where Northern Francia, Syria, and Palestine are taken as examples of a "complex regional economy based on aristocratic wealth."

43. Ibid., 339.

44. Fernand Braudel [1949/1966], *The Mediterranean and the Mediterranean World in the Age of Phillip II* (2 volumes, London: Fontana, 1975), vol. 1, 20–21.

45. Ibid., vol. 1, 355–642; vol. 2, 657–900.

46. Wickham wrote that he would take a broader approach in what was then his forthcoming contribution to the *Penguin History of Europe* (Wickham, *Framing the Early Middle Ages*, 7), and he has done so. See, for example, *The Inheritance of Rome: A History of Europe from 400 to 1000* (London: Allen Lane, 2009), 50–75, 232–51, 405–26.

47. Wickham, *Framing the Early Middle Ages*, 12.

48. Ibid., 145.

49. Ibid., 260–61, 262, 264. In Egypt, wage labor was mainly employed for harvest work. For more on the absence of slaves in Italy after around 300 AD, see 276–77.

50. Ibid., 435–36.

51. Ibid., 543.

52. Contrary to what is suggested in Chris Harman, "Shedding New Light on the Dark Ages," *International Socialism* 2:109 (Winter 2005/06), 189–90.

53. Chris Wickham, "Productive Forces and the Economic Logic of the Feudal Mode of Production," *Historical Materialism* 16, no. 2 (2008), 6.

54. Wickham, *Framing the Early Middle Ages*, 145.

55. Ibid., 60, 61.

56. Ibid., 304.

57. Ibid., 538–41.

58. See, for example, Maurice Godelier, "The Concept of the 'Asiatic Mode of Production' and Marxist Models of Social Evolution," *Relations of Production: Marxist Approaches to Economic Anthropology*, edited by David D. Seddon (London: Frank Cass, 1978), 241. In my view this is the only way in which the notion of the Asiatic mode can be sensibly applied. See chapter 2 in this volume. Nevertheless, Wickham's notion of a peasant mode is preferable, not only because it is free from the other connotations surrounding the "Asiatic," but also—and more importantly—because it foregrounds the class involved in the production process.

59. Wickham, *Framing the Early Middle Ages*, 56–57 (and note 2 to those pages). See also 303–04.

60. Hal Draper, *Karl Marx's Theory of Revolution*, vol. 1, *State and Bureaucracy* (New York: Monthly Review, 1978), 239–45.

61. Wickham, *Framing the Early Middle Ages*, 304.

62. See Neil Davidson, "Many Capitals, Many States: Contingency, Logic, or Mediation?," in *Marxism and World Politics: Challenging Global Capitalism*, edited by Alexander Anievas (Abingdon: Routledge, 2010), 82–83.

63. Wickham, *Framing the Early Middle Ages*, 563.
64. Wickham, "Productive Forces and the Economic Logic of the Feudal Mode of Production," 6–7, 11.
65. Wickham, "Memories of Underdevelopment," 42–43.
66. See chapter 1 in this volume.
67. Robert Brenner, "The Social Basis of Economic Development," in *Analytical Marxism*, edited by John Roemer (Cambridge: Cambridge University Press, 1986), 53; "Property Relations and the Growth of Agricultural Productivity in Late Medieval and Early Modern Europe," in *Economic Development and Agricultural Productivity*, edited by Amit Bhaduri and Rune Skarstein (Cheltenham: Edward Elgar, 1997), 23; "Property and Progress," 88–89.
68. Wickham, *Framing the Early Middle Ages*, 539.
69. Ibid., 386.
70. Ibid., 572–73.
71. Ibid., 141.
72. Ibid., 140–43, 532.
73. Ibid., 408.
74. Ibid., 529–33.
75. Ibid., 441.
76. Ibid., 350–51.
77. Ibid., 578–88.
78. Brent Shaw, "After Rome: Transformations of the Early Mediterranean World," *New Left Review* II/51 (May/June 2008), 106. The charge gains some traction when Wickham, who at one point included war as one of the four elements of the economic dynamic, subsequently reduces them to three: "fiscal demand, private demand, [and] prior dependence on the Roman world-system." See Wickham, *Framing the Early Middle Ages*, 821; compare ibid., 719.
79. Wickham, "Historical Materialism, Historical Sociology," 77. For Marxist analysis of war and military competition more generally, see Alex Callinicos, *Theories and Narratives: Reflections on the Philosophy of History* (Cambridge: Polity Press, 1995), 116–25.
80. Wickham, *Framing the Early Middle Ages*, 87, 711.
81. Ibid., 827.

Chapter 4: Scotland: Birthplace of Passive Revolution?

1. For a discussion of the different meanings ascribed to the term by Gramsci, see Adam David Morton, "Reflections on Uneven Development: Mexican Revolution, Primitive Accumulation, Passive Revolution," *Latin American Perspectives* 37, no. 1 (January 2010), 7–10, and Alex Callinicos, "The Limits of Passive Revolution," *Capital and Class* 34, no. 3, special issue, *Approaching Passive Revolutions*, edited by Adam David Morton (October 2010), 492–500.
2. See chapter 1 in this volume.
3. Gramsci to Tania, June 6, 1932, in *Letters from Prison*, vol. 2, edited by Frank Rosengarten (New York: Columbia University Press 1994), 181–82.
4. Antonio Gramsci [1929–34], "Notes on Italian History," in *Selections from the Prison Notebooks*, edited by Quintin Hoare and Geoffrey Nowell-Smith (London: Lawrence and Wishart, 1971), 115, Q10II§61.
5. Ibid., 61, Q19§24.
6. Antonio Gramsci [1927–34], "The Modern Prince," in *Selections from the Prison Notebooks*, 182, Q13§17.

7.   There is only one, indirect, reference to Scotland in Gramsci's writings, in a passage commending the "tendency represented by John Maclean" in a survey of the European revolutionary left for an issue of *L'Ordine nuovo*, although it describes Maclean as being based "in England." See "Vita politica internazionale," *L'Ordine nuovo* (May 15, 1919). In this he was probably following Lenin's wartime identification of the key individuals and organizations that could be the basis of a new International. See, for example, Vladimir I. Lenin [1916], "An Open Letter to Boris Souvarine," in *Collected Works*, vol. 23, *August 1916–March 1917* (Moscow: Foreign Languages Publishing House, 1964), 201. A more tenuous connection can be traced from a reference in the prison notebooks to the Italian liberal educationalist Ferrante Aporti. As the editors of the 1971 *Selections* point out, Aporti was influenced by Robert Owen's Scottish infant-school experiments after the Napoleonic Wars; it is, however, unclear the extent to which Gramsci was aware of this influence. See Hoare and Nowell-Smith, note to Gramsci, "Notes on Italian History," 103, note 94.

8.   Antonio Gramsci [1922], "Origins of the Mussolini Cabinet," in *Selections from the Political Writings, 1921–1926*, edited by Quintin Hoare (London: Lawrence and Wishart, 1978), 129. The importance of this passage was first highlighted in Adam David Morton, "Disputing the Geopolitics of Global Capitalism," *Cambridge Review of International Affairs* 20, no. 4 (December 2007), 599.

9.   Supporting evidence for the argument that follows can be found in Neil Davidson, "Scotland's Bourgeois Revolution," in *Scotland: Class and Nation*, edited by Chris Bambery (London: Bookmarks, 1999); *The Origins of Scottish Nationhood* (London: Pluto Press, 2000); *Discovering the Scottish Revolution, 1692–1746* (London: Pluto Press, 2003); "The Scottish Path to Capitalist Agriculture 1: From the Crisis of Feudalism to the Origins of Agrarian Transformation (1688–1746)," *Journal of Agrarian Change* 4, no. 3 (July 2004); "The Scottish Path to Capitalist Agriculture 2: The Capitalist Offensive (1747–1815)," *Journal of Agrarian Change* 4, no. 4 (October 2004); "Popular Insurgency during the Glorious Revolution in Scotland," *Scottish Labour History* 39 (2004); and "The Scottish Path to Capitalist Agriculture 3: The Enlightenment as the Theory and Practice of Improvement," *Journal of Agrarian Change* 5, no. 1 (January 2005).

10. Gramsci, "Notes on Italian History," 105, Q15§59.

11. Ibid., 58–59, Q19§24.

12. *Public General Statutes Affecting Scotland from the Beginning of the First Parliament of Great Britain, 6 Anne AD 1707, to the End of the Fourteenth Parliament of the United Kingdom, 10 and 11 Victoria, AD 1847* (3 volumes, Edinburgh: William Blackwood, 1876), vol. 1, 5.

13. Ibid., 107.

CHAPTER 5: THE FRENCH REVOLUTION IS NOT OVER

1.   Georg Lukács [1923], "Towards a Methodology of the Problem of Organization," in *History and Class Consciousness: Essays in Marxist Dialectics* (London: Merlin Press, 1971), 308.

2.   See, for example, Isaac Deutscher [1959], *The Prophet Unarmed: Trotsky, 1921–1929* (London: Verso, 2003), 260–65, and Eric J. Hobsbawm, *Echoes of the Marseillaise: Two Centuries Look Back at the French Revolution* (London: Verso, 1990), 48–66.

3.   Albert Cobban [1955], "The Myth of the French Revolution," in *Aspects of the French Revolution* (London: Paladin, 1971), 95–106. Cobban developed these arguments in *The Social Interpretation of the French Revolution* (Cambridge: Cambridge University Press, 1964).

4.   Jacob L. Talmon [1952], *The Origins of Totalitarian Democracy* (London: Mercury Books, 1961), 80.

5. Hobsbawm, *Echoes of the Marseillaise*, 109; Alasdair MacIntyre, "The End of Ideology and the End of the End of Ideology," in *Against the Self-Images of the Age: Essays on Ideology and Philosophy* (London: Duckworth, 1971), 4.

6. The phrase sounds rather more elegant in the original French: "*le derapage de la revolution.*" See François Furet and Denis Richet [1965], *La Révolution française* (Revised edition, Paris: Gallimard, 1970), 126.

7. François Furet [1978], "The French Revolution Is Over," in *Interpreting the French Revolution* (Cambridge: Cambridge University Press, 1981), 5–6, 12.

8. David Bell, "Class, Consciousness, and the Fall of the Bourgeoisie," *Critical Review* 16, nos. 2–3 (2004), 333.

9. Donald M. G. Sutherland, *France, 1789–1815: Revolution and Counter-revolution* (London: Fontana, 1985), 140, 442.

10. Benno Teschke, "Bourgeois Revolution, State Formation and the Absence of the International," *Historical Materialism* 13, no. 2 (2005), 5.

11. See chapter 1 in this volume.

12. George C. Comninel, *Rethinking the French Revolution: Marxism and the Revisionist Challenge* (London: Verso, 1990), 182, 193, 200, 202.

13. Henry Heller, *The Bourgeois Revolution in France, 1789–1815* (Oxford: Berghahn Books, 2006), viii.

14. Henry Heller, *The Conquest of Poverty: The Calvinist Revolt in Sixteenth-Century France* (Leiden: E. J. Brill, 1986); *Iron and Blood: Civil Wars in Sixteenth-Century France* (Montreal: McGill-Queen's University Press, 1991); *Labour, Science and Technology in France, 1500–1620* (Cambridge: Cambridge University Press, 1996).

15. Heller, *The Bourgeois Revolution in France*, 1.

16. Ibid., 149.

17. Ibid., 26–28.

18. Paul McGarr, "The Great French Revolution," *International Socialism* 2:43 (Summer 1989); Albert Soboul [1965], *A Short History of the French Revolution, 1789–1799* (Berkeley: University of California Press, 1977). .

19. Heller, *The Bourgeois Revolution in France*, 22.

20. To be fair to Guérin, his conclusions about the prospects of working-class power in the French Revolution were ultimately more realistic than those of his followers: "The objective conditions of the time did not allow the [sans-culotte] vanguard to beat the bourgeoisie at their own game." Daniel Guérin [1946], *La lutte de classes sous la Première République* (Revised edition, 2 volumes, Paris: Gallimard, 1968), vol. 1, 405.

21. Heller, *The Bourgeois Revolution in France*, 23.

22. Ibid., 89, 93.

23. Ibid., 23.

24. Georges Lefevre [1951], *The French Revolution*, vol. 1, *From its Origins to 1793* (London: Routledge and Kegan Paul, 1962); [1957], *The French Revolution*, vol. 2, *From 1793 to 1799* (London: Routledge and Kegan Paul, 1964); Albert Soboul [1962], *The French Revolution, 1787–1799: From the Storming of the Bastille to Napoleon* (London: Unwin Hyman, 1989).

25. Heller, *The Bourgeois Revolution in France*, 23.

26. Ibid., 74.

27. Ibid., 150.

28. Ibid., 7.

29. Ibid., 31. See, for example, Immanuel Wallerstein, *The Modern World System*, vol. 2,

Mercantilism and the Consolidation of the European World-Economy, 1600–1750 (New York: Academic Press, 1980), 87–90.

30. Heller, *The Bourgeois Revolution in France*, 34.
31. Ibid., 36.
32. Ibid., 5–6, 36, 45–48.
33. Ibid., 51.
34. Ibid., 37–38.
35. Ibid., 67.
36. See, in general, Perry Anderson, *Lineages of the Absolutist State* (London: New Left Books, 1974), 19–20, and, specifically in relation to France, Robert Brenner [1976], "The Agrarian Roots of European Capitalism," in *The Brenner Debate: Agrarian Class Structure and Economic Development in Pre-industrial Europe*, edited by Trevor H. Aston and C. H. E. Philpin (Cambridge: Cambridge University Press, 1985), 286–91.
37. See, in general, Michael Mann, *The Sources of Social Power*, vol. 1, *A History of Power from the Beginning to A.D. 1760* (Cambridge: Cambridge University Press, 1986), 475–83, and, specifically in relation to France, Theda Skocpol, *States and Social Revolutions: A Comparative Analysis of France, Russia, and China* (Cambridge: Cambridge University Press, 1979), 52–54.
38. Heller, *The Bourgeois Revolution in France*, 66.
39. Ibid., 67.
40. Ibid., 67–69, 70, 147.
41. Ibid., 54–60.
42. Teschke, "Bourgeois Revolution, State Formation and the Absence of the International," 12. See also Ellen Meiksins Wood, *The Origin of Capitalism: A Longer View* (London: Verso, 2002), 63.
43. See chapter 1 in this volume.
44. Heller, *The Bourgeois Revolution in France*, 72. For Gramsci's original discussion of "organic intellectuals," see Antonio Gramsci, "The Intellectuals," in *Selections from the Prison Notebooks*, edited and translated by Quintin Hoare and Geoffrey Nowell-Smith (London: Lawrence and Wishart, 1971), 14–21, Q8§22, Q12§1.
45. Heller, *The Bourgeois Revolution in France*, 86.
46. Ibid., 88, 89.
47. Ibid., 91.
48. Ibid., 96, 103, 119, 129.
49. Ibid., 76–78.
50. Ibid., 110.
51. Ibid., 94, 99–103.
52. Ibid., 113.
53. Ibid., 137.
54. See, for example, my discussion of the transition to capitalism in rural Scotland, "The Scottish Path to Capitalist Agriculture 2: The Capitalist Offensive (1747–1815)," *Journal of Agrarian Change* 4, no. 4 (October 2004), 415–16, 423–31.
55. Benno Teschke, *The Myth of 1648: Class, Geopolitics, and the Making of Modern International Relations* (London: Verso, 2003), 263.
56. Heller, *The Bourgeois Revolution in France*, 126.
57. Robin Blackburn, *The Making of New World Slavery: From the Baroque to the Modern, 1492–1800* (London: Verso, 1997), 300–301.
58. C. L. R. James [1938], *The Black Jacobins: Toussaint L'Overture and the San Domingo Revolution* (New edition, London: Alison and Busby, 1980), 85–86.

59. Heller, *The Bourgeois Revolution in France*, 139.
60. Simon Schama [1977], *Patriots and Liberators: Revolution in the Netherlands, 1780–1813* (Second edition, London: Fontana, 1992), 12–15.
61. Jerome Blum, *The End of the Old Order in Rural Europe* (Princeton: Princeton University Press, 1978), 362, 370; Terence J. Byres, *Capitalism from Above and Capitalism from Below* (Houndmills: Macmillan, 1996), 27–28.
62. Heller, *The Bourgeois Revolution in France*, 7.
63. Ibid., 11.
64. Ibid., 149.
65. Ibid., 65.
66. Geoff Eley, "The British Model and the German Road: Rethinking the Course of German History before 1914," in David Blackbourn and Geoff Eley, *The Peculiarities of German History: Bourgeois Society and Politics in Nineteenth-Century Germany* (Oxford: Oxford University Press, 1984), 85, 154. These conclusions are supported by most serious contemporary histories of Nazi Germany. See, for example, Ian Kershaw, *Hitler, 1889–1936: Hubris* (London: Allen Lane, 1998), 73–75, and Richard J. Evans, *The Coming of the Third Reich* (London: Allen Lane, 2003), 2–21.
67. Brian Manning, "The English Revolution: The Decline and Fall of Revisionism," *Socialist History* 14 (1999), 46 and 44–46 more generally.
68. Heller, *The Bourgeois Revolution in France*, ix.

CHAPTER 6: THE AMERICAN CIVIL WAR CONSIDERED AS A BOURGEOIS REVOLUTION

1. The major exceptions are: Herman Schluter [1913], *Lincoln, Labor and Slavery: A Chapter in the Social History of America* (New York: Russell and Russell, 1965); W. E. B. Du Bois [1935], *Black Reconstruction in America* (New York: Athenaeum, 1969); Bernard Mandel [1955], *Labor, Free and Slave: Workingmen and the Anti-slavery Movement in the United States* (Urbana: University of Illinois, 2007).
2. Eugene Genovese, *Roll, Jordan, Roll: The World the Slaves Made* (New York: Vintage Books, 1972); Eric Foner, *Reconstruction: America's Unfinished Revolution, 1863–1877* (New York: Harper and Row, 1988).
3. See, for example, David Williams, *A People's History of the Civil War: Struggles for the Meaning of Freedom* (New York: The New Press, 2005), 12.
4. Peter Novick, *That Noble Dream: The "Objectivity Question" and the American Historical Profession* (Cambridge: Cambridge University Press, 1988), 95–96, 155.
5. Compare Charles and Mary Beard [1927], *The Rise of American Civilization* (New edition, two volumes in one, revised and enlarged, New York: Macmillan, 1935), vol. 2, *The Industrial Era*, 52–121, and Louis Hacker, *The Triumph of American Capitalism: The Development of Forces in American History to the End of the Nineteenth Century* (New York: Columbia University Press, 1940), 280–400.
6. For a selection, see Peter Camejo, *Racism, Revolution, Reaction, 1861–1877: The Rise and Fall of Radical Reconstruction* (New York: Monad Press, 1976), 13; James McPherson [1982], "The Second American Revolution," in *Abraham Lincoln and the Second American Revolution* (New York: Oxford University Press, 1991), 10–22; Mandel, *Labor, Free and Slave*, 202; and George Novack, introduction to *America's Revolutionary Heritage*, edited by George Novack (New York: Pathfinder Press, 1976), 16.
7. Comer Vann Woodward, *Reunion and Reaction: The Compromise of 1877 and the End of*

Reconstruction (Boston: Little, Brown, 1951), ix, 215.

8. See, for example, Camejo, *Racism, Revolution, Reaction, 1861–1877*, 11, 216–17, 228–32.

9. Barrington Moore [1966], *The Social Origins of Dictatorship and Democracy: Lord and Peasant in the Making of the Modern World* (Harmondsworth: Penguin Books, 1973), 427–28.

10. Ibid., 112.

11. Ibid., 149–52; Kevin Anderson, *Marx at the Margins: On Nationalism, Ethnicity, and Non-Western Societies* (Chicago: Chicago University Press, 2010), 263, note 1; Eugene Genovese [1968], "Marxist Interpretations of the Slave South," in *In Red and Black: Marxian Explorations in Southern and Afro-American History* (New York: Vintage, 1972), 345–48; McPherson, "The Second American Revolution," 9–10.

12. John Ashworth, *Slavery, Capitalism, and Politics in the Antebellum Republic*, vol. 1, *Commerce and Compromise, 1820–1850* (Cambridge: Cambridge University Press, 1995), 498.

13. John Ashworth, *Slavery, Capitalism, and Politics in the Antebellum Republic*, vol. 2, *The Coming of the Civil War, 1850–1861* (Cambridge: Cambridge University Press, 2007), 647.

14. Gerald Runkle, "Karl Marx and the American Civil War," *Comparative Studies in Society and History* 6, no. 2 (January 1964), 138–41.

15. A third letter from the IWMA, "To the People of the United States," emphasizing the need for blacks to be granted full equality, was not written by Marx but by one of the International's trade-unionist leaders, William Cremer. See Anderson, *Marx at the Margins*, 193–94.

16. John Cairnes, *The Slave Power: Its Character, Career, and Probable Designs* (New York: Carleton, 1862); Frederick Law Olmstead, *The Cotton Kingdom: A Traveler's Observations on Cotton and Slavery in the American Slave States* (New York: Mason Brothers, 1862).

17. Perry Anderson [1976], "The Notion of a Bourgeois Revolution," in *English Questions* (London: Verso, 1992), 106; David Fernbach, introduction to Karl Marx, *Political Writings*, vol. 2, *Surveys from Exile*, edited by David Fernbach (Harmondsworth: Penguin Books/New Left Review, 1974), 31–32; Genovese, "Marxist Interpretations of the Slave South," 321–35.

18. Karl Marx [1867], *Capital: A Critique of Political Economy*, vol. 1 (Harmondsworth: Penguin/New Left Review, 1976), 90.

19. Karl Marx and Friedrich Engels [1848], "Manifesto of the Communist Party," in *Political Writings*, vol. 1, *The Revolutions of 1848*, edited by David Fernbach (Harmondsworth: Penguin/New Left Review, 1974), 69, note 15; Friedrich Engels [1885], "Preface to the Third German Edition of *The Eighteenth Brumaire of Louis Bonaparte* by Marx," in *Collected Works*, vol. 26 (London: Lawrence and Wishart, 1990), 302–03.

20. See, for example, in relation to the Meiji Restoration, Eric J. Hobsbawm, *The Age of Capital: 1848–1875* (London: Weidenfeld and Nicolson, 1975), 151, and Albert Soboul [1965], *A Short History of the French Revolution, 1789–1799* (Berkeley: University of California Press, 1977), 167–68.

21. Geoff Eley, "The English Model and the German Road: Rethinking the Course of German History before 1914," in David Blackbourn and Geoff Eley, *The Peculiarities of German History: Bourgeois Society and Politics in Nineteenth-Century Germany* (Oxford: Oxford University Press, 1984), 85.

22. Andrew Abbott [1997], "On the Concept of Turning Point," in *Time Matters: On Theory and Method* (Chicago: Chicago University Press, 2001), 250.

23. Alex Callinicos, "Trotsky's Theory of 'Permanent Revolution' and Its Relevance to the Third World Today," *International Socialism* 2:16 (Spring 1982), 110.

24. See chapter 1 in this volume.

25. Geoffrey de Ste Croix, *The Class Struggle in the Ancient Greek World: From the Archaic Age to the*

Arab Conquests (London: Duckworth, 1981), 52.

26. Jairus Banaji, "Modes of Production in a Materialist Conception of History," *Capital and Class* 3 (Autumn 1977), 4–5, 30–31; Karl Marx [1857–58], *Grundrisse: Foundations of the Critique of Political Economy (Rough Draft)* (Harmondsworth: Penguin/New Left Review, 1973), 463. See also the useful summary of Banaji's position in Abigail Bakan, "Plantation Slavery and the Capitalist Mode of Production: An Analysis of the Development of the Jamaican Labor Force," *Studies in Political Economy* 22 (Spring 1987), 75–77.

27. See chapter 4 in this volume. For a more detailed account, see Neil Davidson, *Discovering the Scottish Revolution, 1692–1746* (London: Pluto Press, 2003), 73–285.

28. James Garfield, *Garfield's Words: Suggestive Passages from the Public and Private Writings of James Abram Garfield*, edited by William Ralston Balch (London: Sampson Low, Marston, Searle, and Rivington, 1881), 161.

29. Mike Davis [1980], "How the US Working Class is Different," in *Prisoners of the American Dream: Politics and Economy in the History of the US Working Class* (London: Verso, 1986), 12.

30. James Redpath, *The Roving Editor, Or, Talks with Slaves in the Southern States* (New York: A.B. Burdic, 1859), 300–301.

31. Georges Clemenceau, *American Reconstruction, 1865–1870, and the Impeachment of President Johnson*, edited by Fernand Baldensperger (New York and Toronto: Dial Press and Longmans, Green, 1928), 226.

32. Perry Anderson [1987], "The Figures of Descent," in *English Questions*, 155–56. See also, specifically in relation to the US, Alex Callinicos, "Bourgeois Revolutions and Historical Materialism," *International Socialism* 2:43 (Summer 1989), 153–54.

33. See, for example, Leo Panitch, *Renewing Socialism: Democracy, Strategy, and Imagination* (Boulder: Westview Press, 2001), 21, 40.

34. See, for example, Gordon S. Wood, *The Radicalism of the American Revolution* (New York: Vintage, 1992), 175–76.

35. See, for example, Gareth Stedman Jones, "The Specificity of US Imperialism," *New Left Review* I/60 (March/April 1970), 63–65.

36. See, for example, "The Trouble with Revolutions," *The Economist* (July 8, 1989), 14.

37. *Independent Chronicle* (September 5, 1776), quoted in Elisha Douglas, *Rebels and Democrats: The Struggle for Equal Political Rights and Majority Rule during the American Revolution* (Chapel Hill: University of North Carolina Press, 1955), 153.

38. John Adams [1765], "A Dissertation on the Canon and Feudal Law," in *The Works of John Adams, Second President of the United States: With a Life of the Author, Notes, and Illustrations, by his Grandson Charles F. Adams*, vol. 3, *Autobiography, Diary, Notes of a Debate in the Senate, Essays*, edited by Charles F. Adams (Boston: Charles C. Little and James Brown, 1851), 454–55, 464.

39. Rowland Berthoff and John M. Murrin, "Feudalism, Communalism, and the Yeoman Freeholder: The American Revolution Considered as a Social Accident," in *Essays on the American Revolution*, edited by Stephen G. Kurtz and James H. Hutson (Chapel Hill and New York: University of North Carolina Press and W. W. Norton, 1973), 261–86; Terence J. Byres, *Capitalism from Above and Capitalism from Below* (Houndmills: Macmillan, 1996), 165–86.

40. Hal Draper, *Karl Marx's Theory of Revolution*, vol. 2, *The Politics of Social Classes* (New York: Monthly Review Press, 1978), 17–21.

41. Beard, *The Industrial Era*, 54.

42. Michael Merrill, "The Anticapitalist Origins of the United States," *Review* 13, no. 4 (Fall 1990), 481–93.

43. Forrest McDonald, *Alexander Hamilton: A Biography* (New York: W. W. Norton, 1979), 3.

44. William Drayton, *The South Vindicated from the Treason and Fanaticism of the Northern Abolitionists* (Philadelphia: H. Manly, 1836), 179–81.

45. *Macon Telegraph* (November 8, 1860), quoted in Michael Johnson, *Toward a Patriarchal Republic: The Secession of Georgia* (Baton Rouge: Louisiana State University Press, 1977), 46.

46. *The Congressional Globe*, new series, 68 (March 6, 1862), 1077.

47. Karl Marx [1844], "Economic and Philosophical Manuscripts," in *Early Writings* (Harmondsworth: Penguin Books/New Left Review, 1975), 340; Karl Marx [1848], "The Bourgeoisie and the Counter-revolution," in *The Revolutions of 1848*, 192–93.

48. Karl Marx [1861], "The Civil War in the United States," in *Surveys from Exile*, 351.

49. Robin Blackburn, *The Overthrow of Colonial Slavery, 1776–1848* (London: Verso, 1988), 9, 383–84; Moses I. Finley, *Ancient Slavery and Modern Ideology* (Harmondsworth: Penguin Books, 1983), 11, 80–81.

50. Marx, *Grundrisse*, 224.

51. Ibid., 513.

52. David Roediger, "Precapitalism in One Confederacy: Genovese, Politics, and the Slave South," in *Towards the Abolition of Whiteness: Essays on Race, Politics, and Working Class History* (London: Verso, 1994), 49.

53. Marx, *Capital*, vol. 1, 878.

54. Peter Kolchin, *American Slavery, 1619–1877* (Harmondsworth: Penguin Books, 1993), 6.

55. Robin Blackburn, *The Making of New World Slavery: From the Baroque to the Modern* (London: Verso, 1997), 374.

56. Banaji, "Modes of Production in a Materialist Conception of History," 15–17.

57. Mark Twain [1883], *Life on the Mississippi* (Teddington: Echo Press, 2006), 46.

58. Andrew Hook, "Scott and America," in *From Goosecreek to Gandercleugh: Studies in Scottish-American Literary and Cultural History* (East Linton: Tuckwell Press, 1999), 103–10, and "The South, Scotland, and William Faulkner," ibid., 193–201.

59. James McPherson, *For Cause and Comrades: Why Men Fought in the Civil War* (New York: Oxford University Press, 1997), 27.

60. Elizabeth Fox-Genovese and Eugene Genovese [1979], "The Slave Economies in Political Perspective," in *Fruits of Merchant Capital: Slavery and Bourgeois Property in the Rise and Expansion of Capitalism* (Oxford: Oxford University Press, 1983), 39–40.

61. Kolchin, *American Slavery*, 190.

62. Vladimir I. Lenin [1911], "The 'Peasant Reform' and the Proletarian-Peasant Revolution," in ·*Collected Works*, vol. 17, *December 1910–April 1912* (Moscow: Foreign Languages Publishing House, 1963), 128.

63. Byres, *Capitalism from Above and Capitalism from Below*, 27–28.

64. Hobsbawm, *The Age of Capital*, 188.

65. Jerome Blum, *The End of the Old Order in Rural Europe* (Princeton: Princeton University Press, 1978), 362, 370; Byres, *Capitalism from Above and Capitalism from Below*, 105–08.

66. Kolchin, *American Slavery*, 99–105.

67. Elizabeth Fox-Genovese and Eugene D. Genovese [1975], "Yeoman Farmers in a Slaveholder's Democracy," in *Fruits of Merchant Capital*, 263.

68. Theodore Allen, *The Invention of the White Race*, vol. 2, *The Origin of Racial Oppression in Anglo-America* (London: Verso, 1997), 249.

69. Shearer Davis Bowman, "Antebellum Planters and Vormärz Junkers in Comparative Perspective," *American Historical Review* 85, no. 3 (October 1980), 783, 785–86, 795, 806–07.

70. Viken Tchakerian, "Productivity, Extent of Markets, and Manufacturing in the Late

Antebellum South and Midwest," *Journal of Economic History* 54, no. 3 (September 1994), 519–20.

71. Kolchin, *American Slavery*, 153.

72. Bakan, "Plantation Slavery and the Capitalist Mode of Production," 86–91; Gavin Wright, "Capitalism and Slavery on the Islands: A Lesson from the Mainland," *Journal of Interdisciplinary History* 17, no. 4 (Spring 1987), 865–73.

73. David Turley, "Slave Emancipations in Modern History," in *Serfdom and Slavery: Studies in Legal Bondage*, edited by Michael Bush (London: Longman, 1996), 187–89.

74. Blackburn, *The Making of New World Slavery*, 492–93.

75. William Howard Russell, *My Diary North and South* (Boston: T. O. H. P. Burnham, 1863), 179.

76. Richard Ransom and Richard Sutch, "Capitalists without Capital: The Burden of Slavery and the Impact of Emancipation," *Agricultural History* 62, no. 3 (Fall 1988), 138–39.

77. Albert Gallatin Brown [1858], "Speech Delivered at Hazlehurst, Mississippi, on the 11th of September, 1858," in *Speeches, Messages, and Other Writings*, edited by Michael W. Cluskey (Philadelphia: Jas. B. Smith, 1859), 594–95.

78. Robert Fogel, *Without Consent or Contract: The Rise and Fall of American Slavery* (New York: W. W. Norton, 1989), 414–15.

79. Wright, "Capitalism and Slavery on the Islands," 863.

80. Vladimir I. Lenin [1917], "The Tasks of the Proletariat in Our Revolution," in *Collected Works*, vol. 24, *April–June 1917* (Moscow: Progress Publishers, 1964), 59.

81. Leon D. Trotsky [1932–33], *The History of the Russian Revolution* (London: Pluto Press, 1977), 223.

82. Andrew Dawson, "Northern Manufacturers and the Coming of the American Civil War," in *New Approaches to Socialist History*, edited by Keith Flett and David Renton (Cheltenham: New Clarion Press, 2003), 115.

83. Engels to Marx, May 12, 1862, in *Collected Works*, vol. 41 (London: Lawrence and Wishart, 1995), 364.

84. Marx to Lion Phillips, May 6, 1861, in *Collected Works*, vol. 41, 277.

85. Probably the most balanced assessment of Lincoln by either man can be found in Karl Marx [1862], "Comments on the North American Events," in *Collected Works*, vol. 19 (London: Lawrence and Wishart, 1984), 249–51.

86. Carl Schurz [1865], "Report on the Condition of the South," in *Speeches, Correspondence, and Political Papers*, vol. 1, *October 20, 1852 to November 26, 1870*, edited by Frederic Bancroft (New York: G. P. Putnam's Sons, 1913), 354.

87. See, for example, Foner, *Reconstruction: America's Unfinished Revolution, 1863–1877* ("unfinished revolution") and Camejo, *Racism, Revolution, Reaction, 1861–1877*, 169–87 ("Republican betrayal").

88. James McPherson [1964], *The Struggle for Equality: Abolitionist and the Negro in the Civil War and Reconstruction* (Princeton: Princeton University Press, 1995), 430–31.

89. Lisa Lowe, *Immigrant Acts: On Asian American Cultural Politics* (Durham: Duke University Press, 1996), 27–28.

90. Beard, *The Industrial Era*, 115.

91. James McPherson, *Battle Cry of Freedom: The Civil War Era* (New York: Oxford University Press, 1988), 861.

92. Davidson, *Discovering the Scottish Revolution*, 272–75.

CHAPTER 7: WHEN HISTORY FAILED TO TURN

1. Broué, *The German Revolution, 1917–1923*, edited by Ian Birchall and Brian Pearce (Leiden: E. J. Brill, 2005), 449.
2. Chris Harman, *The Lost Revolution: Germany, 1918 to 1923* (London: Bookmarks, 1982), 12.
3. *The German Revolution* is fifth in an excellent book series from the journal *Historical Materialism*, consisting of out-of-print classics, books hitherto untranslated into English, and new works of Marxist scholarship. One subsidiary reason for wishing this volume every success is that it might encourage some enterprising publisher finally to translate Broué's biography, *Trotsky* (1988), into English.
4. I discuss the problem of periodization in relation to the bourgeois revolution in *Discovering the Scottish Revolution, 1692–1746* (London: Pluto Press, 2003), 9.
5. A. J. P. Taylor [1945], *The Course of German History: A Survey of the Development of German History Since 1815* (London: Methuen, 1961), 69.
6. Broué, *The German Revolution*, 899.
7. Leon D. Trotsky [1923], "The Lessons of October," in *The Challenge of the Left Opposition (1923–1925)*, edited by Naomi Allen (New York: Pathfinder Press, 1975); Paul Levi [1923], "Introduction to Trotsky's *The Lessons of October*," *Revolutionary History* 5, no. 2 (Spring 1994).
8. There are two main exceptions, both of which are highly recommended. One is by Franz Borkenau, an Austrian Comintern functionary turned Social Democrat, in a study of the Third International originally published in 1939. See Franz Borkenau [1938], *World Communism: A History of the Communist International* (Ann Arbor: University of Michigan, 1962), chapter 14, "Germany in 1923." Despite his reformist politics, Borkenau's exhilarating account of the revolutionary upheavals in Europe at the end of the First World War is more evocative of the excitement, more alive to the possibilities of those days than many more tediously correct versions, although Broué rightly subjects Borkenau's Kautskyite views on the supposed inescapable patriotism of the masses in August 1914 to a brief but searching criticism in *The German Revolution*, 47–49. The other is by E. H. Carr, the senior civil servant turned *Times* leader-writer turned historian, in his *History of Soviet Russia*. See E. H. Carr [1954], *The Interregnum, 1923–1924* (Harmondsworth: Penguin Books, 1969), chapter 9, "The German Fiasco." Carr's book is, for me at any rate, the outstanding volume in his entire *History of the Bolshevik Revolution*.
9. Broué, *The German Revolution*, 450–51.
10. Ibid., 857.
11. Ibid., 577.
12. Ibid., 840.
13. Ibid., 855. For details of the earlier arguments of Levi and Radek, see 302–04 and 309–13.
14. Ibid., 308–09
15. Ibid., 3–5, 289. This was also the view of at least some of the German revolutionaries during the November revolution of 1918. See ibid., 131.
16. Leon D. Trotsky [1930], introduction to the first Russian edition of "Permanent Revolution," in *The Permanent Revolution & Results and Prospects* (New York: Pathfinder Press, 1969), 7. A similar view was actually taken in 1957–58 by internal KPD critics of the Stalinist interpretation of November 1918. See Broué, *The German Revolution*, 844–45. The classic statement of the case for the bourgeois nature of German society before 1914 remains David Blackbourn and Geoff Eley, *The Peculiarities of German History: Bourgeois Society and Politics in Nineteenth-Century Germany* (Oxford: Oxford University Press, 1984).
17. Broué, *The German Revolution*, 280–81.

18. Harman, *The Lost Revolution*, chapter 7, "The Bavarian Soviet Republic."
19. Perry Anderson, "Communist Party History," in *People's History and Socialist Theory*, edited by Raphael Samuel (London: Routledge and Kegan Paul, 1981), 148.
20. Eric D. Weitz, foreword to the English edition of Broué, *The German Revolution*, xv.
21. Broué, *The German Revolution*, 872.
22. Ibid., 355, 356.

CHAPTER 8: FROM UNEVEN TO COMBINED DEVELOPMENT

1. Michael Löwy, *The Politics of Combined and Uneven Development: The Theory of Permanent Revolution* (London: Verso, 1981), 52, 89–90.
2. Perry Anderson, *Lineages of the Absolutist State* (London: New Left Books, 1974), 236; Edward A. Brett, *The World Economy since the War: The Politics of Uneven Development* (London: Macmillan, 1985), 58–59; Isaac Deutscher [1957], "Four Decades of the Revolution," in *Ironies of History* (Berkeley: Ramparts Press, 1971), 55; George Novack [1957], "Uneven and Combined Development in History," in *Understanding History: Marxist Essays* (New York: Pathfinder Press, 1980).
3. Alex Callinicos and Justin Rosenberg, "Uneven and Combined Development: The Social-Relational Substratum of 'the International'? An Exchange of Letters," *Cambridge Review of International Affairs* 21, no. 1 (March 2008), 101; Robert Brenner, "The Agrarian Roots of European Capitalism," in *The Brenner Debate: Agrarian Class Structure and Economic Development in Pre-industrial Europe*, edited by Trevor H. Aston and C. H. E. Philpin (Cambridge: Cambridge University Press, 1985), 255.
4. Giovanni Arrighi, *Adam Smith in Beijing: Lineages of the Twenty-First Century* (London: Verso, 2007), 102.
5. Leon D. Trotsky, "The Draft Program of the Communist International—A Critique of Fundamentals," in *The Third International after Lenin* (London: New Park, 1974), 15, 61; [1932], "Uneven and Combined Development and the Role of American Imperialism: Minutes of a Discussion," in *Writings of Leon Trotsky [1932–33]* (New York: Pathfinder Press, 1972), 116.
6. Robert Brenner, *The Boom and the Bubble: The US in the World Economy* (London: Verso, 2003), 9–24; [1999], *The Economics of Global Turbulence: The Advanced Capitalist Economies from Long Boom to Long Downturn, 1945–2005* (London: Verso, 2006), 32–40; Doreen Massey, *Spatial Divisions of Labour: Social Geography and the Geography of Production* (Houndmills: Macmillan, 1995), 118–19; Neil Smith [1984], *Uneven Development: Nature, Capital and the Production of Space* (Oxford: Blackwell, 1990), 135–54.
7. Gottfried von Leibniz [1712], "On an Academy of Arts and Science," in *Selections*, edited by P. P. Wiener (New York: Scribner, 1951), 596–97.
8. Anne-Robert-Jacques Turgot [1750], "A Philosophical Review of the Successive Advances of the Human Mind," in *Turgot on Progress, Sociology and Economics*, edited by Ronald L. Meek (Cambridge: Cambridge University Press, 1973), 5.
9. For examples, see Neil Davidson, "The Scottish Path to Capitalist Agriculture 3: The Enlightenment as the Theory and Practice of Improvement," *Journal of Agrarian Change* 5, no. 1 (January 2005), 33–36.
10. "A Supplement, Containing an Account of the Present State of Agriculture, and the Improvements Recently Introduced," in Lord Kames, *The Gentleman Farmer: Being an Attempt to Improve Agriculture by Subjecting It to the Test of Rational Principles* (Sixth edition,

Edinburgh: Bell and Bradfute, 1815), 537.

11. Walter Scott [1806/1814], *Waverley; Or, 'Tis Sixty Years Since*, edited by Andrew Hook (Harmondsworth: Penguin Books, 1972), 492.

12. Eric J. Hobsbawm [1965], introduction to Karl Marx, *Pre-capitalist Economic Formations* (New York: International Publications, 1965), 38.

13. Karl Marx and Frederick Engels [1845–46], *The German Ideology: Critique of Modern German Philosophy according to Its Representatives Feuerbach, B. Bauer and Stirner, and of German Socialism according to Its Various Prophets*, in *Collected Works*, vol. 5 (London: Lawrence and Wishart, 1976), 49, 51.

14. Marx to Engels, October 8, 1858, in *Collected Works*, vol. 40 (London: Lawrence and Wishart, 1983), 346–47; see also Friedrich Engels [1895], "Introduction [to Karl Marx's *The Class Struggle in France, 1848 to 1850*]," in *Collected Works*, vol. 27 (London: Lawrence and Wishart, 1990), 513.

15. Karl Marx [1867], *Capital: A Critique of Political Economy*, vol. 1 (Harmondsworth: Penguin Books/New Left Review, 1976), 91.

16. See, for example, Karl Marx [1854], "The Future Consequences of the British Rule in India," in *Political Writings*, vol. 2, *Surveys from Exile*, edited by David Fernbach (Harmondsworth: Penguin Books/New Left Review, 1974), 323.

17. Karl Marx [1877], "[Letter to *Otechesivenniye Zapiski*]," in *Collected Works*, vol. 24 (London: Lawrence and Wishart, 1989), 199, 200. See also Marx to Zasulich, March 8, 1881, in *Collected Works*, vol. 46 (London: Lawrence and Wishart, 1992), 72.

18. Karl Marx and Friedrich Engels [1882], "Preface to the Second Russian Edition of the 'Manifesto of the Communist Party,'" in *Collected Works*, vol. 24, 42.

19. Engels to Danielson, October 17, 1893, in *Collected Works*, vol. 50 (London: Lawrence and Wishart, 2005), 214; Friedrich Engels, "Afterword (1894) [to *On Social Relations in Russia*]," *Collected Works*, vol. 27, 423, 424, 431.

20. Marx and Engels, *The German Ideology*, 83.

21. Karl Marx [1857–58], *Grundrisse: Foundations for the Critique of Political Economy (Rough Draft)* (Harmondsworth: Penguin Books/New Left Review, 1973), 490; Engels to Schmidt, March 12, 1895, in *Collected Works*, vol. 50, 565.

22. Friedrich List [1841], *The National System of Political Economy* (New edition, London: Longmans, Green, 1904), 156.

23. Karl Marx [1845], "Draft of an Article on Frederick List's Book, *Das nationale System der politischen Oekonomie*," in *Collected Works*, vol. 4 (London: Lawrence and Wishart, 1975), 281.

24. Karl Marx [1859], "Preface to *A Contribution to the Critique of Political Economy*," in *Early Writings* (Harmondsworth: Penguin Books/New Left Review, 1975), 425–26.

25. Quoted in Isaiah Berlin, introduction to Franco Venturi, *Roots of a Revolution: A History of the Popular and Socialist Movements in Nineteenth-Century Russia* (London: Weidenfeld and Nicolson, 1960), xx.

26. Georgi Plekhanov [1883], "Socialism and the Political Struggle," in *Selected Philosophical Works*, vol. 1 (Moscow: Progress Publishers, 1961), 79.

27. Georgi Plekhanov [1884], "Our Differences," in *Selected Philosophical Works*, vol. 1, 364–66.

28. Ibid., 357–58.

29. Georgi Plekhanov [1895], "The Development of the Monist View of History," in *Selected Philosophical Works*, vol. 1, 704, 705.

30. See the contributions extracted from the Congress record, "Congress Debate on Colonial Policy [1907]," in *Lenin's Struggle for a Revolutionary International: Documents, 1907–1916*,

edited by John Riddell (New York: Pathfinder Press, 1984), 9–15.

31. Karl Kautsky [1906], "The American Worker," *Historical Materialism* 11, no. 4 (2003), 16.

32. Antonio Labriola [1896], "Historical Materialism," in *Essays on the Materialistic Conception of History* (Chicago: Charles. H. Kerr, 1909), 240; Leon D. Trotsky [1929], *My Life: An Attempt at an Autobiography* (Harmondsworth: Penguin Books, 1975), 123–24, 133.

33. Smith, *Uneven Development*, xiv.

34. Vladimir I. Lenin [1916], "Imperialism, the Highest Stage of Capitalism: A Popular Outline," in *Collected Works*, vol. 22 (Moscow: Foreign Languages Publishing House, 1964), 241.

35. Ibid., 263–64.

36. Leon D. Trotsky [1907–09], *1905* (Harmondsworth: Penguin Books, 1973), 68; Rudolf Hilferding [1911], *Finance Capital*, edited by Tim Bottomore (London: Routledge, 1981), 322; Antonio Gramsci [1917], "The Revolution Against 'Capital,'" in *Selections from the Political Writings*, edited by Quintin Hoare and Geoffrey Nowell-Smith (London: Lawrence and Wishart, 1977), 6.

37. Thorstein Veblen [1916], *Imperial Germany and the Industrial Revolution* (New York: Viking Press, 1939), 65–66, 85–86.

38. Leon D. Trotsky [1906], "Results and Prospects," in *The Permanent Revolution & Results and Prospects* (New York: Pathfinder, 1969), 65–66, 105–106.

39. Leon D. Trotsky [1932–33], *The History of the Russian Revolution* (London: Pluto Press, 1977), 27.

40. See, for example, Otto Kuusinen et al., *Fundamentals of Marxism-Leninism* (London: Lawrence and Wishart, 1961), 386.

41. Ernest Mandel, *Trotsky as Alternative* (London: Verso, 1995), 1.

42. Leon D. Trotsky [1940], "A Serious Work on Russian Revolutionary History," in *Writings of Leon Trotsky Supplement (1934–40)*, 858.

43. The only real forerunner here is Rosa Luxemburg in a brilliant early article on the Ottoman Empire; see [1896], "Social Democracy and the National Struggles in Turkey," *Revolutionary History* 8, no. 3, *The Balkan Socialist Tradition and the Balkan Federation, 1871–1915* (2003), 38–40.

44. Leon D. Trotsky [1929], "Permanent Revolution," in *The Permanent Revolution & Results and Prospects*, 241.

45. Peter Curtin, *The World and the West: The European Challenge and the Overseas Response in the Age of Empire* (Cambridge: Cambridge University Press, 2000), 150.

46. Peter Gowan, *The Global Gamble: Washington's Faustian Bid for World Dominance* (London: Verso, 1999), 167.

47. Trotsky, "Permanent Revolution," 148–50, 252–60; "The Draft Program of the Communist International—A Critique of Fundamentals," 14–19.

48. Trotsky, *The History of the Russian Revolution*, 27–28.

49. Trotsky, "Revolution and War in China," in *Leon Trotsky on China* (New York: Monad Press, 1976), 583.

50. Michael Burawoy, *The Politics of Production: Factory Regimes under Capitalism and Socialism* (London: Verso, 1985), 99.

51. Jamie Allinson and Alexander Anievas, "The Uses and Misuses of Uneven and Combined Development: An Anatomy of a Concept," *Cambridge Review of International Affairs* 22, no. 1 (March 2009), 52.

52. Vladimir I. Lenin [1899], *The Development of Capitalism in Russia*, in *Collected Works*, vol. 3 (Moscow: Foreign Languages Publishing House, 1960), 191–210.

53. Trotsky, *The History of the Russian Revolution*, 30. And see, for example, Alfred Rieber,

Merchants and Entrepreneurs in Imperial Russia (Chapel Hill: University of North Carolina Press, 1982), 224.

54. Burawoy, *The Politics of Production*, 99.

55. Trotsky, "The Draft Program of the Communist International—A Critique of Fundamentals," 159–60; [1928], "Summary and Perspectives of the Chinese Revolution," in *Leon Trotsky on China*, 324–25.

56. See chapter 9 in this volume.

57. Georg Lukács [1924], *Lenin: A Study in the Unity of his Thought* (London: New Left Books, 1970), chapter 1.

58. Leon D. Trotsky [1932], "In Defense of the Russian Revolution," in *Leon Trotsky Speaks* (New York: Pathfinder Press, 1972), 251.

59. Trotsky, *The History of the Russian Revolution*, 27.

60. Clive Treblicock, *The Industrialisation of the Continental Powers, 1780–1914* (London: Longman, 1981), 208.

61. Trotsky, *The History of the Russian Revolution*, 55. And see, for example, Peter Gatrell, *Government, Industry and Rearmament in Russia* (Cambridge: Cambridge University Press, 1994), 15.

62. See, for example, Alexander Gerschenkron, *Economic Backwardness in Historical Perspective* (Cambridge, MA: Harvard University Press, 1962), 127–28.

63. Leon D. Trotsky [1924], "For the Internationalist Perspective," in *Leon Trotsky Speaks*, 199. See also Trotsky, *The History of the Russian Revolution*, 33.

64. David Cannadine, "The Context, Performance and Meaning of Ritual: The British Monarchy and the 'Invention of Tradition,' c. 1820–1977," in *The Invention of Tradition*, edited by Eric Hobsbawm and Terence Ranger (Cambridge: Cambridge University Press, 1983), 120–50; Christopher A. Bayly, *The Birth of the Modern World, 1780–1914: Global Connections and Comparisons* (Oxford: Blackwell, 2004), 426–30.

65. Leon D. Trotsky [1924], "Radio, Science, Technology, and Society," in *Problems of Everyday Life: Creating the Foundations for a New Society in Revolutionary Russia* (New York: Pathfinder Press, 1994), 257.

66. Trotsky, "The Draft Program of the Communist International—A Critique of Fundamentals," 115.

67. Trotsky, *The Revolution Betrayed: What Is the Soviet Union and Where Is It Going?* (New York: Monod Press, 1937), 300.

68. Allinson and Anievas also have concerns with claims for the transhistorical nature of uneven and combined development, although for different reasons than those expressed here. See "The Uses and Misuses of Uneven and Combined Development," 62–63.

69. Justin Rosenberg, "Why Is There No International Historical Sociology?," *European Journal of International Relations* 12, no. 3 (September 2006), 321.

70. Ibid., 321–25.

71. Marx and Engels, *The German Ideology*, 50–51.

72. John Haldon, *The State and the Tributary Mode of Production* (London: Verso, 1994), 63–69; Chris Wickham, *Framing the Early Middle Ages: Europe and the Mediterranean, 400–800* (Oxford: Oxford University Press, 2005), 57–61.

73. Trotsky, *The History of the Russian Revolution*, 28.

74. Trotsky, "The Draft Program of the Communist International—A Critique of Fundamentals," 15.

75. Justin Rosenberg, "International Relations—the 'Higher Bullshit': A Reply to the

Globalization Theory Debate," *International Politics* 44, no. 4 (December 2007), 456.

76. Justin Rosenberg, "Globalization Theory: A Post-mortem," *International Politics* 42, no. 1 (March 2005), 41.

77. Callinicos and Rosenberg, "Uneven and Combined Development: The Social-Relational Substratum of 'the International'?," 99.

78. Colin Barker, "Beyond Trotsky: Extending Combined and Uneven Development," in *100 Years of Permanent Revolution: Results and Prospects*, edited by Bill Dunn and Hugo Radice (London: Pluto Press, 2006), 78. See also Allinson and Anievas, "The Uses and Misuses of Uneven and Combined Development," 54.

79. Trotsky, "Permanent Revolution," 146.

80. Robert Looker and David Coates, "The State and the Working Class," in *The Rise of the Modern State*, edited by James Anderson (Brighton: Harvester, 1986), 112–13; Herman Schwartz, *States versus Markets: The Emergence of a Global Economy* (Second edition, Houndmills: Macmillan, 2000), 95–96.

CHAPTER 9: CHINA: UNEVENNESS, COMBINATION, REVOLUTION?

1. For the following three paragraphs of this section, see chapter 8 in this volume.

2. Jean Chesneaux, *The Chinese Labor Movement, 1919–1927* (Stanford: Stanford University Press, 1968), 50.

3. Lucian W. Pye, foreword to *Shanghai: Revolution and Development in an Asian Metropolis*, edited by Christopher Howe (Cambridge: Cambridge University Press, 1981), xv.

4. David Strand, "'A High Place Is No Better than a Low Place': The City in the Making of Modern China," in *Becoming Chinese: Passages to Modernity and Beyond*, edited by Wen-Hsin Yeh (Berkeley: University of California Press, 2000), 102.

5. Harold Isaacs [1938], *The Tragedy of the Chinese Revolution* (Second revised edition, Stanford: Stanford University Press, 1961), 1.

6. John Gittings, *Real China: From Cannibalism to Karaoke* (London: Simon and Schuster, 1997), 269–71.

7. Beverly Silver, *Forces of Labor: Workers' Movements and Globalization since 1870* (Cambridge: Cambridge University Press, 2003), 147.

8. Dorothy Solinger, *Contesting Citizenship in Urban China: Peasant Migrants, the State, and the Logic of the Market* (Berkeley: University of California Press, 1999), 34, 38–40.

9. R. Bin Wong, *China Transformed: Historical Change and the Limits of the European Experience* (New York: Cornell University Press, 1997), 67.

10. Lei Guang, "Rural Taste, Urban Fashions: The Cultural Politics of Rural/Urban Difference in Contemporary China," *Positions* 11, no. 3, special issue, *Intellectuals and Social Movements*, Part 1 (Winter 2003), 616–17.

11. Wong, *China Transformed*, 185.

12. Mark Selden, "State, Market and Sectoral Inequality in Contemporary China," in *States versus Markets in the World System*, edited by Peter Evans, Dietrich Rueschemeyer, and Evelyne H. Stephens (Beverley Hills: Sage, 1985), 280.

13. Ajit S. Bhalla, *Uneven Development in the Third World: A Study of China and India* (Second revised edition, London: Macmillan, 1995), 297.

14. Raymond Lau, "Economic Determination in the Last Instance: China's Political-Economic Development under the Impact of the Asian Financial Crisis," *Historical Materialism* 8 (2001), 238.

15. David Harvey, *A Brief History of Neoliberalism* (Oxford: Oxford University Press, 2005), chapter 5.

16. United Nations Human Development Program, *Human Development Report 2003: Millennium Development Goals: Compact among Nations to End Human Poverty* (New York: United Nations Organization/Oxford University Press, 2003), 40–41.

17. Graham Hutchings, *Modern China* (Harmondsworth: Penguin Books, 2000), 229.

18. United Nations Human Development Program, *Human Development Report 2003*, 73.

19. United Nations Human Development Program, *China Human Development Report 1999: Transition and the State* (Oxford: United Nations Organization/Oxford University Press, 1999), 62.

20. Shaoguang Wang and Angang Hu, *The Political Economy of Uneven Development: The Case of China* (New York: M. E. Sharpe, 1999), 13–14.

21. Andrew Glyn, "Global Imbalances," *New Left Review*, II/34 (July/August 2005), 17.

22. Jonathan Watts, "Boom City Struggles to Cope as Millions Move In," *The Guardian* (December 6, 2003); Shahid Yusif and Weiping Wu, "Pathways to a Global City: Shanghai Rising in an Era of Globalization," *Urban Studies* 39, no. 7 (June 2002), 1233.

23. Callum Henderson, *China on the Brink: The Myths and Realities of the World's Largest Market* (New York: McGraw-Hill, 1999), 30.

24. Wang and Hu, *The Political Economy of Uneven Development*, 73.

25. Lei Guang, "Rural Taste, Urban Fashions," 618.

26. Wang Danyu, "Stepping on Two Boats: Urban Strategies of Chinese Peasants and Their Children," *International Review of Social History* 45, Supplement 8, *Household Strategies for Survival 1600–2000: Fission, Faction and Cooperation*, edited by Laurence Fontaine and Jürgen Schlumbohm (2000), 181–82, 191–94; John Knight, Lina Song, and Jia Huaibin, "Chinese Rural Migrants in Urban Enterprises: Three Perspectives," *Journal of Development Studies* 35, no. 3, special issue, *The Workers' State Meets the Market: Labor in China's Transition* (February 1999), 87–99.

27. Ya Ping Wang and Alan Murie, "Social and Spatial Implications of Housing Reform in China," *International Journal of Urban and Regional Research* 24, no. 2 (June 2000), 406.

28. Li Zhang, *Strangers in the City: Reconfigurations of Space, Power, and Social Networks within China's Floating Population* (Stanford: Stanford University Press, 2001), 27.

29. Solinger, *Contesting Citizenship in Urban China*, 247.

30. Hutchings, *Modern China*, 339–43.

31. Guo Xiaolin, "'It's All a Matter of Hats': Rural Urbanization in South-West China," *Journal of Peasant Studies* 29, no. 1 (October 2001), 111–20.

32. Peter G. Rowe, conclusion to *Modern Urban Housing in China, 1840–2000*, edited by Lu Junhua, Peter G. Rowe, and Zhang Jie (London: Prestel, 2001), 289.

33. Sarah Cook and Margaret Maurer-Fazio, introduction to *The Workers' State Meets the Market*, 1; Henderson, *China on the Brink*, 39; Lau, "Economic Determination in the Last Instance," 241.

34. Wang Xiaoming, "China on the Brink of a 'Momentous Era,'" *Intellectuals and Social Movements*, 591.

35. Henderson, *China on the Brink*, 47, 50, 258.

36. China Labor Watch, "Reebok's Human Rights Standard and Chinese Workers' Working Conditions" (January 1, 2002), available at chinalaborwatch.org.

37. Feng Chen, "Industry, Restructuring, and Workers' Resistance in China," *Modern China* 29, no. 2 (April 2003), 239.

38. Solinger, *Contesting Citizenship in Urban China*, 284.

39. Trini Leung, "The Third Wave of the Chinese Labor Movement in the Post-Mao Era," *China*

Labor E-bulletin 7 (June 5, 2002), available at http://www.hartford-hwp.com/archives/55/297.html.

40. Donny Gluckstein, *The Western Soviets: Workers' Councils versus Parliament, 1915–20* (London: Bookmarks, 1985), 51–55; Chris Wrigley, introduction to *Challenges of Labor: Western and Central Europe, 1917–20*, edited by Chris Wrigley (London: Routledge, 1993), 5–7, 15–16.

41. Lian Yang, "Dark Side of the Chinese Moon," *New Left Review*, II/32 (March/April 2005).

42. Wang Dan, Li Minqi, and Wang Chaohua, "A Dialogue on the Future of China," in *One China, Many Paths*, edited by Wang Chaohua (London: Verso, 2003), 321–22.

43. Andrew J. Nathan and Bruce Gilley, *China's New Rulers: The Secret Files* (London: Granta, 2002), 235.

44. Ibid., 191–92.

45. Peter Linebaugh [1991], *The London Hanged: Crime and Civil Society in the Eighteenth Century* (Harmondsworth: Penguin Books, 1993), xv.

46. Lian Yang, "Dark Side of the Chinese Moon," 139.

47. Lau, "Economic Determination in the Last Instance," 240.

48. Feng Chen, "Industry, Restructuring, and Workers' Resistance in China," 255–56.

49. Leon D. Trotsky [1932–33], *The History of the Russian Revolution* (London: Pluto Press, 1977), 27.

50. Gregory E. Guldin, *What's a Peasant to Do? Village Becoming Town in Southern China* (Boulder: Westview Press, 2001), 189.

51. Ben Hillman, "The Rise of the Community in Rural China: Village Politics, Cultural Identity, and Religious Revival in a Hui Village," *The China Journal* 51 (January 2004), 73.

52. Deborah Davis, "Social Transformations of Metropolitan China since 1949," in *Cities in the Developing World: Issues, Theory and Policy*, edited by Josef Gugler (Oxford: Oxford University Press, 1997), 177, 199.

53. Stanley Rosen, "The Victory of Materialism: Aspirations to Join China's Urban Moneyed Classes and the Commercialization of Education," *The China Journal* 51 (January 2004), 51.

54. Alexis de Tocqueville [1856], *The Ancien Régime and the French Revolution* (London: Fontana, 1966), 196; Leon D. Trotsky [1921], "Flood-Tide," in *The First Five Years of the Communist International*, vol. 2 (London: New Park Publications, 1974), 82.

55. Henderson, *China on the Brink*, 53.

56. Guldin, *What's a Peasant to Do?*, 269–70.

Chapter 10:
Third World Revolution

1. See chapters 8 and 11 in this volume.

2. There is no entirely satisfactory terminology in which to discuss these issues. None of the binary oppositions that have been used over the last hundred years or so—oppressor/oppressed, West/East, First World/Third World, core/periphery, North/South, advanced/backward, developed/underdeveloped, emergent/established—adequately express current global divisions. Even leaving aside their theoretical adequacy, they all refer to slightly different groups of countries. Vicky Randall argues that, whatever term we use, one "is needed to denote the continuing imbalance of economic and political power between (and not only within) the world's nations. Given this axis of inequality, it also provides an important rallying point as a focus for symbolic identification. In addition it may be desirable to hold onto the idea of a North and South as a corrective to current clash of civilisation arguments." See "Using and Abusing the Concept of the Third World," *Third World Quarterly* 25, no. 1 (2004), 52. I have

continued to use "Third World" for reasons of familiarity and convenience, not because it has any greater scientific provenance than the alternatives.

3. Ernest Mandel, *Revolutionary Marxism Today*, edited by Jon Rothschild (London: New Left Books, 1979), 88–89.

4. Eric J. Hobsbawm, *Age of Extremes: The Short Twentieth Century, 1914–1991* (London: Allen Lane, 1994), 357.

5. Gilbert Rist, *The History of Development: From Western Origins to Global Faith* (New revised and expanded edition, London: Zed Books, 2002), 151.

6. United Nations Human Development Program, *Human Development Report 2003: Millennium Development Goals: A Compact among Nations to End Human Poverty* (New York: United Nations Organization/Oxford University Press, 2003), 31. For a discussion of the differences between East Asia and sub-Saharan Africa in particular, see Giovanni Arrighi, "The African Crisis," *New Left Review* II/15 (May/June 2002), 24–31.

7. Michael Hardt and Antonio Negri, *Empire* (Cambridge, MA: Harvard University Press, 2000), xiii, 335.

8. Roger Burbach, *Globalization and Postmodern Politics: From Zapatistas to High-Tech Robber Barons* (London: Pluto Press, 2001), 50.

9. Hari Al-Kazzaf, "Western Demos Make Big Impact on Islamic World," *Spectrezine*, available at www.spectrezine.org/war/Egypt.htm.

10. Lant Pritchett, "Divergence, Big Time," *Journal of Economic Perspectives* 11, no. 3 (Summer 1997), 9.

11. United Nations Human Development Program, *Human Development Report 2003*, 39.

12. Doug Henwood, *After the New Economy* (New York: The New Press, 2003), 132.

13. Nigel Harris, *The End of the Third World: Newly Industrialising Countries and the Decline of an Ideology* (Harmondsworth: Penguin Books, 1986), 102.

14. Robert Brenner, *The Boom and the Bubble: The US in the World Economy* (London: Verso, 2002), 37.

15. Neil Smith, *The Endgame of Globalization* (New York: Routledge, 2005), 137.

16. United Nations Human Development Program, *Human Development Report 2003*, 39.

17. Hans Kundnani, "Rich Get Even Richer in Third World," *The Guardian* (June 21, 2006).

18. Mike Davis, *A Planet of Slums* (London: Verso, 2006), 157–58.

19. Nigel Harris, *The Return of Cosmopolitan Capital: Globalisation, the State and War* (London: I. B. Tauris, 2003), 244.

20. Henwood, *After the New Economy*, 133.

21. Harris, *The End of the Third World*, 201.

22. Henwood, *After the New Economy*, 134.

23. Richard Wilkinson, *The Impact of Inequality: How to Make Sick Societies Healthier* (New York: The New Press, 2005), 15–16, 18.

24. Greg Critser, *Fat Land: How Americans Became the Fattest People in the World* (Harmondsworth: Penguin Books, 2004), 109–16.

25. Sophie Bessis, *Western Supremacy* (London: Zed Books, 2003), 223.

26. Retort, *Afflicted Powers: Capital and Spectacle in a New Age of War* (London: Verso, 2005), 11.

27. Robert Cooper, *The Breaking of Nations: Order and Chaos in the Twenty-First Century* (London: Atlantic Monthly Press, 2003), 68–70; Niall Ferguson, *Colossus: The Rise and Fall of the American Empire* (London: Allen Lane, 2004), 15–26, 290–95.

28. Quoted in Tyler Marshall, "Bush's Foreign Policy Shifting," *Los Angeles Times* (June 5, 2005).

29. Johan Norberg, *In Defense of Global Capitalism* (Stockholm: Cato Institute, 2003), 47.

30. Stefan Andreasson, "Economic Reforms and 'Virtual Democracy' in South Africa," *Journal of*

Contemporary African Studies 21, no. 3 (July 2003), 385.

31. Bill Emmott, *20:21 Vision* (Harmondsworth: Penguin Books, 2003), 274.

32. William Easterly, "The Lost Decades: Developing Countries' Stagnation in Spite of Policy Reform," *Journal of Economic Growth* 6, no. 2 (June 2001), 154.

33. John Weeks, "Globalise, Global-lize, Global Lies: Myths of the World Economy during the 1990s," in *Phases of Capitalist Development: Booms, Crises and Globalisations,* edited by Robert Albritton, Makoto Itoh, Richard Westra, and Alan Zuege (Houndmills: Palgrave Macmillan, 2001), 272–73.

34. David Harvey, *A Brief History of Neoliberalism* (Oxford: Oxford University Press, 2005), 97, 119.

35. Amy Chua, *World on Fire: How Exporting Free-Market Democracy Breeds Ethnic Hatred and Global Instability* (London: Heinemann, 2003), 125. See also Neil Davidson, "The Trouble with 'Ethnicity,'" *International Socialism* 2: 84 (Autumn 1999), 12–15.

36. Michael Mann, *The Dark Side of Democracy: Explaining Ethnic Cleansing* (Cambridge: Cambridge University Press, 2005), 31. See also 517.

37. Ibid., 526.

38. Harvey, *A Brief History of Neoliberalism*, 97.

39. Peter Gowan [1991], "The Gulf War, Iraq, and Western Liberalism," in *The Global Gamble: Washington's Faustian Bid for World Dominance* (London: Verso, 1999), 127.

40. Chalmers Johnson, *Blowback: The Costs and Consequences of American Empire* (Second edition, New York: Henry Holt, 2002), 8.

41. Ibid., xvi–xvii. See also 17–18.

42. Smith, *The Endgame of Globalization*, 206.

43. He Qinglian, "China's Listing Social Structure," *New Left Review* I/5 (September/October 2000), 86.

44. Mike Davis, "Planet of Slums," *New Left Review* II/26 (March/April 2004), 5–6, 9, 10.

45. United Nations Human Development Program, *The Challenge of Slums: Global Report on Human Settlements 2003* (London: United Nations Organization/Oxford University Press, 2003), 216–18.

46. Larissa Lomnitz, "The Social and Economic Organization of a Mexican Shanty Town," in *Cities in the Developing World: Issues, Theory and Policy*, edited by Josef Gugler (Oxford: Oxford University Press, 1997), 211, 216.

47. Ursula Huws, "The Making of a Cybertariat? Virtual Work in a Real World," in *The Making of a Cybertariat: Virtual Work in a Real World* (London: Merlin Press, 2003), 176.

48. Katherine P. Moseley, "In Defense of the Primitive," in *Rethinking the Third World: Contributions towards a New Conceptualization*, edited by Rosemary Galli (New York: Crane Russak, 1992), 102.

49. Ibid., 90.

50. John McMurtry, *The Cancer Stage of Capitalism* (London: Pluto Press, 1999), 248.

51. Roger Burbach, "Roots of the Postmodern Rebellion in Chiapas," *New Left Review* I/205 (May/June 1994), 113, 114.

52. Roger Burbach, "For a Zapatista-Style Postmodernist Perspective," *Monthly Review* 47, no. 10 (October 1996), 39.

53. See, for example, Burbach, "Roots of the Postmodern Rebellion in Chiapas," 123, and Ana Carrigan, "Afterword: Chiapas, the First Postmodern Revolution," in Subcomandante Marcos, *Our Word Is Our Weapon: Selected Writings*, edited by Juana Ponce de Leon (London: Serpent's Tail, 2001), 441.

54. John Holloway, "The Concept of Power and the Zapatistas," *Common Sense* 19 (June 1996), 21.

55. Subcomandante Marcos, "Punch Card and the Hourglass," *New Left Review* II/9 (May/June 2001), 71.

56. Holloway, "The Concept of Power and the Zapatistas," 23, 24.

57. Jo Tuckman, "Zapatistas Go Back to the Grassroots to Start Again," *The Guardian* (December 27, 2003).

58. Judith A. Hellman, "Real and Virtual Chiapas: Magic Realism and the Left," in *The Socialist Register 2000: Necessary and Unnecessary Utopias*, edited by Leo Panitch and Colin Leys (London: Merlin Press, 2000), 172–73.

CHAPTER 11: FROM DEFLECTED PERMANENT REVOLUTION TO THE LAW OF UNEVEN AND COMBINED DEVELOPMENT

1. Slavoj Žižek, "Afterword: Lenin's Choice," in Vladimir I. Lenin, *Revolution at the Gates: A Selection of Writings from February to October 1917*, edited by Slavoj Žižek (London: Verso, 2002), 305–06.

2. Tony Cliff [1963], "Permanent Revolution," in *Selected Works*, vol. 3, *Marxist Theory after Trotsky* (London: Bookmarks, 2003).

3. Alasdair MacIntyre [1963], "Trotsky in Exile," in *Alasdair MacIntyre's Engagement with Marxism: Selected Writings, 1953–1974*, edited by Paul Blackledge and Neil Davidson (Leiden: E. J. Brill, 2008), 275.

4. Tony Cliff, *A World to Win: Life of a Revolutionary* (London: Bookmarks, 2000), 42, 48.

5. Gonzalo Pozo-Martin, "Reassessing the Permanent Arms Economy," *International Socialism* 2:127 (Summer 2010).

6. Leo Zeilig, "Tony Cliff: Deflected Permanent Revolution in Africa," *International Socialism* 2:126 (Spring 2010), 182.

7. Ibid., 163. The article is part of a growing and impressive body of work by the same author on the rich and complex history of African politics. See also Leo Zeilig, *Revolt and Protest: Student Politics and Activism in Sub-Saharan Africa* (London: I. B. Tauris, 2007); *Lumumba: Africa's Lost Leader* (London: Haus Publishing, 2008); and *Class Struggle and Resistance in Africa* (Chicago: Haymarket Books, 2009).

8. Other writers in the International Socialism tradition have subsequently made this more explicit. See, for example, Alex Callinicos, "Bourgeois Revolutions and Historical Materialism," *International Socialism* 2:43 (Summer 1989), 159–60, and Nigel Harris, *The Mandate of Heaven: Marx and Mao in Modern China* (London: Quartet Books, 1978), 261–82.

9. Tony Cliff, *Trotsky*, vol. 1, *Towards October, 1879–1917* (London: Bookmarks, 1989), 128. For his entire discussion see ibid., 126–28, and Tony Cliff, *Trotsky*, vol. 4, *The Darker the Night the Brighter the Star, 1927–1940* (London: Bookmarks, 1993), 164–65.

10. See Richard B. Day and Daniel Gaido, introduction to *Witnesses to Permanent Revolution: The Documentary Record* (Leiden: E. J. Brill, 2009); Norman Geras, "Between the Russian Revolutions," in *The Legacy of Rosa Luxemburg* (London: New Left Books, 1976); Reidar Larsson, *Theories of Revolution: From Marx to the First Russian Revolution* (Stockholm: Almquist and Wiksell, 1970), 252–304; Michael Löwy, *The Politics of Combined and Uneven Development: The Theory of Permanent Revolution* (London: Verso, 1981), chapter 2.

11. Leon D. Trotsky [1938], "The Death Agony of Capitalism and the Tasks of the Fourth International," in *The Transitional Program for Socialist Revolution* (New York: Pathfinder Press, 1977), 138.

12. Leon D. Trotsky [1938], "Revolution and War in China," in *Leon Trotsky on China* (New York:

Monad Press, 1976), 581, 582–83.

13. Leon D. Trotsky [1938], "Latin American Problems: A Transcript," in *Writings of Leon Trotsky Supplement (1934–40)*, edited by George Breitman (New York: Pathfinder Press, 1979), 784–85.

14. Trotsky, "Revolution and War in China," 582.

15. Trotsky, "The Death Agony of Capitalism and the Tasks of the Fourth International," 138.

16. Cliff, "Permanent Revolution," 188.

17. Löwy, *The Politics of Combined and Uneven Development*, 89.

18. Leon D. Trotsky [1933], "Japan Heads for Disaster," in *Writings of Leon Trotsky [1932–33]*, edited by George Breitman and Sarah Lovell (New York: Pathfinder Press, 1972), 291.

19. Daron Acemoglu and James Robinson, "Why Did the West Extend the Franchise? Democracy, Inequality, and Growth in Historical Perspective," *Quarterly Journal of Economics* 115, no. 4 (November 2000), 1182–86; Goran Therborn, "The Rule of Capital and the Rise of Democracy," *New Left Review* I/103 (May/June 1977), 4, 17.

20. Tony Cliff [1950], "The Class Nature of the People's Democracies," in *Neither Washington nor Moscow: Essays on Revolutionary Socialism* (London: Bookmarks, 1984), 65–66.

21. Alex Callinicos, "Trotsky's Theory of 'Permanent Revolution' and Its Relevance to the Third World Today," *International Socialism* 2:16 (Spring 1982), 110.

22. Cliff, *A World to Win*, 227.

23. Karl Marx [1844], "Critical Notes on 'The King of Prussia and Social Reform. By a Prussian,'" in *Early Writings* (Harmondsworth: Penguin Books/New Left Review, 1975), 419–20; Leon D. Trotsky, *The Revolution Betrayed: What Is the Soviet Union and Where Is It Going?* (New York: Monod Press, 1937), 288. Much the clearest discussion of the subject is in Hal Draper, *Karl Marx's Theory of Revolution*, vol. 2, *The Politics of Social Classes* (New York: Monthly Review Press, 1978), 17–21.

24. Chris Harman, "The Storm Breaks," *International Socialism* 2:46 (Spring 1990), 64–71.

25. See chapter 7 in this volume.

26. Harman, "The Storm Breaks," 38.

27. Fred Halliday and Maxine Molyneux, *The Ethiopian Revolution* (London: Verso, 1981), 62–74.

28. Cliff, "Permanent Revolution," 196–98.

29. Chris Harman [1994], "The Prophet and the Proletariat," in *Selected Writings* (London: Bookmarks, 2010), 344.

30. See chapter 1 in this volume.

31. Trotsky, "Revolution and War in China," 581, 583–84.

32. For this "consequentialist" position, see Callinicos, "Bourgeois Revolutions and Historical Materialism," 124–27, and chapter 1 in this volume.

33. See chapter 1 in this volume.

34. Eric J. Hobsbawm, *The Age of Capital: 1848–1873* (London: Weidenfeld and Nicolson, 1975), 21.

35. John Rees, "The Democratic Revolution and the Socialist Revolution," *International Socialism* 2:83 (Summer 1999), 28; *Imperialism and Resistance* (London: Routledge, 2006), 155.

36. Ellen Kay Trimberger, *Revolution from Above: Military Bureaucrats and Development in Japan, Turkey, Egypt and Peru* (New Brunswick: Transaction Books, 1978), 4–5, 41–45. Trimberger identifies the Meiji Restoration as the first revolution of this type.

37. Cliff, "Permanent Revolution," 194–95.

38. Peter Gatrell, *Government, Industry and Rearmament in Russia, 1900–1914* (Cambridge: Cambridge University Press, 1994), 93; Diane Koenker and William Rosenberg, *Strikes and Revolution in Russia, 1917* (Princeton: Princeton University Press, 1989), 103–10; Jeremiah Schneiderman, *Sergei Zubatov and Revolutionary Marxism: The Struggle for the Working Class in*

Tsarist Russia (Ithaca: Cornell University Press, 1976), 69–140.

39. Cliff, "Permanent Revolution," 196.

40. See chapter 8 in this volume.

41. Tim McDaniel, *Autocracy, Capitalism and Revolution in Russia* (Berkeley: University of California Press, 1988), 41–47.

42. Ibid., 407.

43. Mike Davis, "Sand, Fear and Money in Dubai," in *Evil Paradises: Dreamworlds of Neoliberalism*, edited by Mike Davis and Daniel Bertrand Monk (London: Verso, 2007), 53–54. Indeed, in the case of China, it might be said that the neoliberal turn after 1978 actually resumed the process of uneven and combined development originally detected by Trotsky in the 1920s, which had been consciously halted by a Maoist leadership only too conscious of the explosive effects of uncontrolled urban expansion. See chapter 9 in this volume.

44. Beverly Silver, *Forces of Labor: Workers' Movements and Globalization since 1870* (Cambridge: Cambridge University Press, 2003), 164.

45. Paul Ginsborg, *A History of Contemporary Italy: Society and Politics, 1943–1988* (Harmondsworth: Penguin Books, 1990), 47–53, 223–29; Michael Hardt and Antonio Negri, *Empire* (Cambridge, MA: Harvard University Press, 2000), 287–89.

46. Edward Luttwak, *Turbo-Capitalism: Winners and Losers in the Global Economy* (London: Weidenfeld and Nicolson, 1998), 25–26.

47. Fred Halliday, *Revolution and World Politics: The Rise and Fall of the Sixth Great Power* (Houndmills: Macmillan, 1999), 320–21.

CHAPTER 12: REVOLUTIONS BETWEEN THEORY AND HISTORY

1. This is more common than readers might suppose. "Having been a reviewer myself," confessed the late J. G. Ballard, "I can always tell when somebody has stopped reading the book he's reviewing." See [1975], "James Goddard and James Pringle: An Interview with J. G. Ballard," in *Extreme Metaphors: Interviews with J. G. Ballard, 1967–2008* (London: Fourth Estate, 2012), 95.

2. Alex Callinicos, "The Dynamics of Revolution," *International Socialism* 2:137 (Winter 2013), 135–36, note 19.

3. Neil Davidson, *How Revolutionary Were the Bourgeois Revolutions?* (Chicago: Haymarket, 2012), 575–77.

4. Kevin Anderson, *Marx at the Margins: On Nationalism, Ethnicity, and Non-Western Societies* (Chicago: University of Chicago Press, 2010), chapter 3; Davidson, *How Revolutionary Were the Bourgeois Revolutions?*, 164–70.

5. Jairus Banaji [1977], "Modes of Production in a Materialist Conception of History," in *Theory as History: Essays on Modes of Production and Exploitation* (Leiden: E. J. Brill/Historical Materialism, 2010), 52–65.

6. Callinicos, "The Dynamics of Revolution," 136, note 19.

7. Davidson, *How Revolutionary Were the Bourgeois Revolutions?*, 415–16.

8. Marcel van der Linden, *Workers of the World: Essays towards a Global Labour History* (Leiden: E. J. Brill, 2008), 336–72.

9. Jairus Banaji [2003], "The Fictions of Free Labour: Contract, Coercion and So-Called Unfree Labour," in *Theory as History*, 145.

10. Callinicos, "The Dynamics of Revolution," 136.

11. Donny Gluckstein, "Comment on Bourgeois Revolution," *International Socialism* 2:140 (Autumn 2013), 207.

12. Compare the original plan with the actual structure summarized in Davidson, *How Revolutionary Were the Bourgeois Revolutions?*, xviii.
13. Gluckstein, "Comment on Bourgeois Revolution," 207–08.
14. See the discussion in Perry Anderson [1990], "A Culture in Contraflow," in *English Questions* (London: Verso, 1992), 290–93.
15. Davidson, *How Revolutionary Were the Bourgeois Revolutions?*, 225–36.
16. Ibid., 12–32.
17. Callinicos, "The Dynamics of Revolution," 138.
18. Ibid., 138. My position on the nature of the tributary mode has changed: I originally regarded it as a variant of the feudal mode, but was subsequently convinced by Banaji and by Alex that the *internal* relations among the ruling class were sufficiently different from those of feudalism for it to be regarded as a different mode, even though the process of surplus extraction from the peasantry is similar—hence my reference to the tributary state as a collective feudal overlord, a description that I can now see was misleading in this context. Compare chapters 2 and 3 in this volume with Davidson, *How Revolutionary Were the Bourgeois Revolutions?*, 541–45.
19. And of course there were also states—diminutive Scotland in the West, vast Poland in the East—where the feudal lords were simply too powerful to allow the local dynasties to establish absolutism.
20. Callinicos, "The Dynamics of Revolution," 137.
21. Davidson, *How Revolutionary Were the Bourgeois Revolutions?*, 117.
22. Georges Bataille, *The Accursed Share: An Essay on General Economy*, vol. 3 (Cambridge, MA: Zone Books, 1991), 279; Amy E. Wendling, "Are All Revolutions Bourgeois? Revolutionary Temporality in Karl Marx's *Eighteenth Brumaire of Louis Bonaparte*," *Strategies* 16, no. 1 (2003), 45–46.
23. Alex Callinicos, "Bourgeois Revolutions and Historical Materialism," *International Socialism* 2:43 (Summer 1989).
24. Ibid., 126, 152; Perry Anderson [1983], "Marshall Berman: Modernity and Revolution," in *A Zone of Engagement* (London: Verso, 1992), 44.
25. Callinicos, "The Dynamics of Revolution," 138–40.
26. Gluckstein, "Comment on Bourgeois Revolution," 208, 210.
27. Ibid., 210.
28. See, in relation to the US, Charles Post, "Democracy against Capitalism in the Post–Civil War United States," in *The American Road to Capitalism: Studies in Class-Structure, Economic Development and Political Conflict, 1620–1877* (Leiden: E. J. Brill/Historical Materialism, 2011).
29. Dietrich Rueschemeyer, Evelyne H. Stephens, and John Stephens, *Capitalist Development and Democracy* (Cambridge: Cambridge University Press, 1992), 7, 142–43.
30. Karl Marx and Friedrich Engels [1848], "Manifesto of the Communist Party," in *Political Writings*, vol. 1, *The Revolutions of 1848*, edited by David Fernbach (Harmondsworth: Penguin Books/New Left Review, 1974), 86.
31. Callinicos, "The Dynamics of Revolution," 138–39.
32. But for genuine parallels between Lincoln and Lenin, see "Afterword: We Cannot Escape History," in this volume.
33. Callinicos, "The Dynamics of Revolution," 141.
34. For my discussion of Wickham's analysis of these struggles, see chapter 3 in this volume.
35. Davidson, *How Revolutionary Were the Bourgeois Revolutions?*, 500–502.
36. Callinicos, "The Dynamics of Revolution," 145.
37. Davidson, *How Revolutionary Were the Bourgeois Revolutions?*, 610.

38. See, for example, Theda Skocpol [1982], "Rentier State and Shi'a Islam in the Iranian Revolution," in *Social Revolutions in the Modern World* (Cambridge: Cambridge University Press, 1994), 240–43.

39. Alex Callinicos, "Specters of Counter-revolution," *International Socialism* 2:140 (Autumn 2013), 4.

40. Whether the coup constitutes the counterrevolution is too large a subject to enter into here, but in my view, Hugh Roberts's interpretation—criticized by Alex in "Specters of Counter-revolution"—is the more realistic position. See "The Revolution That Wasn't," *London Review of Books* 35, no. 17 (September 12, 2013), 6.

41. Callinicos, "The Dynamics of Revolution," 145.

42. Neil Davidson, "From Deflected Permanent Revolution to the Law of Uneven and Combined Development," *International Socialism 2:128* (Autumn 2010). See also chapter 11 in this volume, and Davidson, *How Revolutionary Were the Bourgeois Revolutions?*, 144–48, 214–36, 285–308, and 621–29.

43. Ibid., 143.

44. Ibid., 146.

45. Ibid., 144.

46. Alex Callinicos, *Is There a Future for Marxism?* (London: Macmillan, 1982), 4.

47. Neil Davidson, "The Neoliberal Era in Britain: Historical Developments and Current Perspectives," *International Socialism* 2:139 (Summer 2013), 176–77.

48. Alex Callinicos, "Marxism and Philosophy: A Reply to Peter Binns," *International Socialism* 2:19 (Spring 1983), 139. Alex ended his piece by invoking "the words of Oliver Cromwell to the Scottish Estates, 'I beseech ye in the bowels of Christ to think it possible that ye might be wrong.'" Ibid., 140. Since the avoidance of error is a theme of Alex's review, I cannot forebear to point out that Cromwell was actually addressing the General Assembly of the Church of Scotland. See [1650], "Cromwell to the General Assembly of the Kirk of Scotland," August 3, 1650, in *Oliver Cromwell's Letters and Speeches with Elucidations by Thomas Carlyle*, vol. 3 (London: Chapman and Hall, 1871), 18.

Afterword: We Cannot Escape History

1. James Joyce [1922], *Ulysses* (Harmondsworth: Penguin Books, 1982), 40.

2. Abraham Lincoln, "Annual Message to Congress—Concluding Remarks," December 1, 1862, in *The Collected Works of Abraham Lincoln*, vol. 5, edited by Roy P. Basler with the assistance of Marion Delores Pratt and Lloyd A. Dunlap (New Brunswick: Rutgers University Press, 1953), 537.

3. See, for example, James M. McPherson [1986], "Abraham Lincoln and the Second American Revolution," in *Abraham Lincoln and the Second American Revolution* (New York: Oxford University Press, 1991), 29–37. For Marx's views, see chapter 6 in this volume.

4. It is omitted, for example, from Robin Blackburn's otherwise comprehensive collection of statements by the two men, published along with related papers as *An Unfinished Revolution: Karl Marx and Abraham Lincoln* (London: Verso, 2011). For the speeches and proclamations by Lincoln that Blackburn includes, see ibid., 105–22.

5. Garry Wills, *Lincoln at Gettysburg: The Words That Remade America* (New York: Simon and Schuster, 1992).

6. David Bromwich [2001], "Lincoln's Constitutional Necessity," in *Moral Imagination: Essays* (Princeton: Princeton University Press, 2014), 141.

7. Abraham Lincoln, "Speech at Peoria, Illinois," October 16, 1854, in *The Collected Works of*

Abraham Lincoln, vol. 2, edited by Roy P. Basler with the assistance of Marion Delores Pratt and Lloyd A. Dunlap (New Brunswick: Rutgers University Press, 1953), 275, 276.

8.   Lincoln, "Annual Message to Congress—Concluding Remarks," 537.

9.   Karl Marx [1862], "Comments on the North American Events," in *Collected Works*, vol. 19 (London: Lawrence and Wishart, 1984), 250.

10. Bromwich, "Lincoln's Constitutional Necessity," 145.

11. Wills, *Lincoln at Gettysburg*, 145

12. Edmund Burke [1790], *Reflections on the Revolution in France and on the Proceedings in Certain Societies in London Relative to That Event*, edited by Conor Cruise O'Brien (Harmondsworth: Penguin Books, 1968), 107.

13. Wills, *Lincoln at Gettysburg*, 145–47.

14. See, in particular, chapters 1, 11, and 12 in this volume.

15. Hal Draper [1964], "Vladimir Ilyich Jefferson and Thomas Lenin," in *Socialism from Below*, edited by Edward Haberkern (New Jersey: Humanities Press, 1992), 204.

16. Charles Post, "Social-Property Relations, Class-Conflict and the Origins of the US Civil War: Towards a New Social Interpretation," in *The American Road to Capitalism: Studies in Class-Structure, Economic Development and Political Conflict, 1620–1877* (Leiden: E. J. Brill, 2011), 249, 251.

17. Marx, "Comments on the North American Events," 250. By Lincoln's lack of "cothurnus" Marx means that the former did not engage in oratory based on the formal and elevated type of classical Greek drama that bears this name.

18. Lincoln was one of those bourgeois revolutionary leaders, like Cromwell and Robespierre, who "gradually adopted increasingly radical policies under the pressure of events rather than design." See Alex Callinicos, "Bourgeois Revolutions and Historical Materialism," *International Socialism* 2:43 (Summer 1989), 156. But this is less a shared perspective than a common trajectory, which these figures followed in isolation from each other: Robespierre did not model himself on Cromwell, and Lincoln did not seek to emulate either of his predecessors, although some of the "military abolitionists" saw themselves as carrying out a task comparable to that of the French revolutionaries. See Robin Blackburn, *The American Crucible: Slavery, Emancipation and Human Rights* (London: Verso, 2011), 412.

19. Blackburn, *The American Crucible*, 411.

20. Neil Davidson, *How Revolutionary Were the Bourgeois Revolutions?* (Chicago: Haymarket Books, 2012), 225–26.

21. Lars Lih, *Lenin* (London: Reaktion Books, 2011), 132–33.

22. Vladimir I. Lenin, "Two Tactics of Social-Democracy in the Democratic Revolution," in *Collected Works*, vol. 9, *June–November 1905* (Moscow: Foreign Languages Publishing House, 1962), 48–50.

23. Vladimir I. Lenin [1915], "The Collapse of the Second International," in *Collected Works*, vol. 21, *August 1914–December 1915* (Moscow: Progress Publishers, 1964), 250.

24. Vladimir I. Lenin [1915], "Several Theses," in *Collected Works*, vol. 21, 402–04.

25. Vladimir I. Lenin [1917], "Letters from Afar: First Letter: The First Stage of the Revolution," in *Collected Works*, vol. 23, *August 1916–March 1917* (Moscow: Progress Publishers, 1964), 297.

26. Vladimir I. Lenin [1917], "Farewell Letter to Swiss Workers," in *Collected Works*, vol. 23, 372.

27. Davidson, *How Revolutionary Were the Bourgeois Revolutions?*, 226–36.

28. Vladimir I. Lenin [1917], "The Tasks of the Proletariat in the Present Revolution," in *Collected Works*, vol. 24, *April–June 1917* (Moscow: Progress Publishers, 1964), 23, 24.

29. Davidson, *How Revolutionary Were the Bourgeois Revolutions?*, 233–34, 436–37.

30. John Marot, "Lenin, Bolshevism, and Social-Democratic Political Theory," *Historical Materialism* 22, nos. 3–4 (2014), 167, 168.

31. David Lloyd George, *War Memoirs*, vol. 2 (London: Odhams Press, 1936), 1296.

32. See, for example, Antonio Gramsci, "State and Civil Society," in *Selections from the Prison Notebooks*, edited by Quintin Hoare and Geoffrey Nowell-Smith (London: Lawrence and Wishart, 1971), 229–39, Q1§134, Q1§133, Q13§24, Q7§16, Q6§178, Q6§117, Q6§157.

33. Georg Lukács [1924], *Lenin: A Study in the Unity of His Thought* (London: New Left Books, 1970), 83.

34. Daniel Bensaïd [2004], *An Impatient Life: A Memoir* (London: Verso, 2013), 3.

35. Daniel Bensaïd [2002], "Leaps! Leaps! Leaps!," in *Lenin Reloaded: Towards a Politics of Truth*, edited by Sebastian Budgen, Stathis Kouvelakis, and Slavoj Žižek (Durham: University of North Carolina, 2007), 156–57.

36. Vladimir I. Lenin [1917], "The Tasks of the Proletariat in Our Revolution: Draft Platform for the Proletarian Party," in *Collected Works*, vol. 24, 88.

INDEX

"Passim" (literally "scattered") indicates intermittent discussion of a topic over a cluster of pages.

ABOUT THE AUTHOR

Neil Davidson is the author of *The Origins of Scottish Nation-hood* (2000), *Discovering the Scottish Revolution* (2003), for which he was awarded the Deutscher Prize, *How Revolution-ary Were the Bourgeois Revolutions?* (2012), and *Holding Fast to an Image of the Past* (2014). Davidson lectures in Sociology in the School of Political and Social Science at the University of Glasgow, Scotland.